Style

Style

WRITING AND READING AS THE DISCOVERY OF OUTLOOK

THIRD EDITION

RICHARD M. EASTMAN

BRUCE ARDINGER
Editorial Consultant

New York
Oxford University Press

Library of Congress Cataloging in Publication Data
Eastman, Richard M.
Style: writing and reading as the discovery of
outlook.
Bibliography: p.
Includes index.
1. English language—Rhetoric. 2. English language—
Style. 3. College readers. I. Title.
PE1408.E28   1984   808'.0427   83-19404
ISBN 0-19-503395-7 (pbk.)

Printing (last digit): 9 8 7 6
Printed in the United States of America

The New Yorker Magazine, Inc.: for "Our Own Baedeker" by John Updike, copyright © 1956 by The New Yorker Magazine, Inc.; and for "The Reading Machine" by Morris Bishop, copyright © 1947, 1975 by The New Yorker Magazine, Inc. Reprinted by permission.

The New York Times Company: for "Mum's the Word" by Russell Baker from *The New York Times Magazine* (August 29, 1982). Copyright © 1982 by The New York Times Company. Reprinted by permission.

Random House, Inc.: for excerpts from "Prologue" from *Invisible Man* by Ralph Ellison. Copyright 1952 by Ralph Ellison. Reprinted by permission of Random House, Inc.

Saturday Review Magazine Company: for "The Roots of Serendipity" by James H. Austin from *Saturday Review/World* (November 2, 1974), copyright © 1974 by Saturday Review Magazine Co.; and for " 'Learning' To Give Up," by Albert Rosenfeld from *Saturday Review* (September 3, 1977), copyright © 1977 by Saturday Review Magazine Co. Reprinted by permission.

Yvonne Streeter: for "The Ethics of a Housewife" (two drafts of a student paper, 1980). Reprinted by permission of the author.

Time Inc.: for "The Decline and Fall of Oratory" by Lance Morrow from *Time* (August 18, 1980). Copyright © 1980 by Time Inc. All rights reserved. Reprinted by permission from *Time*.

The Tobacco Institute: for an advertisement of 1982.

United Technologies Corporation: for an advertisement of 1981.

Viking Penguin, Inc.: for "On Natural Death" from *The Medusa and the Snail* by Lewis Thomas. Copyright © 1979 by Lewis Thomas. Reprinted by permission of Viking Penguin, Inc.

William K. Zinsser: for "The Transaction" from *On Writing Well,* 2nd edition, by William K. Zinsser (Harper & Row, Publishers, Inc.). Copyright © 1980 by William K. Zinsser. Reprinted by permission of the author.

Style as Outlook

Every style points to a self-interpretation of man, thus answering the question of the ultimate meaning of life. Whatever the subject matter which an artist chooses, however strong or weak his artistic form, he cannot help but betray by his style his own ultimate concern, as well as that of his group, and his period.

PAUL TILLICH, *Theology of Culture*, 1964

Language is the medium in which we are conscious. The speechless beasts are aware, but they are not conscious. To be conscious is to "know with" something, and a language of some sort is the device with which we know. More precisely, it is the device with which we CAN know.

RICHARD MITCHELL, *Less Than Words Can Say*, 1979

Writing as Discovery

For [Conrad] the very act of composition was a way of knowing, a way of exploration.

ROBERT PENN WARREN, Introduction to *Nostromo*, 1951

The process of acquiring technique is a process of modifying one's responses, of learning to see and feel, to hear and observe, to evoke and evaluate the images of memory and of summoning up and directing the imagination; of learning to conceive of human values in the ways which have been established by the great writers who have developed and extended the art. And perhaps the writer's greatest freedom, as artist, lies precisely in his possession of technique; for it is through technique that he comes to possess and express the meaning of his life.

RALPH ELLISON, *Shadow and Art*, 1964

Having a poem, like having a baby, is in large part a matter of exploration and discovery, and both poet and mother are often surprised by what they produce.

B. F. SKINNER, "On Having a Poem," 1972

Foreword to the Teacher

Premises

Two complementary premises underlie this book—that style is outlook and that outlook is discovered through the activity of writing itself.

A writer does not begin with a complete message or experience already imagined, which is then to be wrapped in language as a means of sending it to the reader. Writing is not so much communication as creation. In a real sense, a writer does not have an outlook on anything without first having written on it. That outlook comes into being through the hundreds of tests, choices, and unexpected chances which turn up as one writes on some engaging problem; and most writers agree that the final creation is not anything which they could have precisely anticipated when they first set pen to paper.

This position I believe can advance the learning of composition in these ways:

1. Students may see writing not as a troublesome matter of encoding what they already know, but as *the very way they come to know.*
2. They may see all the issues of vocabulary, syntax, audience, structure, etc. not as pitfalls to be skirted, but as ways to expand their powers of discovery.
3. Students may see that rewriting, usually shirked at reckless cost, is not neat-work, but the extension and final thrust of discovery.

Although I gained this perspective in probably some of the hardest ways possible, I am not, of course, the first to have discovered it. From the epigraphs to this book it can be seen that the perspective is an especially contemporary one which is coming into its own in many creative fields. The bibliography on pages 447–449 will specify my other formal indebtedness.

Uses

Although this textbook is planned for composition courses taught either in the classroom or by tutorial study, it can be used in two other kinds of course.

A creative writing class can use the book for hand reference. It only touches upon narrative and poetic techniques; but creative writing students can profit from Chapter 11 on sentimentality, Chapter 12 on irony, Chapter 20 on sound and rhythm, and the whole book in general matters of detail, tone, emphasis.

A literature class having composition as an auxiliary aim will find that this book draws many of its models from works being studied in English and American literature courses. It also offers a technique—the imitation of models (see Chapter 6)—which fuses composition with literary study.

Practical Features

The chapters have been kept short so that each offers a good but reasonable workout for a single assignment.

Much exercise material is included—much more than any one student would be assigned—so that one may prescribe analysis of models, discussion of principles, writing, or a combination as seems best for any specific class or student.

I regard the imitation of models as a useful art but nearly a lost one, and so I have gone to lengths in Chapter 6 to explain the possible techniques and to provide imitative exercises in subsequent chapters for almost every writing skill.

Chapter 23, "Showing Your Support," can help students in documented writing and even in the much-feared research paper, though this book does not pretend to describe research technique in itself. Chapter 23 is compatible with the *MLA Handbook* (1977).

The appendix, "Usage Reminders," can save individual students from some of the most common confusions in English usage. It is compatible with the Ebbitts' *Index to English*, 6th edition, at present the last of that text to base itself explicitly on linguistic scholarship.

The Plan

The present edition aims at sequentiality—at being used in its own order from beginning to end. The flexible access boasted by the earlier editions seemed to impose needless routing difficulties upon its users, who have been kind enough to recommend solutions which I have adapted. The text now will work straight through, without delaying such key disciplines as invention and revision until coming to "the whole paper." The one exception is Chapter 24, "Reading for Style," which many teachers will draw on early in order to exploit the anthology at the end of the book. The readings themselves follow the sequence of the chapters; their discussion questions generally concentrate on the concept being studied in the corresponding chapter, with occasional additional questions to review previous concepts or to anticipate later ones.

Flexibility is still available in minor ways. If polemically oriented, you might choose to open with Chapters 9 and 10 on writer and audience. If you want to work in a progression from the details of language to the larger shapes of rhetoric, you can open with Part III, "Style and Language," and then join the book at its beginning. The teacher's manual will suggest such alternatives, and for the readings will suggest their thematic correspondences. Where the book is used as reference, students may be sent to individual chapters and will generally find them self-contained. *Style* itself works from the middle scale to the fine scale and then to the large scale as a workable compromise in a discipline where, as the Christensens said, "The commander has to train the troops while the battle is going on." The following summary of development will describe the main sequence which you are invited to exploit.

The five main topics of the book are quickly presented in Chapter 1, "Preview," and are subsequently developed as follows: (1) *Style and outlook* is discussed in Part I through the six criteria put forward in Chapters 2 and 3. Later in the book, the first three criteria receive supplementary discussion in Chapters 13 through 16 (on vocabulary); the second three criteria receive supplementary discussion in Chapters 17 through 20 (on sentence structure, sound and rhythm). (2) *Style and audience* is discussed in Part II (Chapters 9–12), with certain matters receiving supplementary treatment later on, especially in Chapters 15 and 16 (on the vocabularies of feeling and intensification). (3) *Style and language* is treated in Part III, with four chapters on vocabulary (13–16), three on sentence structure (17–19), and one on sound and rhythm (20). (4) *Style and the longer paper* is discussed in Part IV (Chapters 21–23). (5) *Reading for style* is presented in Part V, Chapter 24, on how to extend these principles into one's reading. A small anthology follows, selected to invite the appreciation of various stylistic powers as used in several subject fields.

The Third Edition

Besides the shift to greater sequentiality, I have tried to reinforce the original undertaking in these ways:

Current research on composition has been consulted extensively.

Invention and revision have been pulled out of Part IV (the longer paper) and much more fully elaborated for use early in the book.

Sentence-building has been reconceived with greater benefit from the work of Christensen and his followers, and with exercises tested in the classroom.

Documentation conventions have been moved from an appendix to a new Chapter 23, "Showing Your Support," which integrates the use of secondary sources with the writing process.

About half of the present readings are new.

The appendix, "Usage Reminders," contains a new section on "Sexist Language" (page 446).

Throughout I have hoped and worked for greater clarity, for greater inventiveness of exercise and illustration, to the point where *Style* might appear to be a new generation of itself, a fresh look through the original perspective. The Acknowledgments will partly specify my wide indebtedness to those who helped to show the possibilities.

North Central College   R. M. E.
Naperville, Illinois
1983

Acknowledgments

I am happy to record my debt to the following persons whose reports and suggestions have helped immensely for this edition: Lester Beaurline of the University of Virginia; Joyce Erickson of Seattle Pacific University; Louise Garrison of Oregon State University; Liela Greiman of John F. Kennedy University; Melinda A. Knight of New York University; my own students; and especially Bruce Ardinger of Marshall University, who reinforced my own efforts with much perceptive and inventive commentary.

My special gratitude goes to John W. Wright and George R. Allen, formerly of Oxford University Press, for their discriminating support throughout the history of this book; and to Curtis Church, Kim Lewis, and Nancy Amy of Oxford for sensitive editorial help in the present edition. To North Central College I am thankful for experience, for a sabbatical leave, and for other support.

Finally, I am proud as before to observe a tradition as heartfelt as it is venerable, in dedicating this work to Vivian my wife.

Contents

Style

1   Preview

Style and Outlook

From a person's writing you can determine that writer's way of taking hold of things. Consider two college men who are each writing home about a history test:

> WRITER A Had an American History little exam last week (73 objective ques.–multiple-choice). Another kid and I shared Top Dog (70/73). It wasn't very difficult, needless to say. As I told Jamie, like in spelling, I may not know how to spell a word, but I know when a word is mis-spelled; this makes multiple choice not real difficult for me.

> WRITER B Well, I couldn't tell you whether the Spanish-American War lasted (A) 2 years, (B) 1 year, (C) 6 months, or (D) 10 weeks—and a lot of other ABCD things like that—so I fouled up another of Prof. Harriman's cheapie objective exams in American History. When the hell is that old alphabet-machine going to ask something halfway vital, like whether the U.S. should have been *in* that war? (I passed, barely.)

Presumably neither student thought that he was describing his "educational philosophy." Both were simply reporting a bit of academic news. But look back over their reports. What would you say about their feel for college studies?

You may be struck by Writer A's sense of the American History test as a competitive game. It's a game he is modestly good at. He watches the points like a hawk. He is interested in the flair by which he "won." But

3

the subject matter of the test lies outside his focus. It seems reasonable to guess that Writer A is score-oriented for the moment.

How does Writer B feel about the game aspect of the test? He despises it, doesn't he? ("Cheapie objective exam"; "old alphabet-machine.") Perhaps he's mad because he scored low, but then too he seems to find the game trivial. From him you do learn about the content of the exam and about his own involvement with the ethics of war. It seems reasonable to guess that Writer B is idea-oriented, at least more so than Writer A.

You can't use language without making choices (sometimes unconscious ones) of words, details, sequence, stress, and so forth—and those choices express your values, the experience to which you are most responsive, your judgment of what really counts. If you learn all that you have to choose from, your style can answer more sharply to your own nature. Again, by expanding your knowledge of possible choices you become aware of more in your experience itself. Your style and your experience build into each other: that is why the development of style belongs near the center of a first-rate education. *Chapters 2 and 3 will carry this matter forward.*

Style and Audience

Writing is a social act. It is carried on with readers and because of readers. The presence of your reader—possibly an embarrassment at first—can become your greatest stimulus. In learning exactly how to relate to your audience, you learn more about what you really make of your subject.

Let us concentrate on just one of the letters already cited, the one by Writer B. Return to that letter for a moment and ask how B sees his relationship to the parents who will be reading his letter, and how that relationship enters his thoughts about the history test.

Would you agree that B sees his parents as rather friendly people, to whom he can confess a low score together with his frank indignation ("When the hell . . .")? Quite likely they are also serious people who share B's dislike of superficial education; but they evidently value grades enough for B to reassure them that he did pass.

Imagine that B's audience is different. Suppose that he is addressing another kind of parent—a whip-cracking father who demands top marks and no excuses:

> WRITER B (to changed audience) Dad, I passed that American History test, but honestly I am not satisfied with just passing. These multiple-choice questions should train a man to store a tremendous amount of detailed information, such as how long the Spanish-American War lasted. I know

now that the war lasted 10 weeks, and will know how to master
similar data for the next opportunity.

You may agree that B has timidly catered to paternal tyranny. This again
would be part of his outlook—that in the presence of power-figures, B
tailors his reports to their expectations. If B had known more about himself and his father, he might have written a stronger and wiser account of
his history test. Chapters 9 through 12 will present some of the ways in
which a writer finds the audience and works with it, even in the most
formal, objective writing.

Style and Language

Two small alternatives in B's second letter (the apologetic report to a
stern father) can illustrate the next area of this book:

B MIGHT
HAVE SAID I am *not happy* with just passing.
I am *disgusted* with just passing.
I am *heartsick* over just passing.

B DID SAY I am *not satisfied* with just passing.

What does "not satisfied" say that the other versions don't? It seems to
convey B's hard-headed evaluation of his own low performance which
he hopes his stern father will respect. "Heartsick" wouldn't work; it suggests the crybaby. "Not happy" and "disgusted" would stress B's upset
feelings too much; for such a father he wants to be masterful, not emotional. Thus the slightest variation of words could change the whole feel
of B's report; and if still other word-choices got mixed in, an entirely different experience would be created for both B's father and B. Thus:

I am *disgusted* with *the rotten score.*
I am *heartsick* over *the shameful score.*
I am *in a tizzy over the quantitative insufficiency of my final score.*

For a second case, consider a microscopic variation of sentence structure:

B MIGHT
HAVE SAID Dad, *although* I passed that American History test, honestly I
am not satisfied with just passing.

B DID SAY Dad, I passed that American History test, but honestly I am not
satisfied with just passing.

What is the special effect of "Dad, I passed"? Presumably B wants to begin strong. He did pass the test, and he's not going to downgrade that

success by placing it in a subordinate clause (*"although* I passed"). The "although" signals bad news ahead; it could put his father's hackles up at once.

Your style at this close range is language itself—your words and sentences as they work onto the paper syllable by syllable. It can be compared to the brushwork of the painter in building a canvas. Good style is good choice of words, good choice of sentence structure; from this choice of good "brushstrokes" comes the unique and forceful vision of things that we see in good writing. Therefore you need a cultivated sense for detail in diction and syntax, so that you can make the *principled* choice among *known* alternatives which marks the finest craft of any sort. *The choices open and the effects possible with vocabulary and sentence structure are treated in Chapters 13 through 20.*

From Style to the Larger Scale

Why is it that outlines—so persistently recommended in English courses— are almost never used in writing personal letters? Outlines take extra time, for one thing. Again, no one is pressing letter writers to come up with finished work. But isn't a main reason this, that a person writing to a good friend is absorbed in the letter *as it comes?* The writer feels caught up in the interplay between his or her own recent experience and the listening friend. Not knowing beforehand all that this interplay can bring out, the writer *discovers that experience through writing.* Out of this discovery grows the meaning and the structure of the letter. This is probably why a good letter seems to have a shape and unity even though its writer never thought of organizing it into parts.

Planning and organizing are important, especially for the longer paper dealt with in Part Four of this book. But in all kinds of writing from poetry to the research paper, the significant planning begins at "the moment of style"—the immediate exploration of meaning through the act of writing. What happens in that moment is what counts most. This continual happening can lead you toward the substance, the form, the planning which generate the final whole composition. At these later stages you can best see how to exploit the larger patterns of order which belong to rhetoric.

Reading for Style

Whenever you acquire a new power in writing, that same power strengthens your reading, because you now know where to look for its presence and how to evaluate its effects. The reverse also holds true—that by observantly reading the work of others you can learn new ways to write. Throughout this book, the interplay of writing and reading will appear in the examples and in the short exercise readings for analysis. *Chapter 24 and the following anthology of longer readings will furnish an extended exposure* to be sampled whenever you and your instructor decide.

Exercise 1 (style and outlook)

Each of the following sentences describes the same thing—a young man and a young woman at the theater. What does each version tell you about the narrator's own way of looking at things?

   a. George, Jr., was in the sixth row of the parquet with the daughter of H. B. Carmichael, the third partner of a wholesale dry-goods house. (Theodore Dreiser, *Sister Carrie*, 1900)
   b. Julie was way back in the sixth row, with the son of George Hurstwood, the night manager of a fancy saloon in the Loop.
   c. The svelte honey blonde in the white ermine sat with a sleek, dark-haired youngster in a white tie, in two of the best seats in the house.
   d. Young George Hurstwood had obtained sixth-row parquet seats, as an appropriate setting for the costly Julie Carmichael.
   e. George and I were practically invisible, six whole rows behind the orchestra pit.
   f. He was sitting calmly in the orchestra below us, with a slight bulge over the left side of his chest. His hands stayed in his lap.

Exercise 2 (style and audience)

The speaker in each of the following passages (all taken from well-known fiction) is proposing marriage, or something like it. What can you tell about the speaker's *evident character* (sometimes called "persona")? What can you tell about the listener? What does each speaker do which shows his awareness (or ignorance) of the exact nature of his present relationship to his listener? How would you rate the three proposals as to their probable success?

   a. Almost as soon as I entered the house I singled you out as the companion of my future life. But before I am run away with by my feelings on this subject, perhaps it will be advisable for me to state my reasons for marrying—and moreover for coming into Hertfordshire with the design of selecting a wife, as I certainly did.

   My reasons for marrying are, first, that I think it a right thing for every clergyman in easy circumstances (like myself) to set the example of matrimony in his parish. Secondly, that I am convinced it will add very greatly to my happiness; and thirdly—

which perhaps I ought to have mentioned earlier, that it is the particular advice and recommendation of the very noble lady whom I have the honor of calling patroness. (Jane Austen, *Pride and Prejudice,* 1813)

b. [A gentleman to his housekeeper] You and I know, Mrs. Jimson, at our age, that the really important thing in life is living together in amity and mutual respect and we have that already. Anything more is not really of great importance. As they say, those that have it think nothing of it, and those that have not, think much too much of it. So if you feel that you wouldn't like to go any further in the matter, you'll never hear any more from me. We'll forget that we said anything about it—I'm not going to throw away the solid good fortune I have with you just for the little extra. Pleasant as it would be and convenient, since we do inhabit the same house, and I won't hide it, a great addition to my comforts, I'll think no more of it. What do you say, Mrs. Jimson, shall I drop the subject? (Joyce Cary, *Herself Surprised,* 1941)

c. Sister Elizabeth, when you go down on your knees tonight, I want you to ask the Lord to speak to your heart, and tell you how to answer what I'm going to say.

Sister Elizabeth, the Lord's been speaking to my heart, and I believe it's his will that you and me should be man and wife.

I know, I'm a lot older than you. But that don't make no difference. I'm a mighty strong man yet. I done been down the line, Sister Elizabeth, and maybe I can keep you from making . . . some of my mistakes, bless the Lord . . . maybe I can help keep your foot from stumbling . . . again . . . girl . . . for as long as we's in this world.

And I'll love you, and I'll honor you . . . until the day God calls me home.

And I'll love your son, your little boy, just like he was my own. He won't never have to fret or worry about nothing; he won't never be cold or hungry as long as I'm alive and I got my two hands to work with. I swear this before my God, because He done give me back something I thought was lost.

Sister Elizabeth, will you pray? (James Baldwin, *Go Tell It on the Mountain,* 1953)

Exercise 3 (style and language)

The first proposal from the preceding exercise contains several remarkable choices in diction and syntax, which are italicized in the version below. Show exactly what each choice implies about the speaker's outlook and conception of his listener.

Almost as soon as I entered the house I singled you out as the companion of my future life. But *before I am run away with by my feelings* on this subject, perhaps it will be advisable for me to state my reasons for marrying—and moreover for coming into Hertfordshire with the *design* of selecting a wife, as I certainly did.

My reasons for marrying are, first, that I think it a right thing for every clergyman in easy circumstances (like myself) to set the example of matrimony in his parish. Secondly, that I am convinced it will add very greatly to my happiness; and thirdly—*which perhaps I ought to have mentioned earlier,* that it is the particular advice and recommendation of the very noble lady whom I have the honor of calling patroness. (Jane Austen, *Pride and Prejudice,* 1813)

For each of the two other selections of Exercise 2, mark three or four places where you find the choice of words or sentence structure especially revealing, and be able to show why.

Exercise 4 (outlook, audience, language)

Take any passage of 12 to 20 lines from the work of a writer you are now studying, or a speech of similar length by a character in a play or story. Make as many inferences as you can about:

- a. The evident character of the person writing or speaking.
- b. The outlook of that writer or character.
- c. The way in which the person's relationship to listeners or readers seems to enter into what is said.

For each inference be able to point to exact details of word-choice or sentence structure which make your point. This exercise may either be written as a short paper of analysis (from one to two pages) or prepared as informal notes to support a class discussion.

Exercise 5 (outlook, audience, language)

The purpose of this exercise is for you to discover how outlook, audience, and language shape one another. Choose from the following unfortunate experiences one which you've actually had recently:

- a. An injury or illness.
- b. Running low on money.
- c. Some disillusion with job or education.
- d. Failure to win an expected opportunity.
- e. An auto mishap.
- f. Witnessing a shocking example of misconduct.

Write a letter home covering this experience. Write a second letter to a good friend covering the same experience. Try not to exaggerate or invent the people you're writing to, but imagine them as they really are, and imagine how you would really write them about this incident.

Exercise 6 (outlook, audience, language)

Bring to class any recent writing by yourself or by a friend (perhaps one of the letters you wrote for Exercise 5). Because this exercise could become a bit personal, you may wish to offer a copy with names omitted or disguised. Working either in small groups or as a whole class, discuss one another's samples for the clues they offer as to the way the writer takes hold of the experience being described and the way the writer relates to the reader. Note three or four choices in vocabulary or sentence structure which you find especially significant.

I   STYLE AND OUTLOOK

Style is the ultimate morality of mind.

ALFRED WHITEHEAD, *The Aims of Education*, 1917

Style is organic to the person doing the writing, as much a part of him as his hair, or, if he is bald, his lack of it. Trying to add style is like adding a toupee.

WILLIAM ZINSSER, *On Writing Well*, 1980

2   Three Ways of Seeing

You've already taken notice of several ways by which a writer's outlook takes form through style. This chapter and the next one will systematize the matter by proposing six representative elements of style which most quickly develop the writer's outlook.

Generalizing

Suppose that you have occasion to mention the landscaping of someone's back lawn; but you aren't particularly interested in this lawn except as it indicates, say, its owner's wealth. You might write:

> Behind the Llewellyn manor stretched an ample lawn, magnificently landscaped.

This description contains only two features—manor, lawn—and both are too vague for anyone to picture them. You don't care to specify any further. Instead, you use language which *asserts* the general quality of wealth: "ample," "magnificently landscaped." Assertive language is valuable because it tells your reader what you make of something, what your conclusions are—here, that you infer wealth. It can interpret and control large masses of detail which might otherwise puzzle the reader. You might use your assertion about the ampleness of the Llewellyn lawn as an introduction to numerous substantiating details. Or you might wrap up the details with a final unifying assertion that the lawn was indeed ample and magnificent.

Assertive language used *only by itself* lacks evidence or definition. To put it figuratively, such language communicates "labels" rather than "contents"; therefore it might be called "label language." Label language can indicate your assurance that the matter at hand does not require proof or analysis; hence a summary will do. The word "ample" *could* be supported by mentioning the size of the back lawn as 23.1 acres, but what would be the point if all one cares about is its largeness in general? But remember that *assertions alone prove nothing.* Suppose you write:

> The Llewellyn back lawn was magnificent. Only an enormously rich family could have afforded such a lawn. Its landscape was superb in every way. The total effect was truly imposing.

By the space you give to talking about the lawn you indicate that you find it important, but in support of that evaluation you merely offer repetitive labels: "magnificent," "enormously rich," "truly imposing." This is like saying, "The Llewellyn back lawn was magnificent because it was magnificent." A skeptical reader could hardly be blamed for inferring that you had given the Llewellyn estate little serious thought, that you were claiming an importance for it that you did not feel.

General language is useful, then, for summarizing or sketching out one's outlook on a given topic. It defeats its purpose when it is required to create the outlook too. Other means must be used. (More ideas on the use of general language may be found in Chapter 13, p. 139.)

Detailing

You might open up a direct view of the Llewellyn estate based on what your own eyes can tell you:

> Behind the Llewellyn manor stretched an ample lawn, elegantly bordered with flower beds, arched with grand old elms, lined here and there with finely sculptured hedges.

This description builds upon five features instead of the original two— manor, lawn, flower beds, elms, hedges.

Assertive language does still appear—"ample," "elegantly bordered," "grand old," "finely sculptured"—but now it is linked to concrete detail. Moreover even the assertive language has sharpened, since your mere search for detail has clarified your *general* sense of the scene. Instead of saying "superb hedges," you have stopped to visualize a well-kept ornamental hedge and have come up with the more authoritative "finely sculptured." If you cared enough, you could rework the detail itself, asking what kind of hedge plant it really is, how the eye would actually take it in, thus: "hedges of Hamilton Thorn, dark and waxy, finely sculptured in globes and long bows."

Now suppose that with the same valuation of the magnificence of the Llewellyn back lawn, you want to concentrate on it, to savor it, to create its densely splendid presence. On this large scale you might write several pages, of which we must be contented with this passage for the flower beds alone:

> The flower beds adorned the lawn in elegant festoons, flagged at this season with soft golden iris, clouded with peonies of the faintest pink centered with lemon yellow. Salmon-hued poppies hung indolent near the shiny dark waxy-green myrtle banks. A rich fringe of lavender verbena bordered the beds in long brilliant scrolls and scallops. Advancing onto the lawn, one caught its hot fragrance, so fresh, sweet, and lingering as to seem ambrosial. In the luminous shade under the elms one saw the lucent drops of last night's rain, still poised on the rose leaves.

Here the detail is both intensified and extended on a large scale. These flowers are named, shaped, colored, and scented. Lighting and surface textures are specified. The assertive modifiers still serve the same function as before—of summing up the central quality of opulence: thus "adorned," "elegant," "indolent," "rich," "ambrosial," etc. But the senses of the writer have much more actively noted the particulars which create such impressions. The scene is fully there, a sign of the writer's undivided, educated, and admiring attention, which in turn signifies the high value the writer places on the quality found in it.

In creating your case from particulars rather than from summary assertion, you have two choices: how strong a magnifying glass to use and how wide a glass. The sharper your detail and the larger your scale, the more you're showing that for you it counts.

Notice how your own impression of the Llewellyn estate can be refined and intensified by that process of looking close and noticing. Similarly, your readers when exposed to materials assembled in this way can feel the force of primary concrete evidence. They can respond with much more conviction to the whole impact of the scene.

The two processes used so far—generalizing and detailing—can be clarified by this brief table of comparison:

ASSERTION	DETAIL
He was angry.	His face was red; he began to shout and pound the desk.

It's cold outside.	The temperature is below zero; the ground is white with frost.
Harris was badly in debt.	Harris owed five payments on his car; he was behind on his mortgage; his bank account was overdrawn.

(More ideas on the use of detail may be found in Chapter 14, p. 150.)

Reasoning

How are details and generalizations related? Through reasoning. When you think about a subject, you are linking its generalizations and details using one or both of two logical processes.

1. When you generalize from a body of details, you are using what logicians call *induction*. Thus you survey the Llewellyn lawn and note its details: iris, peonies, poppies, myrtle, verbena, roses. From all your senses tell you, you generalize the impression of loveliness and amplitude.

Scientists use the inductive process when they collect observations in the laboratory and then frame a hypothesis or generalization which brings the detailed observations into some sort of general conclusion. (Of course this explanation of scientific method is much too simple. It doesn't explain how scientists design their experiments in the first place. But the central feature of *generalizing from detail* is there.)

All of us generalize from detail, or we would never learn that fire is hot and that people stepping off cliffs will fall. When someone presents us with an *induction* (that is, a conclusion based on details), we may test it with such commonsense questions as: Were the details *numerous* enough to justify the conclusion? Were they *representative* enough? (Did the writer observe only one corner of the Llewellyn estate in deciding that the estate was magnificent and that the Llewellyns were enormously rich?) Could there be *another and better explanation* of the details? (Maybe a horticultural association had temporarily rented and landscaped the estate for a special exhibit?) You can apply similar tests as you observe the subject you want to write about.

Just as your own outlook can be extended and reinforced by *inductive reasoning*, so can the outlook of your readers, when you expose them to a series of details which call for the same response. (Your doing so can be called *inductive presentation*.) Your readers can respond, not because they receive a summary but because they share in the total impact of the scene.

Writers of fiction, poetry, and drama have mastered the inductive process. They don't *tell* us that their characters are wicked or virtuous. They present the actual living details which *show* the characters' natures. They allow us to *induce* our own conclusion and thus become involved in the action.

2. Instead of drawing your conclusions *from* the details, you may choose to apply some of your previous conclusions *to* the details. This opposite process is called *deduction*.

For example, what standards or assumptions do you have for measuring the magnificence of the Llewellyn estate? How about the opinion of authorities, for one? Then you might reason out the Llewellyn magnificence thus:

> The Chamber of Commerce keeps a list of the most distin-
> guished showplaces in town, for the benefit of tourists. (*General
> statement implying the principle that the Chamber of Com-
> merce is competent to judge "magnificence."*) High on this list
> is the Llewellyn estate. (*Detail from which the inference is to
> be drawn that the Llewellyn estate meets the standard of "mag-
> nificence."*)

Another standard for magnificence might be the size of the estate—thus:

> Most men think themselves opulent if they can landscape their
> homes against half an acre or so. (*General statement implying
> the principle that property of a half-acre and up can often be
> considered "magnificent."*) The Llewellyn place measured le-
> gally at 23.1 acres. (*Detail from which the inference is to be
> drawn that the Llewellyn place meets the standard of "mag-
> nificence."*)

Notice that these general standards (or principles or assumptions) *are* asserted. They are not proved; they are supposed as likely to be conceded by the reader. Logicians will commonly frame a *deduction* in a set format to show what generalization is being applied to what detail—thus:

GENERAL-
IZATION Any place listed by the Chamber of Commerce as a showplace is probably magnificent.

DETAIL The Llewellyn estate is listed by the Chamber of Commerce as a showplace.

CONCLUSION The Llewellyn estate is probably magnificent.

Technically this format is called a *syllogism;* the generalization is called the *major premise;* and the detail is called the *minor premise.* The abstract form of the argument above is this:

A is included in a larger class B.
C is included in A.
Hence, C is included in B.

To test a deduction, one usually applies such questions as these: Is the general assumption (i.e., major premise) *valid?* Can one think of *exceptions* which would weaken the assumption? (Suppose the Chamber of Commerce also lists the broken-down old Hotel Pittsville as a "show place"? Does that make the Hotel "magnificent"?) Or, one can ask, is the *detail accurate?* (Maybe the Chamber of Commerce lists the estate as a showplace merely because it is old?) The advantage of laying out someone's argument in this way is that you clearly pin down each part of the argument so that you can ask whether you accept it and the way it is being used.

Actually, few people think easily in such slow-motion steps, much less write easily in them. You would probably simply imply your general assumptions as you brought forward your details. Thus, in describing the Llewellyn estate, your standards of magnificence would silently enter, as suggested in the left-hand column below:

authority reputation cost care size prestige of users	The Llewellyn estate was listed by the Chamber of Commerce as one of the city's showplaces; and on every fine Sunday, sightseers' cars drove up the Llewellyn road by scores, with license plates from nearly every state. The Llewellyn land taxes would have supported a small college. The chores of planting, pruning, and mowing did support a squad of gardeners. The total estate measured legally at 23.1 acres; not a square foot grew wild; and the long vistas and towering trees had framed many gatherings of governors, businessmen, and scholars.

To check out such a description you (or your reader) will have to extract its buried assumptions and inspect them. Suppose you really don't believe that an estate is magnificent just because of a Chamber of Commerce listing? Or that magnificent size begins with so few acres?

Deductive treatment at its best suggests a judicious mind bringing a wide general experience to bear on its topic—whereas inductive treatment at its best suggests an acutely observant mind rich in concrete evidence. You can choose either or both, depending on how you see your subject.

Exercise 1 (generalizing)

For each passage of detail, substitute a single general assertion about the topic which the details support:

a. My brother Art and I were cracking jokes at the summer cabin breakfast table. Maybe we were getting a bit silly for two grown men. Suddenly he topped one of my jokes just as I was drinking coffee. I snorted, and the hot fluid went down the wrong way. I wheezed furiously to clear my throat, but Art thought I was still laughing. Then I was on hands and knees before the fireplace, gasping in agony for air which would not come until my time had nearly run out. For the rest of that day I was rather quiet.

b. Ferd McDowell's new automobile showroom covered a half-block and, as of July 17, sheltered eighty-three new Oldsmobiles, with another trailer-load on the way. Ferd had six salesmen on his payroll, ten mechanics, two secretaries, and one accountant. For the third week running, fewer than ten prospective buyers had driven into his guest parking lot.

Exercise 2 (detailing)

Identify the "label language" in each passage. Then recast the passage using no label language and supplying the particulars which would demonstrate the original assertion.

a. She was an extraordinarily beautiful woman. Her hair was lovely. Her eyes were enchanting, her complexion exquisite.

b. He was a poor traveling salesman. His samples were shopworn. His person was seedy and unkempt. His salestalk was full of trite slang and insecure humor.

c. The city bureaucracy is maddening. Service to the people is poor. City employees are rude. Delays are endless.

d. My music teacher is terrific. She really understands her students. Her knowledge of music is super.

e. My math teacher stinks. His assignments are hard. He doesn't care about students. His grading is unfair.

f. The strip mining had desolated what used to be lovely landscape. Nothing of its former splendor remained. The countryside was barren, ugly, lifeless.

g. I walked abroad alone, in a solitary place in my father's pasture, for contemplation. And as I was walking there, and looking up on the sky and clouds, there came into my mind so sweet a sense of the glorious *majesty* and *grace* of God, that I know not how to express. I seemed to see them both in a sweet conjunction; majesty and meekness joined together; it was a sweet, and gentle, and holy majesty; and also a majestic meekness; an awful sweetness; a high, and great, and holy gentleness. (Jonathan Edwards, *Personal Narrative*, c. 1739)

Exercise 3 (detailing)

Choose a passage of 12–20 lines from any selection in this book (either an illustration or a reading). Copy it down, underscoring the label language in it. Then recast the passage, using no label language and supplying the particulars which would demonstrate the assertions. Add a paragraph in which you show why your passage is an improvement or why it isn't.

Exercise 4 (detailing)

Work from your own experience in developing one of the following assignments. Base it on close personal observation or memory. Suggested length: from one-half to one page.

- a. Describe the eating of a favorite food in such detail as will substantiate your keen pleasure in eating it. (*Note: Make very little use of assertive language such as "delicious" or "tasty." Instead, concentrate on the details of sight, smell, touch, taste, etc., which actually produce "deliciousness.")*
- b. Describe your final preparations for an important public performance, in such detail as will make clear your intense anticipation or nervousness (or both).
- c. Describe the sights, sounds, and smells of a busy coffee shop or bakery or delicatessen.
- d. Describe approaching your home after a long absence, in such detail as will substantiate your emotion on returning.
- e. Describe an expensive new automobile in such detail as will show its fine materials and craftsmanship.
- f. Describe the first minute of any organized activity which you attend (athletic pep rally, committee meeting, city council meeting, etc.).

Exercise 5 (reasoning: deductive)

In each of the following specimens of the deductive process, a general principle or assumption or standard is being applied so as to state or imply a conclusion. Be able to show what the general principle or assumption or standard is and why you agree or disagree with it. As an alternative, frame each argument as a syllogism (see p. 17), and then judge whether the argument is valid.

SAMPLE You ought to read *Timeweek*—it has twice as many readers as any other weekly newsmagazine.

SOLUTION

MAJOR Any weekly newsmagazine leading the others in circulation (A) PREMISE is a magazine you ought to read (B).

MINOR *Timeweek* (C) is a weekly newsmagazine leading the others in PREMISE circulation (A).

CONCLUSION *Timeweek* (C) is a magazine you ought to read (B).

Evaluation: The major premise (general principle) is weak. Large readership doesn't guarantee quality. Trash can attract large circulation. The minor premise might be challenged for proof. Where did the speaker get evidence of magazine circulations?

  a. Nobody can get ahead as fast as Sally has and still be honest.
  b. I forgive you, honey. You're bound to be tempted by women who throw themselves at you.
  c. "We don't discuss smoking and health," said one tobacco spokesman. "We leave that to those who understand it thoroughly." (*London Times*, 1970)
  d. Crud Breakfast Flakes must be good for you. No other cereal contains PU 57.
  e. (*A motion picture actress*) When someone is spending millions on a film, I don't think it's too much to ask you to take your clothes off. It's not like asking you to change your religion or anything.
  f. Don't tell me the Mayor is innocent of those newspaper charges. She hasn't said a word to refute them.
  g. I fully appreciate that this may be the end of my political career, but I cannot in good conscience stand here and thwart the obvious majority of the House. I therefore request you, Mr. Speaker, to change my negative vote to an affirmative vote.
  h. I oppose gun control because it's just another restriction on our freedom.
  i. Officer, every car on this highway exceeds the speed limit. Why hang a ticket on *me?*
  j. Why does Professor Jenkins stay in the classroom during tests? Doesn't he trust us?
  k. Do you honestly think that Senator Wilkes would make a good President, with all the trouble he's had with his own children?
  l. (*Add one of your own.*)
  m. (*Add another of your own.*)

Exercise 6 (reasoning: deductive)

Here are two mealtimes from fiction. For each, extract the general principles which are being used to judge either the food or the characters:

  a. The girl brought in a big bowl of hot vegetable soup and the wine. We had fried trout afterward and some sort of stew and a big bowl full of wild strawberries. We did not lose money on the wine, and the girl was shy but nice about bringing it. The old woman looked in once and counted the empty bottles. (Ernest Hemingway, *The Sun Also Rises*, 1926)

b. They thanked him, and, entering, were pleased with the neatness and regularity of the place. The hermit set flesh and wine before them, though he fed only upon fruits and water. His discourse was cheerful without levity, and pious without enthusiasm. (Samuel Johnson, *Rasselas*, 1759)

Exercise 7 (reasoning: deductive)

Choose from the following activities one in which you're reasonably expert:

a. Playing in a specific sport.
b. Playing a musical instrument.
c. Working on a piece of machinery or apparatus.
d. Back-packing.

Describe someone performing this activity in a really admirable way—to show not only the specific details which command admiration but to show the general principle by which each detail *is* to be admired. Part of a sample solution involving a tennis player might read thus:

> On each service, her right foot swung forward into an immediate sprint for the net, so that her opponent's return would find her closing in for the put-away.

(The implicit principle is that a tennis player should move toward the net at once on serving, to press home the attack.)

Exercise 8 (reasoning: inductive)

In each of the following specimens of the inductive process, details are being assembled to support (or suggest) a conclusion. Be able to state what the conclusion is, what are the supporting details, and why you agree or disagree with the reasoning. (Tests: Are the details sufficient to make the case? Are they representative enough? Would an alternate explanation make more sense than the conclusion offered?)

SAMPLE TV today has lost all sense of morality. Just last night I watched a drama so full of violence that I turned off the set in protest.

DISCUSSION The conclusion is that TV today has lost all morality. The supporting detail is an unnamed TV drama that the speaker thought was immoral. But one detail isn't enough to make a case. The speaker should have offered a large number of specific examples.

An alternate explanation for this protest may be that the speaker is a prude.

a. Students want stricter rules these days. Wheaton College has tough rules and draws so many applicants for admission that hundreds must be turned away. Our college has permissive rules, and our enrollments have dropped.

b. Women students are obviously performing better at their studies today. Last year the campus Honor Society included 26 women. That was 30 percent of its membership. This year the Society included 46 women or 55 percent of its membership.

c. Ninety-five percent of the employees of Glamour Soap actually use that soap. They must believe in it!

d. I've drawn five blind dates in the last year, and all were real dogs. Don't talk to *me* about blind dates!

3 Three Ways of Focusing

Selecting

So far the Llewellyn back lawn has come to us only through a mind impressed with its opulence. Suppose you were to study the lawn with an entirely different set of values—say those of an infantry officer before a battle during which you'll have to make a stand on the Llewellyn estate. You would forget the opulence. You would now bring military criteria to bear on the terrain before you:

> The long fall of the lawn would allow perfect enfilading fire upon any troops storming from the bottom. The fieldstone wall bordering the patio would serve for a commanding trench. Foxholes behind the hedges would allow machine-gunning through the foliage, while flanking gun nests could be laid among the flower beds on either side.

Of course there is no beauty here, only chances for attack and defense. The glory of the flower beds is irrelevant to their advantages as gun sites.

Or suppose you were an architect commissioned to crown the estate with a cathedral or temple, once the old manor were torn down:

> The Tudor manor, glass conservatory, stables—all that affluence would be swept off the crown of the hill. In its place the temple would rise in a towering thrust, inviting the eyes and thoughts of all within miles. Because the hedges and stone walls blocked off visitors, they would give way to long ascending drives and walks, under the arching elms which would frame both temple and sky. . . .

Notice how quickly the architect disposes of the manor buildings as obstructing the exalted purpose of the new temple. The desired effect is to aspire, to rise, to point earth toward sky, creation toward Creator. Again, the present walls and hedges are seen only as excluding and restrictive. Therefore, they disappear, being replaced by walks and drives which carry the visitors toward the climactic summit. Note how the architect retains the tall elms as reinforcing the new theme. (For further discussion of selection of detail, see "The Catalog," Chapter 14, p. 152.)

Placing

Once you have a selective principle, you can work out your evaluation further by what materials you choose to give prominent placement. The three positions which normally command emphasis are the beginning and ending (of a sentence, paragraph, or composition) and the main clause (of a sentence).

The infantry officer opens his survey with "The long fall of the lawn." This is the key tactical feature from which everything else develops; and such an opening reflects the officer's efficient concentration on the sheer expediencies of war. You can hardly conceive of his neglecting such a fact until the end of his perusal, and you might feel only a limited enthusiasm for following an officer who could do so.

Note how a different opening would change the implied outlook:

> *Any troops storming from the bottom* could receive perfect enfilading fire, thanks to the long fall of the lawn.

Here the stress goes directly to the attackers. The image of troops storming onto the lawn is what triggers the officer's tactical response. He seems to be more defensive in this version, in that his mind seizes upon the danger before coming up on the opportunity.

The power of the second emphatic position, the ending, can be illustrated by supposing that the officer phrases his thought thus:

> The long fall of the lawn might tempt enemy troops to storm upward, only to be greeted by *perfect enfilading fire.*

Delayed until the end, the "enfilading fire" comes as a climactic surprise, just as the officer actually conceives it.

The third emphatic position, the main clause, consists of the three basic parts of the common English sentence: subject (S), verb (V), and whatever complement (C) or additional elements the subject and verb require to obtain minimum grammatical completeness. Since all the rest of the sentence serves to develop this main clause, it logically claims a high rank in the attention of both reader and writer. We can illustrate the range of main-clause emphasis by supposing three infantry officers, each reflecting on the same point:

> 1ST OFFICER The long *fall* of the lawn *would allow* perfect enfilading *fire* upon
>   s   v   c
>   any troops storming from the bottom.

This main-clause structure is FALL–WOULD-ALLOW–FIRE; and it brings out the tactician, the officer who thinks in abstract terms of terrain and text-book moves ("long fall of the lawn," "enfilading fire").

> 2ND OFFICER Because of the long fall of the lawn, the *defenders could open*
>   s   v
>   a perfect enfilading *fire* upon any troops storming from the
>   c
>   bottom.

Main-clause emphasis is now taken by DEFENDERS–COULD-OPEN–FIRE. The same careful means-to-end thinking shows here as in the original, but this variation is more action-centered in that the grammatical subject is no longer the lawn but the defenders. This officer focuses upon men fighting, where the first officer thinks of the play of tactical forces. (Notice that main-clause emphasis can compete with the other emphatic positions of beginning and ending, in which event a delicate balance occurs; or the main clause may coincide with and reinforce one of the other positions.)

> 3RD OFFICER *Troops* soon *would storm the bottom,* only to receive a perfect
>   s   v   c
>   enfilading fire from the upper slopes of the lawn.

This time the main clause is TROOPS–WOULD-STORM–BOTTOM; and it shows the officer concentrating on the enemy, keeping his eye upon the approaching collision.

Which officer would you expect to be entrusted with a major military mission? The answer would depend upon your own values.

(Placement within the sentence is further discussed in Chapters 17–19, pp. 184 ff. Placement as an element in paragraphs is covered in Chapter 7, pp. 62 ff. For placement in longer papers, see Part Four, The Longer Paper, pp. 237 ff.)

Cohering

Young children as well as certain disoriented adults are said to experience life as an unconnected series of vivid separate events. Only the moment counts; it isn't valued above or below other experience. In the language which expresses such an outlook, no subordinate clauses appear, since everything is seen in identical main-clause importance. No connectives are used except maybe for the basic "and" or "then." So everything comes out in the syntax of a textbook for the primary grades:

> My name is Tim. I like candy. Yesterday we went downtown. I bought a bag of candy. Jacky stubbed his toe.

Or perhaps more true to the gushing narrative of the youngster:

> We went downtown and we went into a store and I bought a bag of candy and then Jacky stubbed his toe. . . .

In literature a writer trying to catch this subliterate flow can eliminate even the sense of identities implied by capitalized nouns and pronouns, the elementary organization afforded by sentence division and by clause structure:

> window opens and i step into darkness breathing jumps me breathing hot and putrid and i jab hard with knee everything crashing and screams. . . .

To permit highly civilized thought, language must enable the most sophisticated exposition of connections, guiding values, shades of importance. Consider our architect. An intense mind is at work here, both rejecting and devising resources toward a central goal; but if that mind could emerge only in naive units, it might look like this:

NAIVE STRUCTURES	ORIGINAL
The hedges and walls blocked off visitors. They would give way to long ascending drives and walks. The arching elms would frame both temple and sky. . . .	Because the hedges and stone walls blocked off visitors, they would give way to long ascending drives and walks, under the arching elms which would frame both temple and sky. . . .

The naive version contains three sentences (all simple) for the architect's original one. They are efficient and easy to read, but their point + point +

point sequence would suggest that the architect's mind labors to build the plan. In the original, the whole sentence moves toward a climax—leading through obstructions to final effect. Here the obstructions (hedges, wall) fall away before the ascent of drives, walks, and elms, all pointing toward temple and sky. From such an interlinking of thought, one appreciates the aspiration, determination, and coherent inventiveness of the architect's vision.

Anything you do (or omit to do) in linking your material enters into this element of coherence. The sequence of topics, the amount of subordination, the division of tasks among the sentences—all show the unique way in which your mind joins your ideas and observations in a coherent pattern. Your mind patterns your subject. The same holds true on the larger scale of paragraphs (see Chapter 7, pp. 62 ff.) and longer papers (see especially Chapter 22, pp. 239 ff.).

Summary

When you write, you are working out your outlook. These two chapters have described six major elements of style which enter into that process:

> Generalizing
> Detailing
> Reasoning (inductive; deductive)
> Selecting
> Placing
> Cohering

Other elements of style will emerge later in this book. The more carefully you exploit all these, the more fully and powerfully you can realize your outlook in language and, beyond language, in the imaginations of your readers. *This can happen, whether by "outlook" is meant your total way of life—your philosophy or order of values—or your temporary valuation of a given subject with respect to a given end.* Moreover, by considering these elements as you begin to write, you're asking yourself what your outlook really is. Thus in the *process* of writing, you both create and discover an outlook.

As a reader, you can obtain corresponding benefits. By measuring a writer through such elements as the six discussed here, you can see more clearly the kind of mind which is working toward you. You can respond more accurately to its attractions and dangers, its powers and limits.

A Demonstration

To show how these six elements engage and develop the writer's outlook, a sample analysis will follow this passage from Upton Sinclair's novel on the meat-packing industry, *The Jungle* (1906). Sinclair is describing the slaughtering crew as it kills the cattle.

> They worked with furious intensity, literally upon the run—at a pace with which there is nothing to be compared except a football game. It was all highly specialized labor, each man having his task to do; generally this would consist of only two or three specific cuts, and he would pass down the line of fifteen or twenty carcasses, making these cuts upon each. First there came the "butcher," to bleed them; this meant one swift stroke, so swift that you could not see it—only the flash of the knife; and before you could realize it, the man had darted on to the next line, and a stream of bright red was pouring out upon the floor. This floor was half an inch deep with blood, in spite of the best efforts of men who kept shovelling it through holes; it must have made the floor slippery, but no one could have guessed this by watching the men at work.

1. *Generalizing:* The efficient frenzy of the slaughter is generalized or asserted in such terms as "furious intensity," "on the run," "highly specialized," "swift."

2. *Detailing:* Several lines of detail are devoted to the speed of the knife-work ("one swift stroke, so swift that you could not see it—only the flash of the knife") and to the color and quantity of the blood.

3. *Reasoning:*

   a. *Inductive.* Sinclair is generalizing "furious intensity" from the details shown. A government investigative report would probably include more numerical detail and precise measurements, but enough vivid detail is used to support a strong visual impression for a reader of fiction.
   b. *Deductive.* A strong deductive reasoning power is also at work on each detail to see what it means. Examples:

GENERAL
PRINCIPLE A butchery operation restricted to two or three cuts may be considered highly specialized.

SPECIFIC CASE The tasks of these men were restricted to two or three cuts.

CONCLUSION The tasks of these men were highly specialized.

GENERAL
PRINCIPLE Floors running with blood must be slippery.

SPECIFIC CASE This floor was running with blood.

CONCLUSION This floor must have been slippery.

GENERAL
PRINCIPLE Slaughterers who keep footing on slippery floors must be intensely efficient.

SPECIFIC CASE These men keep footing on a slippery floor.

CONCLUSION These men must have been intensely efficient.

4. *Selecting:* Sinclair says nothing about the appearance or thoughts of the killers here, or of the suffering of the animals. The furious adroitness of the slaughterers is the selective principle by which he controls the description.

5. *Placing:* The idea of "work" opens and closes the passage: "They worked with furious intensity . . . the men at work." The main-clause positions (subject-verb-complement) are given chiefly to the workers ("they worked," "he would pass down," "came the 'butcher,'" "the man had darted") and to the bloody floor ("stream was pouring," "the floor was deep," "it must have made the floor slippery"). On the other hand, Sinclair gives almost no main-clause placement to either the knives or the cutting, as one would expect from the attention he gives elsewhere to those elements. He seems to achieve a slight shock by assigning such casual sentence position to the actual act of killing.

6. *Cohering:* Sinclair manages his sentences as large organizing units, categorically devoting one sentence each to the following topics: the fast pace of the slaughter, the specialization of labor, the illustrative performance of the "butcher," and the bloodiness of the floor. With this much material to control, the sentences are accordingly complicated, containing a dozen main clauses, four subordinate clauses, and numerous phrases.

Summary of "outlook" as inferred from the preceding observations: This passage reveals an unusual blend of sensitive perception and strong nerves. The narrator is capable of analyzing a scene of bloody shambles to see what principles are at work. He is calmly aware of both the spectators' shock and of the imperturbable absorption of the slaughterers.

Exercise 1 (selecting)

Visit a large drugstore. Then:

 a. Write a one-page description of the scene as it might be observed by the manager, proud of the store's success. (*Note: Don't try to sketch in the character of the store manager; this exercise concentrates on selection of observable details.*)
 b. Write a second account of the scene as it might be observed by an old couple trying to cope with poverty and inflation.
 c. (*Alternate*) Write another account of the scene as it might be observed by a playful child.
 d. (*Alternate*) Write another account of the scene as it might be observed by a shoplifter.

Exercise 2 (placing)

Write a sentence of two or three lines to cover (a) an important action you performed, (b) why you performed it, and (c) one reason against it which you rejected. Then try several variations of this sentence, changing the placement of the three elements (a), (b), and (c). Add a brief discussion on how each variation modifies the implied outlook of the writer.

SAMPLE SOLUTION (a) I applied for graduate school (b) to improve my professional training (c) even though my bank account was low. *Discussion:* The speaker stresses decision by opening with it. The low bank account is important to the writer but is downplayed in a subordinate structure. The implied outlook is one of strong, well-motivated initiative.

SAMPLE VARIATION (b) To improve my professional training, (a) I applied for graduate school (c) despite my low bank account. *Discussion:* An even more positive orientation is shown by the speaker's opening on a confident expectation of improvement.

Exercise 3 (cohering)

Here are some scattered thoughts of a paranoid dramatist who is feeling sorry for himself. First write them into a paragraph which shows a highly organized flow of thought and feeling. Modify sentence structure as necessary as long as you retain all the substance. Then write up these thoughts again, this time into a paragraph which shows an incoherent and highly perturbed state of mind.

 a. I am the most brilliant playwright of the age.
 b. My plays are seldom performed.

   c. I won't flatter the critics.

   d. My excellence must be obvious to any unbiased person.

   e. Managers have combined against me.

   f. So have actors and critics.

   g. I am too honest and high-principled to please many people.

   h. My enormous merit stays unrecognized.

   i. I won't kowtow to the influential people of the theatrical world.

   j. The occasional performances of my plays are failures.

   k. My plays contain home truths. When they hit, they hurt.

Exercise 4 (all elements of Chapters 2 and 3)

The death of Marc Antony at Cleopatra's side has been dramatized by William Shakespeare in *Antony and Cleopatra* (1607) and by John Dryden in *All for Love* (1678). Their versions of Cleopatra's immediate response appear below. Using the six elements of these two chapters, describe the significant differences in implied outlook between the two Cleopatras. Incidentally, which version do you think is Shakespeare's?

A

CLEOPATRA: Noblest of men, woo't die?
Hast thou no care of me? Shall I abide
In this dull world, which in thy absence is
No better than a sty? O, see, my women,
The crown o' the earth doth melt. My lord!
O, wither'd is the garland of the war,
The soldier's pole is fall'n; young boys and girls
Are level now with men; the odds is gone,
And there is nothing left remarkable
Beneath the visiting moon.

B

CLEOPATRA: My lord, my lord! speak, if you yet have being;
Sign to me, if you cannot speak; or cast
One look! Do anything that shows you live.

IRAS: He's gone too far to hear you;
And this you see, a lump of senseless clay,
The leavings of a soul.

CHARMION: Remember, madam,
He charged you not to grieve.

CLEOPATRA: And I'll obey him.
I have not loved a Roman, not to know
What should become his wife; his wife, my Charmion!
For 'tis to that high title I aspire;
And now I'll not die less.

Exercise 5 (all elements of Chapters 2 and 3)

Using the six criteria covered in the last two chapters, prepare to discuss the significant differences in outlook between the following two versions of the same material:

VERSION A

The "mass" of today is not active but passive. It is not the rifleman aiming but the target aimed at. Though remarkably literate, the mass does not speak, it listens—to the slick average voices of the *Chicago Tribune,* the New York *Daily News,* CBS, NBC, and ABC. The mass produces no heroes, it simply waits until the ratings and the polls reveal them. But before the "mass" there was the "folk." The folk may have learned its alphabet in one-room schools; it may never have understood the news, but it did have goals. It aimed at getting the vote, at going West, at staking out the private claim. It spoke, through the guitar, the folk tale, the campfire saga. It gave America those giants, Daniel Boone, Abraham Lincoln, Davy Crockett. We treasure the creations of that folk, and we venerate its products in our museum, our libraries, our classrooms.

VERSION B

We have witnessed the decline of the "folk" and the rise of the "mass." The usually illiterate folk, while unself-conscious, was creative in its own special ways. Its characteristic products were the spoken word, the gesture, the song: folklore, folk dance, folk song. The folk expressed itself. Its products are still gathered by scholars, antiquarians, and patriots; it was a voice. But the mass, in our world of mass media and mass circulation, is the target and not the arrow. It is the ear and not the voice. The mass is what others aim to reach—by print, photograph, image, and sound. While the folk created heroes, the mass can only look and listen for them. It is waiting to be shown and to be told.

Exercise 6 (all elements of Chapters 2 and 3)

What experience have you had which changed the way you look at things? (Auto accident, rejection by a lover or employer, betrayal by a friend, loss of loved one, etc.) Describe the experience in a short paper, trying to consider all of the six elements you've studied.

Now imagine that the experience had produced a *much different* change in your outlook. Write up the experience again, accordingly.

Add a paragraph on the significant differences between the two versions in relation to the six elements.

Suggested reading for further illustration, discussion, and writing: "The American Revolution as Seen through Two Foreign Textbooks," page 287.

4   The Blank Page

Poetry and Hums aren't things which you get, they're things which get you. And all you can do is to go where they can find you.

A. A. MILNE, The House at Pooh Corner, 1928

How do you get words onto paper, especially when you don't seem to have much to say? A good deal of research has recently explored the writing process. That, coupled with the general inventiveness of today's teachers of composition, has yielded a wide array of strategies for getting started, ranging from the spectacular to the adventurous to the methodical.

Forced Writing: Jumping In

Try "power-writing" (sometimes called "free-writing"). The would-be writer just starts in, prepared or not, and keeps slogging ahead for 10–15 minutes. No stopping is allowed. Teachers using this tactic often tell their students to write garbage if necessary but write. Any idea can be set down and allowed to lead where it wants.

"Power-writing" sacrifices the deliberate searching and planning which are often thought necessary for "pre-writing," but it does work for many practitioners. The process gets a hesitant writer off and running. Then, on reading over what's been done, a writer will often find one idea to like. A second 10–15 minute session, driving at that one idea, may bring momentum and focus. Some writers urge a third and a fourth session, each working up the best material in the preceding version. Practiced this way, writing is exploratory thought which steadily seeks its most promising channel.

Try brainstorming. Brainstorming is like power-writing except that it *begins* with a specific topic, goal, or problem which a writer wants to get at. For example: "How can I best organize my study time?" or "Why do they package food the way they do?"

One begins writing, always pointing toward the topic, putting down illustrations, solutions, alternatives, letting new ideas enter by free association. No idea should be rejected at this stage, however silly. All should be written down as the writer keeps moving. As one option, a list may be used instead of continuous prose.

By brainstorming, one can generate a store of ideas and details from which to write a coherent paper.

Observation Tactics

People write much from what they see and hear. By sharpening their senses, they find more to write about.

Keep a journal. A journal to many people means a daily record of happenings: "Aunt Meda arrived today. Fantastic pizza dinner. Finished *Brave New World.*" But a writer's journal serves better as a notebook of observation and reflection. Sketches of interesting people, dreams, unusual scenes, complaints, appreciations, theories about why people do certain things—these can sooner or later feed into sustained writing. They strengthen the habit of noticing and valuing experience.

Visit a familiar scene to discover what you haven't noticed before. The visit, perhaps lasting an hour or more, should not be rushed. Notes can be taken as the basis for a report of the visit.

Record an actual dialog. The writer may have to scribble frantically, but the ears should be kept sharp. One can learn about individual speech patterns, thus reinforcing one's sense for language. One can notice how speakers express or conceal their values, how they unconsciously characterize themselves. From the subject-matter of the dialog, a writer may find new topics to think and write about.

The attractiveness of catching others' language on the wing must be balanced with certain difficulties. People may speak self-consciously if they know their words are being taken down. But taping people without their knowledge may be regarded as an intrusion upon privacy. Listening unobserved from another table or booth may work, or one can join the party without note-taking, keeping the memory honed to recall the dialog immediately on departure.

A common format for showing dialog would go like this:

(*Place: Union Lounge. Time: 10:15 p.m., Wed., May 4, 1983.*)
Kevin: Hey, Marilyn. How's the new job?

Marilyn: Great. It lasted three hours.
(After that, for quick transcription, one could use *K* and *M* to designate speakers.)

Interview a person or persons on some issue and write up the results. The exercise makes for good listening and a keener perception of what others are thinking.

For a useful interview, people should be chosen who are thoughtful, articulate, with some originality of viewpoint, and perhaps with enough influence to make others care what they think. The topic should address a live concern such as a current controversy or a prominent news event. Questions should not come from the hip; they are likely to be unreflective and unchallenging. Good interviewers commonly prepare a series of questions to open up lively answers. (Later questions may be framed to pursue new opportunities as they arise.) The interviewer should listen carefully, trying neither to agree nor to win an argument. Answers may be taped if permission is granted; they may be written out on the spot or as soon afterward as possible.

Ask what changes have been taking place in the topic you want to write about. Many shopworn subjects like "capital punishment" or "women's liberation" can take on new life if one asks "What's the latest development here and where can it lead?"

Discover three positive qualities in someone you dislike. Write a short description with illustrations.

Ways of Reflecting

The journal has already been mentioned. As a way of catching the patterns and high points of personal experience it is useful. Writers do need to "think things over"—not in the scattered way of daily life but with concentration. The following tactics may also help to train and direct a reflective mind into a readiness for writing.

Meditate. Meditation itself can be used to think over a current concern such as writing a paper. A secluded place should be found where you can sit without distraction for about 20 minutes. Close your eyes and look downward to cut off visual input. Relax your whole body. Breathe slowly and more deeply than usual. Reflect on a passage of scripture or other significant literature which has been read as preparation. Or simply sit with the mind undirected; directed thinking may afterward flow from this peace of being.

Meditation isn't easy for writers caught up in any rush of duties. It needs to be practiced regularly until it comes naturally.

The following conventional tactics ask writers to ponder specific current problems.

Rank five current aims of your educational program—for example: to prepare for a vocation, to learn who you are, to meet the kind of people you'll spend most of your life with. Then write an essay to explain why these aims are ranked in this way and to defend your choice against possible objection.

Write a letter of recommendation for yourself, addressed to a potential employer in a field you would like to enter. This is a particularly good exercise for members of a group who will share results and offer mutual encouragement toward career exploration.

Show how some personal experience of your own ties into a national controversy such as draft registration, nuclear arms, racism, sexism, ecology.

Write a "Letter to the Editor" about some community issue you feel strongly about—then actually send it. The possibility of an immediate public hearing can evoke one's most mature and resourceful thought.

Describe an imaginary day in which you do everything you've been putting off.

Using Personal Memories

Many writers suppose their own pasts to be jumbles of memories hardly worth writing about. They might be surprised at what a directed scanning may yield.

What would be the title of your autobiography? For example: "The Girl Who Never Gave Up," "Why Did I Have To Be Me?" "Memoirs of a Second-Rate Athlete." Write a brief account to support the title. Use illustration from your actual experience.

Look up several snapshots or yearbook pictures of yourself and describe what you were like at each time.

Search your address book, old yearbooks, or any similar record to find three names you've nearly forgotten. Work your memory as hard as possible to produce a sketch of each person and what he or she once meant to you.

Translate an important early experience into a short narrative. This exercise may work best if you write about yourself in the third person, giving fictitious names to all persons and places. Such a displacement can allow a writer to see the experience more objectively and yet to describe it with greater freedom. Many novelists have begun with such recovery of their pasts, then carried it to much greater length.

Shaking Yourself Up

Wear a football helmet for a half-day and report what happened. Any odd object on the head will do—a feather, a dandelion, a dunce cap.

The point of such stratagems is to project yourself into an eccentric situation which forces you to observe and think the unusual.

Step out of character for one day. If you are usually quiet, then chatter. If normally serious, smile and laugh. If usually neat, become a slob. And so on. The results can then be written up, together with what you make of them.

Design five general-purpose conversation openers. Especially for writers who feel shy and therefore limited in developing their ideas with others, this exercise may answer the complaint "If only I knew how to get started with people." Each conversation-opener can be directed toward different people the writer is likely to meet—professors, new classmates, business clients, attractive strangers of the opposite sex. The writer may then describe these openers, why they ought to work, and how to use them. (Courageous writers may even test them out and report the results.)

Building a Discipline

Above all, writing is a performance skill which has to be practiced, like music or sports. As you undertake to make writing a *discipline,* you may habitually find new ideas for writing, new capacities with language.

Meditation and journal-keeping have already been described as daily rituals which, practiced over a period of time, help to stimulate writing. Others:

Choose the best time, place, and tools for writing. Some writers produce better in early morning, others at night. A certain room or desk may be associated with writing, especially if it allows unbroken solitude. (But some writers like background noise.) Should a piece of writing be drafted with pen or on a typewriter? Some argue that handwriting, being slower, compels more deliberate thinking. Typing may allow momentum, but it discourages crossing-out. The word processor, which allows both fast typing and easy editing, has come into favor with many professionals. A given color, size, or texture of paper may also coax creativity forth.

A writer shouldn't be too compulsive about such arrangements, as helpful as they can be. You can't always enjoy optimum conditions. The pros can produce early or late, in crowds or in bed, on bond paper or on grocery bags—if they have to.

Think writing. Writers' imaginations work verbally. They often daydream dialogs with friends and enemies. When they see, hear, smell, taste, feel something new, they search almost by reflex for the *words* they might use in recording it. Finding the right words is their way of taking hold of experience.

Write often. A writer's "inspiration" seems to work like a well. The more a well is drawn on, the more water it can supply. Anyone who writes only in an emergency is likely to find the well dry sometimes.

Save good ideas. Writers often keep ideas for papers, stories, poems in notebooks or files or even on scraps of paper. Hence they never really run out of projects to work on. Such ideas can strike at any hour anywhere—but they can slide almost instantly into oblivion if not noted on the spot (even in bed).

Start a germination sheet for any project growing beyond the "idea" stage. Many writers begin storing—even days and weeks before any deadline—any material or further idea for expanding, illustrating, or testing their topic. Thoughts need not be organized at this stage. They should be welcomed as fast as they come and in any order. As long as they are gathered in one place, the writer can later pick them over and start putting the best ones together.

Start well ahead of deadlines. Writers under pressure tend to be too result-oriented to use all the energy of the mind at play. If two or three exploratory sessions can take place, the writer's subconscious may warm up to the topic and use the intervals to germinate further ideas.

Learn basic development patterns which can help project any topic into concrete terms. (The chief patterns will be separately described in Chapter 7, p. 62.)

Don't talk about your writing before you've done it. Although it is tempting for a writer to discuss a brilliant idea with a friend, doing so is likely to dissipate creative energy. And if the friend gives the idea a cool reception, the writer may feel utterly dampened even before sitting down to write. In short, a writer is wise not to rush into public without a full draft to show. (Obtaining a supportive critique of a full draft is another matter, to be dealt with in the next chapter, p. 41.)

If you must break off before finishing, remember Ernest Hemingway's advice to stop while "you still have your juice." By waiting until "written out," a writer may find it hard to crank up again. Ideas should still be flowing when one stops. Then is the chance to make a note on how one intends to resume. It will be much easier to start again.

Inexperienced writers often feel a "false block" against getting started. This is often because they suppose that writers must first know everything they're going to say before they begin. Any writer who can do this is a genius or amazingly trained or both. Generally *people write to learn what they make of something.* Writing for most of us is discovery, not the mere taking down of dictation from the brain.

The rest of this book will add many other ways of getting started. All of them can help you to discover what you make of things, including yourself.

Suggested readings for further illustration, discussion, and writing: William Zinsser, "The Transaction," page 293, and Mike Royko, "Four Columns," page 295.

"locate more definitely," he still wants to see more clearly the deep isolation of this countryside; so he tries again:

> 3RD VERSION (penned on scratch paper)
> He made a bet with himself as to the time. From the way the
> shed ~~slipped~~
> breeze ~~flowed~~ softly off the fields, ~~through the curtain~~ from the
> pre-dawn hush of the woods beyond the barns, he guessed at
> three-thirty, ~~as late as Very late, for the~~ He was becoming an
> ~~In this countryside, the nights~~
> expert in the silences of the backlands, and made a bet with
> himself as to the time. From the way the breeze shed

In this tentative, broken-off attack, the writer tries to get at the rural solitude by a rather intrusive assertion ("He was becoming an expert in the silences of the backlands") and by the new detail ("the woods beyond the barns"). He is still trying to catch the feel for a late-night breeze; he tries new wording each time. His next draft shows the benefit of this experimenting:

> 4TH VERSION (penned on scratch paper)
>   dismayed
> Sleepily ~~disappointed~~
> /He lay still, absorbing the faint clues of a night in the back-
>   down
> lands, until he felt the time. From the breeze ~~shedding~~ off the
> fields, from the pre-dawn hush of the woods beyond the barn,
>   L
> he guessed at three-thirty. ~~A bit~~ later than usual.

The *assertion* of locale is now partly submerged in the dramatic detail appropriate to a man tensely aware of the night ("He lay still, absorbing the faint clues of a night in the backlands, until he felt the time"). The man's betting with himself about the time has been eliminated as too playful for such a somber hour. The writer sees a chance to deepen the tone ("Sleepily dismayed") and to imply a mysterious repetitiousness in this nocturnal waking ("Later *than usual*"). His final commitment fixes these matters:

> 5TH VERSION (typed)
> Sleepily dismayed, he lay still, absorbing the faint clues of a
> night in the backlands, until he felt the time. From the breeze
> draining down off the fields, from the pre-dawn hush of the
> woods beyond the barn, he guessed at three-thirty. Later than
> usual.

These revisions concentrate on precision of tone and detail, as might be expected in fiction, and do not illustrate other types of growth, such as

5   Revision

That man is intellectually of the mass who, in face of any problem, is satisfied with thinking the first thing he finds in his head. On the contrary, the excellent man is he who contemns what he finds in his mind without previous effort, and only accepts as worthy of him what is still far above him and what requires a further effort in order to be reached.

JOSÉ ORTEGA Y GASSET, *The Revolt of the Masses,* 1930

What is understood easily and rapidly by the reader may be the result of five or six painstaking revisions by the writer.

E. D. HIRSCH, *The Philosophy of Composition,* 1977

A person's best writing is often all mixed up together with his worst. It all feels lousy to him as he's writing, but if he will let himself write it and come back later he will find some parts of it are excellent. It is as though one's best words come wrapped in one's worst.

PETER ELBOW, *Writing Without Teachers,* 1973

In former days students might be asked to "correct" errors. As the harshest penalty for a weak paper (next to an F), a student might be required to do the paper "all over again." Such treatment of revision as merely *corrective* has changed. So much has been learned about revision as *creative* that revision has come to be taken for granted in much college writing. Students are sometimes asked to revise their own work even before submitting it for the first time.

What Revision Is

Professional writers usually work through a piece at least three times. They may even keep it "around the study," coming back to it at intervals in other work, over months and even years. A blossoming writer has begun to acquire the professional perspective when first troubled by the *need* to revise. When writers feel unfulfilled by their earlier drafts, at bottom they are sensing, however indirectly, that writing is not an end-product of knowledge but a process of knowing—that the final discovery of one's subject can't take place except through dozens of writing choices, many of which are still to be made.

Untrained writers are often handicapped by premature assurance. They equate their own natural pride in completing the first draft with the probable applause of the audience. Why endanger the happy harmony of the piece by tinkering with it? Beyond making a clean copy with a few misspellings cleaned up, such writers do not see what can be done. If their natural gift is large, they may well win high enough marks for first-draft pieces to be convinced that further effort is busywork.

This book frankly insists that writing like all other art comes to its highest quality through disciplined revision (literally, "re-seeing"). The occasional perfection of a spontaneous performance is a miracle to be grateful for, not counted on, and it is most likely to happen to a finely trained craftsman. To put it differently, the better the draft you have in front of you, the more and better choices you will have in writing. In your second and third drafts you can graduate to advanced choices of a kind you couldn't make at first.

The marvelous growth of a piece through revision is hard to demonstrate, since authors rarely save all their scratchwork; but this brief example may help, donated by a contemporary writer of fiction. His five drafts appear exactly as he worked through them, unconscious at the time that he would be watched. The passage introduces a man in terrible danger, as he wakes up alone to wonder what time it is.

1ST VERSION (penned on scratch paper)
He made a bet with himself as to the time~~two-thirty~~. Something about the way the breeze slid off   flowed slowly   the fields, the pre-dawn hush of the nearby woods—well, he guessed at three o'clock.

2ND VERSION (typed)
He made a bet with himself as to the time. Something about the way the breeze flowed slowly off the fields, the pre-dawn hush of the nearby woods—well, he guessed at three-thirty.

These early versions differ on only two points—the time of night (two-thirty, three, three-thirty) and the motion of the breeze ("slid off," "flowed slowly off"). But to judge from the writer's own marginal note to closer definition of general concepts, firming up of organization. The point remains that each new draft can improve the kind of options available to the writer. To take the one instance of the night breeze, if this writer had stopped after one draft, he would have had two options:

> the breeze slid off the fields
> the breeze flowed slowly off the fields

By keeping on, he ended with seven options:

> the breeze   slid off
> flowed slowly off
> flowed softly off
> slipped off
> shed softly off
> down off
> drained down off the fields.

The last attempt (not always the best) in this case catches the slowness of the breeze, the sloping terrain, the sense of the sleeper's being toward the bottom of things. To hit upon all of these contributing qualities on first try would have been almost impossible. Art is intensification, the skill of investing the fewest means with the maximum experience. Revision is a process of intensification.

The following suggestions may help in that process.

Using the Overflow

Often when one has written the last paragraph of a draft, ideas keep welling up. This momentum should be used. One can look over the draft, marking words and passages for which one sees new chances, and adding a note at the end on what to do on returning to the paper. This procedure also works on leaving a draft to be finished later.

Useful Criticism and How to Get It

Revision always begins with a new reading through strange eyes. You yourself can provide this new reading, if a cooling-off period has elapsed (at least overnight), and if you can read your own work with "hostile objectivity"—meaning that you're testing everything for clarity, for fullness of explanation and support. Why "hostile"? Because whatever you overlook at this stage, other readers will not. Writers must learn to be their own severest critics. (Hostility is *not* recommended for writing first drafts, when one needs to feel as positively excited as possible.)

The writer's own silent re-reading, though, is only the first of possible steps. Also try these:

Read your work aloud, with or without a listener. If a real audience is absent, you can imagine one. This exercise helps (1) to project the writing away from oneself to the eventual readers, and (2) to find how tightly and smoothly the sentences work.

Have someone else read the paper aloud. The reader's stumbling will show where the language may be difficult. The reader's successes will confirm your own choices.

Ask a friend-critic to evaluate the draft. What is needed in such a reader is not blind devotion but honesty, good will, and perception. Work should *not* be shown when the writer is so perplexed that any objection would prove depressing. Nor should it be shown when the writer is so exhilarated on finishing it that nothing but praise is expected. No defense against criticism should be attempted at this point. Rather, any adverse comment, however mistaken, should be taken as evidence that *some* problem may need solving.

Use your writing class as an audience. Although it's natural to shrink from public critique, a class using the right ground rules can become a sensitive, supportive reactor for everyone. A writer can be enormously stimulated by a constructive response from a trained group of others who are practicing writing. Some students even come to look forward so much to the reception of their work that they write with all the more energy. Class critiques can be oral or written, group or individual. Authorship can be announced or kept anonymous. Each instructor will have a preference for method.

Not the least valuable reading will be that furnished by your teacher, in written comment, in conference, or both. (One should not wait for this ultimate judgment before beginning to revise. The more advanced a draft is before reaching any critic, the more valuable a good critique can be.)

The Agenda for a Critique

Specific topics to cover in a critique—whether developed through group discussion or by an individual—will always be furnished by the assignment being met or by the concepts under study. But any reader or listener can usefully respond to such questions as these:

1. *What has this writer tried to do?* Unless critics can see the writer's purpose, they can hardly help the writer to meet it.

2. *Just how has the writer gone about it?* The critics' ability to describe the writer's method will confirm the strength or weakness of that method.

3. *Where if anywhere does one have trouble in following or accepting the writer's presentation? What solution might work?* Sometimes a critic's attempt to find and suggest alternatives will clarify and confirm the writer's original choice.

4. *What other suggestions can be made for pushing the paper up a real notch or two in quality?*

The broad questions of 2, 3, and 4 allow the critic to consider the whole range of the paper, from supporting details to tone to word choices to sentence structure to coherence to total structure—in short, all the elements treated in this book.

Breaking the "Revision Barrier"

Suppose that a writer *still* can't see how to change an early draft, despite all comments made? Such a writer may feel that regardless of comment, he or she did say exactly what seemed important, and that the failure of readers to see this is their problem, not the writer's.

A James Joyce or Thomas Pynchon engaged in a radical experiment might justly make such a claim. For most others, the question really isn't whether a particular paper is valid as it stands. The question is whether the writer has enough resourcefulness to develop alternate ways of exploring a topic. Only then can you work up genuine choices. If all else fails—

Imitate your earlier draft without looking at it. A technique for self-imitation is outlined at the end of Chapter 6 (Exercise 6, page 62). When the two drafts are then compared, enough differences will appear to allow choices.

Cut out each paragraph with a scissors; shuffle and try rearrangements. A better structure may leap into light, though a rewrite may still be needed for best continuity.

Switch specifications. Some major condition of the early draft may be changed for the revision. An essay can be translated into a short story or a news item. A different audience can be addressed. Instead of classmates at college level, one could try reaching junior high school readers. If the earlier draft had been written impersonally, the writer may now appear as an "I" with a definite personality. Or one can simply change scale by expanding or contracting the original draft by one-third (without padding or loss of force).

Test the opening. Openings often sprawl because the writer is warming up. Maybe the first paragraph(s) can be omitted, with cruising speed reached much faster. The same principle holds for paragraph openings, which may hem and haw. (See pages 257–258 for other ways of opening strong.)

Check all verb choices, since the verb is the motor of the sentence. A possible way is to circle all verbs and then inspect each. Can a given sentence drive harder if a more exact verb is substituted? Or if the sentence is reorganized to give the verb function to a more important idea? One should especially challenge the verbs *to be* and *to have,* which often lack force and lead to wordiness. Overreliance on these verbs also signals that the writer may be asserting rather than detailing. (For further help, see "Sentence Economy," page 198.)

Actually Writing the Revision

Make notes on the margins of the earlier draft (or elsewhere) as to modifications to try.

Run the whole paper, even those parts which don't seem to need changing, into a clean draft. This practice avoids "patching out"—that is, scratching out certain passages with inserts to be substituted. Patching out, except for minor repairs, can forfeit the possible flow of a genuine revision in which even one's good passages can grow and find better continuity with one's new thinking.

Copy-Editing the Final Draft

Minor slips can weaken the impact of any writing. To put it in baldly mercenary terms, some college students could actually raise their grade by a whole letter if they would invest one more quarter-hour in quality control of their final product. You do make mistakes. No one is immune. Therefore check your final draft severely. Actually try to spot several errors on each page. If your past written work has been averaging three instructor's marks per page, try to make an average of three corrections per page of your final drafts. At the same time keep an eye for last chances to strengthen style.

The following editing marks are commonly used: they are both neat and clear. Unless your page looks peppered, retyping is not usually necessary. Avoid strikeovers and x-ing out.

Delete single letter: ca~~t~~t

Delete one or more words: ~~black cat~~

Substitute letter: bla~~z~~k cat

Substitute word: charcoal ~~black~~ cat

Insert letter or word: the cat and the dg

Transpose: the⌐cat⌐black⌐

Begin paragraph: ¶ him./Afterwards, the

Eliminate paragraph   not the greatest pleasure for him.
indentation: no ¶ ⌐Afterwards, the cat descended the

The Limits to Revision

It is possible to overrevise. A new writer can become so morbidly insecure
about writing—especially after harsh criticism—that everything seems
wrong, the more so with each attempted draft. Professionals develop two
protections against this neurosis. They train themselves to tolerate a high
level of boredom and anxiety about their own work, so that they can keep
at it. And by the continuous practice of writing, they come to trust their
own resources; they know that eventually they *can* finish. The exact moment for declaring that one's composition is "right" is hard to decide,
since in one sense no writing is ever perfect. The British novelist Joyce
Cary once answered this question concerning a novel which had been
delayed: "I said that I had run into difficulties; the novel had indeed
taken nearly three years. But I thought it was nearly finished because
when I changed it for the better in one place, I found I had damaged it
in some other" (*Art and Reality*, 1957). Much beyond that point no one
can expect you to go.

(Special revision agenda for the long or documented paper will be
offered on pp. 250–262.)

Exercise 1

Like Chapter 4, "The Blank Page," this chapter is intended to apply throughout the book to most written composition; hence the usual spectrum of exercise
at chapter's end is omitted. For warm-up, however, you might compare Chapter 4, page 34, with the early outline for it which appears as Figure 1, page

245. Can you identify two or three significant changes which I made in organizing the final draft? What has been the effect of these changes?

Suggested readings for further illustration and discussion: Barbara Hower, "Oh, To Drive in England" (two drafts of student paper), page 305, and Yvonne Streeter, "Ethics of a Housewife" (student documented paper in two drafts), page 408.

6   The Imitation of Models

Nobody would accuse an art student of merely "copying" when drawing from a posed model. Actually, drawing the model can teach a perceptive student how to generalize and differentiate the human anatomy, thus acquiring insight which transfers to the artist's total talent.

Writers also learn from models. Benjamin Franklin described his own practice:

> About this time I met with an odd volume of the *Spectator*. It was the third. I had never before seen any of them. I bought it, read it over and over, and was much delighted with it. I thought the writing excellent, and wished, if possible, to imitate it. With that view I took some of the papers, and making short hints of the sentiment in each sentence, laid them by a few days, and then without looking at the book, tried to complete the papers again, by expressing each hinted sentiment at length and as fully as it had been expressed before, in any suitable words that should come to hand. Then I compared my *Spectator* with the original, discovered some of my faults and corrected them. (*Autobiography*, 1771–1790)

Of course if you imitate slavishly, you'll learn only a bag of tricks. Worse, your writing would become only a xerox of someone else's thought. But if you practice well, imitation opens up these benefits: (1) greater sensitivity to language; (2) broadening of your own stylistic powers; (3) new flexibility in revision of your own work.

Total Imitation

The perfect imitation of a given passage would simply be an exact duplicate of that passage. Some teachers and writing coaches do recommend
the word-for-word copying of selected passages, or writing down such
passages to dictation. One argument for such practice is that language
ought to enter as many channels of the student's perception as possible.
The student *hears* the style of a master, rather than merely scanning it
with the eyes, and *feels* what it is like to write that style. This immersion
of one's hearing and handwriting in a certain author's work can help give
a sense of the way in which the author takes hold of things.

For such direct copying or writing to dictation, the whole passage
should be read aloud first so that one can feel its sweep and strength. The
actual writing should be done by hand slowly, without abbreviation or
scrawling, but not for so long at once that the mind begins to wander.

Selective Imitation

Most imitative writing is selective rather than total. From your model you
would pick out one feature to imitate—such as its distinctive word-
choices, or sentence structures, or approach to audience. This alone is
what you observe and imitate.

You can apply selective imitation to a model passage in two ways. You
can scramble and re-synthesize it. Or you can adapt its distinctive features
to new material.

These techniques will now be illustrated. Since "outlook" is the first
topic of this book to be developed, it will be used as the distinctive feature to imitate. The technique can be used, however, for any later topic
to be introduced. For model, we will take the same passage from Upton
Sinclair's *The Jungle* that was analyzed at the end of Chapter 3:

> They worked with furious intensity, literally upon the run—at a
> pace with which there is nothing to be compared except a foot-
> ball game. It was all highly specialized labor, each man having
> his task to do; generally this would consist of only two or three
> specific cuts, and he would pass down the line of fifteen or
> twenty carcasses, making these cuts upon each. First there came
> the "butcher," to bleed them; this meant one swift stroke, so
> swift that you could not see it—only the flash of the knife; and
> before you could realize it, the man had darted on to the next
> line, and a stream of bright red was pouring out upon the floor.

This floor was half an inch deep with blood, in spite of the best efforts of men who kept shovelling it through holes; it must have made the floor slippery, but no one could have guessed this by watching the men at work.

To scramble such a passage in writing, you can follow Franklin's procedure of writing down "hints" or notes on the contents of the original passage. The original wording should be avoided. So should the original ordering—maybe by using notecards for every sentence or two and then shuffling (scrambling) the cards. Your scrambled notes on the Sinclair passage might look like this on four cards (now in random order):

Blood ½ inch on floor, though men keep shoveling it through holes.
Spectator would not know floor was slippery, men keep at work.

Killing is specialized labor.
Each man specializes in 2–3 cuts, goes down line of 15–20 carcasses.

Killers work furiously and intensely.
Analogy of football game.

"Butcher" comes first.
Bleeds with one fast stroke, very swift, only a flash visible.
Rushes to next carcass as bright red blood streams on floor.

Next, having decided what stylistic feature to imitate, you would return to the model to analyze that element in it. Since "outlook" is our choice for illustration, you would write out an analysis of the six elements of outlook as they appear in Sinclair's passage—exactly as was done on pages 29–30.

Both this analysis and the notecards are then set aside at least overnight, so that you can forget the exact wording of the original. Then without looking at the model, you use the analysis and scrambled notes to write a re-synthesis. A mechanically perfect result of course would be identical with the model. But in re-synthesis the writer's own creative urge comes into play, even in tracking the original material, so that your re-synthesis may show an organic identity of its own, as in the following version which I myself worked out:

RE-SYNTHESIS	ORIGINAL
The work of slaughtering goes on with the fury and intensity of a football game, and also with something of the same high specialization of the players' roles. Each man is an	They worked with furious intensity, literally upon the run—at a pace with which there is nothing to be compared except a football game. It was all highly specialized labor,

expert in two or three cuts, and goes down the line of fifteen or twenty carcasses delivering the same cuts to each. First is the "butcher," who bleeds the carcass with one deep stroke so fast that only a flash of the knife is visible; he has already rushed on to the next carcass by the time the bright red blood streams onto the floor. The floor runs as much as a half-inch deep in blood, despite the men who keep shovelling it through holes; yet you would not suspect the floor to be slippery, so intently do the men press on at the work.

each man having his task to do; generally this would consist of only two or three specific cuts, and he would pass down the line of fifteen or twenty carcasses, making these cuts upon each. First there came the "butcher," to bleed them; this meant one swift stroke, so swift that you could not see it—only the flash of the knife; and before you could realize it, the man had darted on to the next line, and a stream of bright red was pouring out upon the floor. This floor was half an inch deep with blood, in spite of the best efforts of men who kept shovelling it through holes; it must have made the floor slippery, but no one could have guessed this by watching the men at work.

The *difference* between the two versions now allows you to grow as a critic. The final step is to compare the two versions to appreciate the uniqueness of each. For example, you might note that the re-synthesis is 25 words shorter (15 percent less) than the original. Why is this? Mainly because the re-synthesis eliminates several leisurely and even wordy structures of the original—thus:

RE-SYNTHESIS

. . . with the fury and intensity of a football game . . .

Each man is an expert in two or three cuts . . .

ORIGINAL

. . . with furious intensity, literally on the run—at a pace with which there is nothing to be compared except a football game.

. . . each man having his task to do; generally this would consist of only two or three specific cuts . . .

In the original, such structures tend to enhance the calm deliberateness of the writer. The re-synthesis implies more excitement. Again, you might note that the re-synthesis takes the present tense. Evidently its writer forgot that the original passage came from a novel written in conventional past tense. The present tense heightens the immediacy and the excitement of the account. Once again the re-synthesis lacks something of the calm stance of Sinclair's original. And so on. The chief benefit of this final comparison is that you can firm up your earlier analysis: you can see more exactly what outlook Sinclair's style was expressing.

Adaptation of Technique to New Subject Matter

In the second type of selective imitation, you would still need to work out the same analysis of outlook (or other stylistic feature under study). But you don't need to make notes summarizing the content of the model passage. Instead, you search for new subject matter on which you can promote the stylistic trait of the original—new material which will offer the same kind of opportunities.

For example, Sinclair contrasts the shocking violence of cattle slaughter with its systematic procedure. That contrast is central to his way of seeing the meatpacking industry. What other subject might offer the same contrast of violence and system? The mass execution of prisoners? The wreckers' dismantling of a grand old mansion? Police subduing a mob? You might try professional wrestling, which has been called "programmed frenzy."

Your next step would be to look for all the correspondences between your chosen subject and the Sinclair original. In this example you would look for all the parallels between cattle slaughtering and wrestling. You would come up with an informal table like this:

FEATURES OF SLAUGHTERING	PARALLEL FEATURES OF WRESTLING
slaughter of cattle	vanquishing of professional wrestlers
intensity of labor	intensity of labor
analogy of football game	analogy of slaughterhouse
the "butcher"	the "villain" wrestler
his bleeding of a carcass	his demolishing of a foe
bloody floor (brutal disorder)	screaming hall (brutal disorder)

Then, using this table and your analysis of the Sinclair passage, you would write your adaptation. (Don't glance back at the original; that would only encourage mere echoing.) My own result went like this:

ADAPTATION	ORIGINAL
The wrestlers fought the whole evening with the unabating fury of slaughterers in a meat-packing factory; yet this mayhem was a highly organized activity in which each combatant had adopted a specialty—villain, outraged hero, Oriental exotic, Alaskan brute, declassed	They worked with furious intensity, literally upon the run—at a pace with which there is nothing to be compared except a football game. It was all highly specialized labor, each man having his task to do; generally this would consist of only two or three specific cuts, and he would

aristocrat, and so on. Most prominent was the villain, who deftly
slipped past the referee's restraining
arms to slug his unready opponent,
then fell on the limp body to choke
him in plain view of everyone but
the referee, then flopped the victim
on his back for the referee's three-
count which determined victory.
Before the audience fully absorbed
the atrocity the victim was lugged
off stage and the malevolent victor
had duly swaggered through the
ropes. Then despite the enraged
screams of a hall which no referee
nor ushers could still, the next combatants had marched in and faced off
for their own gladiatorial chores.

pass down the line of fifteen or
twenty carcasses, making these cuts
upon each. First there came the
"butcher," to bleed them; this meant
one swift stroke, so swift that you
could not see it—only the flash of
the knife; and before you could
realize it, the man had darted on to
the next line, and a stream of bright
red was pouring out upon the floor.
This floor was half an inch deep
with blood, in spite of the best
efforts of men who kept shovelling
it through holes; it must have made
the floor slippery, but no one could
have guessed this by watching the
men at work.

The final step, once again, is to compare the imitation with the original.
Now the contrast will be harder, since a difference in subject matter was
stipulated. Still, by noting the particulars of *treatment*, you can see, for
example, that the adaptation refers to people by nouns which are more
specific, more dramatic. Where Sinclair restricts his nouns to "men" or
"man" (with "butcher" as the one exception), the adaptation uses "wres-
tlers," "combatants," "villain," "hero," "exotic," "brute," "aristocrat," and
so on. Thus the adaptation lacks some of the abstract impersonality which
creates the tone of understatement in Sinclair's original text.

Again, the adaptation uses much more main-clause emphasis for the
key values of violence and efficiency:

ADAPTATION
This mayhem was a highly organized activity.

The victor had duly *swaggered*
through the ropes. . . . The next
combatants had *marched* in and
faced off. (Three verb positions for
describing the end of the action.)

ORIGINAL
It was all highly specialized labor.
("It" is colorless beside "mayhem.")

The man had *darted* on to the next
line. (Only one verb position for
describing the end of the action.)

So in this second way the overvigorous adaptation misses the understatement of the original; elsewhere it seems reasonably successful.

Parody

You can use this method of imitative adaptation for comic effect if you *exaggerate* (rather than merely copy) the most conspicuous features of the original, applying them to materials which are completely *inappropriate*. The result is *parody*. The titanic but understated violence of Sinclair's slaughterhouse might be unleashed in a campus kitchen:

The University Food Service Opens Its Season
(*with apologies to Upton Sinclair*)

> Back in the Union kitchen the chefs toiled with the savage concentration of a football team on the offensive. Their tactics for the dietitian's favorite main course of Salisbury Steak *au corbeau* were all highly specialized, with each chef having his own "play" to run. Here came the gravy chef to douse the mashed potatoes. This meant one swift dollop from his bucket—so swift that you could see only the flash of his ladle. Then the chef whisked down to the next plate, and a stream of dark brown was pouring on the floor. The floor was inches deep with gravy, potatoes, and gouts of meat despite the best efforts of cooks who kept swabbing it off, often slipping but heaving themselves up again, stained and steamy.

Like most laboratory demonstrations of humor-making, this example may be less than hilarious. But the technique is there. The title and apology give signals, needed early along the line, that a takeoff is under way. The original incongruity of Sinclair's action with his setting is magnified by choosing a campus dining hall, supposedly a center of gracious living, and invading its kitchen with a garbageman's nightmare.

Parody that focuses on a small original sampling, as in that illustration, needs to imitate the original closely. But parody is free to adopt a different scale from the original. It often abbreviates. It may adopt a different literary style, as in using Marcel Proust's luscious prose, say, to relate a rugged incident from Ernest Hemingway—a possible two-way parody. Parody may use a different literary type, as in using a dramatic skit to satirize a novel. In short, parody may use any device which can throw into high relief the target qualities of the original. And these target qualities may range from some quirk of expression to the total personality of the original writer.

By trying such tricks with an author of conspicuous manner, you can enjoy the malicious pleasure of literary takeoff while at the same time enlarging your own stylistic resources. Readers wishing to explore this delightful art might sample the following:

> Donald Ogden Stewart, *A Parody Outline of History* (1921).
> Robert P. Falk, ed., *The Antic Muse: American Writers in Parody* (1955).
> Dwight Macdonald, ed., *Parodies: An Anthology from Chaucer to Beerbohm—and After* (1960).
> S. J. Perelman, various collections of comic pieces including assorted parodies.

The library card catalog under "Parody" may yield other titles as well.

Imitation in Other Stylistic Areas

A summary agenda may help in applying the present chapter to other problems, since imitation exercises are provided for nearly every chapter following.

1. Identify the stylistic quality which is to be imitated. For example, Exercise 6 of Chapter 13 asks you to imitate the definition of "probation" which appears in that chapter.

2. Review the text chapter for the elements which make up that stylistic quality. For definition of terms, the chapter identifies a dozen ways of explaining a given term.

3. Inspect the piece to be imitated to see how it illustrates those elements, and make notes accordingly. The analysis of Sinclair's outlook, pages 29–30, demonstrates the kind of notes worth taking, except that you would be using different topics.

4. If the *scrambling and re-synthesis* technique is to be used, make out notecards which synopsize the original passage but in different words. Shuffle the notecards. Set them aside for a cooling-off period. Then use notecards and your analysis to write the imitation without another look at the original.

5. If the *adaptation of techniques to new subject matter* is to be used, conceive of a new subject matter which lends itself to the elements which you analyzed under number 3, above. Match each such element with some parallel element in the new subject matter. Then develop the imitation without further inspection of the original.

6. Compare your imitation with the original to see what has changed as to the stylistic quality under study. Make your observations as detailed as possible. Only through such microscopic matching of stylistic practice can imitation prove itself as a writing discipline.

Exercise 1 (parody)

a. Which passage below is by Ernest Hemingway and which is a parody of his fiction? (You should be able to make a reasonable guess even if you haven't read much Hemingway.) Be able to point to the details in each which support your identification.

b. What traits of Hemingway's fiction do you think are being parodied?

A

The American was early for the appointment. He came into the bar and he mopped his forehead with a spotted silk handkerchief and he walked across to a table and he picked up more nuts than he could manage and some of the nuts spilled out of his hand and he looked at the carpet for a long time, but he did not stoop to pick up the nuts.

He licked his lips after that, and he mopped his face again, and he walked across to the counter and on the way he knocked over a chair and he apologized even though there was nobody sitting in the chair and nobody to apologize to.

He asked the barman something, and the barman nodded, and pointed to me with a glass he was wiping, and the American buttoned his jacket and unbuttoned it again and walked over to me. He was about fifty and he was going to fat and there was one bead of sweat in the cleft of his chin.

"I am Edward Mankiewicz of Mankiewicz Associates," he said.

"I know," I said.

"May I sit down?" he said.

"Yes," I said.

"I did not intend to sit down at first," he said.

"That's all right," I said.

"At first I thought we might stand at the bar," he said.

"Sometimes it is better not to stand at the bar," I said.

"Yes," he said. "Sometimes it is better to sit at the table."

"That is the way it is, sometimes," I said.

B

When he saw us come in the door the bartender looked up and then reached over and put the glass covers on the two free-lunch bowls.

"Give me a beer," I said. He drew it, cut the top off with the spatula and then held the glass in his hand. I put the nickel on the wood and he slid the beer toward me.

"What's yours?" he said to Tom.

"Beer."

He drew that beer and cut it off and when he saw the money he pushed the beer across to Tom.

"What's the matter?" Tom asked.

The bartender didn't answer him. He just looked over our heads and said, "What's yours?" to a man who'd come in.

"Rye," the man said. The bartender put out the bottle and glass and a glass of water.

Tom reached over and took the glass off the free-lunch bowl. It was a bowl of pickled pig's feet and there was a wooden thing that worked like a scissors, with two wooden forks at the end to pick them up with.

"No," said the bartender and put the glass cover back on the bowl. Tom held the wooden scissors fork in his hand. "Put it back," said the bartender.

"You know where," said Tom.

The bartender reached a hand forward under the bar, watching us both. I put fifty cents on the wood and he straightened up.

"What was yours?" he said.

"Beer," I said, and before he drew the beer he uncovered both the bowls.

(The original Hemingway comes from a short story, "The Light of the World," 1933. The parody is excerpted from Alan Coren's "The Short, Happy Life of Margaux Hemingway," *Harper's*, October 1975.)

Exercise 2 (parody)

Write a parody of about one page on an original sample chosen from one of the following prose sources, which often offer rich opportunities for parody:

  a. Sports interview article.
  b. Advertisement for cosmetics.
  c. Hard-sell automobile advertisement or commercial.
  d. Small-town newspaper coverage of a wedding.
  e. Celebrity gossip in *People, Enquirer,* or similar journal.
  f. Newspaper question-and-answer column on medical advice.

If the original uses visual aids, feel free to design your own as part of the parody. Please attach a clipping, copy, or detailed description of the original so that others may appreciate your treatment of it.

Exercise 3 (expository prose)

a. Imitate this passage for its implicit outlook, following the steps for either a scrambling and re-synthesis or an imitative adaptation:

> Surgeons tell us that a broken arm or leg, if it is correctly set, becomes strongest at the point of the fracture.
>
> I like to imagine an analogy between this and the process I am about to describe, a process that is fundamental in the task we have set ourselves.

Recognition of the value of working especially hard on difficult passages is no new idea in piano teaching: it is one of the oldest and soundest ideas. But my approach to this factor in piano study is perhaps unique. For I don't approach it with emphasis, or stress, or insistence. I approach it with fanaticism, with mania!

I am now looking you straight in the eye and I am speaking slowly and rather loudly:

I believe in marking off, in every piece we study, all passages that we find especially difficult, and then practicing these passages patiently, concentratedly, intelligently, relentlessly—until we have battered them down, knocked them out, surmounted them, dominated them, conquered them—until we have transformed them, thoroughly and permanently, from the weakest into the strongest passages in the piece.

The cat is now out of the bag. My major premise is stated. (Charles Cooke, *Playing the Piano for Pleasure*, 1960)

b. Write a brief analysis (about a half-page) describing the more significant branching-offs of your imitation from the original, and evaluating the resulting difference in impact. (*Important:* Such divergences are almost inevitable in an exercise of this kind. They offer an invaluable chance for close stylistic analysis.)

Exercise 4 (argumentative prose)

Use the instructions for Exercise 3:

Fat people have long known that clothing manufacturers totally ignore us. What sizes are available to the large person come in an array of colors ranging from black to navy blue to gray. I recently discovered another angle to the clothing problem. I'm expecting my first baby next month, but it's impossible to find maternity clothes in a size larger than 18. I get the hint: Fat women don't have babies.

The same thinking applies to wedding gowns. Evidently fat people don't marry, either.

Fat people soon realize they are judged guilty of creating their own deformity. It's their own fault they're fat. Absolutely. They have no self-control. However, the truth is that specialists in bariatric medicine (obesity) found that many fat people eat substantially less than their thin counterparts. These findings prompted still more studies that conclude some people are genetically programmed to burn fat more efficiently than others, thereby needing less food than the thin person who eats like a horse and never gains a pound. For an excellent scholarly treatment of this subject, read Anne Scott Beller's recent book, *Fat and Thin, A Natural History of Obesity*.

But a thousand scientific revelations will never restore the fat person's self-esteem, repeatedly stripped by thoughtless, callous people. It is only when we start to accept and respect ourselves and insist on consideration and politeness from others that the hurts can begin to heal.

It's not true that inside every fat person is a thin person yearning to come out. It is true that inside every fat person is a human being with intelligence and feelings, a being who wants to give love and accept love. We don't feel less pain from an insult because we are cushioned by our fat. A fat person learns at an early age to "laugh at himself," but—hear this—we're not laughing any more. (Kristine A. Schlenzig, "Yes, I'm Fat, But My Patience Is Wearing Thin," 1980)

Exercise 5 (narrative prose)

Use the instructions for Exercise 3:

Paul was killed the last day before he left the Colony. . . . His last evening was spent with us at a party. Usually he controlled his drinking, even when pretending to drink wild with the rest of us. That night he drank himself blind, and had to be put into a bath in the hotel by Jimmy and Willi and brought around. He went back to camp as the sun was coming up to say good-bye to his friends there. He was standing on the airstrip, so Jimmy told me later, still half-conscious with alcohol, the rising sun in his eyes—though of course, being Paul, he would not have shown the state he was in. A plane came in to land, and stopped a few paces away. Paul turned, his eyes dazzling with the sunrise, and walked straight into the propeller, which must have been an almost invisible sheen of light. His legs were cut off just below the crotch and he died at once. (Doris Lessing, *The Golden Notebook*, 1962)

Exercise 6 (self-imitation)

If you're having trouble seeing how to revise your own writing, this exercise can show you one solution.

    a. Choose a paper you've already written, and imitate it, using the technique of scrambling and re-synthesis.
    b. Write a brief analysis comparing your imitation with the original.
    c. Now write a new version of your paper, using the best features of the other two.

7 Basic Development Patterns

This chapter will carry forward Chapter 4 by suggesting further tactics of *invention*—ways of developing one's outlook about a given topic.

Suppose that you would like to write about environmental problems, especially, say, as illustrated by the dramatic Powhatan Creek flood in Appalachia on February 15, 1983. One of two handicaps may block you at the outset. You may know so much that you don't know where to start. Or you may know so little that you don't know how much you still need.

Either way, you can try running the Powhatan Creek flood through a battery of basic development patterns. Each pattern guarantees that you will come up with something—maybe something you didn't know you knew, maybe something you can't agree with, but at least you'll have some working model of your subject which can then be further tested.

Time Order

A natural pattern for any historical happening would be time order, in which events are described from early to late—thus:

Saturday
Tuesday morning

The historic Powhatan Creek flood was set off by three days of heavy rains and melting snow beginning Saturday, February 12. By Tuesday daybreak, the mining company supervisor was alarmed enough to inspect the huge refuse pile which held back a large pond of waste water. He was satisfied, but the new mayor of the nearby village of Sumner was not. The mayor hurried down to the village, warning each household as he went. For the most part, the disaster-hardened villagers smiled at him.

Tuesday
midday

At 11:17 A.M., the refuse pile crumbled, unleashing 20 million
cubic feet of black water upon the five hamlets of Powhatan
Valley. Cresting at 30 feet, the flood crumpled bridges, left
only a handful of homes in its path, carried bodies as far down

Thursday

as the Kitsap River. By Thursday night, the death toll had
reached 90 and was still expected to rise.

Time order is commonly used for narrative, history, and descriptions of
processes. The pattern itself, like all other patterns, serves as a test for
completeness of materials. Here you would check over the whole time
sequence of February 12–17 to see that all key time segments were ac-
counted for. What, for example, happened Tuesday night or Wednesday?
You might return to the Powhatan Creek material to find what if anything
had been overlooked.

Space Order

You might try a space order, in which the discussion is organized by
place—say, as for a tour of the flood aftermath taken from the bottom of
the valley going up.

Kitsap
River

Aside from the occasional corpse floating in the Kitsap River,
the first ravages of the flood did not show until the visitor had

Powhatan
Valley

turned up Powhatan Valley. The creek had subsided, but a
black line running some 20–30 feet high on the valley banks

higher up

showed how deep the flood had been. Broken furniture appeared; battered automobiles; twisted railroad tracks. Higher

near Sumner

up near Sumner, every tree on the footpath was hung with cur-

site of
dam collapse

tains, carpets, dolls, pieces of clothing, family portraits. Sumner
itself, at the foot of the burst dam, was destroyed except for
post office, grade school, and company store.

This particular variety of space order can be called travel or journey
order. It would also serve to describe a building (in the order that one
walks through it) or an elaborate setting. Other space orders would include left to right (as in describing a group photograph), down to up, in
to out, large to small, most to least conspicuous, or some other natural line
of attention as for example a road winding through a landscape. Space
orders help generally to describe visible materials and movements.

Comparison

You might work up a valuable idea by trying a parallel in which you
show how the Powhatan Creek flood resembles similar disasters:

suggested paral-
lel with other
floods Unfortunately the Powhatan Creek flood was by no means
unique in Appalachian coal country. A lesser flood had occurred
at the same site in 1976. Eight mining counties in the neighbor-
ing state had been so badly flooded in September 1982 as to
1st point of
resemblance require a President's Disaster Relief Fund. In each case, the
waste waters from mining operations had been inadequately
2nd point stored behind refuse piles. Heavy weather had increased the
3rd point strain on these facilities. Once the piles gave way, the deep
narrow Appalachian valleys had funneled the rushing waters
4th point onto the houses at the bottom. And in every case, the helpless
communities had required emergency funding from the governments which had failed to prevent the disaster.

You have a choice of drawing the comparison point by point, as this example illustrates; or of first describing the Powhatan Creek flood with all
four of its generic qualities and *then* describing the other floods with their
matching qualities. Such an alternative often serves for brief simple comparisons where the reader covers each whole with one glimpse. The point-
by-point parallel serves better for long or complex comparisons.

A special use of comparison pattern is the *analogy* whereby an event
(or thing) is likened to a more familiar or more vivid event or thing. Thus
the Powhatan Creek flood could be dramatized as a monster running
amok down the valley. Light waves might be clarified by the analogy of
ocean waves. The brain and nervous system might be explained by the
analogy of a telephone network.

Contrast

A similar pattern is the contrast, in which you would point up the Powhatan Creek disaster by showing its differences from other floods to which
it bears an apparent likeness:

possible parallel
with floods else-
where The Powhatan Creek flood began, like many famous floods, with
the bursting of a "dam." But the function of that "dam" explains
the special kind of disaster which so often descends upon Ap-
assertion of im-
portant differ-
ences in dams palachian coal-mining communities. The "dam" at Sumner was
not intended to develop water power or to contain water for use.
as to function Its sole purpose was to use waste solids to hold back a large
pond of acid water and coal slime which otherwise would pol-
as to operation
and construction lute the streams. Therefore, it was neither engineered nor op-
erated as most dams are. The dam at Powhatan Creek was
mainly a growing refuse pile some 70 feet high—of slate, sludge,
silt, slag, coal dust, and low-grade coal.

The contrast pattern can also develop two opposing impressions of an
event or, as in the following example, the pros and cons of an issue:

the issue
1st charge

2nd charge

1st defence

2nd defence

concluding comment

How much was the Boothby Mining Company to blame for the Powhatan Creek flood? Critics charged that the Company had failed to learn its lesson from the early flood of 1976, also caused by the collapse of a refuse pile. A second charge was that the Geological Survey of 1977 had reported 75 poorly constructed refuse piles in the state, including this one, of which the Company was notified. On the other hand, the Boothby Mining Company objected that it had not acquired the Powhatan Creek dam until 1980 and should not be held retroactively responsible. Furthermore, the dam had been inspected since then and found passable under laws which though admittedly vague had been complied with. Altogether, the question of company blame seemed complex; it might therefore need expert and judicious examination by a special grand jury.

Expansion

Probably the most flexible development pattern of all is expansion, which opens with a general statement and then provides amplifying particulars. This pattern (also called *deductive*) could help in several projections of the Powhatan Creek material, as follows:

generalization on extent of poverty
1st particular
2nd particular
3rd particular
4th particular

5th particular

6th particular

GENERALIZATION EXPLAINED BY SUPPORTING PARTICULARS

The 1983 flood left the bleak poverty of Powhatan Valley even bleaker. Even under best conditions, the nearly mined-out hills offer few riches to the five small communities which cling to the creek. The flood carried off all but a handful of the 2,300 homes which house the 5,000 inhabitants of the valley. Bulldozers pushed the wreckage of their belongings into heaps for burning. With the railroad washed out, the mine lost production. A wildcat strike in spring failed to obtain greater compensation to the workers for damages and lost pay. By the next winter, many families had given up and moved out, leaving only a remnant.

Or you could omit the opening generalization and simply supply the details from which a subtle reader might infer the generalization directly. Another expansion pattern:

statement of general principle
examples from history of mining
1st example

2nd example

PRINCIPLE EXPLAINED BY EXAMPLES

Disasters like the Powhatan Creek flood would suggest that man's exploitation of land tends to accelerate as the land is used up. The first step is to mine more deeply after the original coal veins give out. Thus deep-mining began at Powhatan Creek and throughout Ferry County as early as the 1880s. Then, as the deep coal thins out, inferior coal is mined, with lower

3rd example   production and larger problems of waste. Mining companies, running on narrower profit margins, are tempted to downgrade the increased demands for safety and environmental protection.

4th example   Government agencies then fall under heavy pressure to avoid inflicting legal penalties which might halt operations. Perhaps

5th example   the needy miners themselves silently accept these apparent con-

6th example   ditions for survival. So disasters strike, like the Powhatan Creek flood, and the impoverishment of land and man speeds up. Unless unusual strategies are developed, the time hastens on when

7th example   below-surface mining may stop entirely in favor of marginal strip-mining which could complete the denuding of the hills.

Still another expansion pattern:

CONCLUSION SUPPORTED BY REASONS

statement of conclusion   A concerted effort to reclaim Powhatan Valley and similar min-

1st reason   ing communities is evidently demanded of all parties. If the mining companies cannot improve water retention and waste disposal, the further gutting of the land may bring their enter-

2nd reason   prises to a final halt. If state and federal governments cannot close ranks to administer both subsidy and efficient supervision to coal-mining operations, the American people will lose major

3rd reason   energy resources and therefore suffer a reduced standard of living. Finally, if the miners cannot give both voice and energy to better mining conditions, they can expect to subside into apathy and further impoverishment, with emigration as their only escape.

Other expansion patterns would be (1) effect explained by its causes—for example the flood as caused by heavy rain, weak dam, and narrow valley; (2) the converse: a cause being traced out to its effects; (3) definition: the broad definition followed by a series of narrowing qualifiers. (See pp. 141–144 for discussion and demonstration of definition.)

Contraction

With minor adjustments in continuity, any of these expansion patterns can be inverted to an opposite pattern, contraction, which works through the amplification *toward* the generalization, which appears at the end. This pattern (also called *inductive*) works well when you want to get the evidence laid out for both yourself and your reader before drawing a conclusion. It also works when you wish to delay your conclusion for a climax. Here as one illustration is the previous example (conclusion explained by reasons) as it could be remodeled:

REASONS LEADING TO CONCLUSION

1st reason　　If the mining companies cannot improve water retention and waste disposal, the further gutting of the land may bring their

2nd reason　　enterprises to a final halt. If state and federal governments cannot close ranks to administer both subsidy and efficient supervision to coal-mining operations, the American people will lose major energy resources and therefore suffer a reduced standard

3rd reason　　of living. As for the miners, if they cannot give both voice and energy to better mining conditions, they can expect to subside into apathy and further impoverishment, with emigration as

conclusion　　their only escape. In short, the reclaiming of Powhatan Valley and similar mining communities evidently demands a concerted effort by all parties.

If you want the ultimate in emphatic clarity, you can try a fused pattern (expansion-contraction) so that you open with your general proposition, then develop the details, then close on the general proposition restated.

Analysis

The last of the common patterns is analysis, in which you divide your material into a series of essential parts which you then discuss in order. This pattern is also called *classification*, since the material is often divided into classes or categories. It is called *enumeration* when the parts of the topic are numbered.

division of topic　　A natural resource like coal can be lost in at least three ways—

1st point　　more than most people realize. First, we can lose a natural resource by using it up or by using it far faster than it can be re-

2nd point　　plenished. Thus we lose coal by burning it. Second, we can lose a natural resource by letting it be wasted, as when we allow farmland to erode. Coal can be wasted by allowing a mine to become inoperable, or by using inefficient methods of burning it.

3rd point　　Third, we can so mismanage the waste products of a natural resource that they pollute or destroy other natural resources. The draining of coal wastes into a freshwater river would harm wild life as well as needed supplies of pure water. We might

tentative 4th point　　even go a fourth step, to say that human labor is also a natural resource, which can be lost by exhaustion, misuse, or nonuse. Thus the Powhatan Creek flood reduced this resource by putting the inhabitants out of work.

The analysis pattern is apparently easy to apply to almost any material, and it is easy to follow. But the mere numbering of parts doesn't guarantee clarity. The parts must be laid out on some consistent principle.

INCONSISTENT Five kinds of food crops: (1) pears, (2) fruits, (3) wheat, (4) grains, (5) spring crops. (Notice that 1 and 2 overlap, as do 3 and 4; point 5 shifts to a different principle of division.)

CONSISTENT Five kinds of food crops: (1) tubers, (2) stems, (3) leaves, (4) grains, (5) fruits. (Here crops are classified according to one principle—the part of the plant consumed—and then arranged by an approximate space order of down to up.)

These basic patterns of development can overlap a good deal. The space order describing a journey might also be a time order. A single passage might show both analysis and expansion patterns. One pattern might simply fuse into another. The point is that these patterns are textbook models, after all, rarely found neat in living prose. A great advantage of knowing them is that *they can get you started* in conceiving your subject matter. *Form can generate substance.* Given any topic, you can begin by taking a pattern and building up the materials which can fit it. More commonly, your materials, already growing, may suggest a pattern which in turn will tell you what new materials to look for.

The Mosaic or Associative Pattern

An uncommon pattern remains, one which is not recommended except for advanced writers: the mosaic or associative pattern which builds as it goes, each piece finding its own best connection and helping to open a chance for the next piece, until a whole comes into being. Though the completed passage may lack a strong central framework, it nevertheless has the vitality and a bit of the mystery of a living organism.

Suppose that in your reading on the Powhatan Creek flood, you were struck by the half-dozen comments quoted from the victims. You don't make any precise generalization from these speeches, but you want to bring them together into some intense configuration. To begin a mosaic, you don't need an exact plan. The mosaic technique is highly personal. You do need some feel for what your material could mean. For instance, I noted these comments from a large body of magazine and newspaper material because they voiced so honestly the human suffering which lay under the statistics, charges, and counter-charges. So I opened with a broad generalization to this effect, leading into the earliest villager's comment—on the abruptness of the flood:

> The most eloquent commentary on the Powhatan Creek flood came from the plain people for whom the disaster had struck briefly but deep. "The flood came too fast for us to have any warning," said a Sumner resident. "Suddenly it was there—water, mud, and boards from homes." An old woman trying to wipe the muck from a family picture recovered from the rubble explained: "It's about all I have left." In the gymnasium serving as relief center, a woman observed a boy limping past, his face puffy and blotched. "That's the Stevens boy. They found him caught in the branches of a tree. His family is all gone, they say." When the Boothby Mining Company sought immunity weeks later by attributing the flood to an Act of God, a miner observed somberly, "God may have made the rain and snow, but He sure didn't make that dam."

Having only a general intuition to guide you, you literally improvise a mosaic from one piece to the next until it finally collapses (as a good many mosaics do) or until a connecting motif shows up. For me, the one conspicuous motif was the force of the villagers' remarks. That was all there was to start with, except a loose time order. What brought the piece into clearer light was the repeated press reference to this region as a premium coal-producer in the United States. That a prime natural resource should yield such human wretchedness I saw as an irony which pointed up the rest. The irony also dictated the deletion of one sentimental report of a three-year-old survivor who had asked Santa Claus to replace her lost toy forks, spoons, and knives, explaining, "They washed away." (Not every piece needs to be used in a mosaic.) Thus the paragraph got written though its total sense was not apparent to its writer at the beginning.

Not all writing should be mosaic, for the technique sacrifices the planning and design which can support large-scale exposition and argument. But the mosaic does show how the very act of writing can create new meanings, orders, and effects not foreseeable at the outset.

Toward the Larger Scale

A new principle can be drawn from a second glimpse at an earlier example:

division of topic / 1st point / 2nd point   A natural resource like coal can be lost in at least three ways—more than most people realize. First, we can lose a natural resource by using it up or by using it far faster than it can be replenished. Thus we lose coal by burning it. Second, we can lose a natural resource by letting it be wasted, as when we allow

> farmland to erode. Coal can be wasted by allowing a mine to become inoperable, or by using inefficient methods of burning it. . . .

The paragraph as a whole exemplifies *enumeration* as it was intended to do: first the division of the topic into parts, then the enumeration of the parts in turn. But notice the first point:

> First, we can lose a natural resource by using it up or by using it far faster than it can be replenished. Thus we lose coal by burning it.

What is the second sentence doing there? It is providing an illustration, a particular. So this segment by itself shows the *expansion* pattern. *We can give a whole composition one pattern for its chief elements, while giving each element a pattern of its own.* Notice how the second example in the larger enumeration pattern also follows a general-to-particulars pattern by itself:

generalization   Second, we can lose a natural resource by letting it be wasted,
1st particular   as when we allow farmland to erode. Coal can be wasted by
2nd particular   allowing a mine to become inoperable, or by using inefficient
                         methods of burning.

Patterns within patterns—this is what gives you flexibility as you go to the larger scale. You can still have a large pattern, a master structure for the whole; but you may also develop each part by whatever pattern seems best for its own function.

Thus a several-paragraph composition could be designed to argue, say, the need for all parties to join in reclaiming the mining communities. An efficient overall pattern might be contraction (particulars leading toward a generalization):

> I. The destruction caused by recent floods. (1st large detail)
> II. Causes of such flooding. (2nd large detail)
> III. Possible acceleration of deterioration. (3rd large detail)
> IV. Need for concerted action. (Generalization)

Next, notice how each part could accommodate a pattern of its own:

MAJOR PART	POSSIBLE PATTERN
I. The destruction.	Expansion: generalization supported by particulars.
II. Causes.	Expansion: effect explained by its causes.

III. Possible acceleration of
     deterioration.

Expansion: principle explained by
example.

IV. Need for concerted effort.

Expansion: conclusion supported by
reasons.

Going down to the next level, one finds that each sub-part can also benefit from the pattern best suited to it. Under "Destruction," for example, one of several illustrations (like the Powhatan Creek flood) might be developed through time order. Under "Causes," one cause (the poor construction of dams) might be developed through a contrast of refuse piles with engineered dams. And so on. The resulting pyramid of structures for the whole composition might be diagramed:

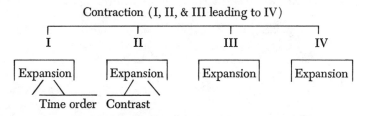

Contraction (I, II, & III leading to IV)

I   II   III   IV

Expansion   Expansion   Expansion   Expansion

Time order   Contrast

If you admire the neat intricacy of a Swiss watch, this is all very nice. Certainly the demonstration is intended to show how many options start spinning as you develop a subject. However, a piece of writing is not a Swiss watch but is a process of growth which often moves beyond any pattern set in advance. When that happens, be ready rather than dismayed. The true proof of the process will always be the illumination and impact which that process creates in your mind and in that of your reader.

Exercise 1 (all elements)

Determine the pattern or patterns used for each passage:

a. One of the interesting things to me about our spaceship is that it is a mechanical vehicle, just as is an automobile. If you own an automobile, you realize that you must put oil and gas into it, and you must put water in the radiator and take care of the car as a whole. You begin to develop quite a little thermodynamic sense. You know that you're either going to have to keep the machine in good order or it's going to be in trouble and fail to function. We have not been seeing our Spaceship Earth as an integrally-designed machine which to be persistently successful must be comprehended and serviced in total. (R. Buckminster Fuller, *Operating Manual for Spaceship Earth*, 1969)

b. As the thunder of bombs and the war of collapsing masonry ebbed, there emerged through it the high-pitched scream from thousands of voices. A stunned shopper whimpered as she searched through shards of glass that had been a display counter. She was an exquisite young woman clothed in the Western "Shanghai" mode, an ankle-length dress of green silk slit to above the knee, and a stiff little collar standing around her curved, porcelain neck. Her extreme pallor might have come from the pale rice powders fashionable with the daughters of rich Chinese merchants, but it did not. She was searching for the ivory figurine she had been examining at the moment of the bombing, and for the hand in which she had been holding it. (Trevanian, *Shibumi*, 1979)

c. Gentlemen—you are now about to embark upon a course of studies which will occupy you for two years. Together they form a noble adventure. But I would like to remind you of an important point. Some of you, when you go down from the University, will go into the Church, or to the Bar, or to the House of Commons, to the Home Civil Service, to the Indian or Colonial Services, or into various professions. Some may go into the Army, some into industry and commerce; some may become country gentlemen. A few—I hope very few—will become teachers or dons. Let me make this clear to you. Except for the last category, nothing that you will learn in the course of your studies will be of the slightest possible use to you in after life—save only this—that if you work hard and intelligently, you should be able to detect when a man is talking rot, and that, in my view, is the main, if not the sole purpose of education. (Cited by Harold Macmillan in the *London Times*, 1975?)

d. The great advantages of simulation and dissimulation are three. First, to lay asleep opposition, and to surprise. For where a man's intentions are published, it is an alarum to call up all that are against them. The second is, to reserve to a man's self a fair retreat. For if a man engage himself by a manifest declaration, he must go through or take a fall. The third is, the better to discover the mind of another. For to him that opens himself men will hardly shew themselves adverse; but will . . . let him go on, and turn their freedom of speech to freedom of thought. And therefore it is a good shrewd proverb of the Spaniard, *Tell a lie and find a truth*. As if there were no way of discovery but by simulation. There be also three disadvantages, to set it even. The first, that simulation and dissimulation commonly carry with them a shew of fearfulness, which in any business doth spoil the feathers [from] flying up to the mark. The second, that it puzzleth and perplexeth the conceits of many, that perhaps would otherwise co-operate with him; and makes a man walk almost alone to his own ends. The third and greatest is, that it depriveth a man of one of the most principal instruments for action; which is trust and belief. The best composition and temperature is to have openness in fame and opinion; secrecy in habit; dissimulation in seasonable use and a power to feign. if there be no remedy. (Francis Bacon, "Of Simulation and Dissimulation," 1625)

e. Suppose that we were approached by galactic travelers with a very advanced technology who offer us the following opportunity. They guarantee to double the standard of living of *everyone* on Earth for one thousand years. At the end of that time they will arrange that humans will become painlessly sterile; when the last human is gone, the galactic travelers will occupy the planet. We check and find their references are impeccable. The question I now ask each person is whether they would accept this deal. I have not yet had a positive response. Yet if we apply standard cost-benefit thinking to this proposition we find it very attractive. (Ronald A. Howard in *Operations Research*, 1980)

f. The dominant modern belief is that the soundest foundation of peace would be universal prosperity. One may look in vain for historical evidence that the rich have regularly been more peaceful than the poor, but then it can be argued that they have never felt secure against the poor; that their aggressiveness stemmed from fear; and that the situation would be quite different if everybody were rich. Why should a rich man go to war? He has nothing to gain. Are not the poor, the exploited, the oppressed most likely to do so, as they have nothing to lose but their chains? The road to peace, it is argued, is to follow the road to riches. (E. F. Schumacher, *Small Is Beautiful: Economics as if People Mattered*, 1973)

g. As individuals, then, we are created by sexual reproduction and social conditioning and are what we are, not by our free choice, but by the accident of birth and economic necessity. As individuals we do not act; we exhibit behavior characteristic of the biological species and social group or groups to which we belong. As individuals we are countable, comparable, replaceable.

As persons, who can, now and again, truthfully say, *I*, we are called into being—the myth of our common descent from a single ancestor, Adam, is a way of saying this—not by any biological process but by other persons, our parents, our siblings, our friends. As persons we are not willy-nilly members of a society, but are free to form communities, groups of rational beings, united, as St. Augustine said, by a love of something other than themselves, God, music, stamp-collecting or what-have-you. As persons we are capable of deeds, of choosing to do this rather than that and accepting responsibility for the consequences whatever they may turn out to be. As persons we are uncountable, incomparable, irreplaceable. (W. H. Auden, *Secondary Worlds*, 1968)

h. Towards the middle of the morning the sky lightened and lifted, the rain thinned to a drizzle, then stopped altogether. The clouds rolled back, the sky was suddenly blinding blue and there were shadows on the water. Rapidly, their gurgling soon lost in the awakening everyday din, canals subsided, leaving a wash of twigs and dirt on the road. . . . Roads and roofs dried, steaming, areas of dryness spreading out swiftly, like ink on a blotter. And presently roads and yards were dry, except for the depressions where water had collected. Heat nibbled at their edges, until even the depressions failed to reflect the blue sky. And the world was dry again, except for the mud in the shelter of the trees. (V. S. Naipaul, *A House for Mr. Biswas,* 1961)

Exercise 2 (all elements)

Rewrite the following defective paragraphs to show how you would clarify their patterns:

a. During our world tour we briefly visited India. We spent five days in London. For a whole week we gaped at the many civilizations of Istanbul. The Japanese visit extended to ten days because of illness. We covered the whole of Italy in two whirlwind days.

b. Burglaries can be discouraged by several precautions. Lawns should be kept mowed in the owner's absence. An extra car can be parked in the drive. Police should be informed of exact duration of absence. Burglary has become one of the most costly crimes in the U.S. today. It is increasing in the cities, in the suburbs, in the countryside, especially with homes which are vacant and unguarded. A professional burglar could probably hit such a home regardless of protective schemes.

c. The exoneration of Congressman Michael Klom restored one of the ablest younger legislators to the service of his party. The Republicans of this state feel new life. People have regained a confidence in them that had badly eroded. The indignant backlash at Klom's accusers will help other Republicans in the coming election.

Exercise 3 (analysis patterns)

Diagnose the inconsistency of principle in each of the following schemes for analysis pattern and propose a solution. Your proposal may combine items, eliminate unnecessary items, or add any item needed to complete the pattern.

a. *Reasons for Monica McKellar's business success*
   flair for finding new markets
   excellent education

company's interest in women executives
talent for sales
first-rate preparation

b. *Homework*
take-home exam
assigned readings
need for quiet
how to prepare for tests
regularity of effort
written exercises

c. *Elements of a sound taxation policy*
past scandals in tax waste
identifying needs for public funding
identifying sources of tax income
how taxes deprive us of freedom
identifying alternate sources of income
fair distribution of tax burden

d. *Elements of the game of tennis*
balls to use
tennis clothing
rules
racquet
strokes
tactics in singles
choosing a doubles partner

Exercise 4 (all elements)

To show your inventiveness with development patterns, first select any one of the following topics:

a. Gourmet food
b. Dueling
c. Homosexuality
d. Women's sports
e. Denims

f. Powerboats
g. Multiple sclerosis
h. A current world crisis
i. Computer games
j. Space exploration

Second, blindly draw two patterns from the following:

1. Space order
2. Comparison
3. Contrast
4. Contraction: effects to cause
5. Analysis
6. Time order

7. Expansion: generalization to particulars
8. Expansion: principle to examples
9. Expansion: cause to effects
10. Mosaic

Third, for each pattern taken, write one independent paragraph on your topic. Use library sources if necessary.

Exercise 5 (patterns within patterns)

To extend the concept of patterns into longer compositions, apply a two-part pattern (either comparison or contrast) to one of the topics below. As you write, develop each part by some different but appropriate pattern. In the margin, show what pattern(s) you are using.

  a. The computer versus the calculator. (*Example:* Each topic in this contrast pattern could be separately developed by *expansion: generalization to particulars*—e.g., the distinctive function of the machine followed by explanatory details.)
  b. Nuclear disarmament.
  c. A success and failure in someone's life.
  d. How would I feel about my best friend's having an abortion?
  e. Scientific fraud.
  f. A specific type of music then and now.
  g. Our nation's best response to industrial competition from Japan.
  h. My parents and I on marriage.

Option: Use a master pattern with *more* than two parts if your thinking keeps leading you that way.

Suggested readings for further illustration, discussion, and writing: William Carlos Williams, "The Use of Force," page 308; Augusto Monterroso, "Three Fables," page 312; James H. Austin, "The Roots of Serendipity," page 314.

8   Coherence

Usually your thoughts shift as you write, simply because writing itself is thought looking for new chances. Your thought may sometimes veer so sharply that you will want to break off to start over in a new direction. More often you can weld your thoughts into a *coherent* unity—especially if you will keep inserting signals to yourself to show how each new idea relates to the preceding ones.

The coherence tactics discussed in this chapter can help you think more tightly; moreover, they will help your reader to follow you. Try imagining the reader's mind as it runs along your sentences. Think of that mind as curious but easily distracted, ready to leap for connections *at any hint whether intended or accidental,* and in the absence of hints ready to invent connections. Anticipate where that mind may stumble or swerve. Such a discipline will help to keep your own mind on track.

Coherence from Sentence to Sentence

Relationship signals announce first of all whether you're continuing in the same direction or shifting direction—and second, what kind of continuity or shift to expect.

The following are signals to show continuation in the same direction:

> *To show that the same topic continues:* this, these, that, such, the same
> *To introduce another item in the same series:* another, again, a

second (a third, etc.), further, furthermore, moreover, similarly, likewise, too, finally, also

To introduce another item in a time series: next, then, later on, afterwards, finally

To introduce an example or particularization of what has just been said: for instance, for example

To introduce a consequence of what has just been said: accordingly, thus, therefore, then, as a result, hence

To introduce a restatement of what has just been said: in other words, to put it differently, that is to say

To introduce a concluding item or a summary: finally, altogether, all in all, the point is, in conclusion, to summarize

These are signals to show a shift of direction:

To introduce material which opposes what has just been said: but, however, on the other hand, on the contrary

To introduce a concession to an opposing view: to be sure, granted, of course

To show that the original line is about to resume after a concession: still, nevertheless, nonetheless, all the same

Such signals need not always come first in a sentence; they are often delayed to allow initial emphasis to something else. A less obtrusive coherence can be built through the *repetition of key words* (or pronouns or synonyms for these words), so that every sentence is made to point toward the central notion. Note the recurrence of the key word "myth" and its equivalents in this sample passage:

Myth as it exists in a savage community, that is in *its* living primitive form, is not merely a *story told* but a *reality lived. It* is not of the nature of fiction, such as we read to-day in a novel, but *it* is a *living reality,* believed to have once happened in primeval times and continuing ever since to influence the world and human destinies. This *myth* is to the savage what, to a fully believing Christian, is the Biblical story of Creation, of the Fall, of the Redemption by Christ's Sacrifice on the Cross. As our sacred story lives in our ritual, in our morality, as it governs our faith and controls our conduct, even so does his *myth* for the savage. (Bronislaw Malinowski, *Myth in Primitive Psychology,* 1926)

You can channel the reader's attention through a crucial passage by using *parallel sentence structures* which not only reduce your syntactical complexity but bind the passage together with their own natural rhythm. Parallel structures often work together with the repetition of key words, as in this celebrated passage from Matthew Arnold's *Culture and Anarchy* (1869). Both techniques are indicated: parallel rhythms are boxed, key terms are italicized. Arnold's key terms—"sweetness," "light," "machinery," "culture"—have been defined by him earlier.

> The pursuit | of perfection, then, is
> the pursuit | of *sweetness and light.*

> He who | works | for *sweetness and light,*
> | works | to make reason and the will of God prevail.
> He who | works | for *machinery,*
> he who | works | for hatred,
> | works | only for confusion.

> *Culture* looks | beyond *machinery,*
> *culture* hates | hatred;
>
> *culture* has | one | great | passion,
> | | the | passion | for *sweetness and light.*
> *It* has | one | even yet greater! —
> | | the | passion | for making *them* prevail.

Still one more technique of coherence is *dovetailing,* in which a new sentence is made to begin with the same topic which closed the preceding sentence—that is, the new sentence may begin with the same phrase, a synonym or paraphrase of it, or a pronoun referring to it. The tightness of the resulting splice is illustrated by this example:

NOT
DOVETAILED   The will to win is what we must never neglect. A man's resources
             can be extended up to 50 percent by his determination to pre-
             vail, perhaps even more.
DOVETAILED   What we must never neglect is *the will to win. The determina-
             tion to prevail* can extend a man's resources up to 50 percent,
             perhaps even more.

These techniques of coherence should not be idolized. Many a writer has learned to conceal a habitual muddle of thought under a tidy veneer of transition signals, repetitions, parallel structures, and dovetails. The truest coherence is the internal coherence of your own conception—your awareness of a distinct central meaning toward which all your arguments, illustrations, reservations, and asides converge. Moreover seasoned read-ers who follow you may resent being over-urged into a path they have already anticipated. Many prefer the intellectual excitement of making their own leaps over the gaps. I myself tend to over-use these signals in writing first drafts, just to keep on course. In later drafts many signals can be omitted, since their job has been done. Mastery of the externals of coherence is simply one discipline which helps you toward the ultimate goal—a lucid comprehension of your subject, of yourself, and of your reader.

Non-Coherence

A few words should be said on the actual values of non-coherence—that is, the intentional refusal to show connection. Wit and irony depend on the reader's delight in joining pieces which have been pointedly left disconnected. Compare:

> A Alderman Bulstrode survived his plunge into the empty swimming pool. He was fortunate enough to land head first.
>
> B Alderman Bulstrode survived his plunge into the empty swimming pool *because* he fortunately landed on his head.

Though B is beautifully coherent, specifying the cause for survival, it lacks the mildly comic shock which A produces in its abrupt second sentence, where the causal connection is left implicit.

Non-coherent language can also express a prelogical or sublogical awareness of experience. In the stream of consciousness technique that was sampled earlier in this book (p. 27), the ordinary links of syntax, even the common punctuation signals, may be omitted to convey that rush of the mind which carries sensations, memories, fantasy, and reflection all together. For example:

> wait theres Georges church bells wait 3 quarters the hour wait 2 oclock well thats a nice hour of the night for him to be coming home at to anybody climbing down into the area if anybody saw him Ill knock him off that little habit tomorrow first Ill look at his shirt to see or Ill see if he has that French letter still in his pocketbook I suppose he thinks I don't know deceitful men all their 20 pockets arent enough for their lies then why should we tell them even if its the truth they dont believe you (James Joyce, *Ulysses*, 1922)

And if the writer sees not only the awareness of experience but experience itself to be disordered, fragmented, futile, a non-coherent language can intensify that vision through its own discontinuities, as in this passage from Samuel Beckett:

> Given the existence as uttered forth in the public
> works of Puncher and Wattmann of a personal
> God quaquaquaqua with white beard
> quaquaquaqua outside time without extension
> who from the heights of divine apathia divine

> athambia divine aphasia loves us dearly with
> some exceptions for reasons unknown but time
> will tell and suffers like the divine Miranda with
> those who for reasons unknown but time will tell
> are plunged in torment plunged in fire whose fire
> flames if that continues and who can doubt it will

(Waiting for Godot, 1954)

These opening lines of a wild discourse on the human condition fail to evolve into a recognizable sentence, they stutter on the Latin *"qua,"* they stumble on "apathia" and its alternatives, they leave off one structure to begin another. All this expresses a chaotic perspective. Notice that you can't give the reader such an experience of disorder merely by writing nonsense. Here highly formal structures are begun ("Given the existence as uttered forth") and recognizable clauses appear here and there ("time will tell"). The art of writers like Beckett is to create definite *fragments of meaning* so that the reader both expects a coherence and is shocked by its absence.

Coherence Among Paragraphs

The left-hand margin break which opens a paragraph is an important and flexible coherence device. Mainly it has served to divide a long composition into blocks which are short enough to be grasped after a minute or two of attention, long enough to hold together all the material supporting a significant point. For just these reasons you would avoid writing so that you must indent the left-hand margin too often; such paragraphing fragments the reader's attention and your own. And you would avoid running an unbroken left-hand margin page after page; such long paragraphs strain the reader by denying a sense of completeness, and will tempt you yourself to neglect the structure of your thought.

But the margin break may support other ends than logic.

Extraordinary emphasis can be given to a sentence by setting it off as a brief paragraph as was just done with the preceding sentence. Again, the margin break is now used in fiction to announce any change of speaker in dialog passages; thus it acts as a transition signal. Really you can indent to signal any shift, such as a shift in tone from light to serious. You can signal a shift in type of support, as when moving from an anecdote, say, to statistics. Again, because the margin break has trained readers to freshen their attention, you can occasionally use it when you wish to enhance the next sentence, no matter how logical the paragraph division may seem at that point.

For examples, consider the flexibility of margin break which can be practiced with a passage from William James' *Pragmatism* (1907). The author's version, which follows, used the margin break traditionally, for a logical division of one topic from a second topic:

FUNCTION OF
PARAGRAPH BREAK
introduction of
new topic
(nature of
metaphysics)

Metaphysics has usually followed a very primitive kind of quest. You know how men have always hankered after unlawful magic, and you know what a great part in magic *words* have always played. If you have his name, or the formula of incantation that binds him, you can control the spirit, genie, afrite, or whatever the power may be. Solomon knew the names of all the spirits, and having their names, he held them subject to his will. So the universe has always appeared to the natural mind as a kind of enigma, of which the key must be sought in the shape of some illuminating or power-bringing word or name. That word names the universe's *principle,* and to possess it is after a fashion to possess the universe itself. "God," "Matter," "Reason," "the Absolute," "Energy," are so many solving names. You can rest when you have them. You are at the end of your metaphysical quest.

introduction of
new topic (con-
trasting nature
of pragmatism)

But if you follow the pragmatic method, you cannot look on any such word as closing your quest. You must bring out of each word its practical cash-value, set it at work within the stream of your experience. It appears less as a solution, then, than as a program for more work, and more particularly as an indication of the ways in which existing realities may be *changed.*

Quite another series of margin breaks could have been used:

FUNCTION OF
PARAGRAPH BREAK
emphasis on
single sentence
(to stress "primi-
tive" quality of
metaphysics)

Metaphysics has usually followed a very primitive kind of quest.

You know how men have always hankered after unlawful magic, and you know what a great part in magic *words* have always played. If you have his name, or the formula of incantation that binds him, you can control the spirit, genie, afrite, or whatever the power may be.

satiric emphasis
on single example

Solomon knew the names of all the spirits, and having their names, he held them subject to his will.

So the universe has always appeared to the natural mind as a kind of enigma, of which the key must be sought in the shape of some illuminating or power-bringing word or name. That word names the universe's *principle,* and to possess it is after a fashion to possess the universe itself. "God," "Matter," "Reason," "the Absolute," "Energy," are so many solving names. You can rest when you have them. You are at the end of your metaphysical quest.

emphasis on
single sentence
(to stress
contrast)

But if you follow the pragmatic method, you cannot look on any such word as closing your quest.

You must bring out of each word its practical cash-value, set it at work within the stream of your experience. It appears less as a solution, then, than as a program for more work, and more particularly as an indication of the ways in which existing realities may be *changed*.

You may judge such paragraphing to be eccentric, and it does come close to being so, mainly to exhibit the variety of margin breaks possible. The rule of thumb would be neither to neglect the potential of the margin break nor to strain it.

One word on what follows the margin break. Your indentation has signaled both your reader and you to be especially alert for new things. Thus you should never squander the opening of a paragraph on dull language or material—thus:

SLACK
OPENING Of the many symptoms which may herald the onset of a coronary heart attack, a prolonged sense of fatigue is one of the commonest.

Until coming to "coronary heart attack," the reader has no idea where the paragraph is really heading. The first eleven words are unspecific, slow. Here is a revision:

STRONGER
OPENING Warning of a coronary heart attack is commonly signaled by a prolonged sense of fatigue.

The first words of the revision pull the reader forward, with attention fully focused for what follows. So especially in revising, you might well work over your paragraph openings to establish immediate orientation, relevance, movement.

For achieving coherence among the sections of a long paper, see Chapter 22, especially pages 254–260.

Exercise 1 (coherence from sentence to sentence)

Review the selections under Exercise 1 of the preceding chapter (p. 71) to identify all examples of relationship signals, repetition of key terms, parallel sentence structure, and dovetailing.

Exercise 2 (coherence from sentence to sentence)

Copy the following paragraph, inserting enough relationship signals to make the connections of thought unmistakably clear. Do not combine sentences. (The sentences are numbered to aid class review of the solutions.)

> (1) When learning a new skill such as tennis or word processing, people dread making mistakes. (2) A mistake may be felt as punishment for ignorance. (3) People often feel guilty after a bad game of tennis or a bungled session at the word processor. (3) If made in public, a mistake can be felt as humiliation. (4) The mistake may be perceived as a costly delay in reaching the objective, which is mastery. (5) One doesn't have all season to perfect one's service or to set a margin. (6) A repeated mistake can perpetuate itself, so that one is actually practicing bad habits. (7) Mistakes call our attention to something important, whereas an uneventful success might put us to sleep. (8) We are forced to analyze our technique, to see what went wrong. (9) When we set a mistake right, we have learned a lesson not easily forgotten. (10) We are protected against that mistake in the future and may go on to learn from more sophisticated errors.

Exercise 3 (dovetailing)

Rework each group of sentences to dovetail them. Do you find the new version stronger or weaker, and why? (Dovetailing which sacrifices simplicity or emphasis may not be worth the coherence which is gained.)

> a. St. Vincent's school does not allow children to have guns. Children are not even allowed to pretend that they have any kind of firearm.
>
> b. A single drawing was all that remained of Leonard's lifetime research. The history of medical research would be changed by that drawing before another decade had passed.
>
> c. It's never hard to find sensitive indicators of the time of year. Some insects emerge, some birds arrive or depart, some flowers bloom in time with the rhythm of the seasons.
>
> d. The composer and the writer can earn royalties over the years for the sale and use of songs, books, musicals, and plays. The visual artist—the painter or sculptor—is paid only for the original sale of the work.

Exercise 4 (coherence from sentence to sentence)

Although the following paragraph is pure nonsense, its sentences cohere so beautifully that simply by following the relationship signals you should be able to come up with a neat outline of its contents. Try it.

> The new drug porocin has proved both dangerous and beneficial. As a cure for creopsis it has far exuded other treatments for that terrible disorder. Again, long-time sufferers from polysclerosis have reported unusual ternsequences after only small dosages. Even the common cold has fraccisured when confronted with porocin. Other illnesses, however, do not respond in this unaculous way. Against arthosis, for example, this new drug exerts no perceivable ostrix. And porocin can positively bradicate the damages of spanditis. Altogether, we must welcome this addition to the doctor's pharmacopoeia, though surely it must be used with caution.

Exercise 5 (coherence and non-coherence)

Take the stream-of-consciousness fragment from James Joyce (p. 80) and edit it for maximum coherence, using sentence division, punctuation, and relationship signals as needed. (Note: In this passage Molly Bloom is sitting up after midnight wondering about her husband.)

Exercise 6 (non-coherence)

Using the non-coherence principles mentioned in this chapter, write from one to two pages on one of the following:

a. The consciousness of a person of titanic intellect laboring through some trivial daily problem, such as whether to cross the street.
b. The consciousness of a student wandering into the campus Union (or coffee house), gloriously elated over a professor's compliment for high performance.
c. The consciousness of a churchgoer on the verge of a breakdown while sitting through a service.

Exercise 7 (margin breaks)

Copy out two or three pages from some prose you've been reading, using *different* margin breaks where appropriate. Number these breaks and in correspondingly numbered notes at the end, explain why you think each break might be effective. (Also indicate where the original breaks occurred.)

Suggested readings for further illustration, discussion, and writing: Hiram Walker and Sons, advertisement, page 321, and James Burke, "Inventing the Future," page 323.

II STYLE AND AUDIENCE

Writing is not just getting things down on paper, it is getting things inside someone else's head. If you wish to improve your writing you must also learn to do more business with other people.

PETER ELBOW, *Writing Without Teachers*, 1973

The relationship of message and audience is a dynamic one, for a shift in audience often leads to a corresponding shift in the way a message is presented, the strategies that are used to persuade.

PATRICK HARTWELL, *Open to Language*, 1982

9   The Audience as Creative Force

Writing is discovery. Because this discovery takes place publicly in the sense of being shared with an audience, different audiences will shape different discoveries. For example, you may hold fairly consistent views on divorce, but when you're writing to a newly divorced friend, you may come up with different reflections than when you're writing to a friend about to marry—not because you're hypocritical or wishy-washy but because different audiences press you to explore your meanings in different terms. Hence you need to know how this relationship to an audience can work.

Two qualities of an audience to which a speaker or writer should respond are its knowledge of the subject at hand, and its present disposition toward that subject.

What the Audience Already Knows

The knowledge of an audience comes from its past experience of the subject and from its general command of information and language. All this you ought to get clearly in mind because it can open up the levels of material and language you can use. Suppose that as a college student, you're making a research report to your classmates on a new cure for some disease. You might open:

> Despite a common belief that Morse's Disease is a minor childhood ailment, medical research has uncovered the serious damage which often sneaks up on the victim after the mild primary

> symptoms have vanished. Weakened vision, slowed-up reflexes, and even brain damage may occur, but so slowly that heretofore they have been ascribed to other causes. [*Drop a footnote to show source.*] The cause lies in a secondary virus which slowly multiplies after the primary virus has temporarily depleted the white blood corpuscles. . . .

Your language here can be mature ("primary symptoms," "ascribed," "virus," "white blood corpuscles"). Your classmates are both intelligent and skeptical enough to expect documentation of your facts, so that you have actually accumulated sources which you can cite. If your audience already knows Morse's Disease by its common symptoms, you are spared from a detailed recital of them and can go directly to more advanced matters.

As a medical student a few years from now, you might be asked to report again on the same topic. You would naturally reach much deeper for conceptions and terms which would answer the professional interests of a medical school audience:

> Morse's Disease is one of a small number of known diviral diseases in which the primary and secondary stages are caused by two separate viruses or by two morphologically distinct stages of one virus. (See Strauss et al., *JAMA*, 1983.) The primary virus, designated TK-112, retards diffusion of beta-keto acids from cells, particularly in the epidermis. The secondary virus, TK-113 . . .

Still later as a doctor yourself, you might be explaining a school health program to a first-grade audience. You might find yourself proceeding thus:

> For most kids Morse's Disease isn't bad. You get a pimply skin which itches. During the next couple of days you may feel almost too weak to cross the room. Then it's over. But some kids aren't that lucky. Morse's Disease sometimes leaves behind a slow poison in the body which . . .

The basic topics for all three openings are the same—the hidden dangers in Morse's Disease. Each audience helps the writer to discover a different significance in the topic—the college student's intelligent but general concept, the medical student's technical comprehension, the child's simple concrete awareness. Each meaning is a different *human* projection of what began as objective information.

The Disposition of the Audience

The disposition of an audience means its initial readiness to feel and to act on the issues you will be treating. People do not feel and act from knowledge and logic alone. They feel and act from their virtues and vices as engaged by specific hopes and fears.

There is nothing complicated about virtues and vices considered as abstract lists. The time-honored virtues are generosity, courage, self-control, justness, reverence, and so forth; the vices are their opposites. These qualities do become alive and complicated through what people most hope or fear, praise or condemn. Most commonly praised are health and youth, friendship and love, independence, wealth, prestige, knowledge, group welfare. We most commonly fear and condemn their opposites.

What you would need to learn, then, is what are the morally sensitive areas in your topic which a given audience will press you to cover. Suppose that you want your community to adopt a public vaccination program against Morse's Disease. Taking the lists of virtues, vices, hopes, and fears just proposed, try applying them to the vaccination issue:

QUESTION What objects do people usually hope for that vaccination would favor?
ANSWER Health. Community welfare.

QUESTION What virtues would be needed to obtain these objects?
ANSWER Courage to be vaccinated. Generosity with time and money. Loyalty to community.

QUESTION What would people fear about a vaccination program?
ANSWER Government regulation. Impoverishment by taxes. Pain of being vaccinated.

For a really full understanding of the moral pressures exerted on you by the audience, you *could* map out this systematic coverage (though most writers work more informally):

	AMONG SUPPORTERS OF A PUBLIC VACCINATION PROGRAM	AMONG OPPONENTS OF A PUBLIC VACCINATION PROGRAM
WHAT WOULD BE HOPED FOR	Health	Freedom from government regulation
	Community welfare	Wealth by avoidance of taxes

WHAT WOULD BE FEARED	Sickness Loss to community through disease	Loss of freedom Impoverishment by taxes Pain of being vaccinated
WHAT VIRTUES WOULD BE NEEDED	Courage to be vaccinated Generosity with time and money Loyalty to community	Independence Courage to resist
WHAT VICES MIGHT ENTER IN	Injustice (invasion of others' rights)	Selfishness (indifference to welfare of others) Avarice (unwillingness to give)

Having surveyed the "moral field" of the vaccination issue, you would be equipped to respond to your particular readers. Some common-sense questions to ask about them would be: To what important group do they belong? What are the special interests and anxieties of that group, and which need primary consideration? What is that group's power to affect the outcome of the vaccination question?

"Membership in an important group" can be defined by any connection you find relevant according to the issue before you. Age, nationality, political party, social level, occupation, place of residence, religion, sex, tastes—any of these could affect audience disposition at one time or another. For example, if you're addressing first-graders on the value of a vaccination program, you would do well to reflect that they belong to the group of those to be vaccinated. Accordingly, their special hopes are to avoid pain and to secure health. Their power is to accept the vaccine cheerfully. Their good will toward your subject can increase if you show how they can use this power to realize their interests.

But if you're writing to old retired people, you ought to remember that they belong to an age group which is exempt from this vaccination. Their special hope is to save money by avoiding new taxes. Their power is to vote in a vaccination referendum. Still, old people also need and hope to be recognized for their experience and their record of civic contribution. Their good will can increase if you show how they can realize their best interests by using this power.

What if your audience is really hostile? You may be lucky. An enthusiastic, "sweetheart" audience could tempt you to think sloppily, as happens to many speakers at political rallies. It is the hostile reader, the skeptical reader, or at least the normally biased reader who helps you test out the subject. True, if you and your readers are *too* far apart, the communication process will break down. Maybe you oppose further taxation so strongly yourself that you can't respect any willingness of your readers to endorse new programs. Or if your readers are dead set against new taxation no matter how urgent the cause, you may despise their shortsightedness too much to take their views seriously. Then you've discovered the limits of any "meaning" you can find with that audience.

You still have several choices. You can just quit trying to communicate, and save your energy. Or you can take the tough abrasive tone of the extremist who is determined to confront, to shatter, to intimidate the audience where a reasoned approach would fail. The frontal assault at least wins attention, and if severe enough may shock the audience into concessions. (This last tactic is rarely tried, and then usually in political crises where a power takeover threatens to occur.) Or without hoping either to win your readers' support or to crush them into submission, you can at least try to get them to take a bigger view of the issues. That tactic may pay off later.

The Relative Importance of the Audience in Different Kinds of Writing

Many inexperienced writers (and some experienced ones) have trouble with this measurement of audience, or else feel that it will take care of itself. One response is "Really, I write for just a general audience, not a specific one." The notion of a general or universal audience can work in many instances—especially if you imagine readers who are essentially like yourself (in your slower or more skeptical moments).

Your subject may develop more sensitively, however, if you consider how these different audiences might shape what you write:

The self as audience. Some writers meet any criticism with the reply, "Oh, I just write for myself." Of course one writes for oneself. It can bring much self-knowledge, self-release, self-satisfaction. But to deny the need to reach any other audience is to admit that one's writing is purely private—just as private as the inscrutable scrawling of an autistic child. One shouldn't complain if others say, "Well, if it's entirely private, you don't need my response."

The instructor as audience. Writing teachers sometimes loom up as grim experts of enormous learning, armed with red pencils, poised for the kill. Students with such a bleak perspective are likely to risk as little as possible, voicing only conventional ideas and concentrating on the avoidance of grammatical errors.

This is too bad, for few people can think or write productively for such an audience. Your best approach is to assume the best: that teachers are skilled and sympathetic readers who are used to putting themselves in the place of other possible readers. Hence you can become your best writing self without fear of a repressive reception. Even if this assumption doesn't always work, it remains the only bet ever likely to pay off.

The small face-to-face audience. Where writers can face their readers, all share the same situation at the same time, with audience response immediate. Common knowledge can be referred to confidently. Questions and unintended reactions can be easily dealt with in revision. Such audiences are found in writing clubs and writing classes. They do much to foster the writer's awareness and use of readers.

The larger audience. The larger and more remote your audience, the less it shares the context in which you write. You need to think harder about its range of knowledge and dispositions, and to modify your thinking and your approach accordingly.

In explanatory writing, by imagining the readers' possible ignorance you may better see the key features of what is to be explained; and by imagining their needs and interests you may see how the topic can become important to them.

Especially in persuasive writing—that which seeks both judgment and action from the audience—a studied insight into the knowledge and disposition of your readers can increase your power. Nowhere is this truer than in advertising, which must seize upon limited space to generate maximum appeal, seeking results from the reader's pocketbook. An ethical question arises somewhere in persuasive writing, as to where an honest address to the interests of the audience gives way to an exploitation of its ignorance, hopes, fears, and biases. You must both resolve such questions for yourself and guard yourself against being manipulated by others.

When writing poetry, fiction, and drama, you may not be explicitly addressing your readers at all. Still, their knowledge and disposition must have much to do with your creation if you're to realize all the impact possible in imaginative writing. Remember that the readers of one great writer said, "He talks from our hearts, not his."

Exercise 1 (the knowledge of the audience)

a. Describe the general command of information and language which the speaker evidently expected to find in his audience. Point to details which support your inference.

Let me say, too, that I have been heartened by the conduct of this convention. You have argued and disagreed because as Democrats you care and you care deeply. But you have disagreed and argued without calling each other liars and thieves, without despoiling our best traditions. You have not spoiled our best traditions in any naked struggles for power.

And you have written a platform that neither equivocates, contradicts, nor evades.

You have restated our party's record, its principles, and its purposes in language that none can mistake, and with a firm confidence in justice, freedom, and peace on earth that will raise the hearts and the hopes of mankind for that distant day when no one rattles a saber and no one drags a chain. (Adlai E. Stevenson in accepting nomination for the Presidency at the Democratic convention of 1952)

b. Write another version of the same material and address it to an audience assumed to be at a much lower educational level.

Exercise 2 (the knowledge of the audience)

Choose a specific topic on which you regard yourself as reasonably expert, such as jogging, gourmet cooking, personal computers, ceramics, dieting, racquet ball. Explain some element of this topic to any three of these different audiences (using one page or less for each version), taking due care to develop your material in response to the presumed knowledge of that audience:

      a. An audience sharing much of your familiarity with that field. (You may want to bone up on your topic a bit, to make sure of having something to offer.)

      b. An audience of high school freshmen.

      c. An audience of your classmates.

      d. An audience of intelligent strangers from another planet.

Exercise 3 (the disposition of the audience)

a. Take a question of campus or city reform on which you have strong convictions. (For example, the grading system or the parking situation.) Then extract from that question a yes-or-no proposition. (For example: "Should the grade of F be used?" "Should parking meters be used in the downtown shopping area?")

b. Assuming that you'll be writing a forceful letter to the appropriate newspaper, map out the "moral field" of this issue in a table like that appearing on pp. 91–92.

c. Discuss the probable good will toward this issue of the following: the administration; and two segments of the campus (or city) population who you think would be strongly affected by the issue.

(Note: For a sequel which builds on this analysis, see Exercise 4 of the next chapter.)

Exercise 4 (all elements)

a. Discuss the view evidently taken of the knowledge and disposition of the reader addressed in this famous letter by Mark Twain (1891):

> To the Gas Company
>
> Dear Sirs:
>
> Some day you will move me almost to the verge of irritation by your chuckle-headed Goddamned fashion of shutting your Goddamned gas off without giving any notice to your Goddamned parishioners. Several times you have come within an ace of smothering half of this household in their beds and blowing up the other half by this idiotic, not to say criminal, custom of yours. And it has happened again today. Haven't you a telephone?
>
> Ys
S L Clemens

b. Write a version of the same letter addressed to a hypothetical gas company president for whom Mark Twain had the highest esteem.

Exercise 5 (a parallel to Exercise 4)

a. Discuss the view evidently taken of the knowledge and disposition of the reader addressed in this excerpt of a form letter sent to wives of mail-order customers by "Duke Habernickel" of the Haband clothes company (1981):

> My Dear Friend,
>
> I love you! There. I said it. I love you! "Holy Smokes!" you say. "These men are all alike! I hardly even know this character and now he says he loves me!" Well that is what you get for giving me a bit of encouragement.
>
> Yes you did! You know that Haband has been doing business with men like your husband for over 55 years. But it wasn't until last year that I dared ask if maybe we could be of service to you ladies too. . . .
>
> And you said yes! Now we are *both* famous for our sensational looking solid color American Beauty slacks. You can't beat the price. You can't beat the quality, or the extremely flattering good looks.
>
> Oops, no! Wait a minute. I almost lied. I do have something better! My friend, if they loved you in those basic solid color

slacks, they'll simply *swoon* when they see you in Seersuckers! And have I got a proposal for you! . . .

b. Write another letter addressed to women with much different knowledge about clothing and with much different disposition toward clothing sales.

Exercise 6 (a parallel to Exercise 4)

a. In this letter from a daughter at college, discuss the view she evidently takes of the knowledge and disposition of her parents:

Dear Mother and Dad:

Since I left for college I have been remiss in writing and I am sorry for my thoughtlessness in not having written before. I will bring you up to date now, but before you read on, please sit down. You are not to read any further unless you are sitting down. Okay?

Well, then, I am getting along pretty well now. The skull fracture and the concussion I got when I jumped out of the window of my dormitory when it caught on fire shortly after my arrival here is pretty well healed. I only spent two weeks in the hospital, and now I can see almost normally and only get those sick headaches once a day. Fortunately, the fire in the dormitory, and my jump, were witnessed by an attendant at the gas station near the dorm, and he was the one who called the Fire Department and the ambulance. He also visited me at the hospital and, since I had nowhere to live because of the burnt-out dormitory, he was kind enough to invite me to share his apartment with him. It's really a basement room, but it's kind of cute. Brent is a very fine boy and we have fallen deeply in love and are planning to get married. We haven't got the exact date yet, but it will be before my pregnancy begins to show.

Yes, Mother and Dad, I am pregnant. I know how much you are looking forward to being grandparents, and I know you will welcome the baby and give it the same love and devotion and tender care you gave me when I was a child. The reason for the delay in our marriage is that my boyfriend has a minor infection I carelessly caught from him which prevents us from passing our pre-marital blood tests.

I know that you will welcome Brent into our family with open arms. He is kind and, although not well educated, he is ambitious. Although he is of a different race and religion than ours, I know your often-expressed tolerance will not permit you to be bothered by that.

Now that I have brought you up to date, I want to tell you that there was no dormitory fire, I did not have a concussion or skull fracture, I was not in the hospital, I am not pregnant, I am not engaged, I am not infected, and there is no boyfriend in my life. However, I am getting a D in History and F in Science, and I want you to see those marks in their proper perspective.

Your loving daughter   (source unknown)

b. Supposing that you are the student with low grades, write a fictitious letter to your own parents—to help them see things in "proper perspective."

Exercise 7 (all elements)

The librarian of a certain campus actually received the following two letters on the same day treating the same question: Should new freshmen be given a library tour? (Names have been changed.) Discuss the view which each letter evidently takes of the librarian's knowledge and disposition. Which writer do you think made more progress toward a total grasp of the educational, administrative, and personal elements of the question?

LETTER A
Miss Cora Nims
Director of the Library

Dear Miss Nims:

This is to inform you that the final decision of the Orientation Committee is that there shall be no library tours in connection with the freshman orientation program. While I appreciate your arguments as to reasons for such tours, it is the consensus of those faculty with whom I have visited regarding this matter that the library tours are not of sufficient value to warrant the time taken by such tours. The Chairman of the Department of English, Dr. Tenk, has been asked to consider the possibility of structuring the freshman English courses so that there is an introduction to the uses of the library.

This is also to request that the library prepare for the college certain items that will aid students and faculty in the use of the library.

1. Prepare a library guide sheet giving the information which the librarians think is necessary to all library users. This should preferably be done in a handbook.
2. Prepare a diagram to be prominently and attractively displayed in the lobby showing the general placement of the various materials in the stacks and elsewhere.

It is my understanding that these things have been discussed for some time; in fact, several graduates of years back have indicated to me that these are needs which have never been met by the library and that they would be more valuable than a tour during the freshman orientation week.

Sincerely yours,
Ian Canfield
Chairman, Orientation Committee

LETTER B
Miss Cora Nims
Director of the Library

Dear Miss Nims:

At a recent meeting of the Freshman Orientation Committee, much interest was expressed in your plans to assist the Library newcomer through such aids as stack signs to show Dewey numbers, a lobby map of the Library, free brochures at the desk to explain library resources, rules, and layout.

As chairman of the Library Committee I was asked by Dr. Canfield to pass along this interest to you, together with the College hopes that these valuable aids can be put into use for the new academic year.

Such aids, it was felt, can serve all College students better than any initial Library tour, since they would come to the student's attention at the exact time and place which he needs to use the Library for some concrete problem. A formal tour may serve its own purpose later on in the year; I will be in touch with you on this possibility.

Our staggered vacations will prevent our meeting personally until late August. Therefore I am taking up these matters by letter. Soon after returning on August 22, I will call on you to see if you need further suggestions or help.

Sincerely,
J. P. Hulterstrum
Chairman, Library Committee

Exercise 8 (all elements)

This exercise calls for you to measure a specific audience of your own classmates, to take account of their position on a sensitive issue.

a. Choose an important controversy on which you have strong conviction and on which some of your classmates are almost sure to differ. Possible: gun control, abortion, gay rights, nuclear freeze, a current conflict on campus or in the community.

b. Use part of a class period (as your instructor will arrange) to circulate among the class to discover how 2–4 members think and feel about that issue. Listen carefully and take notes, trying neither to agree nor to argue. Note such matters as: your classmate's knowledge of the issue; disposition toward it; virtues or vices which the member thinks will be called into play; hopes, fears, and special interests felt toward it. Don't talk to others about what you are learning, since premature discussion might interfere with what you and others are finding out.

c. Write a paper of about two pages supporting *one* main argument involved in the issue, in such a way as to use what you have learned about the people you have interviewed.

d. (If papers are submitted for critique) For any paper presented to the class, suggest where the writer made or could make the most effective approach to this audience.

Suggested readings for further illustration and discussion: Isaac Asimov, "The Case Against Man," page 332; Elisabeth Kübler-Ross, "On the Fear of Death," page 337; the advertisements, pages 321, 364, 396, and 402.

10   The Possible Responses to Audience

Once the audience is understood, a writer can best engage his or her own corresponding qualities of knowledge and disposition—the best result being a kind of friendship between writer and reader which can both define the topic and stimulate its development. The same relationship can predispose the reader to expect and affirm what is eventually said.

The Writer's Knowledge

The writer's knowledge hardly shows to best advantage through a flaunting of degrees earned, offices held, or big names known. Rather, one proves one's knowledge by use of a vocabulary and syntax obviously capable of illuminating a topic to the full scope of the reader's interest. Knowledge can also appear in one's continuous but quiet respect for substantiation, a modest familiarity with the sweep of one's subject. Notice how much knowledge glows through this unassuming passage from Charles Darwin, perhaps the greatest biologist of the nineteenth century:

> We will now discuss in a little more detail the struggle for existence. In my future work this subject will be treated, as it well deserves, at greater length. The elder De Candolle and Lyell have largely and philosophically shown that all organic beings are exposed to severe competition. In regard to plants, no one has treated this subject with more spirit and ability than W. Herbert, Dean of Manchester—evidently the result of his

great horticultural knowledge. Nothing is easier than to admit in words the truth of the universal struggle for life, or more diffi-cult—at least I found it so—than constantly to bear this conclu-sion in mind. . . . (*The Origin of Species,* 1859)

The phrase "in my future work" makes clear that Darwin's interest is serious and large-scaled. His references to the botanist De Candolle, to the geologist Lyell, and to the horticulturist Herbert—these show Dar-win's familiarity with current research. (In modern scholarship such ref-erences are usually supported by footnotes; that and related matters are discussed in Chapter 23, "Showing Your Support," page 267.) Elsewhere in *The Origin of Species,* Darwin's range of allusion—from dozens of ex-amples in all parts of the world from hundreds of plant and animal spe-cies—attests his solid foundation in biology. The precision of his detail underscores the thoroughness of this knowledge. Darwin cites exact sta-tistics and uses technical nomenclature, but almost never so as to bewil-der and always in the easy course of a calm discussion. The sentence structure is highly organized, with a remarkable number of parenthetical expressions (for example, "at least I found it so") which express a judi-cious reserve of a kind to win a serious reader's respect.

When you read the work of others, surely you sometimes ask "How does she know this?" or "Wherever did he come in touch with such ma-terial?" Such skepticism easily arises whenever the author's credentials show thin, whether in argument, explanation, or fiction. The soundest safeguard, as Darwin's example shows, is to provide the kind of detail and vocabulary which establish authenticity. The very process of doing so can enlarge your own grasp of your topic.

The Writer's Disposition

The writer's good disposition can be exaggerated by assuming the stock virtues of humility, piety, patriotism, and respect for motherhood, for in-fancy, and for the common man. But in everyday life a good person neither boasts of being admirably disposed toward important matters nor apologizes for it. One is content to be known by what one hopes and fears, by what one will support or resist, and by the principles on which one does so. A tactful writer will avoid a needless parade of those traits which may disturb readers of opposite conviction. A sensible writer will frankly express those hopes and fears held in common with the audience, since in this mutuality of feeling, a real collaboration between writer and reader can begin. Here a twentieth-century scientist, Harrison Brown, is introducing a book on the critical limits of the earth's capacity to support human life:

> I believe that man has the power, the intelligence, and the imagination to extricate himself from the serious predicament that now confronts him. The necessary first step toward wise action in the future is to obtain an understanding of the problems that exist. This in turn necessitates an understanding of the relationships between man, his natural environment, and his technology. I hope that this study will in some measure contribute to that understanding. (*The Challenge of Man's Future*, 1954)

Notice Brown's honest presence as a man with values: "I believe," "I hope." His respect and hope for humanity are evident. He plainly advocates a rational examination of the overpopulation problem, thus acting as the prudent man in face of danger. He ends with a touch of modesty—"I hope that this study will in some measure contribute"—which alleviates a possible impression of his arrogance in attacking such a huge question as global survival. Such openness of good disposition is no substitute for evidence. But it can help you to enter your subject with ease and force.

The Writer's Image

So far, so good. More is possible. Whereas the audience usually lies half-hidden behind a piece of writing—not distinctly visible even though constantly felt—the writer or speaker comes plainly before us as a human being intent on joining us. Hence the author necessarily assumes a character, a personality best suited to the occasion, much as you might project a certain aspect of yourself on being introduced to a friend's family. This "character" can range from the almost invisible "author" who never says "I" or displays any emotional presence, to the "author" dramatized as a strongly defined "I" whose traits and manner may even differ from those of the actual writer. (The actual use of fictitious "authors" in rhetoric and literature will be touched on later.)

To the image of the writer which appears in a composition the term *persona* is sometimes applied, from the ancient theater term for an actor's "mask." Of course you may not want to be "staged" as the term suggests. Nonetheless you should consider at least these three questions in deciding how you may best appear to your audience: To what extent should you appear directly as "I" or "we"? To what extent should you address the intended audience with authority or with deference? How formal should you seem? A test passage from the science essayist Loren Eiseley can illustrate such choices:

> We think we learn from teachers, and we sometimes do. But the
> teachers are not always to be found in school or in great labora-
> tories. Sometimes what we learn depends upon our own powers
> of insight. (*The Unexpected Universe*, 1969)

Directness of address. In this, the original passage, Eiseley has entered
a partnership with the reader as "we," so that he and the reader seem to
be reflecting together. He might have effaced both reader and writer,
thus:

> People think they learn from teachers, and they sometimes do.
> But the teachers are not always to be found in school or in great
> laboratories. Sometimes what people learn depends upon their
> own powers of insight.

Neither an "I" nor a "you" appears in this second version. "We think we
learn" becomes "people think they learn"; "our own powers" becomes
"their own powers," and so on. A writer's personality is still present—that
of a reflective and sensible man—but you feel much less aware of his
voice talking at your side. The impersonality of the second version encourages you to consider learning as an abstract, universal subject; the
immediacy of the first encourages you to consider learning as a highly
personal experience.

Similarly, the author can appear in direct but solitary view:

> I thought that I learned from teachers, and I sometimes did. But
> my teachers were not always to be found. . . .

Now the account is autobiographical; a man is telling how learning came
to him individually. Finally, the reader can be shown as a listener and
participant present on the scene:

> You think you learn from teachers, and you sometimes do. But
> the teachers are not always to be found in school or in great
> laboratories. Sometimes what you learn depends upon your own
> powers of insight.

Taking such personal notice of your reader easily leads toward a conversational kind of writing; and of course it usually does occur in personal
letters. In argument and instruction-giving, you so definitely need an explicit response that the direct "you" form of address helps to keep the
reader's attention immediate; you're addressing a *person*, not a general,
more or less uninvolved public.

Vantage point. In Eiseley's original partnership with his reader ("We
think *we* learn"), he used another control which can be called *vantage*

point, the position of relative authority which the writer takes with the reader.

The "we" language of Eiseley implies a shared authority in which the writer is "with" the reader, neither above nor below. This *with*-relationship can help a writer who identifies with the audience and wants to speak for and as a member of that audience—hence its frequent use in sermons, campaign speeches, reflective essays. "We" talk should be saved, however, for occasions of real mutual identification; in other situations, it can easily sound Sunday-schoolish and patronizing. (A different use of "we" should be noted—the "editorial we" in which the writer clearly speaks, not as the reader's companion, but as the official voice of the publication itself. Such a "we" usually suggests a moral leadership to which the reader is expected to look up.)

If Eiseley had pictured himself as "above" his audience in age or experience, he might have used an authoritative tone:

> Only sometimes do students learn from teachers. The fact is that genuine instruction is not always to be found in school or in great laboratories. Sometimes what you learn must depend upon your own powers of insight. (Or "Sometimes what *one* learns" if impersonality is desired.)

Notice the dogmatic positiveness of "The fact is" and "must." Eiseley is confidently assuming authority. He might have reinforced the effect by alluding to his years of experience, by characterizing his readers as young and untrained, or the like. Taking the "above" position need not open Eiseley to charges of snobbishness or arrogance. A reader goes to certain writers because they do have superior wisdom on certain matters. In some matters people need *your* knowledge, and you would confuse both them and yourself by pretending to be humbly ignorant. Vantage point identifies your vertical relationship with your reader on a scale of authority or knowledge.

The opposite or "below" position might affect Eiseley's passage thus:

> It is commonly thought that people learn from teachers, and maybe that is sometimes true. But perhaps the teachers are not always to be found in school or in great laboratories. Isn't it possible that learning may sometimes depend upon one's own powers of insight?

By softening his assertions with "commonly thought," "may sometimes be true," "perhaps," and "Isn't it possible," Eiseley would be deferring to his readers. He might do much more so by assuming the marks of inexperience and by characterizing his audience as wiser, older, or the like.

Again, the word "below" need not connote obsequious humility. Deference toward people entitled to your honest respect and courtesy can express a true and natural tact. It would imply moreover a right judgment of human excellence, such as can't be made by a person who respects nothing.

Degree of formality. A writer also chooses how informally to appear before the audience. The choice resembles the selecting of clothes for a party. One may go in jeans, in slacks, in dinner jacket or gown, or even in costume—and in each will find oneself bearing a different manner through the evening, probably even saying different things. In style, the comparable choices are called "informal," "general," and "formal," of which "general" is used by most educated people for most of their writing. Eiseley's original passage is an example:

> We think we learn from teachers, and we sometimes do. But the teachers are not always to be found in school or in great laboratories. Sometimes what we learn depends upon our own powers of insight.

The tone is easy but not offhand. The sentence structure is straightforward but not childish, and so is the vocabulary. The flexibility of general English allows it to be loosened or stiffened as one needs, until it shades into informal English at one end and formal at the other. Your degree of formality identifies your nearness to the reader on a horizontal scale; your writing reveals you as more relaxed, intimate, and informal as you approach your reader.

The most relaxed informal English is seldom met in nonfictional prose; it is the language of careless onrushing speech:

> You know, people are always saying they learn from teachers! OK, so they do, sometimes. But what I want to get across is this— you don't always find your teachers in schools or in labs either. No sir! Sometimes you find the teacher right in your own eyes and ears and brains. That's where it's at!

The breeziness of this version rises from the exclamatory sentences, the personal pronouns, the contractions ("don't," "that's"), and the slack syntax of daily conversation. The informal style can be further loosened by slang, profanity, and nonstandard usage. Though it can help toward a chatty intimacy with your reader, it would clearly hinder you in subject matter in which exact vocabulary and highly coherent organization is essential.

In formal English, on the other hand, Eiseley's passage might read like this:

> Although learning is judged to require teachers (and sometimes
> indeed it does), the real instructors may be found not so much in
> school or in great laboratories as in the student's own powers of
> insight.

The vocabulary is more literary ("judged," "indeed"). The sentence structure involves much more subordination and some inversion as in opening
the first sentence with an *although*-clause. You wouldn't converse in formal English, but you would find it readily responsive to your thought and
mood when composing a term paper or serious address. Formal English
admits the learned, technical, and even foreign vocabularies, besides the
sophisticated syntax for developing subject matters for highly trained
audiences.

The kind of language answering to a given degree of formality does
change from age to age, so much so that an inexperienced reader of
literature may feel baffled by a formal author of another century. For
example, a truly formal style of the early nineteenth century might have
soared like this:

> Whatever the Muses may have to teach my soul—be it Clio with
> her chronicle, Erato with her lyre, or Calliope with heroic song—
> I often cannot hear these wise goddesses in ivied cloister or
> cluttered laboratory. Instead, they speak to me from within.

The elaborate allusions to the classical Muses of learning, and the man-
nered inversion ("be it" instead of "whether it is")—these express the
high or "grand" style often affected in the Romantic period, when a writer
like Thomas Carlyle in his most earnest moods would feel impelled into
flights of sonorous fancy. In Samuel Johnson's measured formality of the
mid-eighteenth century, the passage might have read:

> To some scholars, instruction emanates from lectern or labora-
> tory; to others it radiates from within. No scholar is so well
> taught as he who can teach himself.

For the Age of Reason in which Johnson wrote, the formal mood called
for the vocabulary of impersonal abstraction ("scholars," "instruction,"
"lectern") and the syntax of balanced clauses.

The formality you may choose for writing will hardly follow the elegant
styles just illustrated. They really do not accommodate a twentieth-century way of seeing. Still, you might consciously practice imitating them
to expand your own responsiveness to language, and through becoming
familiar with these past ways of looking, you can absorb older literature
with something of the same vital impact felt by its first readers.

Special Applications to Persuasive Writing

In arguing to obtain immediate or eventual action, one must recognize that people act from *logic fused with feeling*. The evident personality of the writer or speaker becomes far more central than if one is merely explaining, say, how chlorophyll produces sugar. You have several tactics available.

A first step is to review the "moral field" which the preceding chapter has helped you to project for the virtues, vices, hopes, and fears which engage your readers—and then to appear before them sympathetically oriented to their concerns. For example, in supporting a public vaccination program to a politically conservative audience, you would only waste time by appealing to your readers' courage to endure vaccination. Physical pain would not be the issue for such readers. They would be concerned with taxes and government competition with the private sector. Therefore your most effective role might be that of champion of individual initiative, ready to show how further taxes could be minimized and how private doctors might participate in the program leadership.

Next, you might show the same tact in ordering your arguments that you would use in approaching a friend over a touchy issue. Such use of a *psychological ordering* (rather than a logical ordering) might lead you first to remove or reduce a threat to your readers so that they may then respond constructively. Thus you might *first* address a vehement fear of government control *before* outlining the positive benefits of a public vaccination program. Similarly, an intense desire—say, for community health—might offer you the best lead-in, the hope being that a strengthened desire would overcome later objections. Only a ready and sensitive sympathy with a particular audience can guide one in finding the most workable ordering of arguments.

A third tactic grows out of the very dramatic nature of argument, which does cast the writer as one character, the audience as another, allies and opponents as still others—with the plot consisting of the issue under debate and its final resolution. Therefore, you can well assume a far more visible personality than in expository writing. Your allies and opponents can be named and characterized. The time and place of the argument can become a "setting" imbued with dramatic interest. Above all, your audience can be invoked as an active character capable of virtues, hopes, struggle—with the knowledge and disposition to resolve the problem (or "plot") laid before it. The greatest orators and forensic writers have developed this rhetorical drama into an art which deserves study.

For example, in diverting a hostile audience from its own hostility, you could address a substitute audience—an imaginary reader of a kind you can approach with special advantages which you couldn't take with your actual readers who are listening in. The classic example is Edmund Burke's *Reflections on the Revolution in France* (1790), written to check the pro-French liberalism which was invading England in the opening year of the French Revolution. Though Burke wrote for his fellow Englishmen, he framed his *Reflections* as a letter to a French correspondent, thus taking the role of a patriotic defender of England against dangerous alien doctrine. Many of Burke's English readers, one supposes, reconsidered their liberalism and dissociated themselves from the imaginary Frenchman to whom the letter was addressed. A direct assault on these readers in such a tense time might well have failed.

In another use of this oblique-address technique, you could ostensibly face one audience while in fact expecting to reach another, more refractory one. Thus you might present your fellow students with an argument you really wanted the campus administrators to read.

Supposing an audience to be split in attitude or interests, a diplomatic writer distinguishes the opportunities, in turn joining each group of readers and developing the concerns most important to them. The success of the famous evangelical preachers rises partly from their moving through such a wide spectrum of appeals that every listener in a packed hall can at some time feel directly and personally called upon.

Special Applications in Fiction and Poetry

In fiction and poetry the "writer" may appear as the teller of a story or speaker of a poem, it being understood that such teller or speaker is a created character whose identification with the actual author is neither necessary nor accurate.

In older fiction, the "author" often talked with the reader on the side, acting both as a guide and as a chorus to the events of the story. Though the author-guide has passed largely out of vogue, a story or poem may be told in first-person by some "I" whose apparent knowledge and disposition shape the reader's rapport. The exact choice of this narrator's identity and personality affects the whole piece and is therefore one of the most exciting and delicate decisions you would have to make. (A special effect in this line is the irony you can obtain by using an *unreliable* narrator whose intelligence or moral qualities are so clearly inferior to those of the audience as to provide a steady but unconscious self-exposure.)

Occasionally the poet or storyteller goes even further, to create a fictional audience and a fictional setting. Joseph Conrad's *Lord Jim* purports to be the after-dinner reminiscence of a sea captain among good friends. And Robert Browning's "The Bishop Orders His Tomb at St. Praxed's Church" purports to be the deathbed ramblings of a Renaissance bishop surrounded by his illegitimate sons.

Exercise 1 (the writer's qualities)

For each of the following selections, point to the exact details which establish the knowledge, disposition, and image of the writer or speaker. Be sure to consider personality, directness of address, vantage point, and degree of formality.

a. I accept your nomination—and your program.

I should have preferred to hear those words uttered by a stronger, a wiser, a better man than myself. But after listening to the President's speech, I even feel better about myself.

None of you, my friends, can wholly appreciate what is in my heart. I can only hope that you understand my words. They will be few.

I have not sought the honor you have done me. I could not seek it because I aspired to another office, which was the full measure of my ambition. And one does not treat the highest office within the gift of the people of Illinois as an alternative or as a consolation prize.

I would not seek your nomination for the presidency because the burdens of that office stagger the imagination. Its potential for good or evil now and in the years of our lives smothers exultation and converts vanity to prayer.

I have asked the merciful Father, the Father to us all, to let this cup pass from me. But from such dread responsibility one does not shrink in fear, in self-interest, or in false humility.

So, "If this cup may not pass from me, except I drink it, Thy will be done."

That my heart has been troubled, that I have not sought this nomination, that I could not seek it in good conscience, that I would not seek it in honest self-appraisal, is not to say that I value it the less. Rather it is that I revere the office of the presidency of the United States.

And now that you have made your decision I will fight to win that office with all my heart and my soul. And with your help, I have no doubt that we will win. (Adlai E. Stevenson in accepting nomination for the Presidency at the Democratic convention of 1953.)

b. I do not know what effect my accusers have had upon you, gentlemen, but for my own part I was almost carried away by them; their arguments were so convincing. On the other hand, scarcely a word of what they said was true. I was especially astonished at one of their many misrepresentations: I mean when they told you that you must be careful not to let me deceive you—the implication being that I am a skilful speaker. I thought that it was peculiarly brazen of them to tell you this without a blush, since they must know that they will soon be effectively confuted, when it becomes obvious that I have not the slightest skill as a speaker—unless, of course, by a skilful speaker they mean one who speaks the truth. If that is what they mean, I would agree that I am an orator, though not after their pattern.

My accusers, then, as I maintain, have said little or nothing that is true, but from me you shall hear the whole truth; not, I can assure you, gentlemen, in flowery language like theirs, decked out with fine words and phrases; no, what you hear from me will be a straightforward speech in the first words that occur to me, confident as I am in the justice of my cause. (Socrates opening his defense against charges of heresy and corrupting the young, in Plato's *The Apology of Socrates*, c. 399 B.C.)

C. LAZY MILLIONAIRE WANTS TO SHARE THE WEALTH

. . . .
I remember when I lost my job. Because I was head over heels in debt, my lawyer told me the only thing I could do was declare bankruptcy. He was wrong. I paid off every dime.

Now, I have a million dollar line of credit; but I still don't have a job. Instead, I get up every weekday morning and decide whether I want to go to work or not. Sometimes I do—for 5 or 6 hours. But about half the time, I decide to read, go for a walk, sail my boat, swim, or ride my bike.

I know what it's like to be broke. And I know what it's like to have everything you want. And I know that you—like me— can *decide* which one it's going to be. It's really as easy as that. That's why I call it "The Lazy Man's Way to Riches."

So I'm going to ask you to send me something I don't need: money. Ten dollars to be exact. Why? Because I want you to pay attention. And I figure that if you've got $10 invested, you'll look over what I send you and decide whether to send it back . . . or keep it. And I don't *want* you to keep it unless you agree that it's worth at least a hundred times what you invested. . . . (Joe Karbo in newspaper advertisement, July 22, 1982.)

d. Before I proceed a line further, let me make it clear that I enjoy physical exercise and sport as much as any man. I like to bat a baseball, dribble a basketball, kick a soccer ball and, most of all, swat a tennis ball. A man who scorned physical activity would hardly build a tennis court on his summer-house grounds, or use it every day.

Having made this obeisance, let me now confess that I am puzzled and upset—and have been for many years—by the almost obsessive interest in sports taken by the average adult American male.

Athletics is one strand in life, and even the ancient Greek

philosophers recognized its importance. But it is by no means the whole web, as it seems to be in our society. If American men are not talking business, they are talking sports, or they are not talking at all. . . . (Sydney J. Harris, daily column for December 24, 1981.)

e. We know that you highly esteem the kind of learning taught in those Colleges, and that the Maintenance of our young Men, while with you, would be very expensive to you. We are convinced, that you mean to do us Good by your Proposal; and we thank you heartily. But you, who are wise must know that different Nations have different Conceptions of things and you will therefore not take it amiss, if our Ideas of this kind of Education happen not to be the same as yours. We have had some Experience of it. Several of our young People were formerly brought up at the Colleges of the Northern Provinces: they were instructed in all your Sciences; but, when they came back to us, they were bad Runners, ignorant of every means of living in the woods . . . neither fit for Hunters, Warriors, nor Counsellors, they were totally good for nothing.

We are, however, not the less oblig'd by your kind Offer, tho' we decline accepting it; and, to show our grateful Sense of it, if the Gentlemen of Virginia will send us a Dozen of their Sons, we will take Care of their Education, instruct them in all we know, and make Men of them. (Indians of the Six Nations, 1744, replying to an invitation from the commissioners of Virginia to send boys to the College of William and Mary.)

Exercise 2 (the writer's knowledge)

As an exercise in conveying your credentials to the reader, write a one-page introduction for any of the following topics, in such a way as to subtly persuade a fellow undergraduate of your ability to deal with that topic. Bone up on your topic in the library as necessary.

a. A solution for peace in the Middle East.
b. Present status of the female athlete in intercollegiate sports.
c. Prospects for a stock market recession or boom in the next months.
d. New directions in automobile design.
e. The paintings of Andrew Wyeth.
f. What genetic engineering is.

Exercise 3 (directness of address, vantage point, formality)

Choose any selection from Exercise 1 and rewrite it to make decided changes in:

    a. Directness of address.
    b. Vantage point.
    c. Degree of formality.

Add a paragraph evaluating the difference between what happens in the original version and what happens in the second.

Exercise 4 (all elements)

(*This exercise is a sequel to Exercise 3 of the preceding chapter.*) Taking your analysis of audience done for the preceding chapter, now consider the best ways in which you as writer can respond, using the concepts of this chapter. Then write a letter to the appropriate newspaper to implement your viewpoint.

Exercise 5 (all elements—imitation)

Choose any selection from Exercise 1 and, having analyzed the ways in which the writer's qualities are implied, write an imitation using the adaptation-to-new-material method described in Chapter 6 (pp. 54–55). Suggestion: Take notes on the writer's knowledge, disposition, and image, including directness of address, vantage point, degree of formality.

Exercise 6 (special cases: the use of occasion in persuasion)

At St. Martin's Hall, London, on January 7, 1866, the scientist Thomas Huxley gave an address "On the Advisableness of Improving Natural [i.e., scientific] Knowledge," opening with the paragraphs below. His aim was to advance the cause of scientific education. Point to the details by which he exploited the time and the place of his speech, showing how they might contribute toward his goal.

> This time two hundred years ago—in the beginning of January, 1666—those of our forefathers who inhabited this great and ancient city, took breath between the shocks of two fearful calamities, one not quite past, although its fury had abated; the other to come.
>
> Within a few yards of the very spot on which we are assembled, so the tradition runs, that painful and deadly malady, the plague, appeared in the latter months of 1664; and, though no new visitor, smote the people of England, and especially of her capital, with a violence unknown before, in the course of the following year. The hand of a master has pictured what happened in those dismal months; and in that truest of fictions, *The History of the Plague Year*, Defoe shows death, with every

accompaniment of pain and terror, stalking through the narrow streets of old London, and changing their busy hum into a silence broken only by the wailing of the mourners of fifty thousand dead; by the woeful denunciations and mad prayers of fanatics; and by the madder yells of despairing profligates.

Exercise 7 (special cases: persuasion)

Deep Valley Airlines has had several crashes since opening its airport in your community. The latest occurred a week ago, on July Fourth, killing three adult citizens, two children, and destroying the town's chief factory. Sentiment runs strong for closing down Deep Valley Airport. Take either side; assume that you belong to one of the following groups; and write out the remarks which you might deliver at an open City Council meeting debating the issue.

a. An executive for Deep Valley Airlines.
b. A worker from the wrecked factory.
c. A wife or mother of one of the victims.
d. A member of the Chamber of Commerce.
e. A member of the American Legion post.
f. (Choose an identity of your own.)

Exercise 8 (special cases: fiction and poetry)

To show what can be done through the personality assumed by the narrator, write a first-person short story (of two or three pages) or a poem, using one of the following situations:

a. A child reporting either the split-up or the reunion of its parents.
b. A thoroughly dull leading citizen proudly describing his encounter with an equally dull important visitor.
c. A thoroughly rotten company president boasting of having clawed his way to the top.
d. A twisted mind describing an especially horrid crime which it sees as normal and justifiable.

Suggested readings for further illustration, discussion, and writing: Lance Morrow, "The Decline and Fall of Oratory," page 344; Frederick Douglass, "The Meaning of July Fourth for the Negro," page 350; Ralph Ellison, "From Invisible Man," page 356; Lewis Thomas, "On Natural Death," page 360; the advertisements, pages 321, 396, and 402.

11   Urging and Over-Urging the Audience: Sentimentality

Emotion is easy to talk about but hard to transmit. One might best begin negatively, to see how *not* to try it. Writers usually fail when they pelt the reader with loud assertive signals of the emotion they want the reader to feel. Heavy reliance upon such signals is often condemned under the name of *sentimentality*. Sentimentality should not be confused with the direct expression of emotion which often permeates a vigorous piece of writing. The large differences will be dealt with in this chapter. The next chapter treats the contrasting strategy of *irony*, whereby the reader is *indirectly* encouraged to participate in the emotion.

Both the directness and force of your approach to the reader's feelings can shape your way of thinking about your subject—in some ways restricting you and in other ways deepening your sense of what you are about.

The Use and Misuse of Simple Emotional Assertion

If a man says "Ouch!" you don't call him sentimental. If he says "That hurts!" you still don't call him sentimental. He is asserting what for him is a fact, and he is informing you of that fact. People do state their emotions at all sorts of times. At funeral homes they state their sorrow; at weddings they state their happiness. People need to be aware how other people feel simply because they all live together.

But suppose a man in reporting a row with his girl friend says, "I tell you, I'm suffering the torments of the damned. God, what agony! For me this town is nothing but—(choke)—a vast torture chamber!" Now you can probably call him sentimental—not for informing you about his misery but for trying in such a bulldozing way to stir your own compassion. The diction is general and assertive ("I'm suffering," "what agony," etc.); it doesn't produce or even select the detail from which the man himself draws pain. The line, "God, what agony!" seems borrowed from nineteenth-century melodrama. The check in the voice before "a vast torture chamber" seems a bit pat. Of course the susceptibility to such broad signaling varies from person to person and from age to age, but a credible twentieth-century response to it might be, "For heaven's sake, Clyde, where did you get *that?*"

This over-urging of the reader through purely assertive signaling can be found in highly literate form, as in this book-jacket endorsement of a bestseller book-club selection:

> In a blend of complete sincerity and delicacy, so uniquely her own, Carol Akins Calloway shares with the reader her awareness of the many frustrating elements we face today: the restlessness, the unending pressures and demands, the denial of leisure and silence, the threat to inner peace and integration, the uneasy balance of the opposites, man and woman. With radiant lucidity she makes visible again the values of the inner life, without which there is no true fulfillment. She does this without the overtones of preaching, but herself as a seeker, echoing—only clearer and stronger—our own small still voice.

Presumably the writer of this passage wants us to approach Mrs. Calloway and her book with admiration, reverence, and affection. But the writer bases the endorsement almost exclusively on assertive language, on terms which merely label the emotional force of Mrs. Calloway's book—and which fail to offer any details which might communicate that force. Neither the book's "complete sincerity" nor its "delicacy" is illustrated or expanded upon. Other label expressions are "radiant lucidity," "makes visible again the values of the inner life," "without the overtones of preaching." Connoisseurs of book-jacket euphoria will recognize too a kind of cant vocabulary here, a reliance upon an overworked diction of uplift (100 Words To Make People Feel Warm Inside)—thus "sincerity," "uniquely her own," "share," "awareness," "inner peace," "the inner life," "true fulfillment," "seeker," "still small voice," and so forth.

Though assertive language and generalizing summary serve necessary functions elsewhere and even though they can help to guide the reader's response in such material as this, they can't *create* that response. The writer who leans upon such language at such a time seems to betray both a real lack of sufficiently observed detail and an underestimation of the reader's sensitivity. The ultimate cheapness of most sentimentality is just this, that it can be so easily faked. It doesn't require the writer to be concretely engaged with experience. One can spin off emotional label-language without raising the pulse by a single beat. The writer and the reader who deal in such signals as the real thing can be condemned as emotionally promiscuous. They should be urged to develop that discrimination which can eventually open them and their language to really powerful feeling.

Detail: Original and Stock

For another kind of broad emotional signal, consider this news item:

> WIFE STILL LOVES CALLOWAY
> Mrs. Carol Calloway gave three quick gasps. Her head sank forward.
> Her husband had just been found guilty of planting a bomb on an airliner in which she and 60 others were passengers.
> Mrs. Calloway, thin from a recent operation, clutched a black leather purse as federal Judge Harold M. Whitney sentenced her husband to two concurrent 20-year terms in prison.
> After the sentencing, she rose from her second-row seat, rushed toward her husband and threw her arms around him. Her eyes filled with tears.
> Looking around at the judge, she said in a soft, shaken voice, "My husband is innocent."

Besides the same kind of assertive language already commented on ("soft, shaken voice"), this article employs *stock detail,* the hackneyed detail perennially used in sketching such scenes. The "three short gasps," the sinking forward of the head, the clutching of the purse, the rushing forward to embrace the husband, the eyes welling with tears, and quavering profession of faith in her husband's innocence—all these may have actually occurred in the courtroom, but they are the average details, the predictable details which an unimaginative observer would notice (or even unconsciously invent) simply because they might be expected. A more perceptive observer would notice what made these details unique with Mrs. Calloway. Such an observer would keep pushing the extraordinary questions of such a criminal case. How does a man face his wife just after being sentenced for trying to kill her? What kind of loneliness in a wife could muffle her suspicions of such a husband, or what kind of devotion or fear, concealed hatred, or personal drabness had kept her at his side? How much acting went on, and what are the clues in face or gesture by which one might tell? Something like this might at least introduce the real enigmas of the scene:

> In the courtroom noise after the sentencing, Mrs. Calloway found her way to the husband who had evidently been willing to blow up sixty-one people in order to kill her.
>
> Carol Calloway is perhaps forty, with a meek bony face, a short dumpy body, and little else to notice except for a set intensity of the gray eyes. She belongs to no church or club; she has hardly ever spoken to her neighbors. She enters contests of all sorts and occasionally has been reported as winner of a steam iron, a year's supply of soap pads, etc.
>
> She hugged her husband about his stocky waist and called out to the judge in a pinched voice: "My husband is innocent." The man's thick hairy hands cupped her shoulders as he stared through his black horn-rims at the crowd pushing to get out. The round face was calm, almost benign, like that of any businessman saying good-bye at a station or airport.

From stock detail is generated the *stock character*, the flat familiar personality-type whose appeal to the emotions is simple and predictable. In the original Calloway news story the heroically faithful wife is the stock character, inviting a conventional response of compassionate admiration. Stock characters (often called "stereotypes") constitute a kind of shorthand for bypassing the complexities of personality. The stock characterization allows both writer and reader to see an instant pattern; this is both its power and its danger. Not surprisingly, the stock characterization appears most often in those areas where real life threatens or confuses people. Minority groups are often seen as stereotypes—thus the shiftless black, the volatile Italian, the grimly authoritarian German. Family roles are commonly stereotyped—thus the wisely protective mother, the amiable but ineffective suburban father, the sweet baby calling for an automatic murmur of tenderness. Certain occupations are so stereotyped that a mere listing will call to your mind the stock traits of professors, librarians, ministers, doctors, artists, and so forth.

A first-rate novelist or dramatist can use stock minor characters to clarify themes, to satirize common foibles, to help define the central, fully developed characters. In such ways the stock character points up the patterns of human life rather than blurs them. But the ad writer, the propagandist, the demagogue, and the sentimentalist in general use the stock character to oversimplify, to obtain an emotional reaction without justifying it. Despite their unquestioned success with naive audiences, a careless use of stock characters must narrow the kind of discovery which any writer can make in the writing process.

Simple Intensifiers

The sentimentalist, already banking on the *assertion* of emotional content, readily extends the mechanical perspective through certain handy devices for magnifying signals to the reader. Repetition is one such device. In the original "Wife Still Loves Calloway," Mrs. Calloway gives *three* gasps, not just one. The reporter is taking no chances. And although "gasps" are rapid breaths by definition, the adjective "quick" is added just to make sure that no one misses the agitation of Mrs. Calloway.

Another device is the stacking up of tender detail. Mrs. Calloway is "thin from a recent operation" as she listens to the sentencing of her husband. A sentimental novelist exploiting this scene would have no trouble inventing a toddling Calloway infant, a brother on furlough from the armed forces, a cross hung about Mrs. Calloway's neck, and so on.

A utility vocabulary of superlatives and intensifying modifiers can be tapped to boost the general assertiveness of such writing—for example: "very," "utterly," "enormous," "terrible," "tragic," "thrilling," "suddenly." (For others, see p. 140.)

In sentimental poetry, heavy rhythms, hammered rhymes, and reiterated key phrases can furnish even louder demands for the reader's emotional surrender.

The Question of Degree

If emotional overassertiveness can alienate the trained reader, are all trained readers alike? Of course not. Some people do "feel" more unguardedly than others. Some ages, like the Victorian, have enjoyed the release of emotion—particularly the tender emotions—far more than others. Therefore they have responded much more readily to the mere information that an emotion is present, and they have candidly opened themselves to appeals which have become familiar and dear. Moreover, the assertive devices described in this chapter may appear only secondarily in writing which contains much precise observation. Thus the writer comes through as a person whose heart and head are forcefully and harmoniously engaged. Here is Dr. Paul Ehrlich introducing his book *The Population Bomb* (1968):

> I have understood the population explosion intellectually for a long time. I came to understand it emotionally one stinking hot night in Delhi a couple of years ago. My wife and daughter and

I were returning to our hotel in an ancient taxi. The seats were
hopping with fleas. The only functional gear was third. As we
crawled through the city, we entered a crowded slum area. The
temperature was well over 100, and the air was a haze of dust
and smoke. The streets seemed alive with people. People eating,
people washing, people sleeping. People visiting, arguing, and
screaming. People thrusting their hands through the taxi window,
begging. People defecating and urinating. People clinging to
buses. People herding animals. People, people, people, people.
As we moved slowly through the mob, hand horn squawking,
the dust, noise, heat, and cooking fires gave the scene a hellish
aspect. Would we ever get to our hotel? All three of us were,
frankly, frightened. It seemed that anything could happen—but,
of course, nothing did. Old India hands will laugh at our reaction. We were just some overprivileged tourists, unaccustomed
to the sights and sounds of India. Perhaps, but since that night
I've known the *feel* of overpopulation.

Much assertion of emotion is present here: "hellish aspect," "all three of
us were frightened." The common trick of a suspense question is used:
"Would we ever get back to our hotel?" The word "people" is pounded in
heavy rhythm. But such signals are backed up by a catalog of the exact
sights, noises, smells, and heat of a swarming slum. These bring home the
sense of Ehrlich's revulsion and alarm at overpopulation witnessed in the
flesh.

Surely you wouldn't condemn every taste in emotions but your own.
And one can respect the fresher uses of assertive devices more highly
than their cheap and hackneyed uses. As a reader, you have the right to
discriminate among these calls upon your feelings. As a writer, you would
presumably refrain from using emotional signals which you would not
honor yourself. Above all, the sentimental perspective should never distort one's own interest in life as it really is or in the language which gets
closest to it.

Such language is treated on a larger scale in Chapter 15, "The Vocabulary of Feeling," page 159, and Chapter 16, "The Vocabulary of Intensification," page 173.

Exercise 1 (all elements)

Point to details in each of the following passages on which a charge of sentimentality might be based. How would you rank these passages on a "sentimentality scale" from most to least sentimental? How many of these selections
would you defend as being honest and sensitive in their approach to emotion?

a. She stared down and *oh, dear God.* It was her daughter all right and she was dead. The mother's lips moved in her cold face, and a chill came. *Angel, Angel,* she wept as she gagged in her reeling shock.

   No, my baby's only 12 . . . .

   But it surged up like the blur of a microscope's field swimming toward focus. Angel, tied to a tree, her new panties stuffed snowy white in her mouth. There was no way to wake from this. Not with splashes of blood on the weeds and pieces of girl in the dirt. . . . (*Chicago Sun-Times,* November 16, 1980)

b. The bustle in a house
   The morning after death
   Is solemnest of industries
   Enacted upon earth—

   The sweeping up the heart,
   And putting love away
   We shall not want to use again
   Until eternity.

   (Emily Dickinson, "1078," c. 1866)

c. Indeed, she had forgotten! With the sublime selfishness of a woman who loves with her whole heart, she had in the last twenty-four hours had no thought save for him. His precious, noble life, his danger—he, the loved one, the brave hero, he alone dwelt in her mind. (Emmuska Orczy, *The Scarlet Pimpernel,* 1905)

d. Many elderly people are afraid to venture forth, afraid of crime, afraid of icy pavement. Helen was found on the pavement in December. "I fall down," she says, obviously thinking that exhausts the subject. "I can't see or hear or walk so well. I'm what you call a handicapped," she says, and laughs loudly. A wilting poinsettia, a souvenir of her hospital stay, is the only patch of color in her room. But a cloth flower flies like a defiant flag from her wool-knit cap as she heads for a long sit in the "lobby," a barely furnished and unspeakably drab and drafty place where two cops have just quieted a drunk woman. But Helen is uncomplaining, as people are who have much dignity and no illusions, who only dimly remember when things were better and who can't imagine things getting better. . . . (George Will, "A Flower Grows in Concrete," *Newsweek,* March 3, 1980)

e. I did not lose my heart in summer's even
      When roses to the moonrise burst apart:
   When plumes were under heel and lead was flying,
      In blood and smoke and flame I lost my heart.

   I lost it to a soldier and a foeman,
      A chap that did not kill me, but he tried;

That took the saber straight and took it striking,
   And laughed and kissed his hand to me and died.

(A. E. Housman, "37," *More Poems*, 1936)

f. Above their wreath-strewn graves we kneel,
      They kept the faith and fought the fight.
   Through flying lead and crimson steel
      They plunged for Freedom and the Right.

   May we, their grateful children, learn
      Their strength, who lie beneath this sod,
   Who went through fire and death to earn
      At last the accolade of God.

   In shining rank on rank arrayed
      They march, the legions of the Lord;
   He is their Captain unafraid,
      The Prince of Peace . . . Who brought a sword.

(Joyce Kilmer, from "Memorial Day," 1911–1917)

g. Yesterday, I laid a wreath at the cemetery which commemorates
   the brave people who died during the siege of Leningrad in
   World War II. At the cemetery, I saw the picture of a 12-year-
   old girl. She was a beautiful child. Her name was Tanya. The
   pages of her diary tell the terrible story of war.
      And then, finally, these words, the last words in her diary: "All
   are dead. Only Tanya is left."
      As we work toward a more peaceful world, let us think of
   Tanya and of other Tanyas and their brothers and sisters everywhere.
      Let us do all that we can to insure that no other children will
   have to endure what Tanya did and that your children and ours
   and all the children of the world can live their full lives together
   in friendship and in peace.
      Spasibo i do svidaniya. [Thank you and good-by.]

(President Richard M. Nixon, address to Soviet people, 1972)

h. Much later, several men came and dragged Miss Sasaki out. Her
   left leg was not severed, but it was badly broken and cut and it
   hung askew below the knee. They took her out into a courtyard.
   It was raining. She sat on the ground in the rain. When the
   downpour increased, someone directed all the wounded people
   to take cover in the factory's air-raid shelters. "Come along," a
   torn-up woman said to her. "You can hop." But Miss Sasaki could
   not move, and she just waited in the rain. Then a man propped
   up a large sheet of corrugated iron as a kind of lean-to, and took
   her in his arms and carried her to it. She was grateful until he
   brought two horribly wounded people—a woman with a whole
   breast sheared off and a man whose face was all raw from a
   burn—to share the simple shed with her. No one came back. The
   rain cleared and the cloudy afternoon was hot; before nightfall

the three grotesques under the slanting piece of twisted iron began to smell quite bad. (John Hersey, *Hiroshima*, 1946)

Exercise 2 (all elements—parody)

Write a parody of one of the more sentimental passages from Exercise 1, using
the general instructions of Chapter 6, especially pp. 56–57.

Exercise 3 (all elements)

Choose some movie, television show, advertisement, poem, or fictional passage
which has either revolted you with its sentimentality or else moved you with
its genuine understanding of human feelings. Write an essay evaluating the
presence or absence of sentimentality, using the concepts brought forward in
this chapter. (If it is not feasible to include the whole text of your selection,
summarize it and cite enough details to show its tone.)

Exercise 4 (all elements)

a. Choose at least three of the following and combine them into one or two
   pages of tear-jerking fiction which pulls out all the stops described in this
   chapter:

a dog	a community disaster
a mother	wretched poverty
a Bible	illness
an infant	lovers
the national flag	alcohol

b. Take these same elements and write a second passage of similar length in
   which the emotion dealt with in part *a* is realized without the slightest
   recourse to sentimentality. (This assignment can be varied, if your instructor
   chooses, by your taking what some classmate has written for part *a*.)

Exercise 5 (all elements)

a. Write the copy for a deodorant advertisement aimed at an audience extremely sentimental about romance, or—
b. Write the copy for a laxative advertisement aimed at readers sentimental
   about family life, or—
c. Write a one-page brochure for a funeral home explaining its services in a
   way which strikes you as sympathetic, honest, and in good taste.

12   Under-Urging the Audience: Irony

The sentimentalist over-urges or mis-urges the reader to feel emotion. Many good writers simply allow the reader, without urging, to infer the emotion from detail well chosen and carefully drawn. The ironist actually counter-urges in such a way as to draw the reader into active collaboration toward the desired response.

Ironic Assertion

Suppose we have a romantic hero named Chauncey whose sweetheart, Birdene, has departed leaving him in grief. This gripping drama can be rendered in these ways:

SENTIMENTAL The departure of his only sweet Birdene left Chauncey in aching desolation. He wept bitter salt tears throughout the dull harassing duties of each day.

Note the assertive language ("aching desolation," "dull harassing duties") and the stock romantic detail ("bitter salt tears").

STRAIGHT-
FORWARD Throughout Chauncey's conference with the realtors, his Rotary lunch, his bargaining at the lumberyard, and his nine holes of golf, the fact of Birdene's departure remained fixed in his mind.

Note the careful specification of all the duties which fail to distract Chauncey; thus his grief is not asserted but dramatized.

> IRONIC Birdene's departure was troublesome enough, but Chauncey thanked heaven a hundred times daily that he also had duties which kept him from thinking of it.

The trick of this last version is that apparently it says one thing while actually it says the opposite. Apparently Birdene's departure is a mere mishap—it is only "troublesome." Apparently Chauncey is happy—he is thanking heaven for being able to put Birdene out of mind. Actually Chauncey is wretched. The tip-off is "a hundred times daily," far too often for a carefree man to feel relieved of his cares.

Here is the rudimentary pattern of irony: an assertion pointing in one direction together with some signal to the reader that the real sense lies in another. Thanks to the tip-off, the reader becomes the writer's partner. The reader's own intelligence and imagination can complete the real meaning and in doing so become excited through making the creative response and through the shock of seeing that the truth of an assertion can run counter to its appearance. Probably the reader's response to Chauncey, above, is one of compassionate amusement that a man can think himself free of grief just when he is most possessed by it.

Another example:

> Conscience is the inner voice which warns us that someone may be looking. (H. L. Mencken, 1949)

The apparent direction of Mencken's sentence is moral and reverent. Apparently only the highest ethical principles could be invoked by such a sonorous opening as "Conscience is the inner voice which warns us. . . ." The tip-off is the sudden collapse of tone into the vulgar consideration that "someone may be looking." Once again, the reader's response is probably one of amusement that people can make such a moral strut with such grubby principles.

The ironic partnership of writer and reader need not be amusing. It can also work for pathos or indignation or horror.

> In the evening the wounded boy was taken to a Burmese doctor, who, by applying some poisonous concoction of crushed leaves to his left eye, succeeded in blinding him. (George Orwell, *Burmese Days,* 1934)

As Orwell apparently describes a humane attempt to treat a wounded boy, the reader sees by the phrase "poisonous concoction" that the medical treatment is doubtful, and by the final contrast (*"succeeded* in *blinding* him") sees how terribly the diligence of a bungling doctor can actually magnify human misery.

Irony attracts many writers because it begins with critical detachment as opposed to the uncritical immersion of sentimentality. This detachment then makes possible an ultimately stronger and more complex emotional response, in contrast with the simple response of the sentimentalist. You can't be ironic about everything; but every writer with wisdom and experience will find irony in some things, which can be appreciated all the more in the company of a discerning reader.

Large-Scale Irony

The writer can use irony as a sustained strategy of indirect attack—by praising something which should obviously be condemned, by urging a ridiculous solution as a means of calling for a sane solution, etc. The most famous example in English is probably Jonathan Swift's *A Modest Proposal* (1729), in which the narrator calmly and reasonably proposes to solve the overpopulation of Ireland by exporting Irish babies as food for human consumption. In more compact form the indirect attack is illustrated from Mark Twain's "The War Prayer" (1904–5):

> O Lord our Father, our young patriots, idols of our hearts, go forth to battle—be Thou near them! With them—in spirit—we also go forth from the sweet peace of our beloved firesides to smite the foe. O Lord our God, help us to tear their soldiers to bloody shreds with our shells; help us to cover their smiling fields with the pale forms of their patriot dead; help us to drown the thunder of the guns with the shrieks of their wounded, writhing in pain; help us to lay waste their humble homes with a hurricane of fire; help us to wring the hearts of their unoffending widows with unavailing grief; help us to turn them out roofless with their little children to wander unfriended the wastes of their desolated land in rags and hunger and thirst, sports of the sun flames of summer and the icy winds of winter, broken in spirit, worn with travail, imploring Thee for the refuge of the grave and denied it—for our sakes who adore Thee, Lord, blast their hopes, blight their lives, protract their bitter pilgrimage, make heavy their steps, water their way with their tears, stain the white snow with the blood of their wounded feet! We ask it, in the spirit of love, of Him Who is the Source of Love, and Who is the ever-faithful refuge and friend of all that are sore beset and seek His aid with humble and contrite hearts. Amen.

You can see the same constituents of irony here as in the shorter examples. The prayer seems to go one way—toward an expression of the meek suppliancy of the good Christian. The signal to the reader is the incongruous brutality of the actual petitions (e.g., "help us to tear their soldiers to bloody shreds"). The actual direction of the prayer is to expose the bloodthirstiness of supposedly Christian nations once they go to war. Mark Twain amplifies the signal by his full and sympathetic reference to the humanity of the enemy ("their patriot dead," "their humble homes," "their little children," "their unoffending widows")—this kind of sympathy being quite out of tune with the divine butchery which the speaker is pleading for. In noting the contrast between surface and inner meanings, the reader sees and feels the horrid hypocrisy of any people which masks its wartime fury under such sanctimonious cant to a tribal god. The tone of course is neither subtle nor comic but savage and bitter.

The Signals of Irony

Because irony does build on the reader's collaboration in redirecting whatever is said, the writer's signals for that collaboration must be clear, or else the collaboration can't begin. At the same time the signals must be reasonably indirect, or else they will deny the reader the pleasure of exercising ingenuity. The crudest possible signal would consist of bluntly asserting the extreme opposite of what is really meant—thus:

> HOW TO BE A RELIGIOUS HYPOCRITE
>
> Always go to church but never listen to the sermon. Talk to everybody about the needs of the Christian enterprise but don't put a red cent in the collection plate. Always be the first to assume the position of prayer so that your fellow worshipers will notice you, but never think of what the prayer actually means . . .

No reader could miss this irony. Few readers could enjoy it. By shouting, so to speak, that everything you say is to be reversed, you've robbed the reader of active participation.

The finest irony is plausible and coherent at its surface level. It *can* be taken just as it stands, as an argument conceivably efficient toward such an end as people really might wish. In Swift's *A Modest Proposal, plausible* grounds are advanced for slaughtering and eating the infants of Irish poor people. Poverty would be alleviated. The Irish children would only be corrupted if allowed to grow up in slums. Infant flesh would provide a nourishing diet. Ready markets for such flesh would be waiting. Irish mothers would prosper rather than sink under their burdens, etc. Actually Swift built his monstrous proposal so persuasively that he horrified some of his more naive readers with his evident depravity. But they had missed his signals. Therefore they missed sharing Swift's greater horror at the awful misery of Ireland which cried out for a really humane solution.

Probably the best signal for an ironic reception is a slow-burning one—just enough of some disparity to ignite and then to feed gradually the reader's suspicions of a second level of meaning. The disparity may occur between tone and subject, between adjacent details, between the writer's evidence and conclusion. In this example the early American writer Washington Irving is describing his admiration of Europeans:

> . . . I was anxious to see the great men of Europe; for I had read in the works of various philosophers, that all animals degenerated in America, and man among the number. A great man of Europe, thought I, must therefore be as superior to a great man of America, as a peak of the Alps to a highland of the Hudson; and in this idea I was confirmed, by observing the comparative importance and swelling magnitude of many English travellers among us, who, I was assured, were very little people in their own country. I will visit this land of wonders, thought I, and see the gigantic race from which I am degenerated. ("The Author's Account of Himself," 1819)

The ironic reading is signaled for, gradually, by the American's wide-eyed faith in the superiority of foreigners. The more that Irving stresses this amazing readiness to downgrade his own countrymen, the more one suspects it. The signal comes in strong with Irving's citing "the *comparative importance and swelling magnitude* of many English travelers among us, who, I was assured, were *very little people* in their own country." The real theme—that English travelers are often inflated with conceit—fits the signals much more clearly than does the strained notion of New World deterioration. Thus the reader joins Irving in actually laughing at the smugness of foreign visitors, and enjoys Irving's fun in saying, "I will visit this land of wonders [Europe] . . . and see the gigantic race from which I am degenerated."

You might return to the crude "How To Be a Religious Hypocrite" and ask how an ironic attack on religious hypocrisy might be effectively set up. A first step would be to choose an *apparent* goal which people often aim at—for example: "How To Improve the Religious Tone of Your Community by Your Personal Example." The tone adopted might be that of a concerned expert addressing a practical-minded audience on a goal which all find sensible—national religious vigor. For example:

> The United States is great because of her public piety. She has been governed by churchgoing presidents (with one unnotable exception during the Civil War). As a distinguished Chief Executive has said, "It doesn't matter what you believe as long as you believe in something."
> Probably the best defense against communism is to present the

united front of all believers publicly professing their faiths. Some first steps by which the reader can march on this national crusade are proposed below.

By physically attending the church of your choice, you help to provide direct and statistical proof of your community's spiritual solvency. Last year 49,427,603 worshipers were present in the nation's churches each Sunday on the average, a gain of 1.402 per cent over the previous year. Clergymen draw vital sustenance from this progress and often demonstrate the power of their ministry by the rising peaks of their attendance charts. A United States citizen who stays home a single Sunday is "letting down the side."

Secondly, by letting your neighbors know that you hold private family prayers you can add immeasurably to their sense of religious obligation. Although the actual fact of private prayer is not easily advertised, a tactful revelation can be managed by . . .

Your readers will probably grant that most people want their community to have firm religious values. And they can agree that one ought to live one's faith. But the title has already begun the signaling with a clash between true religion and "religious tone" (which suggests mere display). Another clash occurs in the complacent phrase, "by your personal example." The signal is amplified in the parenthetical slur of Abraham Lincoln as an "unnotable exception." Under the methodical advice to become patriotically religious, one sees the real point—an exposure of the hypocrisy by which nations, churches, and individuals exploit external trivia as supposed proof of spiritual force.

Irony in Fiction, Drama, Poetry

An audience can become so strongly involved whenever it detects the countermovements of surface and inner meaning that writers of imaginative literature often use irony in two special other ways—dramatic irony and situational irony.

Dramatic irony, presumably so called for its frequent use in the theater, gives to the audience certain important information lacked by one of the characters. Thereafter what the character says or does will take two levels of meaning—the one intended by the character and the larger one seen by the audience in the full dramatic context. For example, the spectator of Sophocles' tragedy *Oedipus the King* knows very early that Oedipus, king of Thebes, is unknowingly that same criminal whom he has sworn to track down. So every move that Oedipus makes to prove his fitness to rule is actually a move which exposes his unfitness.

A common device for projecting dramatic irony is the incompetent narrator. In Ring Lardner's story "Haircut," the narrator is a talkative, rambling, small-town barber who describes to his customer the death of the town practical joker without realizing (as the reader does) that a well-deserved execution has taken place. The irony arises from the contrast between the barber's own notion of what happened and the actual significance of what he reveals without knowing it. As with the examples given earlier, the reader is signaled early—here by the barber's repeated failure to see the cruelty or humor in the events he relates.

The incompetent narrator is illustrated again by Henry Fielding's novel *Jonathan Wild*, the fictional biography of a complete scoundrel told by an admiring "author" who seems to see in Wild's depraved nature the qualities of "GREATNESS." The narrator's upside-down values create a comic irony in which the reader enjoys discovering the real viciousness of the hero. Sometimes the unwitting narrator can expose himself, as in Robert Burns' poem, "Holy Willie's Prayer," in which Willie, a church elder praying for vengeance on his enemies, actually betrays his own spite, pride, and lust.

Situational irony occurs when a character lined up to do one thing actually does the opposite, as when a lifeguard becomes killer, a fireman becomes arsonist, a clergyman becomes corrupter—or, to take the example of *Oedipus*, the first defender of a kingdom becomes its arch criminal. Or else a character thinking to receive one thing may receive its opposite, as when a lover takes from his beloved a gift which turns out to be a curse. The contrast between the expected and actual outcomes of the role or action invites the audience into the shock of the two-level understanding which is characteristic of irony.

Exercise 1 (ironic statement)

For each of the following be able to show the *apparent* direction of the statement, its *real* point, and the signal which tells you that irony is present.

   a. You can't accuse Duncan of not respecting women. . . . He has
      respected at least four since we came here. (Pamela Hansford
      Johnson, *The Unspeakable Skipton*, 1959)
   b. Inflation isn't all bad. After all, it has allowed every American
      to live in a more expensive neighborhood without moving. (Senator Alan Cranston, 1981)
   c. The amount of women in London who flirt with their own husbands is perfectly scandalous. It looks so bad. It is simply washing one's clean linen in public. (Oscar Wilde, *The Importance of Being Earnest*, 1895)
   d. To bear other people's afflictions, every one has courage enough
      and to spare. (Benjamin Franklin, 1736)

e. May you be in heaven a half-hour before the Devil knows you're dead. (Sign in Irish inn)

f. The last time I was wrong was when I thought I had made a mistake. (Unknown)

g. No poet or novelist wishes he were the only one who ever lived, but most of them wish they were the only one alive, and quite a number of them fondly believe their wish has been granted. (W .H. Auden, *The Dyer's Hand,* 1962)

h. Suicide is a belated acquiescence in the opinion of one's wife's relatives. (H. L. Mencken, *Chrestomathy,* 1949)

Exercise 2 (large-scale irony)

For each of the following selections, be able to point out:

1. The apparent aim of the speaker and the apparent plausibility of the discussion.
2. The speaker's real aim and argument.
3. The signals which call for an ironic reading.
4. Any details which you think sharpen or weaken the total impact.

a. HOW TO BE EFFICIENT WITH FEWER VIOLINS

The following is the report of a Work Study Engineer after a visit to a symphony concert at the Royal Festival Hall in London:

For considerable periods the four oboe players had nothing to do. The number should be reduced and the work spread more evenly over the whole of the concert, thus eliminating peaks of activity.

All the twelve violins were playing identical notes; this seems unnecessary duplication. The staff of this section should be drastically cut. If a larger volume of sound is required, it could be obtained by means of electronic apparatus.

Much effort was absorbed in the playing of demi-semi-quavers; this seems to be an unnecessary refinement. It is recommended that all notes should be rounded up to the nearest semi-quaver. If this were done it would be possible to use trainees and lower-grade operatives more extensively.

There seems to be too much repetition of some musical passages. Scores should be drastically pruned. No useful purpose is served by repeating on the horns a passage which has already been handled by the strings. It is estimated that if all redundant passages were eliminated the whole concert time of 2 hours could be reduced to 20 minutes and there would be no need for an interval.

The conductor agrees generally with these recommendations, but expresses the opinion that there might be some falling off in box-office receipts. In that unlikely event, it should be possible to close sections of the auditorium entirely, with a consequential saving of overhead expenses, lighting, attendance, etc. If the worst came to the worst, the whole thing could be abandoned and the public could go to the Albert Hall instead.

Following the principle that "There is always a better method," it is felt that further review might still yield additional benefits. For example, it is considered that there is still wide scope for application of the "Questioning Attitude" to many of the methods of operation, as they are in many cases traditional and have not been changed for several centuries. In the circumstances it is remarkable that Methods Engineering principles have been adhered to as well as they have. For example, it was noted that the pianist was not only carrying out most of his work by two-handed operation, but was also using both feet for pedal operations. Nevertheless, there were excessive reaches for some notes on the piano and it is probable that re-design of the keyboard to bring all notes within the normal working area would be of advantage to this operator. In many cases the operators were using one hand for holding the instrument, whereas the use of a fixture would have rendered the idle hand available for other work.

It was noted that excessive effort was being used occasionally by the players of wind instruments, whereas one air compressor could supply adequate air for all instruments under more accurately controlled conditions.

Obsolescence of equipment is another matter into which it is suggested further investigation could be made, as it was reputed in the program that the leading violinist's instrument was already several hundred years old. If normal depreciation schedules had been applied the value of this instrument should have been reduced to zero and it is probable that purchase of more modern equipment could have been considered. (Unknown British, c. 1952)

b. HOW TO RUN AWAY FROM AN EDUCATIONAL PROBLEM

Most educational discussions become, sooner or later, a desperate attempt to escape from the problem. This is often done clumsily, causing unnecessary embarrassment and leaving the group without the comfortable feeling of having disposed of the problem. A "cultural lag" is evident in this situation. Educational leaders have long since worked out an adequate battery of techniques for dodging the issue.

In the course of a misspent youth, the writer and his friends have sat at the feet of many eminent practitioners of this art and have compiled a list of their devices. The list, of course, is only tentative, partial, incomplete, a mere beginning, etc., but it should at least give group leaders a command of alternate means of retreat, enabling them to withdraw their forces gracefully and to leave the problem baffled and helpless. In the interest of promoting the Christian spirit, we must dispense with acknowledging the sources of the following items. Additions to the list will be gratefully received.

1. Find a scapegoat and ride him. Teachers can always blame

administrators, administrators can blame teachers, both can blame parents, and everyone can blame the social order.

2. Profess not to have *the* answer. This lets you out of having *any* answer.

3. Say that we must not move too rapidly. This avoids the necessity of getting started.

4. For every proposal, set up an opposite and conclude that the "middle ground" (no notion whatever) represents the wisest course of action.

5. Point out that an attempt to reach a conclusion is only a futile "quest for certainty." Doubt and indecision "promote growth."

6. When in a tight place, say something that the group cannot understand. . . . (from Paul B. Diederich in *Progressive Education,* March 1942)

C. TO THE EDITOR, CHRONICLE OF HIGHER EDUCATION:
In the interest of helping young psychologists who are striving for advancement, I offer the following as a model of the style to be used when submitting manuscripts for publication. It follows the guidelines laid down in the *Publication Manual of the American Psychological Association* and is consistent with the style required by all the learned journals of the A.P.A.

"We hold these truths (Locke, 1696) to be self-evident (Socrates—see Plato, 365 B.C.), that all *persons* (Friedan, Steinem, Millett, 1975) are endowed (Darwin, 1859) with certain unalienable Rights (Rousseau, 1759) among which are Life (Mill, 1863), Liberty (Locke, 1696) and the pursuit of happiness (Epicurus, 280 B.C.). That to secure these rights, Governments (Hobbes, 1670) are instituted (Magna Carta, 1215) among *persons* (Friedan et al., 1975), deriving their just powers (Machiavelli, 1520) from the consent (Rousseau, 1763) of the governed (Voltaire, 1779)."

This elegant style gives clear evidence that the writer is conversant with the literature and is not so arrogant as to have opinions of his own. If Jefferson had followed it he might have become an associate professor of psychology instead of devoting his talents to the writing of undocumented polemics. If John B. Watson had followed it when he submitted his famous "Psychology as the Behaviorist Views It" to the *Psychological Review* in 1913 he might have lived out his life in happy obscurity instead of in the center of a storm. (Paul Woodring, 1982)

d. (*Here the writer is describing "The Good Duke," a Renaissance ruler.*) Nevertheless, like many great princes, he realized that political reasons might counsel at times an abatement of rigour. He could relent and show mercy. He could interpose his authority in favour of the condemned.

He relented on one celebrated occasion which more than any other helped to gain for him the epithet of "The Good"—when an entire squadron of the Militia was condemned to death for some supposed mistake in giving the salute. The record, unfortunately, is somewhat involved in obscurity and hard to disentangle; so much is clear, however, that the sentence was duly promulgated and carried into effect within half an hour. Then comes the moot question of the officer in command who was obviously destined for execution with the rest of his men and who now profited, as events proved, by the clemency of the Good Duke. It appears that this individual, noted for a child-like horror of bloodshed (especially when practised on his own person), had unaccountably absented himself from the ceremony at the last moment—slipping out of the ranks in order, as he said, to bid a last farewell to his two aged and widowed parents. He was discovered in a wine-shop and brought before a hastily summoned Court-martial. There his old military courage seems to have returned to him. He demonstrated by a reference to the instructions laid down in the Militiaman's Yearbook that no mistake in saluting had been made, that his men had therefore been wrongfully convicted and illegally executed and that he, *a fortiori*, was innocent of any felonious intent. The Court, while approving his arguments, condemned him none the less to the indignity of a double decapitation for the offence of leaving his post without a signed permit from His Highness.

It was at this point that the Good Duke interposed on his behalf. He rescinded the decree; in other words, he relented. "Enough of bloodshed for one day," he was heard to remark, quite simply.

This speech was one of his happiest inspirations. Instantly it echoed from mouth to mouth; from end to end of his dominions. Enough of bloodshed for one day! That showed his true heart, the people declared. Enough of bloodshed! Their enthusiasm grew wilder when, in an access of princely graciousness, he repaired the lamentable excess of zeal by pinning the Order of the Golden Vine to the offending officer's breast; it rose to a veritable frenzy as soon as they learned that, by Letters Patent, the entire defunct squadron had been posthumously ennobled. And this is only one of many occasions on which this ruler, by his intimate knowledge of human nature and the arts of government, was enabled to wrest good from evil, and thereby consolidate his throne. . . . (Norman Douglas, *South Wind*, 1917)

Exercise 3 (large-scale irony—imitation)

Imitate the ironic method of the selection in Exercise 2a, taking one of the following topics:

   a. How football can be played more efficiently. (Hint: Why this enormous horsepower to advance the ball such a short distance?)

b. How *Hamlet* can be staged for maximum results per production dollar.
c. How to reduce the energy waste in taking exams.
d. (Choose your own.)

Exercise 4 (large-scale irony—imitation)

Imitate the ironic method of the selection in Exercise 2d, taking one of the following topics:

a. An unscrupulous celebrity.
b. A scientist of high reputation and rotten character.
c. A hypocritical, nasty boss.

Exercise 5 (large-scale irony)

Determine your own real position on one of the following issues:

a. Censorship of pornography.
b. How to solve the federal budget deficit.
c. Freeze of nuclear arms.
d. Equal opportunity for women.
e. Limits to genetic engineering.
f. A campus regulation.

Then write an indirect attack to make your point. Possible strategies: Defend a competing point of view in such a way as to demolish it. Or criticize your own position in such a way as to show that the possible criticisms of your position are stupid. Or argue for some ridiculous alternative so as to make clear what really concerns you. (Remember that your *apparent* argument should *seem* plausible.)

Exercise 6 (dramatic irony)

Write a mistaken-identity skit with three characters, using this vintage formula:

a. (You name the characters.) A is expecting the most important arrival of D, whom A has not met yet. A tells this to B and then leaves.
b. Enter C, who is someone definitely and comically *other than D*. C reveals this information in conversation with B, who then leaves.
c. Re-enter A, who mistakes C for D. The irony is now set up so that the audience can appreciate the errors being made. Have

as much fun with the situation as you can before finally clearing (or completely muddling) it up.

Sample solution: A is about to sell his or her business firm to a potential buyer, D, using as sales pitch its extremely lucrative income which can easily be concealed from the income tax people. A mistakenly gives the sales pitch to C, who turns out to be a government tax investigator.

Exercise 7 (dramatic irony through incompetent narrator)

Choose one:

a. You are a sports coach apparently encouraging your team to show good sportsmanship at all times, while actually you want them to do anything to win. Write out the resulting peptalk, to be delivered just before the big game.

b. As a parent with an excellent opinion of yourself despite very real faults (such as laziness and gluttony), write a letter to your son or daughter in college, advising the virtues which are the opposites of those faults. The irony of course will grow out of your self-exposure—the reader seeing, as you presumably don't, the gap between your preaching and your practice.

Suggested reading for further illustration, discussion, and writing: American Cancer Society poster, "Smoking Is Very Glamorous," page 364; Russell Baker, "Mum's the Word," page 365; Aaron Wildavski, "The Theory of Preemptive Revolution," page 367.

III STYLE AND LANGUAGE

When we genuinely speak, we do not have the words ready to do our bidding; we have to find them, and we do not know exactly what we are going to say until we have said it, and we say and hear something that has never been said or heard before.

w. h. auden, *Secondary Worlds*, 1968

Those for whom words have lost their value are likely to find that ideas have also lost their value.

edwin newman, *Strictly Speaking: Will America Be the Death of English?* 1974

Our behavior is a function of the words we use. More often than not, our thoughts do not select the words we use; instead, words determine the thoughts we have.

weller embler, *Metaphor and Meaning*, 1966

13 The Vocabulary of Generality

The Need for Both Specific and General Vocabularies

The student who takes a Sunday drive past the springtime woods is likely to refer cheerfully to "springtime flowers" or "woods in bloom." A nature-lover will have learned the woods plant by plant, so as to speak of "red trillium," "wild geranium," etc. A specific vocabulary is a sign of both the speaker's authentic experience and respect for detail in a given area. The master of any subject knows its particulars and their proper value, and knows the names for those particulars.

But general language need not be bad language. We've seen that such terms as "spring flowers" and "woods in bloom" do very well when you want merely to label an experience in order to get on to other matters.

Moreover, you won't master any subject unless you *can* generalize from its details—until you can see in it the patterns, classes, orders, laws by which it makes some kind of sense. The linguist S. I. Hayakawa illustrates by supposing an isolated primitive village with only four dwellings, of which the first is called "maga," the second "biyo," the third "kata," and the fourth "pilel" (*Language in Thought and Action*, 2nd edition, New York: Harcourt, Brace and World, 1964, p. 180). Although these four terms would do until the villagers decided to build more dwellings, sooner or later they would see the need to invent a single general term—something like "house"—which expressed the essential qualities common to "maga," "biyo," "kata," and "pilel."

So, to return to springtime flowers, a professional botanist would need

139

to know not only the specifics ("red trillium" or *"trillium erectum"*) but the botanical family, *"liliaceae,"* and the general terminology by which individual plants can be discussed: "sepals," "petioles," "axils," for example. Though such terms are general, they are exact. They derive from the disciplined consciousness of botanists who have found sense in the lush profusion of nature.

In short, you need a specific vocabulary to come to hard grips with any kind of experience, and you need a general vocabulary to define, measure, and analyze it. This chapter and the next will explain some ways of developing these vocabularies.

Sloppy Generalizations from the "Utility Vocabulary"

The worst blurring of diction occurs at the general end of the word spectrum. In daily life people have to speak so quickly and often with so little thought that they resort to the *utility vocabulary*—a body of common words and expressions so broad and pliable as to say something *roughly* right without straining either speaker or listener. Examples:

PRAISE WORDS wonderful, terrific, fabulous, intriguing, lovely, nice, cute, swell, pretty good, not bad, OK, creative, dynamic, vital, challenging, fantastic, meaningful

DISAPPROVAL
WORDS awful, terrible, a mess, horrible, lousy, turkey, wimp

ALL-PURPOSE
TERMS situation, deal, factor, angle, aspect, outfit, bottom line, viable, basically

Of course everyone sharpens such words by nuances of voice and facial expression. Utility words do lubricate ordinary conversation because they make light demands and because they encourage a sense of relaxed informality. But writers who rely upon them steadily for all serious occasions are simply stunting their own vocabulary, let alone their power to think with any precision.

A large branch of utility vocabulary consists of *clichés*—expressions once eloquent but used so often that their impact has dwindled. Examples:

> bored to tears
> it goes without saying
> last but not least
> let's face it

view with alarm
welcome to [the club, the College, the company, or whatever]
would you believe?

Though some clichés do use specific diction ("happy as a *clam*"), they are so commonly applied to whole classes of events that they do serve as generalizers and often as thoughtless ones. You could call the cliché a conditioned reflex of language: your reader can finish the expression if you open with any part of it. Thus the test of a cliché is its anticipatability, as you can prove by supplying the following blanks:

> Like a bolt from the ———, our sales manager strode into the meeting. In a calm, cool, and ——— manner, he told us that results were the name of the ———. Since the campaign was failing, it was back to square ——— in order to strike while the iron was ———. In other words, we were to get in there and ———. He certainly proved a tower of ———. Thanks to his giving us a ——— in the arm, we threw caution to the ——— and pushed the division sales record over the ———.

Clichés as utility words make for easy, light communication; they appear in the everyday conversation of nearly everyone. But they also appear in the serious thinking of second-hand minds. If you want to satirize a bigot, a square, or an old fossil, you can catch and imitate the clichés on which that person's mind is tracked. Moreover, the cliché is relative. Your ear for the hackneyed expression keeps growing more acute as your vocabulary enlarges, so that the cleverness of yesterday can sometimes sound like today's corn. Sooner or later you'll detect your own private clichés— the handy little turns of phrase which have been easing you through daily communication. The big thing is to know when you can relax with a cliché and when you need to distrust it in order to do some new looking and thinking.

The Well-Defined Term

The need for a precise command of general language is readily illustrated by the dormitory argument in which the speakers are miles apart, not because they really disagree but because they are unwittingly using the same terms in divergent senses. For example:

> A: Did you hear the news? They've just put Dennis on probation and there goes his chance to make a football letter.
> B: Dennis can still play football! Probation is just a warning. He'll have all semester to raise his grades.

A: Probation is *not* just a warning. If you're on probation, you can't play football, period.

B: Listen, *I* was on probation last spring. But the Dean himself said the school wouldn't drop me as long as I could bring up the grades by June, and I did.

A: But you weren't on any athletic team. That's what probation is all about!

This argument could heat up indefinitely unless the speakers checked out the term "probation," now being confused by one or both of them with "ineligibility." (The practical difference will be seen presently.)

We can't get anywhere with general language unless we sharpen our terms—the more general the discussion, the tighter the definitions. To catch the full idea of probation, or to use it exactly in an academic context where your own future might be involved, you would need to rough out the concept and then to keep challenging it until you had got hold of everything the concept should contain and fenced out anything accidental or merely similar. The process might start like this:

1ST TRY Placing a student on probation means placing him on warning.

1ST CHALLENGE What kind of student—high school, college, graduate? In the United States, England, France?

2ND TRY Placing a student on probation, as the term is used in colleges and universities of the United States, means placing him on warning.

2ND CHALLENGE Warning for what? Getting drunk? Flunking? Cutting classes?

3RD TRY Placing a student on probation, as the term is used in colleges and universities of the United States, means placing him on warning that his grades must improve.

3RD CHALLENGE Is any academic warning the same as placing on probation? Suppose my teacher tells me I've got to crack the next quiz or get out of the course?

4TH TRY (*Added to previous try*) Probation differs from other kinds of academic "being on trial," such as being privately warned by a professor, in that the status of probation is formal, official, and applied according to certain institutional regulations governing minimum grade-point averages, usually at the end of a school term.

Of course no one is going to break off at every abstract term in order to hammer out an extended definition. Nevertheless the discipline of defining should be constant as a mental process whether you're speaking, listening, writing, or reading; and a few exercises in full formal definition can develop your feel for the kind of topics to cover. "Probation" is defined at length in the following example, with the *topics of definition* labeled in the margin:

special context of term in present sense — Placing a student on probation, as the term is used in colleges and universities of the United States, means placing him on

genus or general class of thing being defined — warning that his grades must improve. The word derives from

origin of term — the Latin *probatio* or "proof" and means just that, that the stu-

synonyms for term — dent is on trial as a student and must prove himself. Sometimes

contrast between thing being defined and other things resembling it — the term "academic probation" is used in distinction from "disciplinary probation" where a student found guilty of misbehavior must show unbroken good conduct as the condition for remaining in school. Probation differs from other kinds of academic

difference between thing being defined and other things in same general class — "being on trial," such as being privately warned by a professor, in that the status of probation is formal, official, and applied

process by which thing occurs — according to certain institutional regulations governing minimum grade-point averages, usually at the end of a school term. Often the failure to keep at least a C average will result in the dean's placing a student on probation. (Sometimes freshmen and sophomores are allowed to fall lower than upperclassmen before being placed on probation.) The student on probation is given a deadline, usually the end of the next term, in which to regain the satisfactory minimum grade average. If he succeeds, he is "off probation"; if he fails, he is subject to dismissal.

difference between thing being defined and other things resembling it — Academic probation is sometimes confused with the "ineligibility" of athletes and others to participate in intercollegiate activities. Both probation and ineligibility do hinge on grades, and many a student has found himself in both statuses; but

they serve different purposes. The status of probation is de-

function of thing
being described signed to improve a student as a student. The status of ineligi-

difference be-
tween thing being
defined and other
things resem-
bling it bility is designed to protect a code of intercollegiate activity

whereby a school will not represent itself by students who fall

markedly below its published scholastic standards. It has been

cynically noted that the standards of athletic ineligibility are

specific examples
of thing being
described often lower than those of probation. At my school, for example,

a freshman tackle could go on probation with a 1.6 average

(where D is 1 and C is 2) but still play football in certain

cases as long as he did not slip below 1.33.

This list of topics in the margin above is enough to generate a full and useful definition of almost any concept you may need to work with. Of course you might vary the order of attack in any way suitable, and you would select only so many topics as would realize your concept beyond any blur. The most important steps of definition are probably:

1. Specifying the context in which the term is used in its present sense.
2. Assigning the thing to its general class.
3. Differentiating it from other things in the same class (or from any other thing it might become confused with).
4. Giving examples of it or showing how the thing works—in short, showing how the thing can be recognized in specific terms.

Dictionaries can help, but since dictionaries aim only to approximate a term as it is most widely used, your own continual testing of a term will be needed to bring it to maximum serviceability as *you* are using it.

Exercise 1 (utility vocabulary)

a. Study the following bit which appeared in *Newsweek* for May 6, 1968:

HOW TO WIN AT WORDMANSHIP

After years of hacking through etymological thickets at the U.S. Public Health Service, a 63-year-old official named Philip

Broughton hit upon a sure-fire method for converting frustration into fulfillment (jargonwise). Euphemistically called the Systematic Buzz Phrase Projector, Broughton's system employs a lexicon of 30 carefully chosen "buzzwords":

COLUMN 1	COLUMN 2	COLUMN 3
0. integrated	0. management	0. options
1. total	1. organizational	1. flexibility
2. systematized	2. monitored	2. capability
3. parallel	3. reciprocal	3. mobility
4. functional	4. digital	4. programing
5. responsive	5. logistical	5. concept
6. optional	6. transitional	6. time-phase
7. synchronized	7. incremental	7. projection
8. compatible	8. third-generation	8. hardware
9. balanced	9. policy	9. contingency

The procedure is simple. Think of any three-digit number, then select the corresponding buzzword from each column. For instance, number 257 produces "systematized logistical projection," a phrase that can be dropped into virtually any report with that ring of decisive, knowledgeable authority. "No one will have the remotest idea of what you're talking about," says Broughton, "but the important thing is that they're not about to admit it."

b. Construct a similar Buzz Phrase Projector using the "in" vocabulary of any field where you're especially conscious of utility words—for example, art criticism, music criticism, literary criticism, baseball, sports cars, educational theory.

Exercise 2 (clichés)

Write a page or two of dialog using one of the following situations and giving the speakers all the clichés you can possibly cram in:

a. A star athlete being interviewed by a sportscaster.
b. A man and woman, just met, as they bemoan the difficulty of achieving truly creative individuality in the culture of today.
c. A writing instructor lecturing on the need for freshness and originality.
d. A campaigning politician being interviewed by a reporter.

Exercise 3 (definition of terms)

As the brain of your crowd, settle the following late-night arguments by showing which terms need defining, and how:

1ST ARGUMENT

A: I say that if the sexes are equal, women should receive the same pay as men.

B: You mean for doing the same amount of work?

A: Right. Eight hours' work, eight hours' pay, no matter which sex.

B: But take physical labor like garbage collection, where most women can't keep up with men. Should they get the same pay per hour?

A: Can all *men* work at the same pace at the same job? No. But they get the same pay, and nobody talks about inequality . . .

2ND ARGUMENT

A: I say that if the U.S. joins a world government, it will surrender its sovereignty.

B: Not at all! The nation would retain its democratic form of government just as now.

A: But suppose your world government didn't want it to? Suppose it declared a universal dictatorship?

B: Look. Pennsylvania is one of the United States. Can the national government dictate how state governments are set up?

A: Why not?

B: The Constitution wouldn't allow it. The world government would also have a constitution.

A: But that constitution would probably forbid the U.S. to maintain armed forces. Then how would the nation make sure of its sovereignty?

B: The U.S. would too have armed forces! Don't the states each have a state police and a militia to preserve order?

A: But that's different . . .

Exercise 4 (definition of terms)

How would you challenge each of the following definitions, and how would you sharpen it to meet that challenge? (You might try your solution on a friend, to see if your friend can challenge it further.)

    a. A truck is a vehicle designed to carry heavy loads.

    b. A true hypochondriac isn't merely one who is forever taking his own temperature. It's one who refuses to believe the thermometer when it registers normal. (Sydney Harris, 1979)

    c. Happiness is the smell of bacon on your first morning home.

    d. You are "routing" when you use the machine called a router.

    e. Terrorists [are what] people who fight back are still called the world over by those who are against people who fight back. (Jens Kruuse, *War for an Afternoon*, 1967)

    f. The question "Who ought to be boss?" is like asking "Who ought to be tenor in the quartette?" Obviously, the man who can sing tenor. (Attributed to Henry Ford)

g. The clavichord is a stringed instrument.
h. Loquacity: A disorder which renders the sufferer unable to curb his tongue when you wish to talk. (Ambrose Bierce, *The Devil's Dictionary*, 1911)
i. Spanish moss is a bromeliaceous plant which grows in the southern United States.
j. To cut a class means to be absent from it.
k. An antimacassar is named for a kind of hairdressing called "Macassar Oil."

Exercise 5 (definition of terms)

Be able to describe the various methods used for each of the following definitions. What questions would you raise to show where further tightening is needed?

a. When a bit of behavior is followed by a certain kind of consequence, it is more likely to occur again, and a consequence having this effect is called a reinforcer. Food, for example, is a reinforcer to a hungry organism; anything the organism does that is followed by the receipt of food is more likely to be done again whenever the organism is hungry. Some stimuli are called negative reinforcers; any response which reduces the intensity of such a stimulus—or ends it—is more likely to be emitted when the stimulus recurs. Thus, if a person escapes from a hot sun when he moves under cover, he is more likely to move under cover when the sun is again hot. The reduction in temperature reinforces the behavior it is "contingent upon"—that is, the behavior it follows. (B. F. Skinner, *Beyond Freedom and Dignity*, 1971)

b. Culture can be loosely defined as the body of nongenetic information which people pass from generation to generation. It is the accumulated knowledge that, in the old days, was passed on entirely by word of mouth, painting, and demonstration. Several thousand years ago the written word was added to the means of cultural transmission. Today culture is passed on in these ways, and also through television, computer tapes, motion pictures, records, blueprints, and other media. Culture is all the information man possesses except for that which is stored in the chemical language of his genes. (Paul R. Ehrlich, *The Population Bomb*, 1968)

c. ABSOLUTE ZERO: Temperatures lower than it are unattainable. The precise point itself ($-459.7°$ F) is almost impossible to reach, because volume would vanish there. Wondrous properties occur near absolute zero. Electrical resistance disappears from some metals (superconductivity). Liquid helium climbs over the edges of containers to reach a lower level (superfluidity). (Wayne Biddle, "From Alpha to X-Ray: A Glossary of Scientific Terms," *Harper's*, August 1979)

d. The term "socialism" is used in a variety of ways in a number of contexts. There is the Russian kind of state capitalism organized under the banner of the Union of Soviet *Socialist* Republics. There is "democratic socialism" (Sweden, Britain), with "socialistic" measures (health, welfare, unemployment benefits, and such) instituted through democratic, parliamentary procedures. There are also "socialistic" measures imposed by armed dictatorships with the help of informers and secret police (for example, the collectivization of farms in Russia and China). Then there are all the measures *called* "socialistic" by their opponents: prepaid medical care, the income tax, social security, aid to dependent children, or whatever. The frightened individual's reaction to all of these *different* measures is *to see them as alike:* "One is just as bad as the other"—they are all "socialism," which means that they are all "communism": the fluoridation of the public water supply, abstract art, or the Negro demand for civil rights. According to Rokeach, *this inability to see the differences among the various things you do not believe in characterizes the closed mind.* (S. I. Hayakawa, *Language in Thought and Action,* 1964)

Exercise 6 (definition of terms—imitation)

Define one of the following, imitating the "probation" definition in the text of this chapter and using the adaptation-of-techniques method described in Chapter 6 (see page 54):

a. Confidentiality
b. Sin
c. Slander
d. A patent
e. A cadenza
f. Novice (in religious sense)

Exercise 7 (definition of terms)

Write a full definition of one of the following terms, taking care to distinguish your concept from any other concept which might resemble it. (Thus, if you choose "cowardice," be sure to show how it differs from "discretion" and "restraint," for example.)

a. Cowardice	h. Depreciation (in accounting)
b. Nanosecond	i. Poverty
c. To politicize	j. Death
d. Prayer	k. Solenoid
e. Ownership	l. Cathode ray tube
f. Money market fund	m. Parsec (in astronomy)
g. Cantilever	n. Caucus

Exercise 8 (combining general terms; instruction writing for assembly)

The writing of clear directions is a rare art, too seldom found in the ordinary instructions which come with devices which we buy. The art requires: 1) exact definitions of parts and steps; 2) an exact schedule for putting things together and into operation.

Take some non-electrical machine or mechanical object which you can later bring to class. Disassemble the device. Then write out instructions by which someone else can assemble it. Bring both device and instructions to class, together with any needed tools, to see how a classmate succeeds or fails in following instructions. Revise instructions accordingly.

Sample devices for this exercise: faucet, stapler, Rubic cube, mechanical toy, drape rod-and-rigging, any contrivance built with Erector set, puzzle (other than jigsaw).

Exercise 9 (instructions for process)

(This exercise is an extension or alternate to Exercise 8.) Write out instructions on how to perform a common task you are familiar with—for example, how to change a tire, how to carve a turkey, how to iron an item of clothing, how to replace a lawn mower blade. Be sure, as for Exercise 8, to define all special parts and terms, to provide an exact schedule of steps to take.

Although you can hardly bring the necessary materials to school for your classmates to test out, you can try your instructions on a group of classmates to see what questions might arise; your work can be revised accordingly.

Suggested readings for further illustration, discussion, and writing: Germaine Greer, "Security," page 370; Aldous Huxley, "Knowledge and Understanding," page 376; George Orwell, "The Principles of Newspeak," page 380.

14   The Vocabulary of Detail

It isn't easy to see things in detail. The "detail vision" requires discipline in knowing what to look for, and an ample vocabulary from which to pick the word for the exact color, texture, shape, intensity, nuance, etc. Compare for example what detail *you* would catch in a minute's glimpse of the fresh vegetable section of a supermarket with what the store manager would catch. Moreover, for the harassed or unimaginative student, writing in detail means simply to get all possible mileage out of a few barren notions; hence every expression is inflated to expand a very few ideas into a great many syllables.

How to Increase the Amplitude of Written Passages in a Highly Verbose Manner

If you're ever bankrupt for real detail in front of a sufficiently gullible audience, you might try out these simple rules of verbosity:

1. *Use a roundabout expression for a plain English equivalent.* Instead of "decide," say "reach a decision." Instead of "try," say "make an attempt."
2. *Replace a word by a synonym with more syllables.* For "start," say "activate." For "begin," say "initiate." For "go," say "proceed."
3. *Replace a plain word with a euphemism* (i.e. an elegant variation which adds both length and a certain stuffy gentility). Instead of "spit," say "expectorate." For "die," say "pass away." For "cemetery," say "memorial park."
4. *Couple a plain word with a needless noun showing its category.* Say "round in *shape*," "red in *color*," "sweet in *taste*," "the *condition* of despair," "the *state* of Wisconsin."

5. *Use the vaguer qualifiers and intensifiers* (and incidentally achieve the illusion of judiciousness and force). Say *"somewhat* angry," *"rather* quiet," *"quite* attractive," "interesting to *some extent," "very* sincerely."

6. *Choose verbs which are vague enough to require adverbs.* Don't say "he *crawled";* say "he *moved slowly"* (or better yet, "he *proceeded very slowly").* Instead of "he *bolted* his breakfast," say "he *ate* his breakfast *very quickly."*

7. *Couple the assertion of a fact with a demonstration of it,* thus getting double length. Thus: "her lips *curled* in *scorn"* or "the man *tugged* at the *heavy* boulder."

8. *Simply be redundant, by repeating your meaning over and over after you have already said what you initially meant in the first place.* Where "essential" is enough, say *"vitally* essential." Don't stop with *"evident";* say *"clearly* evident." Stretch "fundamentals" into *"basic* fundamentals."

The Ladder of Specification

On the other hand, you may wish to see things clear and solid, blurring nothing. A warm-up exercise is to run as far up the "ladder of specification" as you can for a given word. The idea is to start with a fairly general word like "animal" and then step by step to substitute more specific terms until you can't tighten your coverage any further—thus:

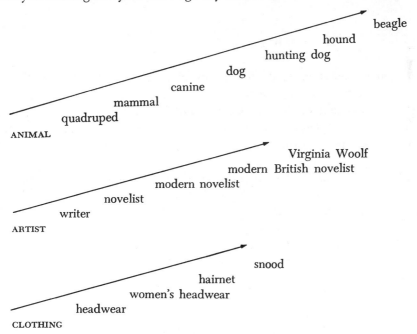

For a finer exercise you could go over anything you've written so far (or your next rough draft) and try running selected terms one or two steps higher on the ladder of specification—thus:

$$
\text{The boy,}\
\begin{array}{l}\uparrow\ \text{crouched on}\\ \textsc{seated in}\end{array}\ \text{his}\
\begin{array}{l}\uparrow\ \text{nail keg}\\ \text{box}\\ \textsc{place}\end{array}\ \text{at the back of the crowded}
$$

$$
\begin{array}{l}\uparrow\ \text{store}\\ \textsc{building},\end{array}\ \text{knew he smelled}\
\begin{array}{l}\uparrow\ \text{Liederkranz}\\ \text{strong cheese}\\ \textsc{cheese}.\end{array}
$$

Notice incidentally what this kind of tightening could do for an essay exam:

$$
\text{A great breakthrough in genetics came}\
\begin{array}{l}\uparrow\ \text{in 1953}\\ \text{in the early 1950's}\\ \textsc{after world war ii},\end{array}
$$

$$
\text{when}\
\begin{array}{l}\uparrow\ \text{Crick and Watson}\\ \textsc{scientists}\end{array}\ \text{first suggested a physico-chemical model for}
$$

$$
\text{the}\
\begin{array}{l}\uparrow\ \textsc{dna}\ \text{molecule}\\ \text{molecule}\\ \textsc{structure}\end{array}\ \text{which carries genetic information from cell}
$$

to cell in all living things.

The difference between the first and final versions is roughly the difference between a C+ and an A paper.

The Catalog

A second discipline would be the inventory or catalog. Try choosing a setting which you can observe at leisure—say, a corner of your room, a store, a desk—and list its contents as minutely as if you were preparing an auctioneer's list. Here for example is the inventory of an open-shelf cabinet in a suburban bathroom:

white wallpaper at back, with bouquets of pinks in blue ribbons; pink, blue, and green butterflies

top shelf: Johnson's Baby Powder
Desert Flower Talcum
fat-bellied jar with cotton wads inside
tiny three-legged porcelain receptacle for jewelry
Chanel No. 5 Bath Powder
amber wine-glass with tiny flowers painted on; soft-yellow candle inside

second
  shelf: bottle of Beauty Shoppe Nail Polish Remover
bottle of Figurine Cologne

can of Right Guard deodorant

plastic bottle of Coty l'Aimant hand and body lotion (Intro-
ductory Special, $2.00)

box of Puffs pink facial tissues (Special 5¢ Off)

small clock, set in Victorian metal stand painted a flaking ivory
with bas relief flowers and foliage painted in many colors—
not working

bottle of 4711 Cologne

bottle of OFF! insect repellent

small bottle of Oh! de Cologne

pocketbook perfume dispenser-tube, lavender, with gold cap

bottom
shelf: jar of Get Set hairsetting gel

box of Mr. Bubble with Lanolin

hand mirror, face down, back in off-white with painted brocade
of flowers

1 bobby pin

bottle of Chantilly hand lotion with push-dispenser

square ash tray containing Diamond matches, 1 large safety pin,
1 small safety pin, 1 rubber band, 1 match folder from Chateau Louise, Dundee, Illinois

But merely scooping in raw materials isn't writing, and certainly though
this raw material is highly specific, you would only clog a description by
using all of it. To finish the exercise you need the sort of selective principle described in Chapter 3—some central or prevailing impression which
your material makes upon you (or some purpose which you in turn want
to impose upon your material). Then you write, selecting only that which
most forcibly sustains that impression or purpose. In looking over the
contents of this suburban cabinet, you might take up the clash between
its elegance and its clutter:

[SELECTIVE
PRINCIPLE]   SUBURBAN TOILET CABINET

ELEGANCE Pink, green, and blue butterflies hover near blue-ribboned
bouquets on the idyllic wallpaper at the back. A dainty Victorian clock stands without ticking, ivory paint flaking off its
CLUTTER   rococo flowered case. No less than three bottles of cologne grace
the upper shelves (Figurine, 4711, and Oh! de Cologne), to-
ELEGANCE gether with three boxes of powder (Chanel No. 5, Desert Flower,
and Johnson's Baby), a bottle of OFF! insect repellent, and can
CLUTTER   of Right Guard deodorant. On the bottom shelf is a box of Mr.
Bubble with Lanolin and a square ash tray holding two safety
pins, a rubber band, and a match folder from Chateau Louise,
Dundee, Illinois. Near it lies a single bobby pin.

Of course the basic inventory might support other selective principles as
well—the grim pressure upon women to be beautiful, the fundamental
tastelessness of the beauty industry, for example.

The suburban cabinet detail was obtained through a space inventory. You could also try a time inventory in which you list with great particularity all the events within a time interval—for example, everything which happens from the ringing of your alarm clock until you leave the room. Still another inventory is the sensory catalog, the listing of all stimuli to all the physical senses within a given scene or action. The sensory catalog is especially recommended for the young poet or fiction-writer, who too often restricts reporting to sights and sounds only, neglecting the dimensions of smell, taste, touch, besides the visceral sensations within one's own body (tension and relaxation; coldness and warmth; pains and pleasures; etc.).

To see what can be done with density of detail, first observe this *generalized* description of a row of business establishments in a small Midwest town:

> The drugstore on the corner was unattractively fitted and was cluttered with toilet articles, seeds, medicines. A doctor's sign showed in a second-story window. Next door was the movie theater, and then the grocery, displaying stale produce and dingy shelves. Above the grocery showed the signs of various lodges. Next was the meat market, and then the jewelry store, showing second-rate watches.

This is accurate as far as it goes. It's also dull. Now look at this passage from Sinclair Lewis' 1920 masterpiece *Main Street,* from which the above summary was boiled down:

> Dyer's Drug Store, a corner building of regular and unreal blocks of artificial stone. Inside the store, a greasy marble soda-fountain with an electric lamp of red and green and curdled-yellow mosaic shade. Pawed-over heaps of toothbrushes and combs and packages of shaving-soap. Shelves of soap-cartons, teething-rings, garden-seeds, and patent medicines in yellow packages—nostrums for consumption, for "women's diseases"—notorious mixtures of opium and alcohol, in the very shop to which her husband sent patients for the filling of prescriptions.
>
> From a second-story window the sign "W. P. Kennicott, Phys. & Surgeon," gilt on black sand.
>
> A small wooden motion-picture theater called "The Rosebud Movie Palace." Lithographs announcing a film called "Fatty in Love."
>
> Howland & Gould's Grocery. In the display window, black, overripe bananas and lettuce on which a cat was sleeping. Shelves lined with red crepe paper which was now faded and torn and concentrically spotted. Flat against the wall of the second story the signs of lodges—the Knights of Pythias, the Maccabees, the Woodmen, the Masons.

> Dahl & Oleson's Meat Market—a reek of blood.
> A jewelry shop with tinny-looking wrist-watches for women. In front of it, at the curb, a huge wooden clock which did not go.

You can feel almost present on this tacky downtown street. Its smell is here (reek of blood), its many glimpses of tawdry merchandise, its feel of things greasy and pawed over, its trashy taste in movies and jewelry.

Besides cataloging by space, time, and sensation, you could adapt any other surveying principle as long as it works for your topic—thus:

> *The catalog of cases or examples:* useful for substantiating a general observation, for illustrating a general principle.
> *The catalog of categories* (e.g. a list of the classes of articles to be found in a supermarket—soups, bakery goods, fresh vegetables): useful for taking hold of large aggregates, such as crowds, panoramic scenes, complex organisms.
> *The cycle catalog* (basically a time inventory which traces the circuit of any repetitive process): useful for describing a typical work day, a Sunday, a routine week, a life cycle, a complete manufacturing operation, etc.

In short, the cataloging technique can intensify your vision for detail by giving you a plan for observing it which in turn helps to focus your observation on the detail itself.

This chapter may have overenthusiastically suggested here and there that detail is everything. Of course it isn't. A writer who plunges into detail for its own sake can be just as chaotic and boring as your neighbor with total recall for a vacation trip. Again, a specialist can be a "detail-dropper" to score conversational points over laymen in the field. A writer may pile on detail in a kind of fraud to cover a lack of a central idea or development. Worst of all, the writer who *thinks* only in detail may forfeit the chance and the right to analyze, to pull together, to evaluate. Nonetheless, selected detail can project your thinking into three dimensions. It can often point up a generalization—like that summary of the genetic breakthrough by Crick and Watson—to give it precision and authenticity.

Exercise 1 (wordiness)

Revise the following sentences for maximum directness:

> a. One of our sales representatives will soon call upon you to initiate your personal purchase program.
> b. From business reports appearing in the *Daily News*, it would appear that a rise of 26 points materialized in the Dow Index

yesterday, thereby showing an unusual increase in stock exchange activity.

c. Alec's paper I found almost interesting, to some extent, that is.

d. Father Daniel was wheezing and gasping as he reached the top of the stairs, quite winded.

e. She referred back to a previous statement which David had made earlier.

f. She flushed red at my words, spoken as they were in a moment of anger.

g. The word *bus* is a shortened form of *omnibus* which has been abbreviated by dropping the initial prefix from the beginning.

h. The patio floor was made of tiles which were a fiery orange in color and were arranged in formations having the shapes of diamonds and triangles.

i. It is not generally known by most people that Major Jackson lived here at one time.

Exercise 2 (wordiness)

Inflate the following sentences by at least 50 percent, freely using roundabout expressions, flabby synonyms, vague qualifiers, redundancies, and the like:

a. The secret of teaching is good listening.

b. Senator Krueger's advisors have told her to campaign more aggressively.

c. Children's sports are overemphasized.

d. Brevity is the soul of wit.

e. Americans generally fear death.

f. A "polymath" is a person of great or varied learning.

g. Good prose is concise.

Exercise 3 (the ladder of specification)

Run each of the following terms as far up the ladder of specification as you can (at least four rungs):

a. Fish

b. Chinaware

c. Obligation

d. To pull

e. Engine

f. To feel pain in the leg

g. To hit

h. Food flavor

Exercise 4 (the ladder of specification)

Rewrite the following sentences, boosting the italicized terms two or three rungs on the ladder of specification:

a. The unemployed talk *at the curb* late in the day and *watch the passers-by.*
b. *This new alloy,* which includes *traces* of *rare metals,* can remain rigid under *extremely high temperatures.*
c. Sara is fond of *classical music.*
d. The old woman's body, lying in the snow, *looked strangely young.*
e. *The school official* suggested that Eric transfer to *a special school.*
f. *Market researchers* have shown that *consumers* will buy *almost anything* on impulse.
g. *In mid-day,* a young woman *came by, carrying a piece of trash.*
h. Unless taxes are *lowered substantially* in *the immediate future,* the city faces a *serious depression.*

Exercise 5 (cataloging)

Actually observe one of the following, take a written inventory of its details, choose a selective principle, and write about one page drawing upon those details. (If the inventory grows too long, reduce the field of observation as necessary.)

a. A gift shop window
b. A stranger passing on the sidewalk
c. A supermarket cashier taking care of a customer
d. The view through a window, observed from several feet back
e. The desk of someone you know
f. A movie theater in the twenty minutes before the program begins
g. The corridor outside of a busy office

Exercise 6 (cataloging)

Some authors are able to create an authentic description of places and actions they have never witnessed. The chances are that they first use the cataloging technique together with library materials. See what you can do with any of the following topics, the only limitation being that you should *not* have first-hand experience of the topic. Construct the inventory (using the library as needed), then choose a selective principle, and write one to two pages drawing upon those details. (If the inventory grows too big, reduce the field of inventory as necessary.)

    a. A ship of ancient times, sinking
    b. Robbing a pyramid
    c. Fishing for marlin
    d. An evening in Tanzania
    e. The external appearance of a Renaissance queen or princess
    f. Shooting a rhinoceros
    g. A canal in Venice

Exercise 7 (cataloging)

As a test of ingenuity, try a full paragraph of detail on one of these:

    a. A mud puddle
    b. A bare foot
    c. A clock
    d. A wastebasket
    e. Sounds of one minute in the middle of a field or woods

Exercise 8 (cataloging)

This exercise is rigged to compel unusual exploitation of physical senses which would ordinarily be neglected. For any one of the following, write as vivid and exact a description as you can, in each case deliberately *omitting* the details that would be perceived by the sense excluded.

    a. A rock singer performing (minus hearing)
    b. A luscious dessert (minus taste)
    c. A library lobby (minus sight)
    d. A pizza (minus sight)
    e. A talkative person at full blast (minus hearing)
    f. A very cold night (minus touch or sense of cold)

Suggested reading for further illustration, discussion, and writing: John Updike, "Our Own Baedeker," page 386.

15   The Vocabulary of Feeling

The political reputation of Senator Claude Pepper of Florida was alleg-
edly damaged in a 1950s campaign by a leaflet which read as follows
(italics added):

> Are you aware that Claude Pepper is known all over Wash-
> ington as a shameless *extrovert?* He is also reliably reported to
> practice *nepotism* with his sister-in-law, and he has a sister who
> was once a *thespian* in Greenwich Village. He has a brother who
> is a practicing *homo sapiens,* and he went to a college where
> the men and women openly *matriculated* together. It is an es-
> tablished fact that Mr. Pepper before his marriage practiced
> *celibacy.* Worse than that, he has admitted to being a lifelong
> *autodidact.*

This passage was literally harmless provided that its readers understood
the actual reference of such words as "extrovert," "nepotism," "thespian,"
and so on. But its whole shocked tone implied that the Senator and his
family were wallowing in sexual perversions. This chapter will deal with
the emotional power of our language, how it can be used and abused.

Approval and Disapproval

You might speak of the "fragrance" of a certain perfume if you liked it,
of its "reek" if you didn't, or simply of its "odor" if you didn't care. These
variants illustrate the principle that words may refer not only to objective

information but to the feelings of the user (and the feelings which the user wants the reader to share).

The common term for the emotional implication of a word or phrase is *connotation*. "Fragrance," "reek," and "odor" are all used to convey information about "smell." But "fragrance" *connotes* the speaker's approval of the smell, "reek" connotes the speaker's revulsion, and "odor" in this context carries no connotation at all. A few other illustrations:

NEUTRAL	CONNOTING APPROVAL	CONNOTING DISAPPROVAL
overweight	portly	tubby
underweight	slim	skinny
friend	comrade	crony
crowd	gathering, assembly	mob
old person	senior citizen	fossil

Besides connoting your approval or disapproval on a given matter, you may also find yourself using certain intensifiers to *magnify* an item (if you wish to praise or blame it) without in the least affecting the mere information present. Suppose that 46 percent of the electorate voted in a recent election. If you think that was a great turnout, you could say "*Fully* 46 percent of the electorate voted." But if you were disappointed, you could *minify* the item by saying "*Only* 46 percent of the electorate voted." Note these pairs of magnifiers and minifiers:

as much as	as little as
no fewer than	no more than
amply (absolutely, unmistakably, completely)	barely (hardly, scarcely)

You could also use what might be called *nudgers*—words and phrases to ease the reader past a doubtful statement. Samples:

indeed	of course
needless to say	surely
honestly (or, to be perfectly honest)	certainly
	frankly
can anyone doubt that—?	sincerely
who can believe that—?	obviously

To see how the same objective information can take opposite emotional values according to such language, note these news stories in which the only real difference is that Writer A approves what Writer B disapproves in describing essentially the same facts:

VERSION A

No less than 157 citizens presented an ethics-in-government petition to Mayor Isabel Troub requesting the removal of Road Commissioner Herb Sayer for a gross conflict of interests. Sayer has openly admitted to owning a full one-third interest in the Eureka Road Paving Company which is under contract to the City. Nonetheless Mayor Troub threw out the petition, with the glib assurance that Commissioner Sayer has played no part in contractual negotiations with Eureka.

VERSION B

A handful of self-righteous citizens slapped Mayor Isabel Troub with a demand for the outright firing of Road Commissioner Herbert Sayer. Under the coloring of an "ethics-in-government" movement, the petitioners tried to make out a conflict of interests case, accusing Sayer of owning a piece of the Eureka Road Paving Company which does occasional business with the City. Mayor Troub firmly rejected the argument, pointing out that Commissioner Sayer has gone on record about his connection with Eureka and accordingly is excluded from any contractual negotiation with that company.

In particular, note such contrasts as these:

VERSION A

no less than 157 citizens
presented a . . . petition
openly admitted

VERSION B

a handful of . . . citizens
slapped a demand
has gone on record

What exactly makes the differences in connotation? You might extract a few other contrasts from the two versions, just to see what connotations can do.

Nothing is wrong with including your approval or disapproval in what you're describing. The trouble would begin if you confused your own feelings with the facts, and imagined that you were communicating evidence when actually you would be offering mainly your unsupported emotional reaction. (Of course the confusion can be deliberate in order to con the audience.) From the confusion arises the excesses of sentimentality (as was illustrated in Chapter 11) and of propaganda. The controversy over abortion, for example, has unfortunately bogged down in loaded language. Those who would prohibit most or all abortions call themselves "Pro-Life," thereby putting any opposition in the "Pro-Death" camp. Those who want some kind of abortion on demand refer to themselves as "Pro-Choice" and to the alternative as "Compulsory Pregnancy."

For a less bitter example, here is a paid questionnaire run in a suburban newspaper:

DO YOU SUPPORT THE PARK DISTRICT'S DECISION
TO BUILD A REC CENTER?

At their June 15th meeting, the Park District Board voted to proceed with
a recreation center at a projected cost of between $1,250,000 and $2,500,000.
This decision was made despite strong objections from the large group present
at that meeting. Furthermore, the Board refused to conduct a poll of the citizens, citing the results of a previous poll held 2 years ago. At that time there
were only 519 responses out of a total of 8,000 to 10,000 questionnaires sent
out.

The Taxpayers Association feels that the taxpayers deserve another opportunity to express their opinion for or against the expenditure for this
facility.

Are you in favor of the Park District spending between 1.25 and 2.5 million dollars for a recreation center?
        NO———   YES———

Note the implication of Board arrogance: "this decision was made *despite
strong objection from the large group present* . . . the Board *refused* to
conduct a poll of the *citizens.*" By contrast, the Taxpayers Association appears as champions of the plundered public, feeling that *"the taxpayers
deserve* another *opportunity.*" That the questionnaire tilted toward rejection of the proposed expenditure can hardly be doubted, nor could much
confidence be placed in its findings.

A special role in the language of approval and disapproval has been
earned by the *euphemism*—the nice way of putting a supposedly ugly
idea. Many people dislike euphemisms for their lack of plain honest talk;
others use them to upgrade facts they want to feel comfortable about.
Thus old age is referred to as "the Golden Years," and old people as
"Senior Citizens." Employees are not fired, they are "separated," "terminated," "selected out." Other examples:

PLAIN TERM	MATCHING EUPHEMISM
garbage can	ecological receptable
janitor	maintenance man
garbage collector	sanitation worker
toilet	lavatory, rest room, powder room, comfort facility
sweat	perspire
breast	bosom
plumber	plumbing engineer
toilet plunger	plumber's helper
butcher	meat technologist
salesman	accounts executive, product representative
used car	pre-owned car
coffin	casket, demise chest
undertaker	mortician, funeral director

A little hypocrisy, a little pretense, doesn't seem to hurt. But euphemism becomes really deadly when it hides brutality, fraud, dishonor. When a government officer masks a lie by calling it an "inoperative statement," public trust is basically eroded. Such virulent euphemisms appear especially in the cover-up of government scandals and military atrocities, as these examples illustrate:

PLAIN TERM	MATCHING EUPHEMISM
dirty politics	playing hardball
wire-tapping	electronic surveillance
burglarizing the opposition files	surreptitious entry, intelligence-gathering
kill	liquidate, terminate with extreme prejudice
invade	liberate, pacify
bombing raid	air support, protective retaliation
search and destroy mission	reconnaissance in force

Researchers will sometimes avoid a loaded term (like "the poor") in favor of a factual equivalent ("families with less than $_____ annual income") because, after all, they are trying to reach objective conclusions. The dispassionate language appropriate to scholarly method should not be confused with language which prevents your taking hold of life.

Other Emotions

Besides expressing mere approval or disapproval, connotation can express the intensity and coloring of the mood in which you write. Compare:

A I'm going to *invite* Frank Newton to my *home.*
B I'm going to *ask* Frank Newton to my *house.*

Which version would you use if Frank were a warm friend? Most people would probably choose A, since "invite" implies a cordial interest missing from "ask" (one could "ask" the plumber or the piano tuner), and "home" connotes a domestic warmth missing from "house." Again:

A I don't *dig* that, *man.*
B I don't *understand* that, *sir.*

Does it need to be asked which version has the feel of careless frankness? And which has the feel of formal respect? But you might try suggesting still other versions to connote indignation, anxiety, humorous modesty, menace, or some other emotion.

Connotation is the life of advertising, which seeks to communicate not only information about the product but the emotional attitudes which will arouse the reader to buy. See how much force is lost when the following advertisement is recast in language of almost neutral connotation.

ORIGINAL   Magic moment in Madrid. Starlight replaces the savage Spanish sun. Breezes whisper softly through the fountain's cool splash. A nightingale sings. And somewhere in the dark throbs a gypsy guitar. This is the moment that belongs to your hostess. With infinite artistry she has set the scene. And what a magnificent setting for her lovely Lenox China and Lenox Crystal. (Magazine advertisement)

NEUTRALIZED   An occasion in Madrid. Night follows the hot day. Wind blows at 3 mph. The fountain discharges water of 52 degrees Fahrenheit at two gallons per minute. The cry of a *luscinia megarhyncha* is heard. Somewhere in the night a nomad plays a guitar. . . .

Note that the original word, "magic," simply disappears, since it is purely connotative and refers to no verifiable factual information.

Poetry, too (in fact, all imaginative literature), is connotative by its nature, since the writer is not only creating an imagined reality but feeling it as well. Neutralized or purely informative poetry would seem pallid, as in this recasting of Housman's lines from *A Shropshire Lad* (1896).

ORIGINAL   Loveliest of trees, the cherry now
           Is hung with bloom along the bough,
           And stands about the woodland ride
           Wearing white for Eastertide.

NEUTRALIZED   The tree I find most beautiful, the cherry tree, now
             has many blossoms on its branches,
             and can be seen here and there along the roads in the woods
             all in white, the color often displayed at Easter.

Again, note that Housman's "loveliest of trees" cannot easily be neutralized, since the word "lovely" has no factual meaning when applied to the tree. It is so purely connotative of the observer's strong esthetic pleasure that we cannot put it more neutrally that as simple information about the speaker himself ("the tree I *find* most beautiful") or perhaps as information about a class of observers sharing the same emotion ("the tree which *many people find* most beautiful").

Since so much force is lost when the connotations of words are eliminated, you can see how much force you can gain through connotations well chosen. Finding the exact connotative language, in fact, is an act of understanding or uncovering your own feelings about a topic. Will you refer to the speaker's joke as a "jest," a "witticism," a "drollery," or a "crack"? What happens to your image of a college president's house as you variously call it a "mansion," a "manor," a "manse"?

Ultimately connotations will prove more subtle than so far suggested. No word carries a fixed connotation which can be simply measured against the dictionary. The whole context of a word—the surrounding sentence, the writer's tone as already established, the evident audience—refines the emotional content of a word, and needs to be felt as you search for language to define your attitude. Thus many writers will work through second and even third drafts to bring all forces into the most exact balance.

Several kinds of vocabulary book can help in lining up your choice of words. A college desk dictionary will give a general treatment of a word. Thus *The American Heritage Dictionary* (2nd College Edition 1982) would give you this entry for "jest":

> **jest** (jĕst) *n.* **1.** Something said or done to provoke amusement and laughter. **2.** A frolicsome attitude or mood: *spoken in jest.* **3.** A jeering remark; taunt. **4.** An object of ridicule; laughingstock. —*v.* **jest·ed, jest·ing, jests.** —*intr.* **1.** To act or speak playfully. **2.** To make witty or amusing remarks. **3.** To utter scoffs; gibe. —*tr.* To make fun of; ridicule. [ME *geste,* tale < OFr. < Lat. *gesta,* deeds < *gerere,* to perform.]

Cross-references to synonyms are sometimes given and sometimes omitted, depending on the dictionary. If you were to shop around for probable synonyms, *The American Heritage Dictionary* would yield this much more, under "joke":

> **joke** (jōk) *n.* **1.** A brief, amusing story, esp. one with a punch line. **2.** An amusing or jesting remark; pun. **3.** A mischievous trick; prank. **4.** An amusing or ludicrous incident or situation. **5.** Something not to be taken seriously; triviality: *His accident was no joke.* **6.** An object of amusement or laughter; laughingstock. —*v.* **joked, jok·ing, jokes.** —*intr.* **1.** To tell or play jokes; jest. **2.** To speak in fun; be facetious. —*tr.* To make fun of; tease. [Lat. *jocus.*] —**jok'ing·ly** *adv.*
>
> **Synonyms:** *joke, jest, witticism, quip, sally, crack, wisecrack, gag.* These nouns refer to forms of humorous sayings or actions. *Joke* and *jest,* which can denote something said or done, are approximately interchangeable, though *jest* now occurs infrequently in this sense. *Witticism* refers to verbal humor, usually with an intellectual flavor and neatly phrased. *Quip* suggests a light, pointed, bantering remark, and *sally* a sudden, clever, or witty statement. *Crack* and *wisecrack* refer less formally to flippant or mocking retorts or to impromptu remarks in response to a specific situation. *Gag* is principally applicable to a broadly comic remark or, less often, to comic by-play in a theatrical routine.

If you prefer simply to get a long list of leads, you can take a thesaurus, such as *Roget's International Thesaurus,* and use the index under "jest" or "joke" to get to the most relevant word list; but note that the following entry (from the 4th edition, published by Thomas Crowell, 1977) neither defines the synonyms nor distinguishes them. You would still need to check its suggestions against a dictionary.

881. WIT, HUMOR

.1 NOUNS **wit, humor,** pleasantry, *esprit* [Fr], salt, spice *or* savor of wit; Attic wit *or* salt, Atticism; ready wit, quick wit, nimble wit, agile wit, pretty wit; dry wit, subtle wit; **comedy** 611.6; black humor, sick humor, gallows humor; satire, sarcasm, irony; parody, lampoon, travesty, caricature, burlesque, squib; farce, mere farce; slapstick, slapstick humor, broad humor; visual humor.

.2 **wittiness, humorousness, funniness; facetiousness,** pleasantry, **jocularity,** jocoseness, jocosity; **joking,** joshing [informal]; smartness, cleverness, brilliance; pungency, saltiness; keenness, sharpness; keen-wittedness, quick-wittedness, nimble-wittedness.

.3 **drollery, drollness; whimsicality,** whimsicalness, humorsomeness, antic wit.

.4 **waggishness, waggery;** roguishness 738.2; **playfulness,** sportiveness, **levity, frivolity,** flippancy, merriment 870.5; **prankishness,** pranksomeness; trickery, trickiness, trickiness, trickishness.

.5 **buffoonery,** buffoonism, clownery, harlequinade; **clownishness,** buffoonishness; **foolery,** fooling, **tomfoolery;** horseplay; shenanigans *or* monkeyshines [both informal]; **banter** 882.

.6 **joke, jest, gag** [informal], **wheeze,** jape; **fun, sport, play;** story, yarn, **funny story,** good story; dirty story *or* joke, blue story *or* joke, *double entendre* [Fr]; shaggy-dog story; sick joke [informal]; ethnic joke; capital joke, good one, laugh, belly laugh, rib tickler, sidesplitter, howler, wow, scream, riot, panic; visual joke, sight gag [informal]; **point,** cream of the jest; jestbook.

.7 **witticism,** pleasantry, *plaisanterie, boutade* [both Fr]; **play of wit,** *jeu d'esprit* [Fr]; **crack** *or* smart crack *or* **wisecrack** [all informal]; **quip,** conceit, bright *or* happy thought, bright *or* brilliant idea; **mot, bon mot,** smart saying, stroke of wit; epigram, turn of thought, aphorism, apothegm; flash of wit, scintillation; **sally,** flight of wit; **repartee,** retort, riposte, snappy comeback [slang]; facetiae [pl], quips and cranks; **gibe, dirty** *or* **nasty crack** [informal]; persiflage 882.1.

.8 **wordplay, play on words,** *jeu de mots* [Fr], missaying, corruption, paronomasia, *calembour* [Fr], abuse of terms; **pun,** punning; equivoque, equivocality; ana-

gram, logogram, logograph, metagram; acrostic, double acrostic; amphiboly, amphibologism; palindrome; spoonerism; malapropism.

.9 **old joke,** old wheeze, old turkey, **trite joke,** hoary-headed joke, joke with whiskers; **chestnut** *or* corn *or* **corny joke** *or* oldie [all slang]; Joe Miller, Joe Millerism; twice-told tale, retold story, warmed-over cabbage [informal].

.10 **prank, trick, practical joke,** waggish trick, *espièglerie* [Fr], antic, caper, frolic; **monkeyshines** *or* **shenanigans** [both slang].

.11 **sense of humor, risibility,** funny bone.

.12 **humorist, wit, funnyman, comic,** *bel-esprit* [Fr], life of the party; **joker,** jokester, gagman [informal], **jester, quipster, wisecracker** *or* gagster [both informal]; wag, wagwit; zany, madcap, cutup [slang]; **prankster; comedian,** banana [slang]; **clown** 612.10; punster, punner; epigrammatist; satirist, ironist; burlesquer, caricaturist, parodist, lampooner; reparteeist; witling; gag writer [slang], jokesmith.

.13 VERBS **joke, jest, wisecrack** *or* **crack wise** [both informal], utter a mot, **quip,** jape, josh [informal], fun [informal], make fun, **kid** *or* **kid around** [both informal]; **make a funny** [informal]; **crack a joke,** get off a joke, tell a good story; pun, play on words; scintillate, sparkle; **make fun of,** gibe at, fleer at, mock, scoff at, poke fun at, make the butt of one's humor, be merry with; ridicule 967.8–11.

.14 **trick, play a practical joke,** play tricks *or* pranks, **play a joke** *or* **trick on,** make merry with; pull one's leg, put one on [slang].

.15 ADJS **witty,** *spirituel* [Fr]; **humorous, funny; jocular,** joky [informal], **joking, jesting, jocose; facetious,** joshing [informal], **whimsical, droll,** humorsome; smart, clever, brilliant, scintillating, sparkling, sprightly; keen, sharp, rapier-like; pungent, pointed, biting, mordant; salty, salt, Attic; keen-witted, quick-witted, nimble-witted.

.16 **clownish,** buffoonish.

.17 **waggish;** roguish 738.6; **playful, sportive; prankish,** pranky, pranksome; tricky, trickish, tricksy.

.18 ADVS **wittily, humorously; jocularly,** jocosely; **facetiously;** whimsically, drolly.

.19 **in fun, in sport, in play, in jest,** in joke, as a joke, jokingly, jestingly, with tongue in cheek; for fun, for sport.

Probably the fullest discrimination of synonyms is to be found in a synonym dictionary like *Webster's New Dictionary of Synonyms* (1978) in which you would locate this discussion:

joke, jest, jape, quip, witticism, wisecrack, crack, gag are comparable when they mean a remark, story, or action intended to evoke laughter. **Joke,** when applied to a story or remark, suggests something designed to promote good humor and especially an anecdote with a humorous twist at the end; when applied to an action, it often signifies a practical joke, usually suggesting a fooling or deceiving of someone at his expense, generally though not necessarily good humored in intent ⟨everyone knows the old *joke,* that "black horses eat more than white horses," a puzzling condition which is finally cleared up by the statement that "there are more black horses"—*Reilly*⟩ ⟨issues had become a hopeless muddle and national politics a biennial *joke—Wecter*⟩ ⟨a child hiding mother's pocketbook as a *joke*⟩ ⟨the whole tale turns out to be a monstrous *joke,* a deception of matchless cruelty—*Redman*⟩ **Jest** may connote raillery or ridicule but more generally suggests humor that is light and sportive ⟨continually . . . making a *jest* of his ignorance—*J. D. Beresford*⟩ ⟨won fame by *jests* at the foibles of his time, but . . . his pen was more playful than caustic—*Williams & Pollard*⟩ **Jape** is identical with *jest* or *joke* ⟨the merry *japes* of fundamentally irresponsible young men—*Edmund Fuller*⟩ ⟨the *japes* about sex still strike me as being prurient rather than funny—*McCarten*⟩ **Quip** suggests a quick, neatly turned, witty remark ⟨full of wise saws and homely illustrations, the epigram, the *quip,* the jest—*Cardozo*⟩ ⟨many *quips* at the expense of individuals and their villages—*Mead*⟩ ⟨enlivened their reviews with *quips—Dunham*⟩ **Witticism, wisecrack,** and **crack** all apply to a clever or witty, especially a biting or sarcastic, remark, generally serving as a retort ⟨all the charming *witticisms* of English lecturers—*Sevareid*⟩ ⟨a vicious *witticism* at the expense of a political opponent⟩ ⟨merely strolls by, makes a goofy *wisecrack* or screwball suggestion —*Hugh Humphrey*⟩ ⟨though the gravity of the situation forbade their utterance, I was thinking of at least three priceless *cracks* I could make—*Wodehouse*⟩ **Gag,** which in this relation basically signifies an interpolated joke or laugh-provoking piece of business, more generally applies to a remark, story, or piece of business considered funny, especially one written into a theatrical, movie, radio, or television script. Sometimes the word has extended its meaning to signify a trick whether funny or not but usually one considered foolish ⟨*gags* grown venerable in the service of the music halls—*Times Lit. Sup.*⟩ ⟨the *gag* was not meant to be entirely funny—*Newsweek*⟩ ⟨gave a party the other night and pulled a really constructive *gag* . . . had every guest in the place vaccinated against smallpox—*Hollywood Reporter*⟩ ⟨a frivolous person, given to *gags* and foolishness⟩
Ana *prank, caper, antic, monkeyshine, dido: *trick, ruse, wile: travesty, parody, burlesque, *caricature: raillery, *badinage, persiflage: jocoseness, jocularity, facetiousness, wittiness, humorousness (see corresponding adjectives at WITTY): *wit, humor, repartee, sarcasm

If, after all this casting around, you find yourself in Flaubert's famous agony over the *mot juste,* you might scribble in the three or four best synonyms and let the choice wait for a while.

Exercise 1 (connotations of approval and disapproval)

Decide whether each term connotes approval or disapproval. Then supply another term conveying the same factual information but the opposite connotation. Finally, suggest a third term which conveys the same factual information neutrally. (A term may include more than one word if necessary.)

> SAMPLE SOLUTION: womanly (favorable); womanish (unfavorable); female (neutral).

a. Belly
b. Phony
c. To sneak away
d. An antique (piece of furniture)
e. Staunch advocate
f. To flatter
g. Lousy
h. naked
i. Outlandish
j. Childish
k. Whore
l. Frank
m. Stingy
n. Din
o. Dictator

Exercise 2 (connotations of approval and disapproval)

Which terms in each passage most clearly connote approval or disapproval, and how do they do so?

> a. (*The author is describing the furnishings of an English country house owned by the Brigstock family.*) It was an ugliness fundamental and systematic, the result of the abnormal nature of the Brigstocks, from whose composition the principle of taste had been extravagantly omitted. . . . The house was bad in all conscience, but it might have passed if they had only let it alone. This saving mercy was beyond them; they had smothered it with trumpery ornament and scrapbook art, with strange excrescences and bunchy draperies, with gimcracks that might have been keepsakes for maid-servants and nondescript conveniences that might have been prizes for the blind. They had gone wildly astray over carpets and curtains; they had an infallible instinct for disaster, and were so cruelly doom-ridden that it rendered them almost tragic. . . . The house was perversely full of souvenirs of places even more ugly than itself

and of things it would have been a pious duty to forget. (Henry James, *The Spoils of Poynton*, 1897)

b. Fanny was now in the nineteenth year of her age; she was tall and delicately shaped; but not one of those slender young women, who seem rather intended to hang up in the hall of an anatomist than for any other purpose. On the contrary, she was so plump, that she seemed bursting through her tight stays, especially in the part which confined her swelling breasts. Nor did her hips want the assistance of a hoop to extend them. The exact shape of her arms denoted the form of those limbs which she concealed; and though they were a little reddened by her labour, yet if her sleeve slipped above her elbow, or her hand-kerchief discovered any part of her neck, a whiteness appeared which the finest Italian paint would be unable to reach. Her hair was of a chestnut brown, and nature had been extremely lavish to her of it, which she had cut, and on Sundays used to curl down her neck in the modern fashion. Her forehead was high, her eyebrows arched, and rather full than otherwise. Her eyes black and sparkling; her nose just inclining to the Roman; her lips red and moist. . . . Her complexion was fair, a little in-jured by the sun, but overspread with such a bloom, that the finest ladies would have exchanged all their white for it: add to these, a countenance in which, though she was extremely bash-ful, a sensibility appeared almost incredible; and a sweetness, whenever she smiled, beyond either imitation or description. (Henry Fielding, *Joseph Andrews*, 1742)

Exercise 3 (connotations of approval and disapproval)

Rewrite passage *b* under Exercise 2 to produce the *opposite* connotation.

Exercise 4 (connotations of approval and disapproval—imitation)

Scramble your solution to Exercise 3, using the method described in Chapter 6; then re-synthesize it to produce the *original* connotation. Compare your solution with the original to write a brief analysis of the differences and their effect.

Exercise 5 (connotations of approval and disapproval)

Write two versions of the following editorial, the first to connote strong ap-proval of the proposed Hospital for Adolescents, the second to connote strong disapproval. This is primarily an exercise in vocabulary substitution. The *facts* should not be changed, added to, or suppressed; but sentence structure and general phrasing may be modified as necessary. "Magnifiers," "minifiers," and "nudgers" may be used at your discretion. (In its present neutral form, the editorial obviously lacks force either way.)

> In urging the voters of this city to (endorse, defeat) the up-coming referendum to create a Hospital for Adolescents, we point first of all to the newness of the concept. No other city in this region has such a hospital. The proposal exhibits con-spicuous forwardness in public medicine. The publicity to at-tend such a project would have an extraordinary impact on the city image.
>
> Second, consider our need for a medical center exclusively directed to the treatment of adolescents. Young people are known to have problems of their own, unlike those of childhood, adulthood, or old age. One should consider whether they should have special attention. When our young people see how far we're ready to go, the whole morale of this city would change.
>
> The soundness of this Hospital project is further indicated by the qualifications of its designer, champion, and probable future director, Dr. Jeremiah Rodkin. His service as Assistant Director of the City General Hospital shows the degree of his familiarity with city medical administration. Dr. Rodkin is a graduate of West Bristol Medical Institute and a practicing orthopedist. As the father of two adolescent children, he has reason to urge a special facility for adolescent care.
>
> The proposed cost of $30,000,000 falls within the limits of recent City budgets. If this cost is compared with the social loss now caused by adolescent disorders, the value of the project as an investment will be verified by next Tuesday's voters.

Exercise 6 (other connotations)

Neutralize any of the following selections, replacing each connotative expres-sion with as purely objective a term as possible:

> a. In the deserted, moon-blanched street,
> How lonely rings the echo of my feet!
> Those windows, which I gaze at, frown,
> Silent and white, unopening down,
> Repellent as the world; but see,
> A break between the housetops shows
> The moon! and, lost behind her, fading dim
> Into the dewy dark obscurity
> Down at the far horizon's rim,
> Doth a whole tract of heaven disclose!
>
> (Matthew Arnold, "A Summer Night," 1852)

b. SEEN IN SOME OF THE BEST PLACES

Year after year the rich and famous return to St. Moritz, Europe's favorite winter playground.

Situated 5400 ft. in sunny Engadin, the heart of the Swiss Alps, this resort offers the challenge of Olympic slopes and a wide variety of other recreation.

After the day's activities, the Chesa Veglia is one of the most popular meeting places.

This charming old building accommodates a restaurant renowned for its ambience, exquisite cuisine and a fine selection of wines and spirits. Naturally, Asbach Uralt, the great brandy from the Rhine, is available to enhance the perfect day.

Special gift offer . . . (magazine advertisement)

c. Any advertisement or passage of poetry or prose which you've recently noticed and which you find intensely connotative. Be sure to include a copy of the original together with your neutralized version.

Exercise 7 (euphemisms)

Test your sugar-coating powers by describing one of the following in the language which a refined and genteel older person might use in writing to a young relative:

a. A picnic brawl in a nearby park.
b. An X-rated movie seen by mistake.
c. The funeral services for the meanest and rottenest person in town.
d. An explosion in the city sewage disposal plant.

Or describe one of the following in the language which an official public relations office of any nation might use in reporting to the press of that nation:

e. The annihilation of an enemy town through overkill bombing.
f. Elimination of aid to needy students as a budget-cutting measure.

Exercise 8 (synonyms)

Each sentence below is followed by a list of synonyms for the italicized word in that sentence. Show how each synonym would shade the meaning of the sentence if it were substituted.

a. Our foremen *examine* each automobile for defects. (inspect, scan, scrutinize)
b. Their quarterback faked his plays with rare *guile*. (cunning, fraudulence, sneakiness)

c. Our relationship appealed mainly to my *animal* appetite. (physical, sensual, carnal)
d. I was *lured* into joining the conspiracy. (enticed, tempted, inveigled, seduced)
e. The audience responded to the new drama with *eagerness*. (alacrity, enthusiasm, zest)
f. Don seems *infatuated* with Laura. (fond of, in love with, ga-ga over)
g. She gained general confidence by her *forthright* manner. (outspoken, blunt, unrestrained, candid)
h. The bearing of the tribesmen throughout the plague could only be described as *stoic*. (cool, apathetic, stolid)

Suggested reading for further illustration, discussion, and writing: Michael J. Arlen, "Ode to Thanksgiving," page 389.

16   The Vocabulary of Intensification

Analogical Language (also called Metaphoric
or Figurative Language)

When the science writer Isaac Asimov compares a collapsing star to a
"punctured balloon," he is using a most powerful tool of thought and
language, the *analogy*, to help us grasp, through familiar terms, the unfamiliar.

Asimov later speaks of the primordial plasma of the universe as the
"cosmic egg"—another analogy or comparison to boost a strange notion
into the comprehensible. The biologist William Albrecht writes of the
microbes in the surface soil serving as "working crews and salvage agencies" in the recycling of wastes. Light-waves are explained by Sir James
Jeans as acting like stirred-up ripples on a pond. Crane Britton built his
major work, *The Anatomy of Revolution,* around the analogy of fever,
showing how revolutions could be understood as following a kind of
fever cycle.

The first use of analogy is to raise an idea to greater visibility, to
greater aliveness to the senses. Just as the electroencephalograph trans-
lates invisible brain waves onto a screen as a dramatically visible graph,
so in language the analogy amplifies the dimly felt idea into a heightened
picture. Analogy serves to vivify not only explanation but argument:

> America is like a student who is proud of having somehow sur-
> vived without serious work, and likes to imagine that if he
> really put any effort into it he could achieve everything, but is
> unwilling to endanger so lovely a dream by making an actual

> commitment to anything. (Philip E. Slater, *The Pursuit of Lone-liness*, 1970)

The mere assertion that "America is gifted but immature and uncommitted" has been projected into the all-too-human sketch of an underachieving student.

The next illustration brings us a step further:

> She looked at him as if he were a rotten apple on which she had trodden unexpectedly. (Pamela Hansford Johnson, *The Unspeakable Skipton*, 1959)

The bare sense of this goes something like "She looked at him with distasteful surprise." But "distasteful surprise" is abstract, not available to eye or ear. A woman just stepping off a rotten apple, however, *dramatizes* the surprise and makes the abstract concrete. This again is the first function of analogy. The analogy also demonstrates a second function, that of accentuating the emotional value of the idea. The rotten apple image reduces the poor victim to comic embarrassment while nicely defining the woman's frigid reserve. Again:

> A nurse who is cynical is like a bartender who drinks.
>
> (Origin unknown)

The image of the alcoholic bartender flashes over the general term "cynical nurse," thus raising its concreteness—the first function of analogy. The image also connotes the frightening acceleration of self-indulgence which could easily destroy a boozy barkeep as well as a nurse who finds in cynicism a cheap escape from the daily sufferings of patients. The whole statement seems much keener than just saying that "nurses cannot afford to be cynical."

Because analogy is a process of *linking experience*, it serves a third function, of relating our present idea with the rest of our experience and knowledge, as we search for connections by which to furnish the idea with its strongest context. Analogy *generates*. It presses us to pull together new and old, strange and familiar, dull and lively. It allows us to *discover* new relationships, to see new possibilities. The process comes so naturally that people use it daily to link up common events with more vigorous experience:

> Why don't you *zip* your lip? (Analogy of zipper.)
> He *rifled* the ball to home plate. (Analogy of shooting.)
> I couldn't *hack* that book. (Analogy of chopping.)

To see how to extend such language to highly individual expression, imagine that you have received a letter saying that Kevin—a very close friend—has come through surgery after facing almost certain death. You could of course say, "The letter made me very happy." But try thinking of all the exhilarating moments you have known which might provide analogies to your present happiness. Comparisons might turn up like these—each varied in image, in connotation, in the kind of experiential connections implied:

> That letter boosted me like an income tax refund.
> It warmed me like the first spring thaw.
> It lifted me like a space rocket bound for orbit.
> The moment I read the letter, the day began to sparkle like a
> sunlit ocean.

From such stabs as these, you could come closer to a genuine realization of the good news.

The process of analogy can generate comparisons in as many ways as one's ingenuity will allow. Scholars have cataloged these ways under numerous technical terms (simile, hyperbole, synecdoche, and so forth) which, though useful in close textual analysis, do not seem essential here. What may help more readily is to note how variously one can conceive an analogy.

Suppose you said, about the good news of Kevin:

> That letter gave me wings for the rest of the day.

Here the analogy comes directly as literal fact. No *as-if* signals are provided; but the full comparison is clear: "I felt *as if I could fly.*" The analogy as literal statement serves as shortcut to many comparisons otherwise laborious:

> She had so many chins she had to put a bookmark on her face
> to find her mouth. (Tom Watts, *Nighthawks at the Diner,*
> 1976)

This comic miniature could be ruined by stretching it into a full explicit comparison:

> Her face with its many chins was like a book with many pages,
> and her mouth was like one hidden page which required a book-
> mark to be located.

More illustrations of the literal analogy:

> The day was to come when our family was so poor that we would eat the hole out of a doughnut. (Malcolm X, *Autobiography*, 1965)

> A lie can travel halfway around the world while the truth is still putting on its shoes. (Attributed to Mark Twain)

The last example also shows the analogical perspective of personification in which things or animals are seen as having human traits. Thus "a lie" and "the truth"—abstract concepts—are made visible through comparison to travelers. Similarly the good news about Kevin might go this way:

> Kevin, alive and grinning, walked out of that letter, took me by the hand, and lifted me up again.

Often the analogy will link the subject to well-known history, news, literature, mythology, and the like, drawing on the overtones of that material:

> Lazarus stepping out of his tomb could hardly have astounded me as did that news of Kevin's miraculous return. (Allusion to New Testament miracle of Lazarus raised from the dead.)

> The surgeon who brought back Kevin must have been a second Christiaan Barnard. (Allusion to famous pioneer in heart-transplant surgery.)

> The President's economic proposals are like re-arranging the deck chairs on the *Titanic*. (Barbara Mikulski, quoted in *Chicago Daily News*, 1974) (Allusion to historic sinking of the ship *Titanic* in 1912.)

Allusions like this unite writers and readers who have a common background in family, school, club, profession, or culture. Such allusions constitute a pleasant in-group language, but used with an audience lacking this common knowledge, they can confuse and irritate. (Suppose the reader has never heard of the *Titanic*?)

Another analogical perspective:

> The letter *was real Kevin*—warm, cheerful, shrewd.

Here one of the subject's attributes or products (Kevin's letter) is expanded dramatically into his whole personality. We could reverse the technique, compacting the subject's whole identity into an attribute or product of that subject:

> Now that Kevin was recovering, we would soon have our dear old *Razor Brain* back in school. (Compaction of Kevin's identity into one attribute, his intelligence.)

Other illustrations:

> Madge opened her eyes very wide, she turned their *blue surprise* straight on me. (William Sansom, 1949) (Expansion of eyes into Madge's total emotional state.)

> Miss Crevy examined *her face* in a mirror out of a bag like any jeweller with a precious stone, and it was indeed without price, but it had its ticket and this had Marriage written on it. (Henry Green, *Party Going,* 1947) (Expansion of face into her whole identity—a complex analogy also including comparison with jeweler and gem.)

This compression of the total subject into a key detail which then stands for it can charge that detail with symbolic and generalizing force, especially over longer passages. Virginia Woolf is describing the British dandy, Beau Brummell:

> Handsome, heartless, and cynical, the Beau seemed invulnerable. His taste was impeccable, his health admirable; and his figure as fine as ever. His rule had lasted many years and survived many vicissitudes. The French Revolution had passed over his head without disordering a single hair. Empires had risen and fallen while he experimented with the crease of a neck-cloth and criticised the cut of a coat. (*Second Common Reader,* 1932)

The "single hair," "the crease of a neck-cloth," "the cut of a coat"—these trivial attributes represent the aristocratic parasite Brummell. Their very triviality when contrasted with the crushing convulsions of European history in which he lived brings out his delicate, cruel inconsequentiality.

When you strike an apt analogy, you may sometimes find that its image radiates through your thought so that you can easily keep the analogy going, both to intensify and—here is a new function not yet stressed—to bind together a passage. If Kevin has been seen as *Razor Brain*, his recovery might extend the image:

> Old *Razor Brain* had survived another *close shave.*

The term *analogical style* could well be used for such writing. Though it can be distractingly overdone, analogical style when used fittingly can bring wit and point to an abstract subject. In the following example, a newspaper editorial is attacking a state governor, using an old nursery-tale allusion:

> Governor Terry was merely crying wolf when he mobilized the National Guard last week over an "emergency" which he could

easily have solved on his own. But he cried wolf so loud that the wolves heard it. We have no doubt that Governor Terry is the most astonished politician in the United States as he contemplates the pack of troubles he called up. They surround him as far as he can see, sitting patiently with their tongues hanging out and their teeth showing, waiting to see what he will do.

The wolf terms ("cried wolf," "pack of troubles," "tongues hanging out," "teeth showing") provide an additional, metaphoric unity to the whole piece. In poetry, fiction, and drama, a recurring metaphor or cluster of metaphors often does tighten and intensify the literary work—thus the metaphors of disease which run through *Hamlet* subtly reinforcing the central theme of a "rotten Denmark." (The use of analogy as a basic development pattern for longer compositions has been touched upon in Chapter 7, page 84.)

All analogical language uses a certain exaggeration to stress the writer's excitement, but it should never use that exaggeration falsely, to suggest an excitement *not* true to the implicit vision of the writer. A reference to "darling little daisies, nodding blissfully in the breeze" must falsify both the writer's reaction, by claiming an affection for the daisies which can hardly be felt, and the subject, by assigning to the daisies emotions which no adult normally imagines them to feel. To this second misrepresentation, that of attributing emotions to nature, is given the term *pathetic fallacy* (literally, error in conception of feelings). A misguided enthusiasm for personification often produces it in adolescent writing. The skies "weep," the wind "groans," "teardrops" run down the windowpanes. Of course, some impressionable children and certain overwrought adults might actually see nature like this; or a writer might legitimately be conceiving a fantasy in which plants and animals take human roles—then personification could properly be used to present their consciousness or conception.

Shock Effects

The other large source of vocabulary intensification is the shock effect rising from some clash of content or overtone. The clash, of course, ought to be efficient and not random, as in this lurid old specimen of mixed figures:

> Mr. Speaker, I smell a rat. I see it forming in the air and darkening in the sky. Unless we nip it in the bud, there will be a conflagration which will flood the entire country!

The unfortunate rat goes through enough metamorphosis (storm cloud, bud, fire, flood) to bewilder any serious reader. Another illustration, this time involving not a clash of content but one of connotation:

> In a truly heroic recital, the great pianist blasted off with Haydn's Sonata No. 5 in C Major.

The "blast off" metaphor from space rocketry connotes a ponderous violence hardly appropriate to Haydn's polished music.

But mixed images can pinpoint an unusual valuation:

> I no longer glanced at the newspapers each morning, for I knew the state of the world. Doubtless another toothpaste had been exploded in the stratosphere; another Miss Universe had been crowned by the United Nations.

This fusing of the toothpaste ad with the nuclear bomb test, of the beauty contest with the UN, might eloquently reflect the fragmented vision of the daily press, in which trivia and holocausts are scrambled together. Connotations too may clash by way of nice emphasis:

> Every day Professor Jenkins would measure out to us so many grains of yellowed wisdom from his crumbling lecture notes.

The pharmaceutical precision of "measuring out grains" clashes with the senile slovenliness of "crumbling lecture notes," thus exposing the professor's incompetence.

A similar clash arises from a deliberate contradiction of terms, as in "splendid failure," "affectionate hatred," "an immense little fib." Such a yoking of contraries reminds one that the extreme of any experience often resembles in some way its opposite; thus an observant contradiction can point up extreme states, as in these examples:

> [Irene Worth's performance as Hedda Gabbler] is a compassionately balanced mood-portrait of modern woman: *boredom* at the level of *panic*, a *yawn* that comes out a *scream*. (*Time*, 1970)

> Her *absence* was a tremendous *presence* to him. (Richard Stern, *Other Men's Daughters*, 1973)

Understatement provides a subtler clash in which a point is made indirectly by negating its opposite. Thus, instead of "I rushed forward," "I did not hold back." Other examples:

> On coming into political office, *he was not idle* in rewarding his friends.

> Despite his grief, *he did not neglect* to check the telephone coin box on his way out.

A final shock effect involves not a clash so much as a fusion, as when a key term occurs to you in two different senses simultaneously, in a kind of pun:

> A *puppy* love is often the prelude to a *dog's* life.
>
> The essence of hospitality is to make your guest feel *at home* even though you wish he were.
>
> My boy friend put *two and two* together, and got my *number*. (Robert Mines, 1958)
>
> Fish and visitors *smell* in three days. (Benjamin Franklin, 1736)
>
> Senator Jenkins *has the best mind* in Congress until he *makes it up*.
>
> The man who thinks by the inch but talks by the yard deserves to be kicked by the *foot*.

Such puns fly far above the crude substitution of nonsense which happens to sound like the intended meaning. (For example: "*Orange juice* sorry you left me?") Sense—at least possible sense—is kept at both levels. You may have noticed some gems of it in lavatory graffiti:

> Molesting minors is child's play.
>
> Some people carve careers—others chisel them.
>
> Xerox never comes up with anything original.
>
> (All from *The Encyclopedia of Graffiti*, 1975)

The witty pun is perhaps too consciously clever to be sought for often, and when it falls flat it just lies there in plain sight; but an occasional flash of it comes naturally to a lively sense of humor.

In finding the vocabulary of intensification, you'll almost always be working at the same time for a sentence structure of intensification. The next three chapters are addressed to this end.

A postscript on *dead metaphors*. When analogical language finds its way into long common usage, its figurative sense fades out. Who thinks of a "meadow" in speaking of "the *field* of economics"? Or of a winged creature on hearing that "time *flies*"? For such language the considerations for using analogy disappear except when the user unwittingly revives the metaphor, as in "I haven't *settled* on a *walk* of life" or "*Running* for office was *duck soup* for Mayor Gould." Such gratuitous disharmonies fail to intensify what is said, and may actually distract.

Exercise 1 (analogical language)

For each example, first show what is being compared to what. Then restate the meaning in direct literal language, to show that you understand the sense of the analogy. Finally, explain why you find the analogy to be effective or ineffective. (Keep in mind the main functions of analogy: to put an idea into more concrete terms; to intensify connotation; to unify.)

SAMPLE His acquaintances see him as the man who lights up a room when he leaves it.

SOLUTION The "man" is being compared to a cause of darkness. *Restated literally:* His acquaintances see him as the man whose departure from a gathering is a relief. *Evaluation:* The analogy seems effective because of its shock—the man lights up a room *not* by entering it (as one would expect) but by leaving. A climax is achieved by delaying the reversal until the end of the sentence.

a. The small animalcules swam gently among one another, and moved after the fashion of gnats in air. (Microscope observation of bacteria in rainwater; Antony van Leeuwenhoek, 1632–1723)

b. Let's stop running around like chickens with our heads in the sand.

c. After a perfunctory attempt to fit him into their prim, grey jigsaw puzzle they had disliked and rejected him. (John Wain, *Hurry On Down*, 1953)

d. The fiery eye of the sun transfixed the guilty man with a withering gaze.

e. This interpretation of Hamlet's madness adds meat to the very foundation of the play.

f. What the caterpillar calls the end of the world, the master calls a butterfly. (Richard Bach, *Illusions*, 1977)

g. Drop-kick me, Jesus, through the goal posts of life. (Bobby Bare, contemporary country song)

h. He's always sticking his oar into the conversation before it gets off the ground.

i. My language is the universal whore whom I have to make into a virgin. (Karl Kraus)

j. Life is like a pinball machine—we are little balls shot out through an alley, kicked around from place to place, sometimes ringing a bell or flashing a light, and eventually falling into a trough and rolling out of sight. (Weller Embler, *Metaphor and Meaning*, 1966)

k. If [Senator Jackson] ever gave a fireside chat, the fire would go out. (Source uncertain)

l. Our foreign initiative seems pinned down by the quicksands of indecision.

m. I throw caution to the winds when there isn't a breeze. (Joseph Heller, *Something Happened*, 1974)

n. Living had turned up so many bad cards for her that she was refusing any more deals. She was withdrawing and lying down. (David Storey, *This Sporting Life*, 1960)

o. The mayor's efforts to help the flood victims were smothered by a swamp of red tape.

p. Too many people now climb onto the cross merely to be seen from a greater distance. (Albert Camus, *The Fall*, 1956)

q. The languid willow with its tresses waving bent to the affectionate wind, which whispered of lonely lovers and mellowed sorrows of long ago.

Exercise 2 (analogical language)

Recast each of the following statements at least twice, using a different analogy each time.

SAMPLE I was hungry.

SOLUTION My stomach was audibly declaring itself a disaster area.
To me that peanut butter sandwich looked like filet mignon.
I cut such a swath through the menu that the waiter must still be mumbling about it.

a. Lennie was a bit on the stupid side.
b. Senator Krug won the election coming from behind.
c. A scientific discovery advances the whole human race.
d. Most people seem to be secretly afraid.
e. Any problem is also an opportunity.
f. Our city politicians are crooked.
g. I wanted to give him (her) something special.

Exercise 3 (analogical language)

Choose either *a* or *b* below. First write a page of literal prose (with no analogies) to develop your topic clearly with supporting detail. Then write a new version involving analogical language to optimum effect in heightening concreteness, connotations, unity.

a. A stiff attack on the way "they" are managing a given problem (e.g., academic advising, parking, unemployment, nuclear energy, foreign relations).

b. A personal experience with strong emotion but little physical action (e.g., praying, lying sleepless, visiting a funeral home, suddenly seeing a person in a new light).

Exercise 4 (analogical language—imitation)

The following passage from *Lucky Jim* by Kingsley Amis (1954) describes the hero awaking with a terrible hangover:

> Dixon was alive again. Consciousness was upon him before he could get out of the way; not for him the slow, gracious wandering from the halls of sleep, but a summary, forcible ejection. He lay sprawled, too wicked to move, spewed up like a broken spider crab on the tarry shingle of the morning. The light did him harm, but not as much as looking at things did; he resolved, having done it once, never to move his eyeballs again. A dusty thudding in his head made the scene before him beat like a pulse. His mouth had been used as a latrine by some small creature of the night, and then as its mausoleum. During the night, too, he'd somehow been on a cross-country run and then been expertly beaten up by secret police. He felt bad.

Imitate its analogical technique in a comic description of one of the following (using the adaptation of techniques method described in Chapter 6):

a. Someone seized with stomach flu.
b. A romantic adolescent in the throes of first love.
c. The unfortunate winner of a pie-eating (or beer-drinking) contest.
d. A student emerging from a grueling final examination.

Exercise 5 (shock effects)

Clashing metaphors can produce nonsense, or they can produce an unexpected shock of meaning. Write a sensible sentence or two about each topic below, as instructed. (The fields for comparison have deliberately been made grossly incongruous, as a challenge.)

	USING A CLASHING
SAY SOMETHING ABOUT—	METAPHOR FROM—
SAMPLE A bombing raid.	Suburban commuters.

SOLUTION The bombers arrived over Berlin promptly at 8:56 A.M., their commuter run having become a routine they neither feared nor welcomed.

a. A horrible bore	A volcanic eruption
b. A scientist	A rat in a maze
c. Football game	Ballet
d. The "life of the party"	Rodeo rider
e. A disaster-prone person	Computer technology
f. (Make up your own.)	(Make up your own.)
g. (Make up your own.)	(Make up your own.)

Suggested reading for further illustration, discussion, and writing: Suzanne Britt Jordan, "Marriage Is Better," page 393.

17 The Sentence I: Basic Building

A clear sentence is no accident. Very few sentences come out right the first time. Keep thinking and rewriting until you say what you want to say.

WILLIAM ZINSSER, *On Writing Well*, 1980

The most remarkable truth, and the easiest one to forget, is that native speakers of English already have a well-developed sentence sense.

HARVEY WIENER, *The Writing Room*, 1981

The vocabulary choices of the preceding four chapters furnish the *substance* of your outlook. The process of creating *order* in it really starts as soon as your consciousness begins to work on a given topic, becoming fully active as your sentences emerge on paper.

How Sentences Work

The English sentence is extremely plastic. It can be enlarged, combined, adjusted with almost any degree of fineness to accommodate a writer's thought, as can be shown through a review of its operating parts. (Formal grammatical terms have been squeezed to a minimum in the following review. The terms NOUN, SUBJECT, and VERB are taken for granted as part of almost everyone's working vocabulary. Other essential terms, also introduced in capitals, will be largely explained by example or by context.)

At the center of most sentences is a CLAUSE. That clause consists, in its normal order, of a SUBJECT (to be diagrammed below as S), a VERB (V), and whatever COMPLEMENT (C) or additional element the subject and verb require to attain minimal grammatical completeness. Such clauses are found in four main types, as illustrated below:

	s	v	c	
	Cecil	slept.		(Clause is complete as it stands.)

Cecil fed   the aardvark. (The verb acts upon something, the aardvark.)

Dick is   a student.   (The verb connects the subject "Dick" with an identifier, "student.")

Jane is   tired.   (The verb connects the subject "Jane" with a word describing her condition.)

Into this core structure (s-v-c) you can insert other clauses as subjects or complements:

> *That the aardvark had arrived* surprised nobody. (clause as sub-
>   s   v   c
> ject)

> Cecil had known *that it would come.* (clause as complement)
>   s   v   c

Since the powers of sentence structure will soon unfold with geometric rapidity, we may do well to move into exercises as we go, step by step.

Exercise 1 (combining clauses)

Already we can combine clauses by making one serve as part of another. For each pair below, construct a main clause which uses the other clause as its subject or complement.

SAMPLE 1) I had been sick.
               s   v   c
        2) Henry knew that.
               s   v   c

SOLUTION   Henry knew *that I had been sick.*
               s   v   c

a. 1) Everyone heard the news.
   2) Doris got her promotion.
b. 1) The promoters were afraid.
   2) The rain would spoil the race.
c. 1) The boss could not understand it.
   2) I made the sale.
d. 1) Was the waitress angry?
   2) Nobody could tell.

Basic s-v-c structure can be expanded in two other ways: by CO-ORDINATION and by MODIFICATION.

In coordination you can attach, to any element of a sentence, another element (or more) having the same grammatical value. You can thus have two or more subjects (s&s-v-c), two or more verbs (s-v&v-c), two or more complements (s-v-c&c). Examples:

> *Cecil and Henry* fed the aardvark. (subject expanded)
> Cecil *groomed and fed* the aardvark. (verb expanded)
> Cecil fed *the aardvark, the giraffe, and the elephant.* (complement expanded)

Coordinate elements are usually linked by such connectives as *and, or, either . . . or, neither . . . nor.* The additional connectives *but, for, so,* and *yet* can show that the elements, though of equal stress, are related by contrast or by cause-and-effect:

> Cecil *fed* the aardvark *but forgot* the elephant.
>   v   v

For a series of three elements or more, the connective may appear only before the last item ("the aardvark, the giraffe, *and* the elephant") and may even be omitted. For elements describing a noun, sometimes only a comma is used ("the pampered, stupid, overfed aardvark") and, if the elements are short without possible confusion, no comma at all ("the tall red aardvark").

You can use coordination to expand elements of almost any grammatical type: nouns, verbs, even whole clauses or sentences:

> Henry fed the giraffe. Cecil fed the aardvark. (sentences unrelated)
> Henry fed the giraffe, *and* Cecil fed the aardvark. (sentences joined in coordination)

You can coordinate PREPOSITIONS ("government *of, by,* and *for* the people"). You can also coordinate PHRASES (a phrase being a group of words without a subject *and* verb which serve a single function within the sentence):

> The aardvark *liked to eat   fried green bananas,*
>   (v phrase)   (noun phrase as c)   +
> *poached celery,* and   *cold smoked oysters.*
> (noun phrase as c)   +   (noun phrase as c)

A special type of coordination is APPOSITION, in which the added element is *not* a new item; rather, it simply explains or identifies the item already there:

Cecil, *the hired man,* fed the aardvark. ("The hired man" is said to be *in apposition* to "Cecil.")

My uncle Cecil fed the aardvark.

Exercise 2 (expanding sentences by coordination)

Expand each sentence by adding two or more coordinate elements having the same grammatical function as the italicized element. (Do aim for better sense than aardvarks and Cecil.)

SAMPLE I loved *the cool evenings.* (Noun phrase as complement)

SOLUTION I loved *the cool evenings, the quiet nights,* and *the waking sounds of dawn.*

WRONG
SOLUTION I loved *the cool evenings,* with *the fireplace blazing,* and *its logs hissing.* (A nice sentence in itself, but the added phrases are *not* coordinate as asked for. As a test, coordinate elements can usually be transposed; these cannot, because they are *subordinate*—a possibility to be covered next.)

a. *Karen* likes hot chocolate in mid-evening.
b. I could never figure out *what got Douglas through college.*
c. Properly used, drugs can help people *to combat sickness.*
d. The company was ruined *by quick profit-taking.*
e. *Dolly,* are you going to the game tomorrow?
f. *Walking,* the soldiers retreated from the bombed village.
g. Marie, *the oldest girl,* took charge of the bus.

The other way of expanding the basic sentence is by MODIFICA-TION. You can enlarge any element of a sentence by supplying additional information which amplifies it. The element being amplified is often called the HEADWORD; the amplifying term is the MODIFIER. In the examples to follow, the modifiers are circled and joined by arrows to their headwords:

Cecil fed the (red) aardvark.

Cecil (slowly) fed the aardvark.

Note that the modifier "red" and the headword "aardvark" are *not* co-ordinate terms of the same series like "Cecil and Henry" or "red and black." The headword *is* the headword because it is grammatically the more important: it has to be there first in order to receive the modifier. The modifier merely contributes to it, and that contributor relationship is called SUBORDINATION. The fact of subordination can usually be confirmed by a simple test: Whatever can be omitted without breaking sentence structure—*that* is the modifier.

> Cecil fed the _____ aardvark. (Modifier is omitted; the sentence remains whole.)
>
> Cecil fed the red _____. (Headword is omitted; the sentence is broken.)

Modifiers can be single words. They can also be PHRASES.

> Cecil fed the aardvark (every single evening.)
>
> Cecil fed the aardvark (with the double-jointed tail.)

Phrases can modify other phrases, to produce chains of much complexity:

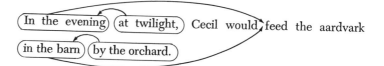

> (In the evening) (at twilight,) Cecil would feed the aardvark (in the barn) (by the orchard.)

Notice that "at twilight" modifies the headword "evening" which is part of the next higher modifier, "in the evening." That phrase in turn modifies "would feed," the main-clause verb.

Modifiers can be whole clauses. Modifying clauses are usually joined to the main clause by a subordinating connective such as *after, although, as, because, if, since, that, unless, when, where, which, who.*

> Cecil, (who had long yearned for this chance,) fed the aardvark.
>
> (As soon as twilight fell,) Cecil would feed the aardvark.

Clause modifiers, like phrase modifiers, can form chains:

> (When he came to the barn) (where the aardvark was stalled,) Cecil entered in great excitement.

A special type of modifier called an ABSOLUTE (i.e., an independent modifier) can be thought of as modifying the sentence as a whole, without subordination to any single headword in it. Note that absolute modifiers are always set off from the rest of the sentence by commas and have no words connecting them to the sentence.

(Cecil,) will you please feed the aardvark? (word of address as an absolute)

(No,) it's not time yet. (negative reply as an absolute)

Cecil, (his lungs straining from the effort,) fed the aardvark. (phrase as an absolute)

(The aardvark fed at last,) Cecil went to the ballet. (phrase as an absolute)

Exercise 3 (expanding sentences by subordination)

Expand each sentence by adding two or more modifiers for each italicized element. You may chain modifiers as you wish, and you may insert them in the sentence wherever seems natural. If you like, go for real length by extending the sentence up to half a page without padding, clumsiness, or nonsense.

SAMPLE I loved *the cool evenings*.

SOLUTION I loved the cool evenings, *with the fireplace blazing*, and *its logs hissing*. (Note that this solution, which had been called "wrong" as a demonstration of coordination, is now perfectly acceptable as a demonstration of subordination.)

    a. Harry *hurried* to the hospital. (Note: You could amplify by showing when Harry hurried, how, why, or in spite of what.)
    b. By saving every *penny*, Molly managed to send her daughter to *college*.
    c. We're interested in buying *the house*.
    d. *The company* has decided to hire eight hundred *technicians*.
    e. Our time of history is *unique*.
    f. The city was *starting to bustle*.

Sentence Variety

Besides expanding a sentence in these ways, you can vary its order and length, thus finding numerous ways of moving key ideas into more emphatic positions.

You invert a sentence by placing into a lead position an element which usually comes later, as when you place the complement before the verb:

That car I'll buy. (c-s-v instead of the normal s-v-c)

What she was really like, I'll never know.

Whatever each man can separately do, without trespassing upon others, he has a right to do for himself. (Edmund Burke, 1790)

(The sentence in normal order would go like this: Each man
has a right to do for himself *whatever he can separately do*
without trespassing upon others.)

Or you can precede a headword with the modifier which normally follows it:

> *Down* she fell, all the way to the bottom.
>
> *With that*, you'll have to be contented.

Such radical inversions are too conspicuous to use often without seeming
stilted. A much commoner type of inversion goes like this:

> NORMAL Cecil fed the aardvark.
>
> INVERTED The aardvark was fed by Cecil.

Here the position of the subject of the clause is given to the *recipient* of
the verb action (the aardvark) rather than to the *doer* (Cecil). Because
the subject is now *acted upon*, this way of stating things is called "the
passive voice" in contrast to the normal "active voice" in which the subject is the doer of the verb. Granted that the passive voice usually lacks
vigor, it serves especially to set up beginnings and endings of sentences
for unusual stress:

> *The money was* not borrowed but *stolen.* (stress at end)
>
> *Your own neighbor was selected* as Most Valuable Citizen.
> (stress at beginning)

The passive voice is also used when the actor is unknown or unimportant (as in the opening clause of this sentence) or where the writer
avoids responsibility for identifying the actor ("The decision has been
reached not to renew your contract").

You delay the normal order of a sentence by inserting an interrupting
element, such as the phrase "more than anything else" in the following
examples:

> *More than anything else* Cecil wanted an aardvark. (subject
> s v c
> postponed)
>
> Cecil *more than anything else* wanted an aardvark. (verb post-
> s v c
> poned)
>
> Cecil wanted *more than anything else* an aardvark. (complement
> s v c
> postponed)

In the following example the long *if*-clause pointedly delays and stresses the complement:

> The changes in our physical environment require, *if they are to*
>   S   V
> *bring well-being,* correlative changes. (Bertrand Russell, 1955)
>   C

Such expansion and manipulation of sentence structure requires the clear use of punctuation—especially the comma—in signaling the exact connection of sentence parts. Section **P** of "Usage Reminders," page 436, offers guidance as needed.

Both order and length of sentence can pace your own thought as it develops, and can pace the reader's attention from boredom to active participation. Look at the following two nearly identical versions. Which version has more interest for you? The stronger one comes from the pen of a professional (Ruth Benedict, *Patterns of Culture,* 1934).

A	B
All cultures, of course, have not shaped their thousand items of behavior to a balanced and rhythmic pattern. Like certain individuals, certain social orders do not subordinate activities to a ruling motivation. They scatter. If at one moment they seem to be pursuing certain ends, at another they are off on some tangent apparently inconsistent with all that has gone before, which gives no clue to activity that will come after.	All cultures, of course, have not shaped their thousand items of behavior to a balanced and rhythmic pattern. Certain social orders like certain individuals do not subordinate activities to a ruling motivation but, instead, scatter. They seem at one moment to be pursuing certain ends but at another will be off on some tangent. This tangent will be apparently inconsistent with all that has gone before and will give no clue to activity that will come after.

Which version sounds better and why? See how each sentence opens in the two versions:

SENTENCE	OPENER IN A	OPENER IN B
1	subject of sentence	subject of sentence
2	phrase modifier	subject of sentence
3	subject of sentence	subject of sentence
4	clause modifier	subject of sentence

Version B will seem duller to most readers partly because its writer opens every sentence with the same pattern regardless of real chances for new emphasis. It does not vary syntactical focus. Again, notice the word lengths of the sentences:

SENTENCE	A	B
1	18 words	18 words
2	14 words	17 words
3	2 words	19 words
4	37 words	23 words

Once more, Version B seems duller, since the required span of attention remains uniform sentence after sentence, whereas the sentences of Version A range from the short and punchy to the long and flowing. Command of syntactical focus enables you to secure this refreshing variety of length and placement, and thus to keep the attention of your reader, since the short sentence and the long one can stress different aspects of the subject they discuss.

The clearest advantages of variety in pattern are obtained most simply by manipulation of the sentence opener. A professional is so used to beginning sentences at almost any point that variety comes easily, with little reflection, by habitual use of the opener to point up a main idea or relationship. Note Karl Menninger's flexibility in sentence openings in this passage from *Man Against Himself* (1938):

MENNINGER'S TEXT	SENTENCE OPENER	IMPLIED ADVANTAGE
The question of suicide in families is one which has received almost no competent scientific investigation.	phrase as subject	stress on immediate topic
Such newspaper accounts as those just mentioned would indicate that in the popular mind the suicidal tendency is hereditary.	same with added modifier ("such")	link to previous evidence
In my own studies I have come upon several families in which it would certainly appear to be so.	phrase modifying verb	similar link to writer's own evidence
For example, one patient came to us at 61 on account of strong suicidal propensities which she had several times attempted to gratify.	phrase as absolute modifier	signal that the preceding generalizations will now be illustrated
Three of the patient's sisters had killed themselves in an identical manner; the patient's mother, and the patient's mother's mother had also killed themselves in the same way.	phrase as subject	stress on the most striking data of the evidence
Moreover, the patient's mother was a twin and the twin brother had also killed himself!	phrase as absolute modifier	stress on piling-up of evidence

As for variety in sentence length, you're hardly going to practice any arbitrary spread of word count (such as aiming for 26 percent of your sentences in the 10–15 word class, 17 percent at 30 words and over, and the rest in between). An effective variety will come through your developing sense of what different sentence lengths can do. The very short sentence, following a series of long sentences, provides a shock, an abrupt shift of energy. Again, several short sentences in sequence can build a rhythmic emphasis:

> The Church is not organized religion. It is not hierarchical authority. It is not a social organization. It is all of this, of course, but it is primarily a group of people who express a new reality by which they have been grasped. (Paul Tillich, *Theology of Culture*, 1959)

Note how the short sentences which open this passage give way to the climactic sweep of the longer sentence which finishes it.

The sentence fragment, so long the terror of remedial English instructors, can express the force of a man hammering home his thought with sharp blows:

> I want to put before you a vision: The Judge our people should have. He who listens with his heart, as well as his head. The Judge who weighs the sins of the malevolent, the sins of the wise, the sins of the crafty on different scales than the sins of the helpless and the weak. The Judge who sees the bench as an altar, rather than a counter, or a ladder. The Judge who. . . . (Talbot Smith, address, 1956)

These noun phrases are not conventional sentences, but Smith punctuates them as such, giving each one heavy stress. Put in parallel, the structures build a rhythm of repetition appropriate to Smith's emotional appeal to his readers' ideals. Moreover, the series is controlled by the strong opening main clause, "I want to put before you a vision," to which all these "fragments" syntactically relate. No new main clause enters to confuse the reader's sense of syntax.

The short sentence, including the fragment, is so much a feature of everyday speech that you may easily shift into these quicker structures when you take a conversational tone. Here is Walter Lippmann, the political essayist, at a warm moment of *The Public Philosophy* (1955):

> Experience since 1917 indicates that in matters of war and peace the popular answer in the democracies is likely to be No. . . . At the critical junctures, when the stakes are high, the prevailing mass opinion will impose what amounts to a veto upon changing the course on which the government is at the time proceeding. Prepare for war in time of peace? No. It is bad to raise taxes, to unbalance the budget, to take men away from their schools or their jobs, to provoke the enemy. Intervene in a developing conflict? No. Avoid the risk of war. Withdraw from the area of the conflict? No. The adversary must not be appeased. Reduce your claims on the area? No. Righteousness cannot be compromised. Negotiate a compromise peace as soon as the opportunity presents itself? No. The aggressor must be punished. Remain armed to enforce the dictated settlement? No. The war is over.

The long sentence, say of twenty words and up, is indispensable to any sophisticated ordering of complex materials. It will be discussed in the next chapter.

Exercise 4 (variety in sentence structure)

Rewrite each sentence below, each time opening it with a different one of the italicized elements. The opening element may be put in different grammatical form or introduced with an article or preposition as necessary.

SAMPLE   Although Mark's grades were *very good,* he found it hard to *settle down* in law school.

SOLUTION   In spite of *very good* grades, Mark found it hard to settle down in law school. *Settling down* in law school was hard for Mark, in spite of his good grades.

a. The child stood quietly and *watched* me as I laid the mother down on the floor, *still unconscious and pale.*
b. He let himself in, *switched on* the light, and *lay down* on the sofa *without even calling* to her.
c. Life in a concentration camp tore open *the human soul* and exposed its *depths.* (Viktor Frankl, 1959)
d. Unless the canoe is *overloaded,* you can pass *the first rapids* without difficulty; otherwise *a mile-long portage* will be necessary.

Exercise 5 (variety of sentence structure)

Revise the news story below for greater variety in pattern and length. At present every sentence opens with the subject; they all fall in the 6-to-12-word range.

38 WHO SAW MURDER DIDN'T CALL POLICE

Thirty-eight citizens in Kew Gardens watched a murder. These citizens were respectable and they were law-abiding. But they watched a killer stalk a woman in three separate attacks. Their chatter interrupted him twice and frightened him off. He returned each time to seek her out and stab her again. No one telephoned the police during the assault. One witness called after the woman was dead. That was two weeks ago today.

With all this structural flexibility, you can move a given idea into almost any position in the sentence, with almost any degree of emphasis. When you find yourself at least occasionally scribbling out a sentence in three or four versions, you've begun to see what can be done with a sentence. The next two chapters will show further possibilities.

The final exercises of this chapter will deal with all these present matters as a whole.

Exercise 6 (failed sentences)

You are surely human enough to feel occasionally smug over the grammatical disasters of others, as in the following botched sentences. Why are they so bad? Can you recast them to make clear sense?

a. In accordance with your instructions, I have given birth to twins in the enclosed envelope.

b. My sister offered a pear to our guest that was half-eaten.

c. This is the squirrel that the dog that the girl that the man loved fed chased. (Cited by Jerome Bruner, 1966)

d. Teri Stalgood reported someone broke into her home during the night of April 12 and took a purse which contained a small amount of cash and a Honda motorcycle.

e. A young Sardinian shepherd recovering in a hospital here with a broken jaw he received when he attacked another shepherd with an ax was knifed to death in his bed by the other shepherd, police said yesterday.

f. His secretary pulled the thick file marked "Commander Corrington, Dismissal Proceedings" out and opened it.

Exercise 7 (variety of sentence structure)

Rewrite each sentence so that each italicized element falls into one of the main-clause positions (subject, verb, or complement). Recasting is allowed as long as information remains complete.

SAMPLE   Because of the weakened condition of the *house*, its collapse was imminent.

SOLUTION   The *house* is about to collapse because of its weakened condition. (Other solutions are possible.)

a. Though *ants* often do take long *rests*, they justify the popular view of them as busy workers.

b. The excitement of that night in London made *sleep* impossible for all but a *few people*.

c. The salesman who is constantly on the road will have real difficulties in fulfilling his duties as *father and husband*.

d. The baby was left to *cry* for hours when hungry, because his mother fed him on a rigid schedule.

Exercise 8 (sentence expanding)

Expand each sentence in three steps, each time adding more information *either through coordination or subordination.* You may use words, phrases, or clauses as you see fit, but keep to one sentence only. Since this discipline can help one to generate exciting new material without loss of control, take special care to avoid padding or awkwardness. The exact wording of the prior version should be kept if possible, but minor changes may be needed.

SAMPLE   The river flowed past us.

STEP 1.   The Kokomak River flowed past us, broad and serene like a vast mirror.

STEP 2.   The Kokomak River, which we had expected to find in a raging torrent, flowed past us, broad and serene like a vast mirror.

STEP 3.   As we crested the hill, the Kokomak River, which we had expected to find in a raging torrent, flowed past us, broad and serene like a vast mirror.

     a. Martha gave up.
     b. The President addressed the nation.
     c. The Tigers won the championship.
     d. The girl was dancing.
     e. The American woman wants a career.
     f. I love to climb.

Exercise 9 (sentence combining)

Combine each pair of sentences into a sensible single sentence. Change structures as needed. Then produce a second solution for the same sentence. Avoid easy solutions which merely yoke two sentences together with a conjunction.

SAMPLE   1) Sometimes you have to play in front of hostile crowds.
          2) At such times it's to your advantage to be a good sport.

SOLUTIONS 1. Good sportsmanship is smart if you play in front of hostile crowds.

       2. You're smart to be a good sport when you play in front of hostile crowds.

   a. 1) The government of a new nation has many demands made upon it.
       2) It should give priority to the education of the nation's young.
   b. 1) Fred Fincher found that with all the village power knocked out, he could charge $10 for one candle.
       2) He couldn't buy a customer for $100 once power was restored.
   c. 1) An enemy ship lay stranded on the shore.
       2) The captain, sighting it, attacked at once.

  d. 1) Your enemy slanders you, and your friend tells you about it.
     2) It takes both, working together, to hurt you to the heart.
  e. 1) The doctor would have stayed awake at the patient's side.
     2) Because of fatigue, he decided to sleep on the couch in the same room.
  f. 1) As the new idea grips the professor, he stops short.
     2) Then he almost jumps with excitement, chalk still in hand.

Exercise 10 (all principles)

a. See if you can write a good single sentence of at least 150 words on some current news item or some fictional action. Either coordination or subordination may be used, but avoid merely stapling clauses together with *and* or *but*.
b. Recast your solution, using an effective variety of shorter sentences, including one or two really abrupt sentences for emphasis.

Suggested reading for further illustration, discussion, and writing: United Technologies Corporation, advertisement, page 396.

18   The Sentence II: Concentration

Sentence Economy

No one is likely to write good long sentences without having learned to write good short ones. But long sentences in themselves come easier because there are so many loose and hodgepodge ways of bolting them together. To build long sentences at their strongest and subtlest, you need to avoid such wasteful structures as this:

> The thing which apparently brought about the President's decision to resign was the emergency caused by the sudden collapse of his wife.

The sentence sprawls. The reason lies in the words placed in the main-clause positions. As written, the subject of the sentence is "thing," the verb is "was," and the complement is "emergency"—thus:

> The thing was the emergency.

If the main clause says nothing, the sentence is doomed. The first principle, then, of syntactical economy is that *main-clause positions should go to main ideas.* Consider the main clause as the highway along which your sentence moves. The more this highway is cluttered by trivia, the more laboriously you'll have to detour. What is the "real" subject of the sentence above? Presumably the President. Then let's put "the President" in the subject position. What does the sentence say *about* the President? That he resigned. Let's put "resigned" in the verb position and try again:

> The President resigned apparently because of the sudden collapse of his wife.

This is much tighter—12 words for the original 22, a savings of 45 percent. But notice how the sentence still thins out at the end ("because of the sudden collapse of his wife"). The key words here are "wife" and "collapse," but they have been pushed into trivial positions within phrase modifiers. If we expand the principle of economy in sentence structure to this—that *important sentence positions should go to important ideas*—we can try "wife" and "collapse" as the subject and verb of a subordinate clause:

> The President resigned apparently because his wife suddenly collapsed.

We have now tightened the sentence to 9 words, a savings of 59 percent over the original. By writing like this, you can put into 9 pages what would take the other writer 22 pages. You can go on to say as much again and more before using up the other's length. You will spare your audience the editorial drudgery of sorting out the junk.

Though the 9-word solution many be the shortest, it need not be the best. You might prefer to stress the wife's collapse by opening with it:

> The sudden collapse of his wife was apparently enough to make
>   s   v   c
> the President resign.

The verb and complement positions are weakened to get this stress, and the sentence has expanded to 14 words; but the sacrifice of space is efficient. Or suppose you want to emphasize the suddenness:

> The suddenness of his wife's collapse apparently led the President
>   s   v   c
> to resign.

Although you've moved "wife" and "collapse" back into phrase positions, you've retained overall strength. In short, the principle of main sentence positions to main ideas doesn't limit you to one solution; it simply suggests that whatever you want to stress can and should be stressed by carefully choosing its sentence position.

Nor does the ideal of economy prohibit the *restatement* of ideas for specific effect:

> The President resigned apparently because his wife suddenly collapsed. Her paralytic stroke evidently added such a personal load to his official burden that he could not do justice to both.

Each sentence does report the same event, but the whole seems neither repetitious nor padded. The second sentence provides detail and explanation; the first has summarized the result. To develop difficult material or to work with a difficult audience, one must often find several ways to open up the same point. In every version, the principle of economy says the same thing—get rid of the flab.

Just as your sentences firm up when your key ideas rise to main positions, your sentences will slacken as you permit key ideas to slip to lower status. Notice the horrendous bloating in the following progression (main-clause positions are italicized):

> Large *scholarships attract* aggressive *athletes*.
> Large *scholarships are* a key *factor* in attracting aggressive athletes.
> The *largeness* of scholarships *is* a key *factor* in attracting aggressive athletes.
> The *largeness* of scholarships *is* a key *factor* in the attraction of athletes with characteristics of aggressiveness.
> The *factor* of the size of scholarship *is* a key *consideration* in the attraction of athletes with characteristics of aggressiveness.
> The *factor* of the size of scholarships *tends to be* a key *consideration* in the attraction of athletes with characteristics of aggressiveness.
> The *factor* of size of scholarships *tends to be* a key *consideration* in the attraction of athletic personnel who are distinguished for the possession of high quotients of aggressiveness.

The original clause has deteriorated badly. Its subject, "scholarships," has ended up in a phrase modifying another phrase ("of size of scholarships"). Its verb, "attract," is now buried in a phrase modifier ("in the attraction"). Its complement, "athletes," has become the inflated "athletic personnel" in a phrase modifying another phrase ("in the attraction of athletic personnel").

In the press of informal speaking, you probably resemble many other people in often starting a sentence before knowing how it will end. Hence the deadwood opener like "A point we might all keep in mind is . . ." or "It has always seemed to me that. . . ." In effect you're marking time while your mind warms up. But in writing and serious speaking you can warm up in advance.

Then, too, you may legitimately hesitate to overcommit yourself. Something like "I never saw a better movie" you may find extravagant. You may prefer the judicious reserve of "This may well be one of the best movies I have ever seen." Qualifiers like *apparently, possibly, usually, may, might* can prevent rashness of expression. Brevity is not the chief virtue in writing; accuracy ranks even higher. But there is a huge difference between the prudently qualified generalization and the habitual fuzzing of all statements in the fear of being caught with a definite opinion.

Though the daily pressure to use slack sentences is real, reflection, habit, and the practice of revision will tighten up your style so that when you speak, others may listen as they did to Francis Bacon. Ben Jonson said of him that

> No man ever spake more neatly, more pressly, more weightily, or suffered less emptiness, less idleness, in what he uttered. No member of his speech but consisted of his own graces. His hearers could not cough or look aside from him without loss. He commanded where he spoke. (*Timber, or Discoveries*, 1641)

Sentence Tension

If you see a group of words like this:

> Priscilla kicked the

you recognize the whole structure of which this is a part. You both expect and want the subject and verb to be rounded off with a complement:

> Priscilla kicked the gong.

The completion of such a grammatical structure we may call—to borrow a term from psychology—*closure*. Generally the human mind wants closure. It seeks to bind together fragments into wholes, to close up gaps in patterns, to bring a given field of observation into a contained order— and thus to reach a sense of completeness, finality, rest. In writing or reading sentences, one accordingly wants to close any uncompleted structure—to fulfil a modifier with its headword, a subject with its verb—and until that closure is reached, both writer and reader experience *grammatical tension:* they are expecting and wanting the closure to take place.

The degree of grammatical tension varies with the types of structure used, the predictability of structures, the number of structures kept open, and the amount of interrupting material included. Grammatical tension usually mounts with the complexity of your thought, since more and more material must be related efficiently within your sentences before you complete them. Certain writers seem to "see" things in tension: that is, they grasp and hold on to all the parts of an observation before committing themselves to the unifying inference, and they naturally present their observation in the same way, delaying the final clue which unites it for the reader. Any writer can deliberately regulate grammatical tension—increasing it to create suspense before a climactic closure, or reducing it to simplify the attention required of the reader by unfamiliar materials. For this purpose, prose syntax can be classified roughly according to three degrees of grammatical tension: low, moderate, high.

Most general English prose is "moderate-tension." Its structures neither prolong grammatical tension nor abbreviate it to any marked degree. For example:

> I have been *wondering* for a month *why you* hardly ever *come*
>
> to our meetings.

Some slight tension does appear here. The verb-complement pattern ("wondering why") is momentarily delayed by the insertion of "for a month"; and one of the subject-verb patterns ("you come") is also briefly delayed. But no unusual postponement of closure occurs which would require extended concentration from writer or reader as in the examples of "high-tension" prose which follow.

The tensest possible syntax is known by the term *periodic*. A periodic sentence delays closure until the period which ends the sentence itself:

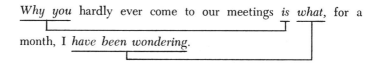

> *Why you* hardly ever come to our meetings *is what*, for a
>
> month, I *have been wondering.*

All structures are kept open here. The opening "why you" signals a subordinate clause which can't come to rest until it has joined the main clause. The final main-clause component, "what," signals another subordinate clause which can't close until it reaches its own verb at the end ("have been wondering"). The tension is further stretched by the modifier "for a month," which by occurring in *advance* of its headword ("wondering") doubles the reader's need for the final verb which is also that headword.

Periodic sentences occur frequently in more formal prose. Their intricacy of subordination and their climactic design are congenial to minds working carefully to bring complex matters to a point. Example:

> One of our perennial troubles is that improvement of the world is undertaken by so many unpolished minds. (Douglas Bush, 1955)

The complement is a *that*-clause arranged in passive voice so that the doer of the verb does not appear until the last word of the sentence. Notice the ironic deflation which this ending achieves. "Improvement of the world" has encouraged lofty expectations which the "unpolished minds" at the ending are quite unable to fulfil.

> If two instincts are in conflict, and there is nothing in a creature's mind except those two instincts, obviously the stronger of the two must win. (C. S. Lewis, 1952)

Here the long *if*-clause delays the conclusion of Lewis' argument, which does not reach completion until the closing verb, "must win." Once again:

> Given the inherent complexities of this form of organization—given the gravity of the matters with which we deal—given the youth of the United Nations—given its extremely rapid growth—it must be said that the General Assembly, with few exceptions, has conducted itself with surprising responsibility and maturity. (Adlai Stevenson, 1962)

Grammatically this sentence is complete just before the ending, at the noun "responsibility"; but the over-all approach is periodic. Notice how the parallel structures—the four phrases each opening with "given"—can help to intensify the delay of closure and thus to build suspense.

Periodic structure trains you to focus on the climaxes of your sentences. The delay can keep your audience "up" for the full revelation of meaning, and it serves excellently to prepare for shocks and reversals. But merely prolonging the expectations of the reader is not the goal. Poor writing may delay grammatical closure simply because the writer isn't sure where to go. Even efficient periodic structure, if used continually, can be tiring and can wear down the reader's capacity for surprise. But the "delay" of good periodic structure provides clues to guide the reader's anticipation; both reader and writer know the kind of structure which the sentence is moving to complete.

At the other extreme from periodic structure is what we may call "low-tension" structure, in which all patterns are closed off quickly to keep down grammatical tension. Thus instead of our original model sentence in "moderate-tension"—

> I have been wondering for a month why you hardly ever come to our meetings

—a low tension version might read this way:

> We have meetings. You attend them rarely. Why? I have been
> wondering about this for a month.

The mild grammatical tension of the original has vanished. By the re-
packaging of the original into four simple sentences, no subject-verb-
complement pattern is interrupted, no long modifier precedes its headword. If you're trying for maximum closure, you would cut down long
phrases and clauses; avoid inversions and interrupters; and keep modifiers close to their headwords. In general, you would make sure that the
reader is never more than a few words away from closure. Here is how
tension could be drained from Bush's sentence:

PERIODIC (original version)	LOW-TENSION
One of our perennial troubles is that improvement of the world is under- taken by so many unpolished minds.	So many unpolished minds try to improve the world. This is one of our perennial troubles.

Writing low-tension prose trains you to break your thought into clear
short units and to lay them out in a logical point-by-point sequence most
easily grasped by the reader. Similarly it spares the reader's energy from
grammatical analysis, to be spent instead on subject matter. It serves excellently in "directions for use" and in exposition for presumably tired or
busy readers. Used extensively, however, low-tension prose sacrifices any
real sophistication in sentence organization. Anyone who reads extended
passages of it is likely to resent being fed a pabulum style which pre-
sumes to nurse one past all difficulties.

The possible range of grammatical tension may be illustrated by working from this passage in moderate-tension syntax to both extremes:

ORIGINAL

Democracy, like liberty or science or progress, is a word with
which we are all so familiar that we rarely take the trouble to
ask what we mean by it. It is a term, as the devotees of seman-
tics say, which has no "referent"—there is no precise or palpable
thing or object which we all think of when the word is pronounced. On the contrary, it is a word which connotes different
things to different people, a kind of conceptual Gladstone bag
which, with a little manipulation, can be made to accommodate
whatever collection of social facts we may wish to carry about
in it. (Carl Becker, *Modern Democracy*, 1951)

PERIODIC	LOW-TENSION
Democracy, like liberty or science or progress, is the kind of word with which we are all so familiar that we rarely take the trouble to ask what we mean by it.	Democracy is a word like liberty or science or progress. We are all so familiar with it that we rarely take the trouble to ask what we mean by it.

| In that no precise or palpable thing or object comes to the minds of all of us when the word is pronounced, the term "democracy" lacks, as the devotees of semantics say, a "referent." | The term has no "referent," as the devotees of semantics say—we do not all think of any precise or palpable thing or object when the word is pronounced. |
| On the contrary, "democracy," connoting such different things to different people, is that kind of Gladstone bag which, with a little manipulation, can be made to accommodate whatever collection of social facts we may wish to carry about in it. | On the contrary, the word connotes different things to different people. It is a kind of conceptual Gladstone bag. We can easily manipulate it so as to accommodate almost any collection of social facts we may wish to carry about in it. |

Notice in particular these contrasts, in which the periodic version keeps the grammatical structures open and the low-tension version seals them off:

PERIODIC	LOW-TENSION
Democracy, like liberty	Democracy is a word like liberty
with which we are	we are
In that no precise or palpable thing or object comes to the minds of all of us when the word is pronounced	we do not all think of any precise or palpable thing or object when the word is pronounced
"democracy," connoting such different things to different people	the word connotes different things to different people
[It] is that kind of Gladstone bag	It is a kind of . . . Gladstone bag

You may prefer the short low-tension sentence for any one utterance. Certainly it is emphatic. But the longer periodic sentence will more readily develop your thought into the advanced patterns to be described next.

Exercise 1 (economy)

Deflate each sentence below into good plain English in which important idea receives important structure.

SAMPLE The number of people who make the trip to Las Vegas in the search for privacy is not very large.

SOLUTION Few people go to Las Vegas for privacy.

a. One leper, who had been handicapped by the loss of his fingers, was given such an efficient course of instruction that he had acquired the skill of knitting as well as any grandmother.

b. If all human behavior were governed by the maxim that "ideas should be lived," such is the confused and inconsistent state which predetermines the mental process of the global population that the earth would soon undergo a transformation into an infernal condition.

c. In recent negotiations conducted between the owner and potential buyers, a figure of $60,000 was mentioned as the asking price for the black coat and suit which had been worn by Abraham Lincoln on the occasion of his assassination.

d. The success of the surgical operation for the transplanting of a human heart is in no small measure dependent upon the efficient functioning of the heart-lung machine.

e. In the area of career selection, Marlene has a definite preference for the field of marketing.

f. The results of polls of opinion recently taken among British citizens would support the inference that dissatisfaction with the Prime Minister has reached a substantial degree in various localities throughout the nation.

g. Improvement of the sales picture this year is currently being expected by all companies of the area, who anticipate that the total volume may be topped off at the 13 million level.

Exercise 2 (economy)

As practice for a career as government bureaucrat or educational administrator, inflate each of the following sentences step by step, each time displacing an important idea into less important structure. Your final versions should double or triple the length of the originals. (See the illustration on page 200 for an example.)

a. Squirrels can climb trees fast.

b. Easy writing makes hard reading.

c. People can telephone much more efficiently today than ten years ago.

d. Many schools really do not expect students to master writing skills.

e. If postal rates go up, the volume of mail may go down.

f. At the Battle of Crécy the French relied too much on armored cavalry.

Exercise 3 (economy)

Find the flabbiest, most inflated prose you can. Try government bulletins, textbooks and professional literature in psychology, sociology, education, physical education. Rewrite it in precise economic prose which misses no essential in-

formation or emphasis of the original. Calculate how many times more efficient your version is than the original by dividing the word length of the
original by the word length of your solution. Submit original passage, revision, and calculation.

Exercise 4 (economy)

As an exercise in making your verbs pull maximum weight, write a one-page
account of the following without using any form of the verb *to be* other than
as auxiliary to another verb.

      a. A deserted street
      b. Why people lose hope
      c. Lying awake
      d. A political issue
      e. A walk beside water

Exercise 5 (tension)

Identify the following examples as high-tension or low-tension. Be able to
explain your answer. Judge each structure for what it is—sentence, clause, or
phrase.

      a. I got the sack and she got promoted.
      b. Do you have any idea, for the love of Pete, what in the ever-
         loving world you're doing?
      c. The aging king could no longer impose his will, though his
         subjects continued to love him as they always had.
      d. That silver, high-flying, never-to-be-forgotten moon.
      e. Excuses, evasions, outright lies—these are what the General heard
         from every member of his staff.
      f. The white cherry tree in the lower orchard in the early eve-
         ning.
      g. That, believe it or not, is absolutely true.
      h. Have you heard the latest? The sales tax has been declared
         unconstitutional! Wow!
      i. Jack's rhubarb pie was delicious—tender-crusted, mouth-melt-
         ing, sweet with the faintest tang of bitterness.
      j. Modern doctors are quick to acknowledge the difficulty of de-
         ciding when a person has actually died.

Exercise 6 (tension)

Would you say that the following passages tend toward high-tension or low-
tension syntax? Be able to show the details of sentence structure which make
your point.

a. The right inherent in society, to ward off crimes against itself by antecedent precautions, suggests the obvious limitations to the maxim, that purely self-regarding misconduct cannot properly be meddled with in the way of prevention or punishment. Drunkenness, for example, in ordinary cases, is not a fit subject for legislative interference; but I should deem it perfectly legitimate that a person, who had once been convicted of any act of violence to others under the influence of drink, should be placed under a special legal restriction, personal to himself; that if he were afterwards found drunk, he should be liable to a penalty, and that if when in that state he committed another offence, the punishment to which he would be liable for that other offence should be increased in severity. The making himself drunk, in a person whom drunkenness excites to do harm to others, is a crime against others. (John Stuart Mill, *On Liberty*, 1859)

b. If you have salespeople calling on prospects, you're spending close to $60 per call today!

Yes, a whopping $60. Twenty years ago it was only $17.24, a recent study shows. But that was yesteryear.

Point: In today's sky-high world, you need to do something fast to decrease that cost. How? Try lead-generating direct mail. Condition the prospect FIRST for that salesman and watch his reception improve. Remember, a promotion letter is the closest thing ever invented to a person-to-person conversation. (Tip: Be sure to enclose a business-reply card. And encourage your sales force to jump on those inquiries FAST—strike while the iron is red-hot! You'll make more money. And that's even better than saving money.) (Clemprint, Inc., *Letter Perfect*, 1975)

Exercise 7 (tension)

Rewrite each selection under Exercise 6 to produce the opposite degree of tension. For example, if the passage is high-tension, rewrite it as low-tension.

Exercise 8 (tension—imitation)

Imitate selection *b* under Exercise 6, using the adaptation of techniques method described in Chapter 6 (see page 54). Concentrate on duplicating the degree of tension. Possible topics:

a. How to organize your time.
b. (To a prospective enrollee) What bartending school can do for you.
c. (To a prospective bride and groom) How to handle wedding gift arrangements.

Exercise 9 (tension)

Choose a prose passage of 12–20 lines from something you've read, and write a brief essay analyzing the tension of its sentence structure and showing how that tension affects the total force of the passage. Be sure to submit a copy of the original passage together with your discussion.

Exercise 10 (all elements)

Both sentences below are virtually unreadable, thanks to inflated structure and inefficient tension. (But both were actually written in all seriousness.) Rewrite each one for optimum economy and tension. Sentences may be divided into smaller units.

a. This is the still important and increasingly critical issue of when and under what circumstances of very serious, apparently irreversible, deterioration of physical and/or mental health of a candidate for kidney dialysis treatment services should such a patient not even be started on dialysis nor recommended for transplantation; or the case of an individual who has been on dialysis for some time, perhaps years, but because of serious physical or mental problems developing deteriorates irreversibly without perhaps death being imminent as long as dialysis is continued—under what criteria could or should such an individual have his/her dialysis terminated by the physician?

b. The current and anticipated County community economic and employment reality, and, Bethlehem's significant participation within this community including the many important ramifications thereof, not the least of which is felt *and* expressed commitment to sustained systematic regularity of charitable giving as a principal means of assuring members of the County community availability of human services potentially having valued family life support (and, perhaps, enrichment) impact, were among the several aspects of your presentation having especially particular interest to me.

Suggested readings for further illustration, discussion, and writing: the advertisements, pages 321, 396, and 402.

19 The Sentence III: Higher Organizations

Balance: Parallel Structure, Antithesis, Symmetry

By repeating certain grammatical structures, you can balance your material so as to order it, to emphasize it, and to make it easier for your audience to grasp. Three kinds of balance can be distinguished: parallel structure, antithesis, and symmetry.

An example of *parallel structure* appeared in the preceding paragraph in the three verb phrases: "to order it, to emphasize it, and to make it easier." The principle consists of expressing similar thoughts in duplicate grammatical structures, and it can be applied to structures of all ranks:

> VERBS I approved,
> admired,
> adored her way of winning a point at tennis.

> NOUNS Power,
> glory,
> profit—these were the aims of the attacking Huns.

> PHRASES I wanted to cry out,
> to complain in courts of law,
> to lead an indignant army.

Notice that merely using three phrases is not enough for parallel structure. The phrases must duplicate each other in their main grammatical features—here, in using the same verb form: *to cry out, to complain, to lead.*

SUBORDINATE
    CLAUSES Give me the man who will speak before he acts,
                  who will think before he speaks,
                  who will listen before he thinks.

      MAIN
    CLAUSES None of them is available: John has gone to the movies,
                         Hiram has gone to the laundry, and
                         Bert has gone home.

  SENTENCES I protest against the manufacturing standards which could permit such a shoddy product to reach the market.
             I protest against the advertising ethics which could conceal such defects in the goods advertised.
             I protest most of all against the public apathy which will tolerate such an abuse of its trust year after year.

The specific uses of parallel structure are to develop a climactic order of ideas (as just seen), to group or link similar ideas, to list the items of a series, or (as in the next example) to organize the details which support a generalization:

          I had rarely witnessed such frenzied activity:
             office boys darting along the aisles,
             clerks scuttling to the file cabinets,
             executives clawing through the heaps of paper before them,
             telephones jangling on every desk.

Parallel structure offers a clear but flexible way of ordering ideas in a sustained passage. Once the rhythm of similar structures is developed, it urges you forward to new parallels. The fullest eloquence of parallel structure can be seen in the following passage (written in 1711) by the essayist Richard Steele, describing a visit to Westminster Abbey. (To show the structural harmonies of this passage, parallel structures are designated by the same letter-symbol; italics are used to show climactic stress.)

        (a) When I look upon the tombs of the great,
          (b) every emotion of envy dies in me;
        (a) when I read the epitaphs of the beautiful,
          (b) every inordinate desire goes out;
        (a) when I meet with the grief of parents upon a tombstone,
          (b) my heart melts with compassion;
        (a) when I see the tomb of the parents themselves,
            (c) *I consider the vanity of grieving for those whom we must quickly follow:*
        (a) when I see kings lying by those who deposed them,
        (a) when I consider rival wits placed side by side, or the holy men that divided the world with their contests and disputes,

(c) *I reflect with sorrow and astonishment on the little competitions, factions, and debates of mankind.*

(a) When I read the several dates of the tombs, of some that died yesterday, and some six hundred years ago,

(c) *I consider that great day when we shall all of us be contemporaries, and make our appearance together.*

Most forceful are the *c*-structures—the first-person main clauses which terminate each block of *when*-clauses. They occur in a rising order which gives to the last sentence—the final recognition of human vanity—an especially moving grace.

Parallel structure of this primary series-type seems so natural under many conditions that you can be jarred when a writer fails to fulfil it:

I was arrested for burglary, on charges of car theft, and because I had exceeded the speed limit.

Although evidently seeing the three criminal charges as a series, the writer shifts structures for each item as if forgetting their similarity. The lost parallelism could be recovered in several ways:

I was arrested for burglary,
            for car theft, and
            for speeding. (three phrases)
I was arrested because I had burgled a home,
            stolen a car, and
            exceeded the speed limit. (three
            verbs + complements)
Because I had burgled a home,
because I had stolen a car, and
because I had exceeded the speed limit,
            I was arrested. (three clauses)

A reader's expectation of parallel structure is especially stimulated by certain pairs of conjunctions: *both . . . and, either . . . or, neither . . . nor, not only . . . but, not so . . . as.* You would therefore take care to honor the expectation.

PARALLEL STRUCTURE ABANDONED	PARALLEL STRUCTURE MAINTAINED
I hope both to see you win and expect to.	I both hope and expect to see you win.
Not only did you come too late but left too early.	Not only did you come too late but you left too early.
Either you will pay down the full fee or leave the tournament.	Either you will pay down the full fee or you will leave the tournament.

A second, less frequent type of parallel structure is illustrated by this example:

> *Forty* ships alone were left to him to defend the banner of the crusade and the honor of Castile; but
>
> *those forty* were the largest and most powerfully armed and manned that he had. (James Anthony Froude, 1895)

What provides the sense of repetition here is not so much any series (as with the parallelism described so far) as the emphatic recurrence of the opening word, "forty," to begin the second clause. This device can be called simply *parallel openers.* Another example:

> *The moment* you abate anything from the full rights of men, each to govern himself, and suffer any artificial, positive limitation upon those rights,
>
> *from that moment* the whole organization of government becomes a consideration of convenience. (Edmund Burke, 1790)

The term *antithesis* applies to a kind of parallelism which repeats structure not to stress similarity but to stress contrast:

> Many things *difficult to plan* prove *easy to perform.*

So effective is antithesis at striking opposites against each other to produce a flash of insight that it is commonly found in those memorable terse statements called *aphorisms:*

> Our promises are made in hope, and kept in fear.
> (La Rochefoucauld, 1678)
>
> The Romans preserved peace by a constant preparation for war.
> (Edward Gibbon, 1776)
>
> Those who are the most distrustful of themselves, are the most envious of others. (William Hazlitt, 1823)
>
> Sex is something you do with an organ; love is something you do with a person. (Unknown)
>
> Marriage is popular because it combines the maximum of temptation with the maximum of opportunity. (G. B. Shaw, 1903)
>
> Fanaticism consists in redoubling your efforts when you have forgotten your aim. (George Santayana, 1906)
>
> It is a sin to believe evil of others, but it is seldom a mistake. (H. L. Mencken, 1949)

(Aphorisms in other structures are illustrated in the following pages.)

The term *symmetry* can be applied to structures which mirror each other—that is, which imitate each other in reverse, as in the series a-b: b-a. Symmetry, too, can lead to aphoristic compactness:

> Where there's *marriage* without *love*, there will be *love* without
>   a   b   b
> *marriage.* (Benjamin Franklin, 1734)
>   a

> Books are the best of things, well used; abused, among the worst. (Ralph Waldo Emerson, 1837)

> America did not invent human rights. Human rights invented America. (President Jimmy Carter, 1981)

> When a man with money meets a man with experience, the man with experience gets the money, and the man with money gets the experience. (William Knudsen)

> Hate and love, after all, are nearly one; a blow can be a kiss out of heaven, and a kiss a blow out of hell. (Dylan Thomas, 1933)

> Ask not what your country can do for you—ask what you can do for your country. (John F. Kennedy, 1960)

> Maybe he wasn't the best President we might have had. But we sure as hell aren't the best people a President has ever had. (Mike Royko, 1968)

Climax

An important effect in all of these patterns is climax, about which a few words may be added. The periodic sentence, by delaying both grammatical closure and the key idea until the end, achieves climax by suspense.

> If you think education is expensive, try ignorance. (Derek Bok)

> I put my face close up to hers and said very low but distinctly, "Redival, if there is one single hour when I am queen of Glome, or even mistress of this house, I'll hang you by the thumbs at a slow fire till you die." (C. S. Lewis, 1956)

You can sometimes add shock to any climax if your ending reverses the reader's expectation.

> You can't cheat an honest man unless he believes that you can't cheat an honest man. (John Finnegan, 1980)

> Sheriff Hunsacker is indefatigable in energy, tenacious in pur-
> pose, a fox for ingenuity, and a lion for courage—in short, he
> has all the qualities of a great defender of the law except one:
> he is pathologically dishonest.

Again, parallel structures in longer series can develop a rhythmic momentum which will intensify if the items come in rising order of importance (climactic order):

> The police captain told his men to prepare for anything—insults,
> looting, arson, murder.

Note how you could weaken that sentence by scrambling the series:

> The police captain told his men to prepare for anything—loot-
> ing, murder, arson, insults.

Like the periodic sentence, climactic series can be used to shock, when
the ending reverses the reader's expectations in tone or subject matter:

> Let thy maid-servant be faithful, strong, and homely. (Benjamin
> Franklin, 1736)

The Flexibility of Sentence Management

Though you've just seen the sentence at its most spectacular, the real aim
of considering all these principles is to multiply your options even in the
most straightforward daily writing. You have before you the choices
which allow you to organize small-scale materials in dozens of ways, to
discover almost any shade of meaning which is available in those materials. For a small demonstration, let us propose these five events, arranged here in simple time order:

> a. The pumps of our ship, *The Flatiron*, had broken down.
> b. Water was pouring over the decks.
> c. We abandoned ship.
> d. Our lifeboat put into Kang Harbor.
> e. The authorities condemned our captain.

Now let us order this material into sentences in several different ways, to
see what can happen to "meaning":

> VERSION 1 After the pumps of *The Flatiron* had broken down and water
> began pouring over the decks, we abandoned ship. When our
> lifeboat put into Kang Harbor, the authorities condemned our
> captain.

There aren't any syntactical fireworks here—no abrupt juxtapositions or protracted climaxes—but the dynamics of sentence structure are operating at every point to establish a clear relationship among the facts. First of all, this objective version keeps the actual time order of the events, dividing them into two sensible phases: events on ship (first sentence), events on shore (second sentence). Main-clause stress is given to the chief action ("we abandoned ship") and to the chief consequence ("the authorities condemned our captain"). This emphasis on major events is accentuated by a periodic syntax which places each main clause at the very end of its sentence. Notice that the version is ethically neutral. It does not favor either the captain or the authorities. It does not try to judge motivation—it says "we abandoned ship" *after* the pumps broke down, not *because* they broke down. Altogether Version 1 seems to express a factual attitude to the events.

> VERSION 2 Even though we had delayed abandoning *The Flatiron* until the pumps had broken down and water was pouring over the decks, our lifeboat had no sooner reached Kang Harbor than the authorities were condemning our captain.

This long periodic sentence builds toward an indignant climax favoring the captain. The opening subordination maximizes the crew's unwillingness to abandon ship (*"even though* we had delayed . . ."); and the parallel structure maximizes the dangers ("the pumps had broken down and water was pouring over the decks"). The "no sooner . . . than" construction of the main clause equates the arrival in harbor with the condemning of the captain implying excessive haste on the part of the authorities. Altogether Version 2 seems to express a defensive championship of captain and crew.

> VERSION 3 Our captain abandoned ship. Granted, the pumps of *The Flatiron* had broken down, but he abandoned ship. True, water was pouring over the decks, but he abandoned ship. He did get us into Kang Harbor by lifeboat, but of course the authorities condemned him—he had abandoned ship.

Another defensive account like Version 2, this version uses parallel main clauses ("he abandoned ship") for sarcastic emphasis on the single-minded severity of the authorities. The series of matching clauses ("the pumps had broken down," "water was pouring over the decks," etc.) all stress the captain's good sense and heroism, again sarcastically, by use of grudging concessionary expressions like "granted" and "true." The polar opposition of captain and authorities is intensified by having the captain the sole actor for the ship (*"he* abandoned ship," not *"we* abandoned ship"). Version 3 can be summarized as more heavily bitter than Version 2, more focused on the unfairness of the authorities than upon their haste.

> VERSION 4   No sooner did the pumps break down than the captain abandoned *The Flatiron* and had us row him off to Kang Harbor while water poured over the decks. The authorities were prompt to condemn him.

Any sailor writing this version would be taking a bleak view of his captain. Only one hazard—the breakdown of the pumps—appears as the cause. The water pouring over the decks is implied to be the *result* of the abandonment. The captain, not the crew, is the agent—and of *two* unheroic acts: abandoning ship prematurely and looking after his own skin ("he had us row *him* off," not "he had *us* row off"). Both shabby acts take main-clause emphasis. The condemnation by the authorities follows in a brief final sentence as their natural and expected consequence.

Many more versions could be improvised, each using a different sentence strategy. You could magnify such choices further by trying different vocabulary, as in saying "*escaped* from the ship" rather than "abandoned ship." You could moreover expand or contract your scale—giving more detail to the dangers, say, and less to the captain's desire to survive.

"It is possible to fail in many ways," as Aristotle said, "but to succeed in only one." For writers his principle might be altered in this way: "It is *necessary* to fail in many ways in order to succeed in one." What's remarkable is not that you can devise so many versions of your material, but that with all this freedom you can at last hit upon the truest way—for you—of seeing the subject. Knowing and trying the options is the best and perhaps the only real preparation for that success.

Exercise 1 (balance)

a. Rework each of the following into three versions each illustrating parallel structure in a different way. Make minor changes in wording as needed.

> SAMPLE   Great opportunities are welcome to most people. The exceptional person makes them happen.
>
> SOLU- (a) *Most people welcome great opportunities. Exceptional people*
> TIONS   *make them happen.* (Parallel structures in italics)
>   (b) Great opportunities, though *welcome to most people*, are *made by the exceptional few*.
>   (c) *Most people welcome*, but *exceptional people make*, a great opportunity.

1. The navy of ancient times moved by oars. Recent navies were moved by sail. Motors move the navy of today.
2. The best college education will teach one how to acquire firm friendships. One may reach one's peak at sports. The mind should be finely extended. Foundations should be laid for a significant career. One should sleep now and then.

b. Rework each of the following into a sentence with parallel openers:

1. On the day that Michael Freimuth took the first dollar out of company funds, he was a ruined man.
2. Those things which are done by brave people are often undone by other brave people.
3. A squad car materializes in the rear-vision mirror whenever I edge just a mile or two above the speed limit.

c. Rework each of the following so as to fulfil the reader's expectation of parallel structure:

1. Any profession should make it possible for its members not only to develop continually as practitioners but as persons.
2. Steve Ingold liked to plow and tending his dairy herd, and above all he liked to move big rocks.
3. Either Susan Trunkey would have to buck the county Democratic machine or give up her stand on property taxes.

Exercise 2 (balance—imitation)

Imitate the sentence patterns of any four of the following passages, using the scrambling and re-synthesis method described in Chapter 6 (see page 52). For each solution, add a brief evaluation of what your imitation preserved from the original and what it may have lost.

SAMPLE It is the nature of words to mean. To consider words only as sounds, like drum taps, or to consider written letters as patterned objects, as in alphabet soup, is the same as to consider a Stradivarius as material for kindling wood. (W. K. Wimsatt, "Style as Meaning," 1941)

SOLUTION *Notes on contents:* (These notes were made on separate cards which were put away overnight and then shuffled, coming up in the order below. In the note-taking, effort was made to vary the original wording.)

1ST CARD: A Stradivarius is not just kindling wood.

2ND CARD: Written letters are not just patterned objects, though in alphabet soup they are such.

3RD CARD: Words have meaning by their very nature.

4TH CARD: Words cannot be considered as just sounds, as drum taps are.

Imitation: Words cannot be thought of as mere sounds, like drum taps, any more than written words can be thought of as mere patterned objects, like letters in alphabet soup, or a Stradivarius violin can be thought of as mere kindling. Words have meaning; that is their nature.

Evaluation: The imitation uses effective parallel structure through clauses, where the original used infinitive phrases ("to consider words . . ."). The original opens with its main point, then supports it with a periodic sentence ending in the climactic analogy of the Stradivarius violin being treated as kindling. The imitation forfeits suspense by opening with a complete clause which states the main idea in negative terms ("Words cannot be thought of as mere sounds"), but ends climactically by stating and re-stating its main point. Both versions seem strong, in different ways. The original climax on the Stradivarius analogy is admittedly lost in the imitation, which proceeds more evenly.

a. The tragedy of the world is that those who are imaginative have but slight experience, and those who are experienced have feeble imaginations. (Alfred Whitehead, 1928)

b. The only way for a woman, as for a man, to find herself, to know herself as a person, is by creative work of her own. There is no other way. (Betty Friedan, 1963)

c. Macaulay complained that Puritans objected to bear baiting not because it caused pain to the bear but because it gave pleasure to men. Macaulay was wrong and the Puritans were right. Pain is bad but pleasure in pain is far worse. (Alan Brien, "Mad Dogmas and Englishmen," 1970)

d. Just as I spent my life trying to find a church or sect liberal enough for me, so Horace spent his seeking for one that was rigorous enough for him. (Walter Allen, *All in a Lifetime,* 1959)

e. The Zen artist sits down very calmly; examines his brush carefully; prepares his own ink; smooths out the paper on which he will work; falls into a profound silent ecstasy of contemplation—during which he does not think anxiously of various details, composition, brushwork, shades of tone, but rather attempts to become the vehicle through which the subject can express itself in painting; and then, very quickly and almost unconsciously, with sure effortless strokes, draws a picture containing the fewest and most effective lines. (Gilbert Highet, "The Mystery of Zen," 1957)

f. When, in the course of human events, it becomes necessary for one people to dissolve the political bands which have connected them with another, and to assume among the powers of the earth the separate and equal station to which the laws of nature and of nature's God entitle them, a decent respect to the opinions of mankind requires that they should declare the causes which impel them to the separation. (Thomas Jefferson, *Declaration of Independence*, 1776)

g. Sit down before fact as a little child, be prepared to give up every preconceived notion, follow humbly wherever and to whatever abysses nature leads, or you shall learn nothing. (Thomas Huxley, letter to Charles Kingsley, 1860)

h. A wise man will dispense with repentance. It is shocking and passionate. God prefers that you approach him thoughtful, not penitent, though you are the chief of sinners. It is only by forgetting yourself that you draw near to him. (Henry Thoreau, *Journals*, c.1850)

Exercise 3 (climax)

Rework each passage to give climactic stress to the italicized element. Make minor changes in wording as needed.

a. Daniel *admired himself* although he did not like himself; it was not in him to like people.
b. The Wall Street crash of 1929 *brutally shocked* those businessmen who had gambled complacently on a vision of infinite prosperity.
c. One can never *measure* the amount of energy wasted by men and women of first-class quality in arriving at their true degree before they begin to play on the world stage.
d. More than a little generosity, a little forbearance, a little detachment, *silence* can make for a long friendship.

Exercise 4 (sentence management)

Choose any two series of statements below and for each series write three separate versions, each stressing a different theme. You are expected to construct and divide your sentences accordingly. Make minor changes in wording as needed, but do *not* add new detail. For each version, add a brief explanation of the theme you were using, and how you think your management of sentence structure supports that theme.

a. Governor Russell took the state out of debt.
   The schools had to cut their budgets.
   The highway program was postponed.
   The Governor made good on his campaign promise.
   The state had been in the red for decades.

(*Possible themes:* the importance of fiscal solvency; the damage done by cutbacks; the importance of education; the Governor's integrity.)

b. 90 percent of all city trial court cases never come to trial.
Often one party defaults.
Often a compromise settlement is reached.
Many parties lack funds.

c. Our enemies are pathologically afraid of us.
Nuclear weapons are the only really effective deterrent to war.
It may be better to be destroyed than to be defeated.
Nuclear weapons can destroy both parties to a war.
Peace is unattainable unless we can permanently deter our enemies.
Our enemies will impose their evil values on us if they can.

d. Early in this century the typical American traveled about 1600 miles a year.
Currently the typical American travels more than 10,000 miles a year.
Our highways have had an astonishing growth.
A national fuel shortage constantly threatens.
Americans now mix travel with almost everything they do.

Exercise 5 (all elements)

To practice for maximum power in single sentences, write two or three pages of aphorisms, each composed of one or more terse sentences explaining your own observations of life. You'll probably need to work each entry over several times to obtain full force. For models, see page 213 or pp. 213–214. You might also enjoy reading extensively in some author known for aphoristic skill. The following are recommended:

W.H. Auden, *The Dyer's Hand and Other Essays* (1962)
Marcus Aurelius, *Meditations* (c. 180)
Benjamin Franklin, *Poor Richard's Almanac* (1732–58)
William Hazlitt, *Characteristics* (1832) and *Commonplaces* (1823)
H.L. Mencken, "Sententiae" in *A Mencken Chrestomathy* (1949)
Michel Montaigne, *Essays* (1580–88)
Blaise Pascal, *Thoughts* (1662)
Coventry Patmore, *The Rod, the Root, and the Flower* (1895)
La Rochefoucauld, *Maxims* (1678)
G.B. Shaw, "Maxims for Revolutionists" in *Man and Superman* (1903)
Jonathan Swift, *Thoughts on Various Subjects* (1727)

Exercise 6 (review of all vocabulary and sentence elements)

This exercise should help to bring together the concepts of Chapters 13–19. Describe the chief differences in vocabulary and sentence structure between the following versions. What differences in meaning and emphasis emerge? Which version do you find more effective, and why? (The original passage appears in the novel *Siddhartha* by Hermann Hesse, 1922, as translated in 1951.)

A

He looked lovingly into the flowing water, into the transparent green, into the crystal lines of its wonderful design. He saw bright
5 pearls rise from the depths, bubbles swimming on the mirror, sky blue reflected in them. The river looked at him with a thousand eyes—green, white, crystal, sky blue. How he
10 loved this river, how it enchanted him, how grateful he was to it! In his heart he heard the newly awakened voice speak, and it said to him: "Love this river, stay by it."
15 Yes, he wanted to learn from, he wanted to listen to it. It seemed to him that whoever understood this river and its secrets, would understand much more, many secrets, all
20 secrets.

But today he only saw one of the river's secrets, one that gripped his soul. He saw that the water continually flowed and flowed and yet
25 it was always there; it was always the same and yet every moment it was new. Who could understand, conceive this? He did not understand it; he was only aware of a
30 dim suspicion, a faint memory, divine voices.

B

The surface of the water was a shimmering green, rippling placidly and forming stunning patterns. Gazing tenderly into the river Siddhartha watched as a stream of 5 bubbles rose to cluster on its transparent surface and reflect the azure sky. Myriad orbs of green, white, crystal and azure returned his gaze. He sensed that by listening and un- 10 derstanding one could comprehend many more mysteries, all secrets. He felt a deep love for this river, a fascination with it, an appreciation for it. From within his heart he 15 sensed a recent awakening which urged him: "Love this river, remain here, study its message." Indeed he yearned to study it, he yearned to understand its wisdom. Yet at this 20 juncture only one of the many secrets was revealed to him, yet one that quickened his heart. Although the river was constantly flowing, it was still always present, always 25 there; it was eternally constant, yet always unique. Could this ever be understood, explained? Siddhartha as yet could not comprehend it, yet he felt a tinge of suspicion, a vague 30 impression of celestial voices.

Suggested readings for further illustration and discussion: Ann Landers, "[Maturity]," page 397, and Max Lerner, "On Being a Possibilist," page 398.

20 Rhythm and Sound

For every syllable written by the human hand, the human mouth speaks thousands of words. Before writing has always come speech. The sounds and rhythms of the speaking voice have shaped the process of creation and discovery—for our culture and for us individually—which writing has extended. Speech invites everyone present to become a community of one time and place. It projects the speaker's whole live human presence upon us as listeners. It can sing to us those attitudes which print can only struggle to convey.

Statesmen, preachers, teachers, and others who speak publicly often do so without script because they know that a livelier truth may come into being through the voice addressing a fresh occasion. The composed styles of written English might arrest the sense of immediate exploration. Even those professionals who speak from manuscript usually try to imitate unrehearsed speech so that the audience may at least feel that a new reality is forming right now as they listen.

Similar reasons have impelled certain writers to "speak" their compositions into being. Henry James dictated some of his work; so did Mark Twain.

You yourself might experiment with using your voice as a "pen." Not having a stenographer, you could speak your thoughts into a tape recorder, then write them down as you hear the playback, then work them out as needed for a reading audience. Your written prose might take on something of the immediacy and authenticity of the voice.

Writing of course does differ basically from speech. What it may lose in spontaneity it can gain in compactness, order, analytic force. What

may help you is to see how certain speech values—rhythm and sound especially—can enlarge a writer's powers.

Rhythm

In English speech, certain syllables are pronounced with more stress than
others. A common symbol for a stressed syllable is ╱. A common symbol
for an unstressed syllable is ˣ. Several additional gradations of stress and
unstress are recognized by linguists and poetry specialists, but these two
will do for our purposes. Examples:

> ╱ ˣ   ╱ ˣ ╱   ╱ ╱   ╱ ˣ ˣ
> stricken happenstance birthday cluttering

While you can't invert the stress pattern of a word without making a
hash of the pronunciation, many syllables are neutral enough—especially
monosyllabic words—to take either stress or unstress according to their
context. Note the word "my" in these examples:

> ╱ ˣ ˣ ╱ ˣ
> This is my ladder. ("My" is unstressed.)

> ╱ ˣ ╱ ╱ ˣ ╱ ╱
> This is my ladder, not yours. (Stress on "my" is required by
> meaning.)

> ╱ ˣ ╱ ˣ╱ˣ
> This is my piano. (Stress on "my" is encouraged by unstresses
> before and after.)

You could generate a relatively simple kind of rhythm by composing
your language so that its stresses and unstresses fall in repeated patterns:

> ˣ ╱ ˣ ╱ ˣ ╱ ˣ ╱ ˣ ╱
> I cannot ease the burden of your fears.

> ˣ ╱ ˣ ╱ ˣ ╱ ˣ ╱ˣ ╱
> Or make quick-coming death a little thing,

> ˣ ╱ ˣ ╱ ˣ ╱ ˣ ╱ ˣ ╱
> Or bring again the pleasure of past years. . . .

> (William Morris, "An Apology," 1868)

The pattern there is rigid and simple (ˣ ╱). You'll rarely find it outside
of traditional verse; but since the older verse patterns open the way to
the more complex rhythms of prose and contemporary poetry, we should
look at them. Traditional poetry in English works with five stress patterns:

STRESS PATTERN (each occurrence is called a "foot")	EXAMPLE	NAME OF FOOT (NOUN)	ADJECTIVAL FORM
x /	x / tonight	iamb	iambic
/ x	/ x handsome	trochee	trochaic
x x /	x x / to the hills	anapest	anapestic
/ x x	/ x x puttering	dactyl	dactylic
/ /	/ / nighttime	spondee	spondaic

Thus a line of iambic verse would consist of several iambic feet, the actual number being set by the scheme adapted for the whole poem. The traditional schemes are as follows:

LENGTH OF LINE IN FEET	TERM USED FOR SUCH LINES
1	monometer
2	dimeter
3	trimeter
4	tetrameter
5	pentameter
6	hexameter
7	heptameter
8	octameter

So the rhythm of a poem in traditional meter can be described first by its dominant stress pattern (e.g., iambic, trochaic) and second by its dominant line length (e.g., tetrameter, pentameter). The following line of Shakespeare is an iambic pentameter: five feet with the stress pattern x / :

x / x / x / x / x /
My mistress' eyes are nothing like the sun

(Sonnet 130)

Variant feet or line-lengths may sometimes appear, in emphatic contrast to the prevailing pattern. But you don't wallop the beats of traditional poetry either in writing it or reading it aloud. *The verse is conceived for its sense and read for its sense.* The rhythm asserts its harmony in the background, without distracting.

The five basic feet serve only as approximators for describing the more intricate patterns of prose and much contemporary poetry. Rather than borrow the clutter of additional terms worked out by specialists, we can find a way into prose rhythm by a plain stress-and-unstress diagramming of those passages which obviously do carry a beat. The following sentence from the Book of Jeremiah (King James Version of the Bible, 1611) is here pieced into lines according to the major pauses which the punctuation and meaning suggest:

```
     /    x x  /   x  /   x  x  /   x x  /   x   /
1 Woe unto him that buildeth his house by unrighteousness,

       x   x  /   x  x   /
2    and his chambers by wrong;

       x  / x  x   /   x   /   x  x x   / x
3 that useth his neighbour's service without wages,

       x  / x  x   /  x x   /
4    and giveth him not for his work;

     x    /   / x  /   / x /   /   x /   /    x
5 That saith, I will build me a wide house and large chambers,

       x  / x   x   x  / x
6    and cutteth him out windows;

       x  x x   /    x  / x
7    and it is cieled with cedar,

       x  / x  x   x  / x
8    and painted with vermillion.
```

(Jeremiah 22: 13–14)

Although you might dispute this scanning of stresses here and there, the following features can be observed:

First, triple rhythms predominate in the opening lines (/ x x or x x /).
Second, lines 1 and 2 are rhythmically echoed by lines 3 and 4—thus (with boxing used to stress the similarity):

```
1 and 2   | / x x / x / x x / x | x  / | x / x x / x x / |
3 and 4 x | / x x / x / xxx / x |      | x / x x / x x / |
```

Third, the smooth flow of the passage suddenly breaks in line 5, which is studded with double stresses (spondees):

```
      x  |  /     | x    |  /    /  | x |  /    /  | x  |  /    /  | x
5 That | saith, I | will | build me | a | wide house | and | large chambers |
```

This double-stressing seems to slow down the line, to pound out the arrogant self-assertion of the unrighteous man.

Fourth, the closing lines reimpose a flow which again is reinforced by parallels (as the boxing indicates):

6	x / x x x	/ x
7	x x x / x	/ x
8	x / x x x	/ x

Just possibly the repeated two-stress lines support a sardonic tone in the writer who sneers at the rich man's affluence:

> 6 and CUTeth him out WINDows!
> 7 and it is CIELED with CEDar!
> 8 and PAINTed with verMILLion!

In such biblical passages the rhythmic schemes do not flow as evenly or steadily as in formal verse, but at least one sees that prose can come in groupings or "lines" which often repeat patterns of stress. Moreover a beat can develop in prose, though obscurely, unevenly, and temporarily. A bunching of stresses can be used to hammer a point. And sometimes the stress patterns can dramatize the meaning (thus the spondees to suggest the strut of the unrighteous man).

Much prose rhythm—both in the Jeremiah passage just quoted and especially in speech—develops from repeated grammatical structure, so much so that the term *grammatical rhythm* is sometimes used, and this rhythm itself is often employed in modern poetry. Actually parallel structure offers such a natural way of building ideas that you may often find yourself falling into grammatical rhythm as you speak or write. Here is a passage in which Jacques Barzun pounds at the horrors of long-term imprisonment in his attack upon those who would abolish the death sentence in favor of a prolonged prison sentence. (Parallel structures are designated by the same letter; italics are used for the stark, unmatched central statement.)

> (a) Despite the infamy of concentration camps,
> (a) despite Mr. Charles Burney's remarkable work, *Solitary Confinement,*
> (a) despite riots in prisons,
> (a) despite the round of escape, recapture and return in chains, *the abolitionists' imagination tells them nothing about the reality of being caged.*
>> (b) They read without a qualm, indeed
>> (b) they read with rejoicing, the hideous irony of "Killer Gets Life";
>> (b) they sigh with relief instead of horror.
>>> (c) They do not see and suffer
>>>> (d) the cell,
>>>> (d) the drill,

>   (d) the clothes,
>   (d) the stench,
>   (d) the food;
>   (c) they do not feel
>   (d) the sexual racking of young and old
>   bodies,
>   (d) the hateful promiscuity,
>   (d) the insane monotony,
>   (d) the mass degradation,
>   (d) the impotent hatred.

("In Favor of Capital Punishment," 1962)

The four series of parallel structures give Barzun's indignation a rising force. (For other illustrations of prose rhythm through parallel structures, see the preceding chapter, pages 210–214).

Your own use of rhythm ought to come most naturally if you *hear what you write as you're writing it*. Rhythm is likely to begin spontaneously as it does in your speaking. Even if it doesn't, you'll avoid stumbling into such twitchy prose as this, whose lack of rhythm inhibits comprehension:

> The President, beyond a doubt, is, for most citizens, the visible symbol of, for better or worse, the American Dream.

With luck you may catch a rhythm which drives you forward reaching for the kind of language needed to fulfil it. As you come to passages you want to hit hard, your rhythms may intensify just as they do in spirited face-to-face discussion, and they will probably answer to the tempo you feel at such times—solemn urgency, rushing vigor, abrupt jabs. For example, notice how much difference the rhythms alone can make in the following two versions of the identical material (try reading them aloud):

VERSION A

Sex has exploded in the popular arts! Can it any longer be ignored as a minor change of fashion? Films now portray sexual intercourse. They can be shown publicly. Day after day they draw full-house crowds. Novels treat sexual conduct in explicit detail. Often they become best sellers. In plain view on the stage sexual intercourse is already simulated. Before long the fact will undoubtedly be featured in full reality. Such a massive overthrow of traditional restraints—does

VERSION B

The explosion of sex in the popular arts can no longer be ignored as a minor change of fashion. Films which portray sexual intercourse not only can be exhibited publicly, but draw full-house crowds day after day. Novels which treat sexual conduct in explicit detail often become best sellers. Sexual intercourse is already simulated on the stage in plain view and undoubtedly will be featured as a full reality before long. Such a massive overthrow of traditional restraints may mean a

it mean a massive depravity in contemporary man? Certainly it means
that cultural values are going
through a very deep shift.

massive depravity in contemporary
man; certainly it symptomizes a very
deep shifting of cultural values.

Which passage seems more heated, and what rhythmic elements make
the difference? In particular, compare the passages where they most coincide:

> VERSION A Certainly it means that cultural values are going through a very
> deep shift.
> VERSION B Certainly it symptomizes a very deep shifting of cultural values.

Apparently very close. But A hits more energetically, with a few more
stresses, and ends with a climactic cluster of stresses on *"very deep shift"*
(/ ˣ / /). In contrast, B seems quiet, unhurried. Which version would
you respond to more favorably, and why?

Besides establishing characteristic tempos and moods like this, rhythm
can produce the highly specialized effect of directly imitating a rhythmic
action being described. Notice how James Joyce portrays a joyfully excited youth in the same surging rhythm of the youth's striding along the
beach:

> He turned away from her suddenly and set off across the strand.
> His cheeks were aflame; his body was aglow; his limbs were
> trembling. On and on and on and on he strode, far out over the
> sands, singing wildly to the sea, crying to greet the advent of
> the life that had cried to him. (*A Portrait of the Artist as a
> Young Man*, 1916)

Though such dramatic rhythms are usually confined to narrative and poetic passages, the rare chance to try them is worth taking.

Sound

A similar effect in sound is brought about by *onomatopoeia*, the use of
words which in their own sound suggest the sound described. For example:

> She skipped through the dry fallen leaves, delighting in their
> CRACKLE and RUSTLE, SCUFFING her heels so as to stir the leaves
> into CRISP WHISPERS and BRITTLE HISSES.

Whether a foreigner would identify the word "scuff" with the sound of a
scuffing shoe is doubtful. Yet most English speakers already knowing the

word would hear in it the sudden crack (the explosive *k* sound) followed by the friction (the *f* sound) of a real scuffing. Certainly "scuff" comes closer to the sound of scuffing than, say, a word like "loom." Several dozen onomatopoeic words are common in English and are readily drawn upon in describing common sounds—for example, "babble," "cough," "mumble," "rattle," "sizzle."

The use of imitative sound can extend from words to phrases:

> the rattling clatter of the cups
> the turbid gurgle of Burger's brook

And imitative sound occasionally runs through longer passages, as in this storm scene from Ted Hughes' poem, "Wind" (1962):

> This house has been far out at sea all night,
> The woods crashing through darkness, the booming hills,
> Winds stampeding the fields under the window
> Floundering black astride and blinding wet. . . .

Still, onomatopoeia remains, like imitative rhythm, a narrow effect.

English makes much wider use of repetitive sound, best known under the broad term *alliteration*. Such repetition comes easily in our language; it can intensify short phrases and make them memorable. Ad writers, politicians, poets, novelists, essayists, and sportswriters use it freely. In the following examples the repeated sounds are capitalized and connected by lines:

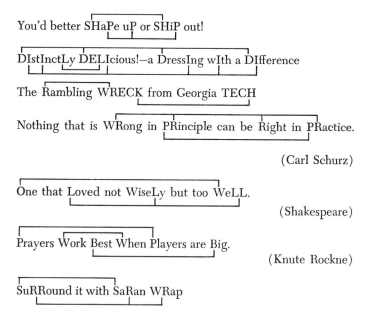

You'd better SHaPe uP or SHiP out!

DIstInctLy DELIcious!—a DressIng wIth a DIfference

The Rambling WRECK from Georgia TECH

Nothing that is WRong in PRinciple can be Right in PRactice.

(Carl Schurz)

One that Loved not WiseLy but too WeLL.

(Shakespeare)

Prayers Work Best When Players are Big.

(Knute Rockne)

SuRRound it with SaRan WRap

Note that what counts is the repetition of *sound* not of written letters. Thus the written WR = the spoken R, KN = N, OUGH = UFF, etc.

If alliteration is not pushed to the point of distraction, it can enhance almost any passage which has emotional content. The enhancement rises from our instinctive pleasure in sound pattern; from the extra stress taken by the language which uses it; most of all from the power of recurrent sound to pull a passage into tighter unity.

You're likely to use recurrent sound most effectively if, once again, *you hear what you write*. A sound may recur accidentally as you write, but once your ear has detected it, you can take up the sound and exploit it in your selection of the next words. Then another sound pattern may rise out of your writing, and you may shift to that—and so on, using sound not mechanically or compulsively but naturally, as a stimulus and guide to your own ear and later to the reader's. The combined richness and quiet intensity of the resulting prose can be illustrated by the following passage from Aldous Huxley, in which one cluster of sounds subtly dominates for a while and then yields to others. (The diagraming intentionally exaggerates the effect.)

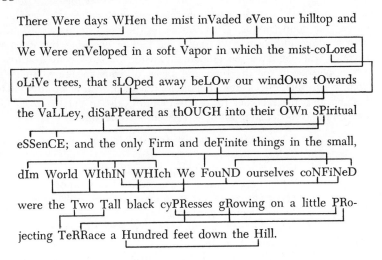

("Young Archimedes," 1924)

Finally, sound contributes in a specialized way to rhythm, by influencing *tempo*, the speed at which spoken English is delivered. In writing meant to be heard, tempo can be built into the language by the amount of work assigned to the voice organs. Vowels which require extreme positions of the jaw or lips (for example, AW, AH, EE, OH) force the speaker to slow down; so do consonant clusters like SKS, RTH, NGST, which impose labor on the tongue, glottis, or lips. By listening to what you write, you can avoid random consonant blockages like "conscienceless choices" or "she frowned at me unfriendlily." And you can obtain highly emphatic decelerations as in these familiar lines:

> Oh, most wicked speed, to post
> With such dexterity to incestuous sheets!

In this tangle of consonants (try saying it fast), Shakespeare has Hamlet's horror and revulsion break from him a syllable at a time, in fitting climax to the grief of his first soliloquy. Of course few writers if any ever start out by saying, "I'm going to slow down this passage with difficult consonant clusters." As with alliteration, the effect probably emerges accidentally, is detected and approved by the trained ear of the writer, and is then consciously strengthened.

Exercise 1 (voice composition)

Take a topic of common discussion like one of those below. Use a tape recorder to "speak" a short essay on the topic, imagining that you are talking with a few good friends. Then transcribe the essay to paper. Then revise it for a reading audience; try to keep the feel of *speaking* but remember that a reader will not have the guidance of your voice or your gestures or your known personality or the time and place of your speaking. Suggestions for taping: Scribble out a few points in advance; warm up by talking your thoughts into the recorder for a few minutes, just to get the hang of recording; use the recorder stop-button as needed. Possible topics:

- a. Why everyone should (or should not) own a personal computer.
- b. What the next great invention will probably be.
- c. What the U.S. should do about nuclear weapons.
- d. The greatness of a contemporary musical artist or group.
- e. Are the movies getting dirtier?
- f. Why the listeners—an executive recruiting team—should hire you for a given position.
- g. The chief virtue of your political party.

Exercise 2 (rhythm)

What rhythmic patterns do you find in the following passages? Explain why you think they are appropriate or not.

- a. What passions cannot be unleashed on a dark road in a Southern night! Everything seems so sensual, so languid, and so private. Desire can be acted out here; over this fence, behind that tree, in the darkness, there; and no one will see, no one will ever know. Only the night is watching and the night was made for desire. Protestantism is the wrong religion for people in such climates; America is perhaps the last nation in which such a climate belongs. In the Southern night everything seems possible, the most private, unspeakable longings; but then arrives the Southern day, as hard and brazen as the night was soft and dark. It brings what was done in the dark to light. (James Baldwin, "Nobody Knows My Name," 1959)

b. Mr. Magruder sailed into his office with a bouncy step. He was healthy. Each morning, he breathed the fresh air at the open window. Out went the chest, in went the chest. The air came in between. He felt good. Very good. Into his office with the jaunty step. "Good morning," he crackled. "Good morning," countered the switchboard girl. She looked surprised. But then that was her way.

Off went his coat. Up rolled the sleeves. Down he sat. . . .

(J. Alvin Kugelmass, "Time out of Mind," 1947)

c. (*In this next passage the young orderly is about to murder his sadistic captain.*) And he heard the sound of the Captain's drinking, and he clenched his fists, such a strong torment came into his wrists. Then came the faint clang of the closing of the pot-lid. He looked up. The Captain was watching him. He glanced swiftly away. Then he saw the officer stoop and take a piece of bread from the tree-base. Again the flash of flame went through the young soldier, seeing the stiff body stoop beneath him, and his hands jerked. He looked away. (D. H. Lawrence, "The Prussian Officer," 1914)

Exercise 3 (rhythm)

Write three different accounts of your moving forward for a confrontation (with, for example, a lover, enemy, judge, teacher, parent, executioner, audience). Choose a different situation for each encounter. Use rhythmic elements to establish a different mood for each account.

Exercise 4 (rhythm)

Write a half-page of description for any two of the following subjects, using whatever rhythmic elements you can to imitate or suggest what is being described.

a. A galloping horse.
b. A six-year-old in the bathtub.
c. An old person dozing before television.
d. A waltz.
e. A firing squad marching to the execution ground.
f. (Choose your own topic.)

Exercise 5 (sound)

Write a half-page of description for any of the following, using onomatopoeia:

    a. Rainstorm at night.
    b. Surf on beach.
    c. Dog show.
    d. Windy day.
    e. Chopping wood.

Exercise 6 (sound)

What sound patterns do you find in the following passage? Explain why you think they are appropriate or not.

> The water-clock marks the hour in the *Ta-chung sz'*,—in the Tower of the Great Bell: now the mallet is lifted to smite the lips of the metal monster,—the vast lips inscribed with Buddhist texts from the sacred *Fa-hwa-King*, from the chapters of the holy *Ling-yen-King!* Hear the great bell responding!—how mighty her voice, though tongueless!—KO-NGAI! All the little dragons on the high-tilted eaves of the green roofs shiver to the tips of their gilded tails under that deep wave of sound; all the porcelain gargoyles tremble on their carven perches; all the hundred little bells of the pagodas quiver with desire to speak. KO-NGAI! All the green-and-gold tiles of the temple are vibrating; the wooden goldfish above them are writhing against the sky; the uplifted finger of Fo shakes high over the heads of the worshipers through the blue fog of incense! KO-NGAI!—What a thunder tone was that! All the lacquered goblins on the palace cornices wriggle their fire-colored tongues! And after each huge shock, how wondrous the multiple echo and the great golden moan and, at last, the sudden sibilant sobbing in the ears when the immense tone faints away in broken whispers of silver,—as though a woman should whisper, *"Hiai!"* Even so the great bell hath sounded every day for well-nigh five hundred years,— *Ko-Ngai:* first, with stupendous clang, then with immeasurable moan of gold, then with silver murmuring of *"Hiai!"* (Lafcadio Hearn, "The Soul of the Great Bell," 1887)

Exercise 7 (all elements)

Describe the specific rhythmic and sound elements of the following passages. Explain why you think these elements are appropriate or not.

a. The skies they were ashen and sober;
        The leaves they were crisped and sere—
        The leaves they were withering and sere;
    It was night in the lonesome October
    Of my most immemorial year.

                    (Edgar Allan Poe, "Ulalume," 1847)

b. How did rice get its romantic reputation? Well. . . . If you
    threw potatoes at a wedding, what kind of reception would you
    have? Rice is romantic. Rice is racy. And it gives you almost as
    much food energy as a small, lean steak. Great with everything—
    especially people. Feel reckless, serve rice! *Switch from routine
    to rice.* (Magazine advertisement)

c. Glory be to God for dappled things—
        For skies of couple-colour as a brinded cow;
            For rose-moles all in stipple upon trout that swim;
    Fresh-firecoal chestnut-falls; finches' wings;
        Landscape plotted and pieced—fold, fallow, and plough;
        And all trades, their gear and tackle and trim.

    All things counter, original, spare, strange;
        Whatever is fickle, freckled (who knows how?)
            With swift, slow; sweet, sour; adazzle, dim;
    He fathers-forth whose beauty is past change:
                    Praise him.

                    (Gerard Manley Hopkins, "Pied Beauty," 1877)

d. The mealy look of men today is the result of momism and so
    is the pinched and baffled fury in the eyes of womankind. I said
    a while ago that I had been a motherless minister's son and im-
    plied that I had been mauled by every type of mom produced in
    this nation. I pointed out that the situation was one on which
    the moms would try to fix their pincers. I did not bother to prod
    at any misgivings they might feel about what the rude minister's
    boy, trained in snoopery by the example of the moms, might
    have found out about the matriarchy and its motivations through
    hanging around sewing clubrooms, hiding in heavy draperies,
    and holing up in choir lofts. (Philip Wylie, *Generation of Vipers,*
    1942)

e. Cowards
    In power
    Prize
    Lies
    And guise.

f. Passing bells are ringing all the world over. All the world over,
    and every hour, some one is parting company with all his aches
    and ecstasies. For us also the trap is laid. But we are so fond of
    life that we have no leisure to entertain the terror of death. It

is a honeymoon with us all through, and none of the longest.
Small blame to us if we give our whole hearts to this glowing
bride of ours, to the appetites, to honor, to the hungry curiosity
of the mind, to the pleasure of the eyes in nature, and the pride
of our own nimble bodies. (Robert Louis Stevenson, "Aes Tri-
plex," 1878)

Exercise 8 (all elements)

Write a page of free verse (no rime, no regular meter, no regular line length)
using rhythm and sound to reinforce your description of either topic below:

   a. A sudden but brief shower as it approaches, breaks, recedes.
   b. A street watched from busy evening to quiet night.

Suggested reading for further illustration, discussion, and writing: The Tobacco Institute, advertisement, page 402.

IV THE LONGER PAPER

Professional writers are often mystified by the way they put together writing. They know it has a form but they seldom know its origin. They are afraid of outlining because they want things to happen to them as they write. Nevertheless their final draft usually possesses sure form, a movement that gives power to the events they have written about. Some emphasize freedom to discover. Some emphasize the need for plan.

KEN MACRORIE, *Telling Writing*, 1980

The craftsman isn't ever following a single line of instruction. He's making decisions as he goes along. For that reason he'll be absorbed and attentive to what he's doing even though he doesn't deliberately contrive this. His motions and [what he's working on] are in a kind of harmony. He isn't following any set of written instructions because the nature of the material at hand determines his thoughts and motions, which simultaneously change the nature of the material at hand. The material and his thoughts are changing together in a progression of changes until his mind's at rest at the same time the material's right.

ROBERT M. PIRSIG, *Zen and the Art of Motorcycle Maintenance*, 1974

21 Building the Long Paper

Longer papers do not involve a different discovery process than short papers, but they do usually take shape much more tentatively to begin with. They usually require more systematic canvassing of supporting materials. Because the complexity of a piece of writing increases with its length, longer papers usually require more development to get all elements working with maximum harmony and force.

Finding a Subject

Your first aim naturally is to fix on something to write about. Possible tactics for the shorter paper appear in Chapter 4, "The Blank Page." They can help with the longer paper but need to be extended.

Let us suppose that you have a general curiosity about censorship. So much debate goes on about child pornography, male striptease, X-rated movies and TV—not to mention extremist political dogmas and their threat to social stability—that the topic could be developed in many ways. Let's suppose further that you are not governed by any assigned guidelines as to what kind of censorship to investigate, or in what place or in what time. Your topic is open.

Begin by welcoming your ideas wherever they start. It is *not* essential to read about all kinds of censorship and then whittle down to a specific topic like "The Censorship of Military Mail." The prescription to squeeze down a broad field to a narrow topic is found in many textbooks on writing, and it has a certain common sense. But ideas for writing can just as readily come the opposite way. For example, your first thought on censorship might be highly explicit: "At Purkey's Drugstore you can't buy *Quickie Hot Romance* magazine except under the counter." A store does exercise a kind of censorship by removing a magazine from the regular racks; and you could work from this point toward the general problem of censorship in the retail marketplace. Again, you might start with a wide conviction which others might condemn as vague: "Censorship interferes with truthful reporting." A perfectly usable springboard. From there you could work out the definitions and collect the evidence which could persuade others.

Think without restrictions during these first reflections. Premature decisions on exact scope or topic can throttle the imagination. The most startling perceptions can flash out from unexpected combinations of ideas. For example, you might catch yourself asking, "How about heroin and marijuana—is it censorship to forbid their sale?" No, the term "censorship" is usually confined to verbal and artistic expression; but in touching on drugs, you're getting at the broader issues of government license and prohibition in *any* field. Maybe *that's* what you want to write about. So an oblique question can sometimes lead to one's real subject.

Try projecting your topic onto the basic development patterns described in Chapter 7 (page 62). These patterns offer possible definitions of topic, possible lines of order and expansion. For example, by applying the time-order pattern to censorship, a writer would be led into censorship history: the Comstock Act of 1873, the controversy over the novels of Thomas Hardy in the 1890s, the 1933 trial over James Joyce's *Ulysses*, and so forth. A space-order pattern might suggest an east-to-west survey of censorship as found in Russia, France, England, the United States.

Ask *why* you want to know about your topic as it is beginning to take shape. Such a question need not take the skeptical tone of "so what?" Rather, it may come as a generating opportunity: "What could a mastery of this topic help me to do?" Surely censorship is more than an intellectual puzzle to play with. An investigation of censorship might clarify your personal standards of taste. It might help you (and your audience) to understand what freedom of expression means, and what the social benefits and dangers of such freedom are. It might help you to deal with some issue in your own community (how far, for example, should you concern yourself with the textbooks your kids read in school?).

Settling on a Main Point

Every successful piece of nonfiction should leave the reader with one provocative thought that he didn't have before. Not two thoughts, or five—just one. So try to decide what point you most want to leave in the reader's mind. It will not only give you a better idea of what route you ought to

follow and what destination you hope to reach; it will also
affect your decision about tone and attitude.

WILLIAM ZINSSER, *On Writing Well*, 1980

At some moment which only you can recognize, you do arrive at a controlling idea, a conviction of having a meaning which is worth working on. This instant of assurance is doubly significant. It puts you on the inside of the creative process rather than on the outside. And it tightens the focus of your exploration. Up to now you've been ranging widely, freely, even playfully. From now on, the search for meaning and the search for material will still interplay, much more than in a short composition; but you will feel more and more sure of what will help and what won't.

This main point can be fixed by framing a single sentence which states your topic *and what you see as important in it*—for example:

> The censorship of pornography does more damage than does the pornography itself.
>
> Selling girlie magazines under the drugstore counter encourages unhealthy attitudes in the purchaser.
>
> Thomas Hardy let censorship scare him out of writing novels.

Such a guiding statement, often called a *thesis* or *thesis sentence,* may later need to be more precisely attuned to the structure and conclusion of your final draft, but a trial thesis serves to launch you forward. You need only to avoid such a vague thesis as would deny your material any shape, as in these examples:

> Censorship is for the birds. (*Why not say instead what the main objection to censorship is?*)
>
> There are many kinds of censorship. (*Why not say instead what kinds there are and why the variety matters?*)
>
> Good censorship must be distinguished from bad censorship. (*Why not say instead how the two can be distinguished?*)

You might write out your trial thesis on a card to keep in front of you as you go further. Whether it appears in your paper labeled *as* your thesis is optional.

Topics for Amplification and Support

Besides whatever leads you've already opened up, try working up some of these traditional phases of an explanation or argument:

> *Background*
> Definition, origin, and illustration of the central question (or event or process or concept).

Contexts of the present subject: Where is it important, how,
why, to whom?
Development
Typical cases.
Possible interpretations or solutions, and the standards for
choosing.
Demonstration of right and wrong choices and their conse-
quences.
Extending of conclusion to some broader application.
Reinforcement
Additional illustration.
Possible questions; answers.
Possible objections; refutations.
Reemphasis of main point and its significance.

You might also give a provisional thought to your audience as you line
up your materials. Not every writer has a keen feel for the reader this
early. Some writers apparently must begin by writing for themselves,
only gradually becoming aware of a real audience which might stimulate
the creative process. What's most important is that you should never accept an audience relationship which requires you to fake. To ask "What
do they want to hear?" rather than "How do we work together?" is to become an intellectual flunkey. In doubt, you probably do best to satisfy
your own values first, and let your picture of the audience develop later.

Still, writing is the public exploration of meaning, and your sense of an
audience can improve your choice of materials and of writing plan *especially when you expect to be read by inexperienced or hostile readers.* If
you plan, say, to *defend* censorship against idealistic readers who hotly
resent it, you need to discover their arguments, to devise rebuttals, to ask
how far you can respect their position, to order your defense so as to
minimize their resistance. The whole business of finding a relationship
with one's audience is treated in Chapters 9 and 10 and should enter
your thinking now if you anticipate facing anything like a difficult
reception.

Note-Taking

A "germination" or storehouse sheet always serves for jotting down any
ideas for expanding, illustrating, or testing a topic. For longer papers
which require extended study, you will soon see the need for systematic
notes which can be efficiently mobilized for the actual writing. Any plan
which works is fine; but some commonsense tips may serve.

*Postpone detailed note-taking until the exploration process is well un-
der way.* A writer who begins too early will take too many notes and bog
down in the necessary orientation. To start with, read widely and quickly.

Classify your notes under broad topics so that you can sort them out for the writing. But before deciding on detailed subtopics, wait until the material takes shape.

Note exactly the source of any notes you take. This precaution is especially important for a documented paper in which you are expected to back up any substantial assertion. (For special conventions of the documented paper, see Chapter 23, page 267.) To save yourself the drudgery of copying out a source reference dozens of times for dozens of notes, you can set up a master bibliography card (or sheet) on which each source is assigned a code letter which you then use for shorthand reference to all reading notes. (In place of code letters, the author's initials or last name may be used.) Thus:

```
                     Bibliography card - 1

A - McDonagh, David E.  Censorship and Literature.  2nd ed.;  New York:
      Macmillan, 1983.

B - Kupke, Doris I.  "Thomas Hardy, Ex-Novelist," Fiction Notes, XXII
      (1982), 451-464.

C - Young, Leslie S.  "The Plotting of Serialized Novels," in The Sociology
      of Fiction, ed. Andrea Calkins.  3rd ed.; New York:  Oxford University
      Press, 1979.
```

In your reading notes, "A 117" can now be used instead of writing out the details for McDonagh's book, page 117. From this card you can later type up your formal bibliography (naturally omitting the code letters, which have merely served your convenience). The bibliography card should therefore describe each item carefully, with all the information conventionally included. See page 275 for instructions on formal bibliographies.

By no means take your notes on large sheets written on both sides. You would waste hours later on in searching, comparing, and recopying scattered materials to bring them together. The great advantage of *notecards* (3 × 5 or 4 × 6) is that you can later arrange them in the exact order you like, and even write your paper taking the notes as they come. For maximum efficiency, follow the principle of *one note per topic per source*—that is, start a new note for each change of topic or source. The slight extra cost for cards will be thoroughly justified by the gain in flexible handling of your materials.

As for the form of your note (or notecard), reserve the top for its

topic. Unless you do use such headings, you will later have to read each
note an extra time to identify it. Some writers may choose to use two
topics—a general one (at upper right, say) and a specific one (at upper
left but lower). Summarize your source wherever possible, but copy
word for word wherever the exact wording of your text would carry unusual authority. When you do copy word for word, take extreme care to
use quotation marks, since failure to do so may lead you into unintentional plagiarism when you do write your paper. Show page numbers,
taking care to show just where you leave one page of your source for another; thus any references in your paper to *part* of your note can be accurate. A sample card:

```
                                                    plot
   sex

   (117)  Explicit sex relationships between unmarried lovers were taboo
   for many magazine editors in the early 20th century.  Fear of puritanical
   readers.  "John Akins rewrote the love plot of A Wild Night three times,
   so that (118) the lovers' baby finally turned out to be adopted."

                        A 117-118
```

Use the back of the notecard if necessary. If you must use two or more
cards for the same note, invent some notation to keep you from later
scattering the cards beyond recall; or staple the cards together.

The Writing Plan

Writers differ so much in their planning of first drafts that a rule would
be foolish. Some prefer the traditional textbook strategy of a formal outline, right down to roman and Arabic numerals. Others feel constrained
by outlining and would rather plunge into a sea of notes, trusting to find
and use its deeper currents as they swim along.

I have used both approaches with reasonable success, but feel most
comfortable with a blend of rough plan and spontaneity, with the final
draft being used to tighten structure. Thus I will jot down the major
headings; under each, I write reminders of the material to use, assign a
rough ordering by use of letters and numbers, and then begin to write.
Figure 1, for example, shows the plan which I used for drafting Chapter
4, "The Blank Page," a new chapter for this edition.

Figure 1.   Writing Plan for a First Draft

(Chapter 4 of the present text. Original was scribbled by hand. The symbols and numbers after certain entries refer to sources to be consulted during the writing.)

Ch. O. THE BLANK PAGE

2
A *Forced writing*
  (jumping in)
Brainstorming
Freewriting

4
B *Observation*
1 Keep journal
4 How is this subj
  changing?
3 Record an actual dialog
5 5 pos quals in disliked
  person
2 Stroll thru fam setting

1
E *Discipline*
3 Think writing 236
5 Save good ideas
  236
6 Start germination
  sheet 237
7 Start well ahead of
  deadline 237
2 Optimum environs
  &c
1 False block RC 100
4 Write often 235

2 (Also: journals; meditation)

5
C *Reflection*
5̸ Ltr to ed.
1 Meditation
2 Rank aims of edn
4̸ Show how you tie
  into natl controversy
x A̸s̸ ̸a̸ ̸r̸e̸s̸ ̸s̸c̸i̸e̸n̸t̸i̸s̸t̸
  /w̸h̸y̸ ̸t̸i̸e̸/
6̸ A day doing delayed
  tasks
3 Ltr of self-rec.

6
D *Springboards*
Answer "so what?" PS453
Answer "for instance"
G̸e̸n̸e̸r̸a̸t̸e̸ ̸f̸r̸o̸m̸ ̸p̸r̸o̸v̸o̸c̸a̸t̸i̸o̸n̸s̸
Interview EPJ 23-
t̸o̸y̸ ̸s̸a̸y̸ ̸p̸r̸i̸n̸t̸
Wear a turkey feather WK
Step out of char WK
Starting a conversation WK

3
F *Memory*
3 Recover childhood
2 5 snapshots
1 address bk;
  forgotten names
4 Title of yr autobiog

NOTE: The order adopted was something like general-to-particular—from the general discipline of a writer to primary sources of material for writing to gimmicks for shaking oneself loose. This order was drastically modified for the actual Chapter 4 as it appears in this book.

The Writing

When you risk your first words on paper, you won't have thought of everything a writer eventually considers. You can, if you wish, preview the next chapter: it deals with the later drafts of a long paper. But Ernest Hemingway's observation of the writing act itself should be kept in mind: "Everything changes as it moves." Only a few authors of exceptionally retentive mind, like Samuel Johnson, have been able to work and rework their compositions in their heads before touching paper. Thus their first written drafts, with only a little re-touching, became their final drafts.

Most writers like me (and perhaps you) are condemned to begin their first drafts on stumbling feet—dashing forward and tripping by turns as they take this gamble and dodge that difficulty. If your rough plan begins to crumble on you, take heart. Stop, scribble out a revised map for what's still ahead, and climb on. You've already caught sight of some luminous heights ahead of you. Such glimpses are discoveries. The whole first draft is an experiment in discovery.

When you've finished the first draft, don't slam your books shut and dash out to celebrate—just yet. Use your momentum. New ideas often keep pouring in as one looks over the first draft. New support may suggest itself, or better ways of putting something. Mark such places with reminders of what to do when you come back to the project. All this will help the next draft to start up much more easily.

Exercise 1 (tentative main point; trial thesis)

Show which of the following statements of main point would be hard to write from, and for each of those, suggest an improved version.

EXAMPLE   *Trial thesis:* I don't want to live past seventy.
Analysis: This sentence shows only a conclusion. To write from this, one needs to know what chief reasons would support the conclusion.
Possible improved version: I don't want to live past seventy, because of the greatly increased odds against continued health, mental capacity, and financial security.

a. Students transfer between colleges for several reasons.
b. Antisocial behavior which surfaces at Christmas.
c. The best reason for men to support the women's movement is

to liberate themselves from the false role expectations which have been imposed upon the male.

d. We don't offer college courses in typing; why should we offer college courses in computer operating?

e. A really safe automobile must prevent the passenger's head from whipping backward, must cushion the head from forward collision, and must prevent the body from shooting out of its seat.

f. One should not sign up with a correspondence school without taking certain precautions.

Exercise 2 (finding amplification and support)

For each statement of main point below, invent the questions which would implement the three traditional functions of background, development, and reinforcement outlined on p. 241 or pp. 241–242:

EXAMPLE Although modern technology imposes greater controls on people, it also gives them larger freedom.

Questions to implement background:
What is meant by "modern technology"?
In what ways are people being "controlled" by technology? Examples?
Why are people excited about this issue? What do they foresee as the worst consequences?
Questions to implement development:
What controls of people does modern technology really make necessary, and why?
What fears of control may be founded or unfounded?
What would constitute "larger freedom" in a modern technological society?
What evidence is there that such freedom actually results?
Questions to implement reinforcement:
Can I come up with a single clincher illustration of some community or company which is "liberated" by technology?
Could a pessimistic critic see a dark side to this illustration? How would I answer?

a. Students are most likely to gain the values of a liberal education if their teachers attractively embody those values.

b. Urgent action is needed to preserve our national parks from damage by overuse.

c. The current revival of interest in early musical instruments rises from three causes: the reaction against the "big music" of modern orchestras and auditoriums; the new historical curiosity as to how early music was actually performed; the wide desire for musical activity which is open to the amateur.

d. If the proportion of carbon dioxide in our atmosphere were doubled, the climate would become warm enough to melt the world's glaciers.

Exercise 3 (note-taking)

Using notecards, take notes on Chapter 20 of this textbook (page 223), taking as your subject how rhythm and sound can be used in advertising. This brief exercise can help you to learn the form of notecards. It can help you to learn how to *select* material to support a given topic which may *not* be the topic of your source. Your instructor may ask you to show or share these notes for critique.

Exercise 4 (all elements)

This exercise is linked with others in the next chapter, to carry you all the way through the three drafts recommended for best college work. It can be adapted to a research paper, to an extended essay, or to a story or play. See Exercises 4 and 5, Chapter 22.

a. Choose one of the following topics on which you would be willing to invest a large block of time. If you're using this book with a literature course, you could tie in many of the topics with a given author or literary period—for example, "The Rights of Women in Socrates' Athens" or "The Censorship of Chaucer's Bawdier Stories."

denim pants
Benjamin Franklin
censorship
the recovery of lost literature
Leonardo da Vinci
eavesdropping
the use of stimulants and
  depressants
Alexander the Great
man-caused changes in climate
domestic architecture
African origins of modern music

genetic engineering
espionage
the rights of women
the writing disciplines of famous
  authors
the concept of hell
ear damage
secret knowledge or practices in
  religion
miniaturization of equipment
professional soccer
computer translation
(*a topic of your own*)

b. (For thinking and discussion rather than writing) Carry your topic through the initial exploration described in this chapter. Remember that you can modify, restrict, or broaden topics to meet your interests.
c. Take notes from sources which can amplify or support your topic.
d. Write a brief evaluation of the audience you plan to address and its probable effect on your approach.
e. Arrive at a trial thesis (single-sentence statement) of what your topic will

mean in this paper. Write it out, and use the reactions of others as your instructor may suggest.

f. Work out a writing plan to show main headings and main support to be used in drafting your paper. Such a plan may range from a formal outline to a roughing out of headings and support as shown in Figure 1, page 245.

g. Write the first draft and submit all working papers with it. (For acknowledging sources by means of footnotes and bibliography, you will need to check out Chapter 23; but instead of full footnotes, you can use parenthetical references at this stage.)

Although much of this work has to be informal and scribbly by the very nature of exploratory writing, do use pen or typewriter for enough legibility to allow responses from your reader(s).

22   Reaching the Final Commitment

A long paper grows as a short paper does, and the agenda proposed on Chapter 5, "Revision," can be useful here. But length multiplies your opportunities so much that you may want to have a first priority for re-working the paper, and then a second priority—perhaps for a later and final draft but at least for helping you to concentrate on first matters first.

First Priorities for Re-Working the Paper

Critique. The long draft needs a close looking-over by you and by members of your audience. See "Useful Criticism and How To Get It," page 44; also apply the relevant matters below.

Sharpening the main point. The gains to be made in this new stage of writing can be illustrated by supposing that a student has already arrived at the trial thesis cited in the last chapter:

> Thomas Hardy let censorship scare him out of writing novels.

Suppose further that the student's first draft can be digested thus:

> Thomas Hardy's *Jude the Obscure* (1895) ran into such furious attacks on its alleged immorality that Hardy was "completely cured of further interest in novel writing."
> Hardy might have expected some protest, since he had dared to open a forbidden issue for those days—the sexual drive in

young people and how it conflicts with traditional attitudes toward marriage. Jude is a brilliant English youth who loses his
chance to enter the university when his sensual sweetheart tricks
him into marriage on the bluff of being pregnant. After separating from this opportunist, Jude falls genuinely in love with
his cousin Sue; but on her discovery that he is already married,
she rebounds into a mismatch with an older man. She recovers
from this mistake and tries to live with Jude. The entanglement
of bad marriages, bad conscience, constant poverty, and unhappy children proves too much. Jude's family breaks apart in
an avalanche of catastrophe; he dies hearing the bells of the
university to which he never gained admission.

But Hardy's moral boldness is not so remarkable as his strange
timidity in first toning down a serialized version of *Jude* for the
editor of *Harper's Magazine*. The Jude of the magazine version
marries his first sweetheart *not* because his sexual drive has
trapped him but because she has resorted to the high school
stunt of arousing his jealousy by exhibiting forged letters from
another admirer. The magazine Jude *never* lives with Sue. They
merely live *near* each other as prudish companions. Naturally
the children have to be manufactured through adoption. And
so on.

In short, Hardy made *Jude the Obscure* acceptable to the
magazine audience of the 1890s by whitewashing the central
sex issue, by reducing the strength of his characters, by mini-
mizing the high stakes for which they had lived.

This summary of Hardy's troubles with *Jude* seems interesting enough
but it sprawls. The exploratory trial thesis (on why Hardy stopped writing novels) dissolved as the writer found new leads on *how Hardy ap-
peased the editor*. A new thesis is now needed to express this new concern, and, because the writer will invest so much energy developing a
new thesis, several thesis statements should be tried and tested—thus:

1. Thomas Hardy evaded censorship by toning down *Jude the
   Obscure* for magazine serialization.

Actually this statement plays with words. If Hardy acted as his own cen-
sor, he really *didn't* evade censorship, he merely complied with it.

2. The toning down of Thomas Hardy's *Jude the Obscure* illustrates what can be called social or editorial censorship as opposed to legal censorship.

A valid point to make. But if "editorial censorship" becomes the topic,
won't many other examples be needed, from other authors as well? That
would mean a new and different paper. After several more tries, the following statement might turn up:

3. In toning down the original version of *Jude the Obscure* to satisfy his magazine editor, Thomas Hardy downgraded a great novel into a pallid romance.

This version strikes exactly the line which the student was approaching in the exploratory draft. *Note that the student's "sprawling" during the first draft shows significant strength, not weakness.* Over-control during the exploration process can actually choke off growth. Digressions can be fruitful. They can lead to the writer's main vein.

The tension between control and sprawl may need to continue through two cycles or more; but eventually one does settle on—or arrive at—an exact idea of main point which brings its own benefits. A precise thesis statement can help you to select and shape the material which goes into the new draft. Because the thesis is restrictive, it excludes material which though associated with the topic does not advance it directly. Any early material on Hardy's life or on his other works can now be stripped down. Second, because the thesis is unified, it tells you how to frame the details. Whatever Hardy did to *Jude the Obscure* for magazine serialization must now be examined in the light of one question: how did it weaken or not weaken his novel? Finally, because the thesis is specific, it tells you what new material you need.

Expanding the support. You can work up a full, commonsense attack on your subject by putting your main point closely and curiously through the same traditional phases already presented for use with the earlier version of your main point: background, development, reinforcement (page 241 or pp. 241–242). Here again is the new thesis:

> In toning down the original version of *Jude the Obscure* to satisfy his magazine editor, Thomas Hardy downgraded a great novel into a pallid romance.

For the background, you ask—if you hadn't already asked in the earlier draft—what briefing your reader would need to understand the basic assertion made by the thesis. Let your present readers help, if they will. Thus:

> Who was Thomas Hardy?
> What is the novel *Jude the Obscure* all about?
> What evidence suggests that the novel was modified under pressure?
> What is the history of this question? What earlier critics have commented on it? Why does it merit further attention? (*Note:* The history of the main problem receives special attention in scholarly research, but in more general writing it will often be taken for granted.)

> What tastes of the Victorian public collided with Hardy's novel, and how are these tastes to be accounted for?
>
> What kinds of hostility to the fictional treatment of sexual matters were being shown at this time, and how serious were the dangers to authors and publishers?
>
> Why did Hardy want to serialize his novel with *Harper's Magazine* and why was *Harper's* interested?

For the development, you ask what evidence would persuade your reader that Hardy did damage his own novel—thus:

> What *are* the "original" and "magazine serial" versions of *Jude the Obscure?*
>
> What toning down did the editor specifically ask for? Did Hardy protest? What compromises did they make, if any?
>
> What did the toning down affect—plot, characterization, style, etc.—and how much of it was done? How did the toning down achieve its objectives in each case?
>
> What virtues of the original were weakened or lost, and how?
>
> Do any critics concur in the judgment that *Jude the Obscure* was impaired by the toning down? What did Hardy himself think?

For the reinforcement, you ask what questions a hostile, skeptical, or confused reader might raise on reading the demonstration—thus:

> By any chance could some of the changes in *Jude the Obscure* be defended as artistic improvements?
>
> Even if the changes failed to improve the novel, did Hardy really make enough of them to cause serious damage?

Such reinforcement backs up the central argument. If the writer's aim were not to argue but to explain a process, then the reinforcement might focus on the details most difficult to grasp or on some alternate way of seeing the process. If the writer's aim were to define a concept, the reinforcement might supply those distinctions which the reader would find hardest to make.

Placing the audience. By fixing your relationship with the reader at this time, you can see what elements of your own subject have the most potential, and which most threaten the success of your paper.

The student who wrote on *Jude,* for example, might have drifted during the exploratory stage—from having no picture of the reader, then to seeing the reader as a partner in indignation at what Hardy did, then to finding the reader a partner in amusement at Victorian prudishness. The writer might relax from a formal, impersonal style to an informal, you-and-I manner. Or vice versa: The writer might see the reader as more skeptical and hostile than supposed, so that a more formal and objective manner would be best.

As you feel in closer touch with a live reader, you can also ask "What would best come first?" "What might come better later?" So you may arrive at a *psychological ordering* for the new draft—that sequence of discussions most likely to find a given audience prepared, interested, and receptive at every point. For example, readers will follow more easily from the familiar to the unfamiliar than the other way around. For potentially hostile readers, consider taking time to reach rapport on those topics least open to question, before proceeding to touchier issues. Psychological ordering becomes especially useful in argumentative writing, in calls for action, in the giving of directions, and in arousing a sluggish audience.

The new writing plan. As long as an explicit outline cramps you, you may be wise to trust the writing process itself to shape your discovery as you go. Sooner or later, a long piece must be more or less *outlinable*—it must be accessible to the reader who tries to see how it all works together. So you may well rough out a plan now, taking more care as your project is longer and more serious. Even so, everything may continue to "change as it moves," and some writers (including me) find that they remap each section of the paper as they actually come to it and see it close at hand.

Particularly with the long formal essay or research paper, three principles will guarantee the clearest structure: *unity of concepts, interrelatedness of subdivisions,* and *consolidation of points.* A paper which neglects them can become so structurally deformed that only extensive rewriting will save it.

Unity of concepts means that the writer's concepts are all necessary and mutually consistent. No concept is introduced which is not required; no concept shifts from one sense to another one. Consider how that principle is violated here:

> I. *Official censorship* (censorship applied by a government agency) should be differentiated from *private censorship* (censorship applied by a private agency through legal suits, boycotting, and so forth).
>
> II. Thomas Hardy toned down *Jude the Obscure* to satisfy the anxieties of his magazine editor over the possible public reception.

One obvious flaw is that neither "official censorship" nor "private censorship" as described in Part I has any bearing upon Hardy's toning-down of *Jude.* Hence the concepts, however interesting in themselves, are useless here. They mislead and squander the reader's attention. Such digressions easily enter the work of any writer who draws heavily upon library sources without subordinating them to a single present purpose. How does this next example violate the unity-of-concepts principle?

> I. *Pornography*, which degrades sex into the single and obsessive aim of life, should be distinguished from *sexual realism*, which treats sex honestly as one element in the total life experience.
> II. D. H. Lawrence's *Lady Chatterley's Lover* can be defended as *artistic pornography*—pornography done with such skill and humanity as to elevate the subject matter.

Both I and II may seem sensible in themselves; but together they are contradictory. Part I conceives of *all* pornography as degrading, whereas Part II conceives of a type of pornography which is not.

Interrelatedness of subdivisions, the second principle, means that the subject is divided so that its parts cleanly work together. You would avoid such overlaps as this:

> I. Victorian standards of personal conduct.
> II. Victorian attitudes toward adultery.

Adultery of course *is* personal conduct; thus the writer seems to be entering the topic just left. A cleaner subdivision would be:

> I. *General* Victorian standards of personal conduct.
> II. Victorian attitudes toward adultery *as a specific* illustration.

Notice how pointedly Part II is made to relate to Part I without trespassing upon it.

The interrelatedness-of-subdivisions principle applies especially to parallel topics, which should be subdivided so as to invite parallel attention. Here they are not:

> HARDY'S "JUDE THE OBSCURE" AND LAWRENCE'S "LADY CHATTERLEY'S LOVER"—A CONTRAST IN LITERARY SUPPRESSION
> I. Hardy's *Jude the Obscure*.
>   A. The suppressing agency.
>   B. The author's response.
>   C. The effect upon the novel.
> II. Lawrence's *Lady Chatterley's Lover*.
>   A. Why the novel was first barred from the U.S.
>   B. The 1959 case in which the ban was voided.
>   C. Implications for literary suppression today.

The color of an apple can't be compared with the shape of a pear; nor can the *agency* for suppressing *Jude* be compared to the *reasons* for suppressing *Lady Chatterley*. Comparisons can be drawn only from features held in common, and the logical solution here would be to replan Part II so that it matches Part I; then a true comparison could be made.

Consolidation of points, the third principle of organization, means that the writer uses a minimum of subdivisions—only those indispensable to a competent analysis of the subject. As a rule of thumb, any long list of equally ranked points should be checked to see what consolidations are possible—thus:

HARDY'S TONING DOWN OF THE MAGAZINE VERSION
OF "JUDE THE OBSCURE"
Splintered
    I. Hardy's modification of Arabella's "pregnancy."
   II. His disinfecting of Jude's motives for marrying Arabella.
  III. His devitalizing of Sue's adulterous passion for Jude.
   IV. His treatment of their later common-law marriage as a platonic friendship.
    V. His sentimentalizing of the main characters.

Here an experienced writer would recognize that Points I–V boil down to two major items—Hardy's plot and Hardy's characterization—and would regroup the points thus simplifying the attention of both writer and reader.

Consolidated
    I. Hardy's cleaning up of plot where sex was involved.
      A. His modification of Arabella's "pregnancy."
      B. His disinfecting of Jude's motives for marrying Arabella.
      C. His devitalizing of Sue's adulterous passion for Jude.
      D. His treatment of their later common-law marriage as a platonic friendship.
   II. Hardy's sentimentalizing of the main characters.

The consolidation-of-points principle can also protect you from "looping back" or reentering a topic previously examined, as in the following example:

    I. The suppression of Lawrence's *Lady Chatterley's Lover*.
      A. . . . .
      B. . . . .
      C. Lawrence's reaction to the suppression.
   II. Lawrence's own view of sex, in *Lady Chatterley's Lover*.
THE "LOOP"   A. . . . .
      B. . . . .
      C. His reaction to the suppression.

Although returning to remake an earlier point can sometimes yield a new level of meaning or an emphatic contrast, the writer may easily seem to be merely rambling back and forth. Here one might do better to consolidate the two accounts of Lawrence's reaction to the suppression—perhaps by dropping I-C and treating the whole of Lawrence's reaction under II-C.

Framing the paper: the beginning. In opening the paper, you can help the reader make a confident, sympathetic, and efficient beginning if you do at least two things:

> Make the topic known.
>
> Show the interest and significance of the topic for the reader.

Treated in such a way, the beginning provides the most important part of the background. In a longer paper, the beginning may also:

> Announce the plan of attack.
>
> Establish the knowledge and disposition of writer and reader (see Chapters 9 and 10).
>
> Emphasize the special associations and pressures of the immediate occasion (see p. 108).

Of these functions, the plan of attack is often omitted for short or informal pieces; the traits of writer and audience may be left to imply themselves gradually; and the immediate occasion may not exert enough pressure to be mentioned at all. A hostile audience, however, requires such diplomacy that a writer may extend the introduction to gain rapport in every way possible.

Three devices which help fulfil these functions are the title, the lead sentence, and the organizing sentence or paragraph. Possible titles here:

> Vague and dull: "The Censorship of a Victorian Novel."
>
> Exact, suitable for a serious audience: "Thomas Hardy's Magazine Version of *Jude the Obscure:* A Study in the Cost of Social Censorship."
>
> Lively, sensational, suitable for the light reader: "Did Thomas Hardy Sell Out to the Victorian Bluenoses?" or "A Great Novel Ruined—An Episode in Victorian Censorship."

The lead sentence(s) can do so much to engage the reader that the modern press has developed lead techniques to open articles energetically and attractively. One might open with a paradox which points up a central conflict:

> In 1894 Thomas Hardy wanted to publish a novel on a topic no
> editor had been willing to touch. Hardy also wanted to be read.

The lead might present a question:

> Was Thomas Hardy's audience of the 1890s finally ready for a
> frank study of the sex drive and its potential damage to a prudish
> society?

The lead can open narratively:

> When I first read Thomas Hardy's *Jude the Obscure,* I could not
> believe that the sexual drive of a good young man could wreck
> his life as terribly as it did in Hardy's nineteenth-century
> England.

A leading quotation, if apt and brief, can introduce the major theme to
be treated:

> "No legal censorship can weaken the fine arts as much as the
> informal restraint imposed by a priggish public taste." (Harold
> O'Rourke, *Courage and Convention,* 1973)

The lead can challenge a common view:

> Though Thomas Hardy is commonly praised for defending the
> English novel against Victorian prudery, he did surrender on
> occasion.

Mechanically applied, such leads are gimmicky and they would insult an
audience by implying that gimmicks are required to hold its attention.
But there is nothing wrong with an honest and tasteful effort to prove
the interest of your topic. Why *should* the reader care about the toning
down of a serialized novel that took place some generations ago? Presumably because society still suffers from social censorship and can learn
from past errors. Or because people still read Thomas Hardy and want a
clearer estimate of his achievement. Or because one can see in the 1890s
a confused and rebellious time like our own. This is the kind of relevance
you should feel when commiting yourself to such a topic in the first
place; your opening should communicate it.

The final opening device, the organizing sentence or paragraph, announces the plan of attack—thus: "In the following pages I will first take
up A, then B, then C." Such an announcement could damage an informal
paper where a spontaneous tone is wanted (imagine starting a personal
letter with such a sentence). In formal essays and research papers, however, systematic attention from both writer and reader is essential, and

the organizing sentence helps to assure it. (Another term for the organizing passage is *programmatic passage,* in that the passage sets down the program to be followed.)

A good beginning does so much for a paper that many writers rework their opening passages more often than any other section of the paper. To fix the topic, to plead its interest, to prepare the reader's attention, and to enter into the optimum writer-reader relationship for that whole process of "public exploration through writing" which this book describes—to do all these at once is more than most of us can manage on first try.

Framing the paper: linking parts. The link is a phrase or passage which signals both you and your reader that one section of the paper is over and another is beginning. The paragraph heading which you've just read is such a link. It announces the new topic—the link—while reminding you of the encompassing subject, "framing the paper."

Major links may begin by recapitulating the section just finished, and then go on to furnish the plan for the next section. Minor links can signal the shift in one passing phrase—for example, *"Another reason* for revising Hardy's novel was that. . . ." Like organizing passages, links are especially appropriate to formal, highly organized exposition or argument. Linkage can be overworked for readers who resist being steered too strenuously; but a good rule of thumb is to employ plenty of links in the first draft—where you need to steer yourself—and then to prune them in later drafts. For discussion of coherence at paragraph level, see Chapter 8, page 77.

Framing the paper: the ending. The conclusion is almost as hard to write as the opening, because in it one is seeking to confirm the sense of discovery achieved by both writer and reader. Moreover, one is making a final bid for the reader's intellectual, emotional, and moral assent. A conclusion therefore ought to do at least this much:

> Restate or imply the main point.
>
> Seek to reinforce the commitment desired from the reader in terms of emotional response, intellectual agreement, moral conviction, will to act.
>
> Satisfy (or pointedly deny) the reader's need for closure.

To satisfy the reader's need for closure is to round off the paper so that it seems complete, finished, done. Thus the reader won't skid past the last page expecting more to follow—as here:

> Hardy's editor did want still other changes to be made in *Jude the Obscure,* but Hardy refused.

Well yes, but what happened then? This writer evidently broke off while still wandering in mid-subject. By revision, the ending could nail down the main point:

> Even though Hardy refused to make the further changes which his editor wanted, the damage was done. In its magazine form, *Jude the Obscure* had been emasculated into a bedtime story— an easily forgettable monument to the everlasting power of editorial timidity.

Closure is almost always achieved in formal conclusions, but a story, poem, or personal essay may end without wrapping things up, sometimes to imitate the inconclusiveness of everyday life and sometimes to provoke the reader to keep on wondering or wanting.

The conclusion can also serve the function of reinforcement if it will do the following:

> Recapitulate main points.
>
> Illustrate or otherwise extend the application of the main point. (Are readers still being spoon-fed by magazine editors? Was Hardy's ordeal a blessing in disguise, in that he turned to writing poetry for the splendid work of his last years?)
>
> (*For argumentative writing*) Intensify the rhetorical drama as described on pages 108–109—the human significance of the issues; the characterization of writer and reader; the pressures of the immediate occasion.

The substantial conclusion of several paragraphs needed to do this may be appropriate to a long serious paper, especially if the audience is hostile or if a large investment is being asked of it.

In coming to the sign-off sentences, you can adapt, if appropriate, the techniques already mentioned for the lead—question, challenge, quotation, narrative, and so on. You can echo your opening lead, to give the sense of wheel-coming-full-circle. Honesty of tone is especially hard to maintain at this moment when you're already drained of your subject but are still trying to end strong. Lame truisms and sonorous uplift are characteristic faults of the closing, which instead should be fresh and thoughtful. In Zinsser's words, "The perfect ending should take the reader slightly by surprise and yet seem exactly right" (*On Writing Well*, 1980).

Second Priorities

The "first priorities" deal with the large organic matters of main point, content, tone, and structure. In writing a long paper you may need to address them more than once to approach final form. In proportion as you resolve such questions, you can think of the following "second priorities"—the checking and refining which will bring your insights into precise focus.

Accuracy of support. Surprising errors can seep into details and references which you may have copied two or three times en route from source to present draft. Professionals will verify each cited fact, each quotation, each page reference by checking back to the source itself. Do this if you can. As a minimal procedure, proofread your notes at the time you write them, quotations especially. Then check your final draft against your notes.

Control over sources. A special problem arises when citing sources which may diverge widely from you in outlook and purpose. The danger in earlier drafts is that you may be dominated by your notes—using *their* scale and emphasis rather than your own.

Suppose that you wish to make the point on Hardy's *Jude the Obscure* that a hostile reception of that novel was a real and present danger, not the bugaboo of timid editors. In support, you might find this passage from Florence E. Hardy's *The Later Years of Thomas Hardy*, 1930, describing the furor which greeted *Jude* when it finally appeared in book form without the toning down applied to the earlier magazine version:

> The *New York World* had been among those papers that fell foul of the book in the strongest terms, the critic being a maiden lady who expressed herself thus:
>
> "What has happened to Thomas Hardy? . . . I am shocked, appalled by this story! . . . It is almost the worst book I ever read. . . . I do not believe that there is a newspaper in England or America that would print this story of Thomas Hardy's as it stands in the book. Aside from its immorality there is coarseness which is beyond belief. . . ."

Excellent evidence. But a poor way to use it would be merely to tuck it into your paper with only a covering sentence like this:

> Among those critics which assaulted *Jude the Obscure,* the most vehement was the *New York World,* whose attack included the following: [*Insert quotation as above.*]

This citation merely echoes the emphasis of the source upon the hostility of the public. It fails to redirect the evidence to your own purpose, which is to stress *the justification of the magazine editor's fears.* The following solution does so:

> The moral indignation feared by Hardy's magazine editor did in fact erupt when *Jude the Obscure* later appeared in unexpur-

gated book form. "I am shocked, appalled by this story!" wrote a critic in the *New York World*. ". . . I do not believe that there is a newspaper in England or America that would print this story of Thomas Hardy's as it stands in the book."

The new solution not only opens more relevantly but pares down the quotation, without distortion, to its essentials.

Students writing research papers sometimes feel that they are copying rather than thinking originally. Such revision as just described will de-emphasize copying; it will restore the paper to its author.

Sharpening of words and sentences. You can lose valuable momentum by stopping dead in mid-sentence of an early draft to rack your word-books for a better vocabulary choice. (My own tactic in early drafts is simply to scribble "w" in the margin for a doubtful word choice—or an "s" for a weak sentence—and to keep moving, with the intention to return later on.) Once your draft lies before you in full dimensions, then you can chip away for perfection in small parts, much like a sculptor who has first blocked out the marble. The concepts to apply have been presented in Chapters 13 through 16 for word-choices, and in Chapters 17 through 19 for sentence structure. Recommended for special attention are definition of terms (page 141), specificity of word-choice (page 151), misuse of emotional language as substitute for proof (page 161), economy and tension of sentence structure (page 198), and sentence management (page 215).

Paragraph beginnings. Nothing will pull your readers forward more surely than paragraph openings which at once provide direction and interest. A succession of paragraphs which drag down the reader with flabby wordage can slacken the whole pace of your paper. Consider re-working your first sentences, as well as redividing paragraphs for optimum guidance of the readers' attention. (See "Coherence Among Paragraphs," page 81.)

Copy-editing. See the counsel already provided in "Copy-Editing the Final Draft," page 47.

Exercise 1 (psychological ordering)

Consider the following statement of main point:

Emphasis on winning can damage boy and girl athletes both physically and psychologically unless it is subordinated to such other values as cooperation and self-realization.

What ordering of the topics below would you propose for reaching each of the following audiences?

a. Parents of Little League players.
b. A group of All-Star athletes being briefed on making speeches to banquets for fans.
c. A grade-school convocation attended by parents and children.

Topics (listed randomly):

1. The value of sports in training the athlete to set personal goals.
2. The national conviction that "winning is everything."
3. Physical injuries caused by the will to win at all costs.
4. The social impact of sports, as furnishing models of community behavior.
5. Psychological damage to "losers" and "winners."
6. The importance of win-records in career advancement of coaches and athletes.
7. The value of sports in developing cooperation and altruism.
8. The virtues of striving to be first.

Exercise 2 (writing plans)

Each plan below embodies at least one structural flaw involving the principles of unity of concepts, interrelatedness of subdivisions, and consolidation of points. Diagnose the flaws and revise the plans accordingly.

SAMPLE I. The Russian mass audience.
    A. Its size.
    B. Its media.
    C. How it is motivated.
II. The United States mass audience.
    A. Its size.
    B. Its motivations.
    C. Its alienation of the individual.

SOLUTION This outline fails to relate its subdivisions. Since "Russian mass audience" and "United States mass audience" are parallel headings, they should be subdivided in parallel, as in this possible version:

I. The Russian mass audience.
    A. Its size.
    B. Its motivations.
    C. Its media.
    D. Its influence.
II. The United States mass audience.
    [Same subdivisions.]

a. I. Types of social protest.
    A. The sustained violent protest which disrupts communications, negotiation, and public security.

B. The calm but earnest protest which uses communication and negotiation without disrupting public security.
C. The brief mass demonstration to let off steam.
II. Causes of social protest.
A. Need to let off steam.
B. Poor housing.
C. Unemployment.
D. Poor educational programs.
E. Dissatisfaction with the whole establishment.

b. I. How certain rich people reduce inheritance taxes.
A. Conversion of wealth into forms on which tax is low.
B. Untaxed gifts to children before death.
II. How certain rich people outrightly avoid inheritance taxes.
A. Establishing legal residence in countries which have no inheritance tax.
B. Conversion of wealth into forms not monitored by tax agencies.
C. Failure to report such wealth.

c. I. Congestion of traffic on urban highways.
II. "Expressway" and "tollway" distinguished.
III. Causes of highway overload.
IV. Solutions.

d. I. Risks in medical research with human subjects.
A. Physical damage to patient from new observational techniques.
B. Poisoning of patient through experimental drug therapy.
C. Withholding of traditional treatments of known value.
II. The element of "informed consent" of patient before experiment is begun.
A. Moral and emotional competence of patient to decide.
B. Patient's knowledge of risks.
C. Patient's conscious desire to participate.

e. I. Types of formal outline.
A. In sentence outlines each heading should be a complete sentence with only one main clause.
B. Topic outlines, using words or phrases for headings.
II. Relative advantages and disadvantages of each type.
A. Topic outlines.
1. Can be quick and brief.
2. Lack of parallel structure in headings can confuse.
B. Sentence outlines may ramble, but at their best they express the writer's thought more fully and exactly.
C. Both types of outline should lead off with a statement of the main point which the outline is to support.

Exercise 3 (openings—imitation)

Choose any three selections from the readings at the end of this textbook. For each, imitate the title and opening, adapting it to a different subject-matter. Be sure to indicate which reading you're working from. (See "Adaptation of Techniques to New Subject-Matter," page 54.)

Exercise 4 (critique)

As groups or individuals, critique the long paper of a classmate, providing written responses to the following questions:

FIRST PRIORITIES

a. What is the evident main point of this paper? (State as a single sentence.)

b. What elements of the paper need to relate more clearly to the main point, and why?

c. What additional questions could the writer answer in order to provide full support for the main point? (Consider the standard functions of background, development, reinforcement.)

d. How does this paper characterize its writer and its audience—as to knowledge and disposition? (For help, see Chapters 9 and 10, page 89 and page 101.) How does this writer-audience relationship help or weaken the paper?

e. Can the paper be outlined? Support your answer by offering an outline of one-half to one page. Why is this structure effective or ineffective? Explain.

f. How has the writer used the framing elements: beginning, linking, ending? Can you suggest any improvements?

SECOND PRIORITIES

(*Note:* Steps g–j may be postponed if this paper is later to be submitted in still a further draft. Go directly to k.)

g. If support from other sources is used, how accurate is the citation? Some library checking may be necessary unless the writer has brought sources to class.

h. Where are word-choices especially exact or inexact? Explain. Cite three examples.

i. Illustrate special strengths or weaknesses in the sentence structure of this paper. Cite three examples of the best or worst sentences. (Give some particular attention to paragraph openings.)

j. Has the paper been carefully copy-edited? Cite any need for further editing.

k. For all critiques: All in all, what do you find to be the strongest elements of this paper? Can you offer one or two additional suggestions which would raise it a real notch in quality?

Exercise 5 (all elements)

This exercise is a sequel to Exercise 4 of Chapter 21, and builds on the exploratory draft done for that exercise.

Write a new draft of the earlier draft prepared for Chapter 21. If you received a critique through Exercise 4 of this chapter, attach the critique together with your written response to the new draft. If no critique was furnished, prepare your own critique according to the instructions for Exercise 4. Also attach the earlier draft and all working papers.

Suggested readings for further illustration, discussion, and writing: Albert Rosenfeld, " 'Learning' to Give Up," page 404, and Yvonne Streeter, "The Ethics of a Housewife" (student documented paper in two drafts), page 408.

23 Showing Your Support

Many students and teachers suffer from nervousness over "documentation," "footnoting," "bibliography," "plagiarism," and so on. They are gloomily convinced that documented papers are mainly tedious ordeals in copying library sources, carrying severe penalties for violation of the least specification for quoting or footnoting.

Documentation simply expresses the common-sense principle of showing where you learned something, for some reader who might want to know.

Levels of Documenting

Suppose that you are wondering—in a personal letter—why people read or don't read, a question which popped up in a book you just finished. So you write:

> Some people won't read anything more than a few years old. They think that just because scientific insights are constantly outdated, all knowledge is soon rancid. Well, that's not what I learned at home.

There's no documentation here at all. You didn't say that the question came up in a book by Mortimer Adler titled *How to Read a Book*. You didn't even say that you got the idea from any source. The friend receiving your letter doesn't expect it, and if you added a formal footnote would laugh at the affectation. You *might* bring in the book title for good reason: if the reader had given you the book for Christmas; if you wanted to recommend Adler's writing; if you wanted to give some idea of what you'd been studying. Otherwise documentation would simply be superfluous in an informal communication developing the writer's personal thoughts for a reader unconcerned with the origin of ideas and materials which have clearly become your own. Often an assigned paper is relaxed enough in its requirements that you could write with similar unconcern for sources.

Now suppose that you are writing a paper or test for a class on methods of study; it has been assigned Adler's book to master. You might write:

> If we are to believe Adler, modern readers have no use for great books of the past. Because science commands universal admiration, and because science is always crossing new boundaries, the same is supposed for all fields of knowledge.

You do make a *mention* of Adler because your reader, the instructor, needs to know whether you read Adler's book with understanding. The source, so to speak, is part of your content. But you don't need a footnote. You don't even need to give the title, if the title would be taken for granted.

Suppose next that your reader knows only that you were studying the subject of reading; hence you must identify Adler in more detail, actually providing a *summary* of his point:

> If we are to believe Mortimer Adler in *How to Read a Book*, most readers suppose that only the latest science has anything to teach. Therefore they ignore anything written in the past, no matter what the subject.

One could even omit the title if the book would be familiar to the reader.

You might go beyond such a summary to a *paraphrase* prepared directly from a passage in the book, but restated in briefer and different language more suited to your own scale and purpose. Key words and sentences from the original source may be retained, but they are placed in quotation marks:

> Such is our faith in the latest science that as Mortimer Adler warns in *How to Read a Book*, "We tend to think that the past can teach us nothing." Great books of the past have become mere museum pieces—of possible interest to the antiquarian but irrelevant to people living and working on today's concerns. Even science itself soon becomes dated.

Here for the first time you should add a *note* usually at the foot of the page (hence a *footnote*), giving the publication facts of Adler's book and the pages referred to. This tells your readers that you are working at close quarters with your source, and that they are invited to verify your citation. *Notice that author and title still appear in the text itself,* so that your readers don't *have* to search out the note if they are satisfied with your information; they can maintain pace of attention. Guidance for notes will be found in Section N, "How to Include Notes," page 271.

A natural question may arise: Why don't we see all kinds of documentation in newspapers, magazines, and even in serious books for the general reader? One answer is that much popular writing aims to entertain rather than to prove. Most readers of Sunday supplements, *People,* or *National Enquirer* want surprise and gossip more than documented reasoning. A second answer is that even a serious popular audience might be distracted by footnotes; therefore the writer and editor find more informal ways of detailing their support. This chapter describes some of those informal ways. A final answer for the most serious writing is that much authority already resides in the earned reputation of author and publisher. When you read an essay in *Atlantic Monthly* by an expert of national reputation, you know that care has already been taken to secure strong support which therefore need not be spelled out at every turn. So you may reserve your challenges for the most debatable points, and here you may find that the author of the essay has anticipated your challenge and provided some sort of documentation.

But you as student or novice writer lack the credentials of established publisher or expert. If you're writing seriously about the world outside your personal life, you must earn your way into the reader's confidence. Documentation provides that way.

The fullest documentation consists of the *direct quotation* of an entire passage, as follows (from Adler's book):

> In the age of science, which is progressively discovering new things and adding to our knowledge every day, we tend to think that the past can teach us nothing. The great books on the shelves of every library are of antiquarian interest only. Let those who wish to write the history of our culture dabble in them, but we who are concerned to know about ourselves, the aims of life and society, and the world of nature in which we live, must either be scientists or read the newspaper reports of the most recent scientific meeting.
>
> We need not bother to read the great works of scientists now dead. They can teach us nothing. The same attitude soon extends to philosophy, to moral, political, and economic problems, to the great histories that were written before the latest re-

searches were completed, and even to the field of literary criticism.

This passage is reproduced word for word from Adler's book (Simon and Schuster, New York, 1967, pages 88–89). The kind of punctuation, format, and footnoting to be used will be described later. In general, quote only when you need the word-for-word statement as exact, primary evidence. For example, if you were citing Abraham Lincoln's views of slavery, you would want his own words on the topic. On the other hand, if you were citing a history book on the same topic it would be more economical and sensible to summarize the historian's comments in your own words. As a general rule, *quoted material will account for only a minor portion of a paper*. Remember that the more you quote, the more risk you run of letting your source determine your own direction. (See "Control Over Sources," Chapter 22, page 261.)

Papers which draw support from several sources will usually include, at the end, a *bibliography* or list of sources used. As a rule of thumb, add a bibliography if more than two sources are cited—because at such a point the readers may want to look over your total background of support. Conventions for the bibliography will be described under "How to Include a Bibliography," page 275.

Plagiarism

Plagiarism, or copying without due acknowledgment, is cheating. If it occurred only when conscious and deliberate, this book could pass it by as too rare for consideration.

Unfortunately most plagiarism is unconscious and unintended. People who have been allowed to think that "research papers" consist mainly of copied passages stitched together can easily go on to regard copying, with little or no acknowledgment, to be a truly academic skill. Thus the topic deserves one hard look.

To define the matter more fully, plagiarism is the offering of someone else's words, pictures, data, ideas, and even conceptions as if they were one's own. Writers are indeed encouraged to draw upon the information and wisdom of others, but in the spirit of intellectual inquiry they are expected to state such indebtedness so that (a) their own creativity can be justly appreciated and (b) their use of sources, like a scientist's experiment, can be verified by others. Plagiarism differs from this productive use of sources in that the similarity of the original to the borrowings is very close; it is acknowledged imperfectly or not at all; and it shows little or no creative application by the borrower.

Plagiarism is a prime intellectual offense in that the borrower is faking the discovery process. No community of writers and readers can thrive if its members counterfeit their achievements, deceive their critics, and take unfair competitive advantage of others.

Luckily such breakdowns are really unusual. The whole of this chapter should guide its readers confidently past any error of the kind just described. One need not defend oneself by "overdocumenting"—spraying a paper with quotations and footnotes. The right thing is to ask yourself, whenever adapting the work of others to your own purpose, "How much detail about my sources does the reader need, to feel confidence in my support?"

How to Include Notes[1] (N)

(The margin symbol **N** for "notes" may be used by you or your instructor to refer to any item of this section. Specific numbered items may thus be referred to as **N1, N2,** etc.)

N1   *Passing acknowledgment.* In addition to footnotes, you should often indicate briefly in the text itself what writer or work you are about to draw from—especially when approaching a major statement. This is done to give the reader advance notice on entering a documented passage, and to reduce the reader's need to consult every footnote. Note how passing acknowledgments were used in the Mortimer Adler examples earlier in this chapter.

N2   *Numbering of footnotes.* Use arabic numerals (1, 2, 3, etc.) without periods. Use one series of numbers for the whole paper; do not start a new series for each page.

N3   *Placing of footnote numeral in the text.* Place the footnote numeral, raised about one-half line, at the end of the passage which it governs and after any terminal punctuation. When you can, avoid inserting the numeral in the middle of a sentence, since it will break the reader's attention. For indebtedness extending beyond one paragraph, further footnoting and passing acknowledgment can be used as reminder of that indebtedness, but rather than spatter your page with notes to a single source, consider the options under **N6** below. For a passage indebted to several sources at once, consider consolidating such references in a single footnote.

---

[1] The remainder of this chapter is compatible with the *MLA Handbook for Writers of Research Papers, Theses, and Dissertations* (New York: The Modern Language Association of America, 1977). Certain fields like biology, chemistry, and psychology publish their own documentation guides, to which your instructor may direct you.

N4   *Placing of the footnote itself.* (See Figure 2, page 277, for a model first page which illustrates this and related matters.) The first footnote for any page begins four spaces (two double-spaces) below the bottom line of the text. Indent five spaces; raise a half-line to print the number of the note, then drop back down; make one space; then begin the note. Subsequent lines of the same footnote should be single-spaced *without* indentation. A double-space should be used between notes.

N5   *The endnote option.* As an alternative, your instructor may allow you to place all notes on a separate sheet or sheets at the end of the paper, to be headed *Notes.* Use the same format for the notes but double-space throughout. The endnote offers three advantages: (a) the reader may simply place the endnotes next to the text while reading; (b) the writer is spared the intricate planning of space at the bottom of each page (or, much worse, replanning); (c) if the paper is later re-copied or printed, one is spared the recalculation of space for footnotes. For these and other reasons, the endnote option is becoming more commonly used.

  In the first drafting of a documented paper, writers seldom bother to work out all such details, which would only need to be repeated or modified later. One shortcut consists of placing the numeral in the text as already described and then, in parentheses, giving a code for the source, such as "A-117," as suggested on pages 243–244. On redrafting later, the code can be expanded to a full reference which will be placed as a proper note.

N6   *The brief-reference option.* Footnoting and endnoting can be avoided where a brief and clear reference can be made in the text. If your paper concentrates on one source, for example, you can say in your first footnote that "subsequent references to this work will appear in the text." Any later page-reference would then appear in parentheses *after* any quotation marks and commonly *before* the sentence period. Again, you can sometimes work in a full reference in the text itself without distracting the reader unduly—for example: "A strong conviction that the United States can create a society of unparalleled excellence appears in Philip Slater's *The Pursuit of Loneliness* (Boston: Beacon Press, 1971, p. 144)." Note that the publication data came at the end of the sentence, so as not to break sentence continuity. But many or long references of this sort could clutter your text, so that footnotes or endnotes might be preferable after all.

N7   *Footnotes for first reference to a source.* There are no universal rules for the exact contents and arrangement of a footnote, except that the information should be complete enough to enable a reader to locate the original source. The examples below provide a workable way of handling the most common types of footnote. For further, specialized cases, consult the *MLA Handbook* or Kate Turabian's *Student Guide for Writing College Papers* or the style sheet of a given profession if your instructor stipulates it; or check a grammar handbook by looking in the index under "footnotes"; or if all else fails, use common sense and be consistent.

A book:

² Henry P. Jones, *Techniques of Sleep Learning* (New York: Macmillan, 1983), p. 24.
³ Sandra L. Deeter and Ruth E. Todd, *The Subconscious Student* (Boston: Little, Brown, 1981), p. 117.

You will usually find the publisher, the place of publication, the year of publication, and the edition (if other than the first) on the title page or its reverse side.

An article or essay (as found in journals or essay collections):

⁴ Henry P. Jones, "Techniques of Sleep Learning," *The Educational Psychologist*, 22 (1982), 438.
⁵ Henry P. Jones and Dora Gresham, "Techniques of Sleep Learning," in *Frontiers of Education*, ed. William Smith, 3rd ed. (New York: Macmillan, 1983), p. 258.

Titles of articles are placed in quotation marks. The volume number (XXII or 22) will be found in front of the periodical or, if the periodical is bound into a volume, on the spine of the book. The page abbreviations "p." and "pp." are not used for periodical articles where the volume number is given. For an anonymous article, begin the note with the title of the article itself.

An article (as found in newspapers and general magazines (date is given, volume number is omitted):

⁶ Henry P. Jones, "Learning While Asleep," *Chicago Sun-Times*, 18 January 1982, p. 38.

An article in an encyclopedia:

⁷ Henry P. Jones, "Sleep Learning," *Encyclopedia Europa*, 4th ed., 1979.

For well-known encyclopedias, only the edition and year are given (sometimes in combined entry, as "1979 ed."). Page numbers should be added at the end of the note if the encyclopedia is not alphabetically arranged, or if the entry runs for more than one page. Author's name should be added at the beginning of the note if identified in the encyclopedia by signature or initials at the end of the entry. (If only initials are given, turn to the key at the beginning or ending of the volume or set, and find the author's full name.)

A source cited in another source:

⁸ Henry P. Jones, *Techniques of Sleep Learning* (New York: Macmillan, 1983), p. 24, as cited in Geoffrey Larkin, "New Powers of the Subconscious," *The Reporter*, XIII (1984), 413.

The second-hand citation of sources is not recommended, however, until you have exhausted reasonable effort to check the original.

A personal interview:

⁹ Personal interview with Henry P. Jones, Associate Professor of Psychology, North Central College, 3 April 1983.

N8   *Subsequent references to the same source.* Use the simplest possible clear reference. "Jones, p. 36" may do nicely. If more than one work by Jones is cited, if another author named Jones is also cited, or if the first reference is a long way back, amplify as necessary:

¹⁰ Jones, *Sleep Learning*, p. 36. (For a book.)
¹¹ Jones, "Sleep Learning," p. 38. (For an article.)

Ibid. ("in the same place"), *op. cit.* ("in the work already cited"), and *loc. cit.* ("in the place already cited") are not recommended for use. Though these Latin abbreviations have served honorably, they involve fine points which are avoided by the common-sense method just described.

How to Include Quotations (**Q**)

(See pages 269–270 on when quotations are most and least valuable.)

Q1   *Short quotations.* Quoted material of less than five typed lines of prose (about 50 words) or three lines of poetry should be enclosed by quotation marks and be run into your text without special spacing or indentation. When quoting poetry in this way, use a slash-mark (/) to show the line divisions of the original.

Q2   *Long quotations.* Longer material is set off from the text by three spaces, indented ten spaces, and typed in double-space without special paragraph indentation if only one paragraph or less is quoted. (If the quotation includes more than one paragraph, additionally indent the second and later paragraphs by three spaces.) *No quotation marks are used in this format* except as they also appear in the original material.

For poetry, preserve the original line divisions and any special margination.

Q3 *Modifications of quoted matter* through skips, inserted explanations, or added emphasis. Though you need to control sources to conform to your own scale and interest, you have an equivalent responsibility not to tailor your source so as to distort its own sense. (By adroit snipping, an unscrupulous writer could obviously make a source mean its opposite.)

Show any omission in your quotation by inserting ellipsis periods: three spaced periods (. . .). If the ellipsis occurs at the end of a sentence, the terminal punctuation is added (usually a fourth period) inside the quotation marks.

Any explanatory words of your own which you include in a quotation should be enclosed in brackets: [ ]. Draw the marks in with a pen if necessary. Parenthesis marks will not serve, since the reader may suppose that they belong to the original material.

If you wish to stress parts of the quotation by italicizing them (or by underscoring them, which is the equivalent in typing or handwriting), insert the parenthetical notice "(italics added)" as you introduce the quotation or else include that notice in the footnote.

Q4 *Grammatical compatibility of quotation and text.* A quotation must fit grammatically with the sentence which introduces or includes it.

> PUZZLING According to Henry P. Jones, "the possibilities of learning while unconscious."
>   CLEAR Henry P. Jones speaks of "the possibilities of learning while unconscious."

The punctuation of a quotation should be consistent with that of its new context.

How to Include a Bibliography (B)

B1 A bibliography is appropriate, as suggested earlier, whenever your paper has explicitly drawn upon more than two sources. It usually includes only sources which you have actually referred to in the text. If you used works that were *not* cited in the paper itself, include them as well, but entitle your bibliography "Works Consulted" to clarify its scope. Don't inflate your bibliography with works which you might have used but didn't.

B2 *Placement and arrangement.* Place the bibliography on a separate sheet at the end of your paper (following the endnotes if used). Center its heading at the top: "Bibliography" or "List of Sources Consulted." Start the first item four lines down (two double-spaces) at the left-hand margin. Double-space throughout. Indent the second and later lines of each entry by five spaces.

Arrange the titles in alphabetical order of the authors' last names. Although a single list is customary, long bibliographies may be divided into sections by any principle which proves serviceable (for example, by different aspects of the topic discussed, by type of source such as "Books" and "Articles," etc.).

B3   *Form and content of entries.* Although the information is almost the same as for footnotes (see **N7**), the notes are customarily punctuated and read as sentences; bibliographies are presented as lists. Bibliography entries are not preceded by numerals; nor do they cite the page numbers actually used. The sample entries below provide a workable way of handling the most common types of source. As with notes, you can consult more specialized guides for further cases.

A book:

> Jones, Henry P. *Techniques of Sleep Learning.* 2nd ed. New York: Macmillan, 1983.
> ----------. *What the Mind Can Do in Sleep: A New Approach to Learning.* Chicago: Scott, Foresman, 1980.

Note that periods separate the elements of book information. If two or more titles by the same author (Jones) are listed, use ten hyphens in place of the author's name for second and later titles. Subtitles should be included even though omitted in the text of your paper.

An article or essay (as found in journals and essay collections):

> Jones, Henry P. "Techniques of Sleep Learning," *The Educational Psychologist,* 22 (1982), 430–437.
> Jones, Henry P., and Dora Gresham. "Tape-Recorder Techniques for Sleep Learning." In *Frontiers of Education.* Ed. William Smith. 3rd ed. New York: Macmillan, 1983, pp. 246–63.

For periodical articles give inclusive page numbers as was just done.

An article in an encyclopedia:

> Jones, Henry P. "Sleep Learning." *Encyclopedia Europa.* 4th ed. (1979).

Page-numbers are unnecessary because of the alphabetical ordering of the encyclopedia.

Figure 2.   Sample first page for a documented paper using footnotes

Charles Hatfield
English 205
December 5, 1985

Primitive Marriage Customs in South Magua: A Problem for U.S. Diplomacy

The act of mating is so important to all cultures that the marriage customs of any society provide a key to its central values. Behind these customs one can see the stabilizing forces of a given culture, the dis-integrative forces most commonly feared, the ideal of individual development, and so on. As Sara Chambers has said, "The history of marriage is in large part the history of humanity."[1]

The specific challenge of the South Maguan tribes has become, for the United States, a political one. According to J. B. Hargrave, who led the 1982 expedition to South Magua:

> No primitive people has resisted Western curiosity so adamantly as have the South Maguans, ever since Captain Pitt discovered their islands in 1829.
>
> Since 1849, when the Navy reported the probable existence of huge uranium deposits there, the inhabitants have greeted every intrusion with bloody violence. Thus America has faced the choice of foregoing the uranium, or of annihilating the South Maguans.... One aim of our expedition, therefore, was to find a way out of the dilemma.[2]

Accordingly, one aim of this paper is to explain Hargrave's findings, in which the South Maguan marriage customs showed the way to a major triumph in American foreign policy. A second aim of this paper is to show how any

[1] Sara Chambers, An Anthropological Case-Book (New York: Macmillan, 1979), p. 16.

[2] J. B. Hargrave, "World Crisis in South Magua," Social Problems Quarterly, 14 (1983), 183–184.

A personal interview:

> Jones, Henry P., Associate Professor of Psychology, North Central College. Personal interview. April 3, 1983.

B4 *The annotated bibliography.* An uncommon but useful feature, the annotated or critical bibliography includes, after each item, an evaluation of such points as the author's evident qualifications; the currency of the material or discussion; the evident quality of support and reasoning; the overall usefulness or limitation of the source for the purpose of the present paper.

Annotation is sometimes assigned to help students in using their library sources with discrimination. It also can lend weight to the paper by attesting to the author's care with the sources. Offered at expert level, annotation can help other scholars in the field to work forward.

No set form governs annotation. The annotation may simply extend the bibliographic entry by a sentence or few; or it may appear under the item as an indented block paragraph.

Exercise 1 (all elements)

For the passage which follows, you will be asked to prepare several kinds of citation as training in different ways of showing support. The passage is taken word-for-word from pages 45 and 46 from a book titled *You and Your Aging Parent: The Modern Family's Guide to Emotional, Physical, and Financial Problems,* by Barbara Silverstone and Helen Kandel Hyman. It was published in New York by Pantheon Books in 1976.

> [P. 45] Your mother may have said over the years, "I will never be a burden to any of my children," but unless she has made some prior arrangements to cover all emergencies as she grows older, she may have no choice. She may be forced to turn to someone in her family for help. In families where there are several children, however, the big question is: *Who will that someone be?*
>
> If you are the only daughter in the family, the chances are that it will be you, rather than one of your brothers. Experts in family relations feel that daughters (usually middle-aged) are more likely to take on the major responsibility for their parents' care. They and other female relatives are normally the ones who contact outside sources of support—family and community agencies—when they cannot cope with the responsibility alone. Even when their parents are getting along well and do not need help from anyone, daughters are usually thought of as keeping in closer touch than sons, who are more likely to become involved on special occasions or with major decisions and financial arrangements.

[P. 46] It could be argued that the behavior of daughters has been determined through the years because women have traditionally been at home and available, and also because housekeeping and nursing duties have always been seen as women's roles. It will not be known until the future whether this pattern will continue as more and more women become involved outside the home in careers, and domestic duties are shared to a greater extent by both sexes.

a. Write a brief paragraph on an appropriate topic in which you *mention* this material. (Sample topics: Who Is Responsible for Aging Parents? Or: Can Women Really Be Liberated from the Home? The same topic can be used to frame the other citations for this exercise.)

b. Write a brief passage of *summary* for this material.

c. Write a passage including a *paraphrase* of some part of this material, adding a footnote or endnote.

d. Write a passage which *quotes* the material at length of five lines or more, adding the necessary footnote or endnote.

e. Write the *bibliography* entry for this material.

f. Write a passage *plagiarizing* this material (to show that you recognize such misuse of a source).

g. Write a passage *misusing ellipsis periods* in quoting this material so as to distort its meaning (again, to show that you recognize such misuse).

Exercise 2 (form of notes and bibliography)

Put each of the following references into (1) proper form for footnote or endnote; (2) proper form for bibliographic entry.

a. Page 53 of a book called The Story of Our Republic written by Melville Freeman and published in 1938 in Philadelphia by Coutts.

b. Page 43 of an article called War Elegy, by Reginald Cowley, which appeared in the Atlantic Monthly, volume 174, June, 1945, pages 40 to 53.

c. Page 48 of a book by Charles Hewett Miller, published by Oxford University Press in 1981. The name of the book is The Assassination of John F. Kennedy and Its Mystery.

d. Page 56 of the same book, in subsequent reference.

e. Page 44 of the Atlantic Monthly article cited in *b*, in subsequent reference.

f. Page 400 of an article on Abraham Lincoln by Harvey Pottle in The Encyclopedia Panamerica published in Houston in 1979.

g. Page 195 of the book by Freeman cited in *a*, in subsequent reference.

Exercise 3 (annotation)

For any one source which you are now using or about to use for a long paper, prepare an annotation of about one page considering whichever of the following questions seem appropriate. (Though most annotations are briefer, this exercise aims to bring out a full range of judgment.)

> What credentials does the author have in this field? (See foreword, introduction, acknowledgments; check biographical references such as *Who's Who*.)
>
> Is the author free of selfish interest in the conclusions being drawn?
>
> Is the author addressing a serious and competent audience?
>
> (If the question is one of history) Does the author consider evidence which originated near the time of the event being studied?
>
> (If the question is one of current knowledge) Does the author use current sources and seem to rely on current information?
>
> Does the source contain a large sampling of facts or observations which seem representative of the field under study?
>
> Does the author consider other viewpoints?
>
> If any *other* conclusion might be drawn from the data offered, does the author show that it is less likely to be sound?

Suggested reading for further illustration and discussion: Yvonne Streeter, "The Ethics of a Housewife" (student documented paper), page 408.

24 Reading for Style

The guiding principle of this book has been that writing is a process of discovering one's outlook. Reading, by extension, is a process of discovering the outlook of someone else. This principle opens up a way of reading which may seem new to you.

The commonest way of reading is "to see what it says" or "how it comes out." Details are culled only as the reader sees a possible use for them (in passing a test or writing a paper, say) or as they simply strike the reader's imagination into the response, "How true that is!" or "Can it be possible?" or just "Wow!" Thus the writing is seen not for itself but for its contribution to the independent needs and curiosity of its user. This approach, which may be called *reader-oriented*, serves very well for limited purposes.

A second way of reading, much favored in college composition courses, is to analyze the selection according to some agenda laid out by the instructor—thesis, organization, apparent traits of audience and writer, diction, sentence structure. Now the reader's immediate personal needs are set aside in order to study the writing both for itself and for the discipline being presented by the teacher. This approach, which may be *classroom-oriented*, serves very well to increase the student's skills both in reading and writing.

Actually, this "agenda for analysis" approach resembles a tennis lesson in which one practices first the forehand, then the backhand, then the other strokes, then movement on the court, then tactics. Each skill is isolated so that it can be seen for itself and practiced without distraction.

This book uses the same approach both in its exercise materials and in the anthology of readings to follow. The discussion questions are intended to help you to focus on the particular powers and problems of style.

Of course a tennis lesson is not the same as *playing* tennis. The actual game will call upon the player's skill in constantly shifting patterns, often unpredictably, revealing its chances in proportion as one has trained to recognize and respond to them.

So reading, in the third way now to be looked at, is not the same as a reading lesson governed by the instructor's agenda, calling upon one skill at a time. For reading at its most sensitive, the chances will also come in shifting patterns, often unpredictably, revealing themselves in proportion as one has trained to see them and to respond. Such reading, which may be called *writer-oriented*, serves to bring the reader closest to *new* wisdom which can substantially enlarge one's mind and purposes. You are now ready for it—not to shop for your own needs or to discharge the teacher's agenda, but to engage *with* the writer in the discovery process. The writing is no longer there as an exhibition of announced stylistic principles. It is there as a skilled and ordered extension of the writer's pursuit of meaning which includes you as a participant.

Not all writing is to be read in this searching way. You would still read most newspapers, magazines, textbooks, and library references for immediate and limited uses. But since the skill to read with intensive discernment is an invaluable means of intellectual and personal growth, the small anthology of readings which follows has been designed to furnish a spectrum of opportunities. These pieces illustrate—in a less clinical fashion than used so far—the widely different ways in which writers discover their outlooks on different topics.

Several suggestions may help you to read in the way which has just been described:

1. *Develop your own agenda* according to the chances appearing in the piece. A few leads may be given by the instructor or by the textbook; but just as a tennis player wants eventually to play without a coach on hand, you want to read on your own. Since you have been acquiring the skills by which a writer gets into the chosen subject, you already have the same skills which a reader needs in order to join the writer. Let the writing itself signal which skills to bring to bear. If your attention is struck by the qualities ascribed to the audience, follow up those qualities and their evident function. If the vocabulary startles you with its singularity, if the sentences seem ornate, if the organization apparently lapses—let such traces of uniqueness draw you into the piece with all the curiosity you have been learning to apply.

2. *Use "negative imagination"* at such points. Notice what the writer is *not* doing as well as what *is* done. Imagine the options which the writer faced, and then ask why the alternatives were *not* used. Such questions as the following can concentrate the process by which the reader joins writer: "Why did she say *rancor* instead of just plain *hatred?*" "Why did he bother with the incident of his near-drowning when he could have got right into his topic?" "Why did she discuss death rate *before* birth rate?"

3. *Use rereading just as you use revision.* Even the most gifted writer may revise—or re-create—a piece several times as a way of delving out the full discovery. The same holds for reading. You may find on the second reading what you missed the first time; you may extend an insight only glimpsed before; you may find a higher level of meaning. One proof of a masterpiece is that it can be read many times with satisfaction, because of the richness which cannot be possessed through the first contact alone. A good piece of writing deserves a bit of the same testing.

4. *Internalize your reading skills* through steady practice so that they become intuitive just as the advanced tennis player learns to play without thinking of each individual element of the game. From every side you have been urged so far to examine these skills, to compare, to drill, to choose, to apply. The purpose was not to mechanize your writing or reading but to make such skills second nature, unforced, often spontaneous. The seasoned writer often works quickly, the acquired skills coming into play without the conscious sorting-out which the beginner must go through. The disciplined reader can work in the same way. Only when an unusual challenge looms up do such craftsmen halt for a deliberate inspection of techniques and alternatives. The full freedom conferred by thorough mastery is rare; but it is partly within sight of any serious student. Your progress toward it can turn reading and writing from strained achievements into immediate pleasures.

5. *Make your reading discoveries your own.* Although the first act of a responsive reader is to become attentively passive under the writer's guidance, the final act is to channel the resulting discovery into one's own wisdom and values. What, in short, does the piece add to your own awareness of life? How does it match other recent discoveries you have made? Does it improve your perception of the issues and potentials in front of you? Such queries go beyond the proper scope of a book on style. One large use of such a book, however, is to equip one to sustain such large personal questions. One excellent way of sustaining these questions is to redirect them to writing—this time your own writing—by which you confirm and expand what you know. Read to write.

Exercise 1 (all elements)

Read Morris Bishop's "The Reading Machine," page 424. *No study agenda is proposed by this textbook,* since the whole point of this chapter is that you now have the power to develop your own. Bring to class whatever you can as to your own observations about any or all elements of Bishop's essay, your responses to it, what further ideas it gives *you* for writing.

Exercise 2 (all elements)

Read from Robert M. Pirsig's *Zen and the Art of Motorcycle Maintenance,* page 427, following the instructions for Exercise 1.

Exercise 3 (all elements)

As a proof of your integration of reading and writing skills, prepare an anthology of the best writing you can find in general-audience publication. Suggested choices of fields: a) any Sunday edition of a metropolitan newspaper; b) a month's issues of any daily or weekly newspaper; c) the issues of any five magazines published the same week. News stories may be chosen, or editorials, columns, advertisements, comic strips—as long as you regard them the best specimens of that kind of writing. The length of the anthology may be suggested by your instructor. A minimum of something like ten selections would probably be needed for an adequate sampling.
　　Write an introduction explaining your choices.

A Spectrum of Readings

Some three dozen readings follow, chosen to display the topics of this textbook in roughly the same order. The Study Opener questions will direct attention first of all to the stylistic element chiefly illustrated and then to other topics of interest. It is to be hoped that you yourself will supply additional questions and comments as encouraged by Chapter 24.

The American Revolution as Seen
Through Two Foreign Textbooks

A. *The War for Independence of the English
Colonies in North America and Formation
of the United States*
by A. V. Efimov

(translated from a U.S.S.R. secondary school
textbook, *Modern History*, Part One, 1970)

· · · ·

In 1774 the American colonies sent their delegates to a congress in one
of the largest cities in the colonies—Philadelphia. This assembly sent the
King a request that he do away with the restriction on trade and industry. The colonists also asked that taxes not be imposed on them without
5   their consent. The King responded by declaring that a "revolt" had begun in the colonies, he sent armed forces to suppress it, and he demanded the complete submission of the colonies.

Commencement of Military Actions

Military engagements between the armed forces of the English King and
10   the colonists began in the spring of 1775. This is the way it happened.
The English sent from Boston two regiments of royal forces to seize rifles,
wagon trains, gunpowder, bullets, and flour—in short, the entire secret
military stores created by the American colonists. A detachment of English soldiers dressed in red uniforms marched out of the city at a mea-
15   sured pace. But the soldiers guessed that someone had informed the population about the military raid. And in fact Paul Revere, a highly skilled
silversmith who was intelligence chief of the Boston Revolutionary Committee, had ridden his horse at top speed from Boston to raise the alarm.
Alarm bells were rung and there were shots along the route of march of
20   the English soldiers. Following a brief skirmish along the way a detachment of royal forces scattered the Minutemen—local inhabitants who
were supposed to run with their arms to a meeting place within a minute after the alarm. The royal forces seized the cache of arms, but on
their return trip the farmers fired upon them from behind trees and
25   houses. The shooting intensified, and the withdrawal of the English became a disorderly flight. That is how the colonists began to use the tac-

tics of extended order, the combat tactics of an armed populace in rebellion.

There was little gunpowder and lead; they used sheets of lead from
roofs, later they even sawed up a lead statue of the English King; they   30
rationed out the lead in sparing portions, and every soldier cast his own
bullets according to the muzzle of his gun.

Congress named Col. George Washington (1732–99), a Virginia planter
known to be a confirmed advocate of the liberation of the colonies from
English oppression, to be commander-in-chief of the armed forces of the   35
rebellious colonies. He was known as an outstanding organizer and the
only important military specialist in the colonies.

In response to the demands of the commercial and young industrial
bourgeoisie, farmers, craftsmen, and workers, one after the other the colonies began to declare their secession from England.   40

Declaration of the Independence of the Colonies

Under the pressure of the masses, on July 4, 1776, the Congress adopted
the Declaration of Independence: i.e., the declaration of separation from
England.

The author of this document was Thomas Jefferson (1743–1826), an   45
advanced thinker for his time and an outstanding political figure. Elected
a member of the Virginia Legislative Assembly, he strove for the aboli-
tion of slavery. In England he was sentenced to death for a pamphlet
against the King.

The Declaration of Independence said that England was oppressing its   50
colonies in America and that the united colonies were seceding from
England and setting up an independent nation. All men are created
equal, the Declaration stated. They are entitled to life, freedom, and the
pursuit of happiness as their inalienable rights. The Declaration announced that the people itself had the right to establish authority and a   55
government: i.e., it proclaimed the idea that the people itself is the
source of power—the idea of popular sovereignty. The proposition that
the people itself can set up a government was aimed against the power
of the King, against the monarchy, and it signified recognition of the
republic. On the other hand, this same idea was aimed against colonial   60
oppression. The Declaration proclaimed the equality of man and nations.
Thus, the founders of the American republic condemned colonial oppression and colonialism.

But the bourgeoisie used the progressive ideas of the Declaration to
reinforce the power of the wealthy, provided also that they were white.   65
The Declaration did not abolish slavery and did not put an end to anni-

hilation of the Indians and their being driven from their land, and it preserved the exploitation of hired workers. The former colonies proclaimed themselves to be States, and they formed a union—the United States of America.

.   .   .   .

[A brief passage takes up the course of military operations.]

Taking advantage of the old enmity between the two colonial states, England and France, the Americans obtained a treaty of alliance and armed aid from France. In order to obtain France's aid, the Congress of the United States sent as its ambassador to Paris Benjamin Franklin, an outstanding scientist, diplomat, and public and political figure who had participated in writing the Declaration of Independence. Progressive social circles in France were ardently sympathetic with the struggle of the Americans to free themselves.

The aristocrat Lafayette, for example, fitted out a warship at his own expense, called it the *Victoire* (Victory) and sailed for America against the King's prohibition, and there he fought in the revolutionary forces.

In 1781 the main forces of the English surrendered to Washington at Yorktown. The peace was signed in 1783. The English recognized the independence of the colonies, 100,000 English aristocrats and members of their families were expelled from the United States, and their land was confiscated and put up for sale. That was the end of the war for independence that Lenin called the revolutionary war "of the American people against the plundering English, who had oppressed America and held it in colonial bondage."

Thus, during the Revolutionary War, in the course of a fierce class struggle, power in the United States passed from one class to another—from the aristocratic landowners to the commercial and industrial bourgeoisie of the North, which ruled in an alliance with the slaveowning planters of the South.

This signified that a bourgeois revolution had taken place in the United States. A republic was set up, the equality of all before the law was proclaimed, and slavery was gradually abolished in the northern States. But the capitalists and slaveowners took advantage of the people's victory to strengthen their own domination.

.   .   .   .

B. *The Formation of the United States*
by Jean Michaud

(translated from a French secondary school textbook,
1715–1870, La Formation du Monde Modern, 1966)

•   •   •   •

THE BREAK WITH ENGLAND

A congress made up of delegates from all the colonies except Georgia
met at Philadelphia in 1774: in a Declaration of Rights, it affirmed the
right of every English citizen not to be taxed without his consent. At the
same time, the colonists were building up supplies of weapons every-   5
where. An English detachment that tried to seize one of these depots
clashed near Boston with some American militiamen and lost about 250
men (1775).

That incident brought the final break. While George III was making
up his mind to reduce the colonies by force of arms, the Philadelphia   10
Congress assumed sovereign authority, raised troops, and gave command
of them to a Virginia planter named Washington. The following year, in
1776, the colony of Virginia declared itself independent of King George
III. A new Congress, on July 4, 1776, adopted the Declaration of Independence of the United States.   15
From then on, the only way to settle the conflict was by force.

BEGINNINGS OF THE WAR FOR INDEPENDENCE

The war lasted almost 8 years. Each of the adversaries ran into serious
difficulties. The English troops, partly composed of German mercenaries,
were good and numerous; but they were fighting in an unknown land, al-   20
most without roads, and covered with immense forests where it was
often impossible to get supplies or engage the enemy. As for the Americans, they were a long way from presenting a united front to the English.
Very jealous of sovereignty, the 13 colonies refused to submit to a single
government even for the duration of the war. Moreover, loyalists, big   25
planters, and wealthy merchants, who wanted to keep an understanding
with the mother country, existed side by side with those who favored
the breach with England. This latter group came mostly from the more
modest levels of society. Finally, the American army lacked arms and
clothing; the volunteers would leave the front as soon as their term of   30
enlistment had expired; the militia were reluctant to fight far from their

homes; the generals were mediocre. Washington himself was no great
military leader; it was rather because of his moral qualities, his firmness
of spirit, his tenacity, and his self-sacrifice that he became the architect
35 of victory.

The first 2 years of the war were bad ones for the colonists: the cities
of New York and Philadelphia were occupied by the English. But, at the
end of 1777, an English army moving down from Canada was encountered in the forest and forced to surrender at Saratoga. This victory re-
40 stored courage to the Americans and, most important, it won them
France as an ally.

The French Intervention

THE FRENCH ALLIANCE AND VICTORY FOR THE INSURGENTS

The American cause was very popular in France; already a number of
45 gentlemen, including the Marquis de Lafayette, had gone to serve under
Washington as volunteers. The [French] Government began by providing for the insurgents—that is what the rebelling colonists were called—
clothing and arms; then in 1778 it signed a treaty of alliance with their
representative in France, Franklin. The following year Spain joined with
50 France, hoping to get Gibraltar and Florida back from the English.

The war went on for 5 more years, in very different theaters. In America, where the struggle was shifting to the South, General Rochambeau's
French corps helped the rebels to blockade an English army in the city
of Yorktown, in Virginia, and to force it to surrender (October 1781). In
55 Europe, the Franco-Spanish fleets managed neither to effect a landing in
England nor to retake Gibraltar. In the Antilles, the French fleet, after
initial victories, in 1782 suffered a severe defeat. Meanwhile, off the coast
of India, [Admiral] Suffren several times defeated the English fleet and
signed a treaty of alliance with a Hindu sovereign who was an implaca-
60 ble foe of the English.

At last, England gave in and signed the Treaty of Versailles [Treaty of
Paris] in 1783. She recognized the independence of the United States,
and ceded to it all the land between the Allegheny Mountains and the
Mississippi; she returned to Spain the island of Minorca and Florida; she
65 restored to France one of the Antilles and a few posts on the Senegal
coast which had been taken from her in 1763, and at long last recognized
France's right to fortify Dunkirk. Out of this long war, which had cost
her enormous sums, France won only minimal advantages, but the Government was content to have restored French prestige and brought Eng-
70 land low.

ORGANIZATION OF THE UNITED STATES

The American war had many consequences. The most important was the
creation of a new state, the United States, the first free state ever founded
by Europeans outside Europe.

After a lot of difficulties—a financial crisis, political and commercial   75
squabbles between colonies, strong social antagonism between rich and
poor—in 1787 the 13 States adopted a Constitution which, in its major
outlines, is still in force today. Like the United Provinces in Europe, the
United States constituted a federal republic. Each State had its own in-
stitutions, but above those 13 State governments there was a federal gov-   80
ernment responsible for their common affairs: war, diplomacy, currency,
and commerce. The executive power was vested in a president; the legislative power, in a Congress made up of two chambers—a Senate, in which
each State has two representives, and a House of Representatives, in
which each State is represented by a number of congressmen propor-   85
tional to its population. Finally, there were the federal courts, the highest
of which is the Supreme Court.

REPERCUSSIONS IN AMERICA AND IN FRANCE

The example of the emancipation of the English colonies had profound
repercussions. As early as the end of the 18th century, there were up-   90
risings in Spanish America and, 40 years after the Treaty of Versailles,
there was nothing left of the Spanish empire on the American continent.
In France, the example of the United States was even more swiftly followed. The principles the French *philosophes* had argued and preached
were the foundations of the Declaration of Rights in 1774 and again of   95
the Declaration of Independence in 1776. The French had made those
principles victorious in America; would they not make them prevail in
France itself? Furthermore, the expenditures connected with the war
had increased the financial difficulties: Louis XVI had to agree to sum-
mon the Estates General into session in 1789. And the convocation of the   100
Estates General marked the beginning of the French Revolution.

                              •   •   •   •

Study Openers

1. How do Efimov and Michaud seem to differ in their outlook on the American Revolution? In answer, look at the selection of historical detail, the

scale and order given to it, the kind of language used. (For example, note how the two authors regard the Treaty of 1783.)

2. Read one or two United States textbook accounts of the American Revolution done on the same scale. Write a report, using details, showing the difference in outlook among the accounts you have studied. What do you conclude about the nature of historianship?

The Transaction
by William Zinsser

(from *On Writing Well*, 1980)

Five or six years ago a school in Connecticut held "a day devoted to the arts," and I was asked if I would come and talk about writing as a vocation. When I arrived I found that a second speaker had been invited—
5 Dr. Brock (as I'll call him), a surgeon who had recently begun to write and had sold some stories to national magazines. He was going to talk about writing as an avocation. That made us a panel, and we sat down to face a crowd of student newspaper editors and reporters, English teachers and parents, all eager to learn the secrets of our glamorous work.
10 Dr. Brock was dressed in a bright red jacket, looking vaguely Bohemian, as authors are supposed to look, and the first question went to him. What was it like to be a writer?

He said it was tremendous fun. Coming home from an arduous day at the hospital, he would go straight to his yellow pad and write his
15 tensions away. The words just flowed. It was easy.

I then said that writing wasn't easy and it wasn't fun. It was hard and lonely, and the words seldom just flowed.

Next Dr. Brock was asked if it was important to rewrite. Absolutely not, he said. "Let it all hang out," and whatever form the sentences take
20 will reflect the writer at his most natural.

I then said that rewriting is the essence of writing. I pointed out that professional writers rewrite their sentences repeatedly and then rewrite what they have rewritten. I mentioned that E. B. White and James Thurber were known to rewrite their pieces eight or nine times.
25 "What do you do on days when it isn't going well?" Dr. Brock was asked. He said he just stopped writing and put the work aside for a day when it would go better.

I then said that the professional writer must establish a daily schedule and stick to it. I said that writing is a craft, not an art, and that the man

who runs away from his craft because he lacks inspiration is fooling   30
himself. He is also going broke.

"What if you're feeling depressed or unhappy?" a student asked.
"Won't that affect your writing?"

Probably it will, Dr. Brock replied. Go fishing. Take a walk.

Probably it won't, I said. If your job is to write every day, you learn   35
to do it like any other job.

A student asked if we found it useful to circulate in the literary world.
Dr. Brock said that he was greatly enjoying his new life as a man of
letters, and he told several lavish stories of being taken to lunch by his
publisher and his agent at Manhattan restaurants where writers and edi-   40
tors gather. I said that professional writers are solitary drudges who seldom see other writers.

"Do you put symbolism in your writing?" a student asked me.

"Not if I can help it," I replied. I have an unbroken record of missing
the deeper meaning in any story, play or movie, and as for dance and   45
mime, I have never had even a remote notion of what is being conveyed.

"I *love* symbols!" Dr. Brock exclaimed, and he described with gusto
the joys of weaving them through his work.

So the morning went, and it was a revelation to all of us. At the end
Dr. Brock told me he was enormously interested in my answers—it had   50
never occurred to him that writing could be hard. I told him I was just
as interested in *his* answers—it had never occurred to me that writing
could be easy. (Maybe I should take up surgery on the side.)

As for the students, anyone might think that we left them bewildered.
But in fact we probably gave them a broader glimpse of the writing   55
process than if only one of us had talked. For of course there isn't any
"right" way to do such intensely personal work. There are all kinds of
writers and all kinds of methods, and any method that helps somebody
to say what he wants to say is the right method for him.

Some people write by day, others by night. Some people need silence,   60
others turn on the radio. Some write by hand, some by typewriter, some
by talking into a tape recorder. Some people write their first draft in
one long burst and then revise; others can't write the second paragraph
until they have fiddled endlessly with the first.

But all of them are vulnerable and all of them are tense. They are   65
driven by a compulsion to put some part of themselves on paper, and
yet they don't just write what comes naturally. They sit down to commit
an act of literature, and the self who emerges on paper is a far stiffer
person than the one who sat down. The problem is to find the real man
or woman behind all the tension.   70

For ultimately the product that any writer has to sell is not his sub-

ject, but who he is. I often find myself reading with interest about a topic that I never thought would interest me—some unusual scientific quest, for instance. What holds me is the enthusiasm of the writer for
75 his field. How was he drawn into it? What emotional baggage did he bring along? How did it change his life? It is not necessary to want to spend a year alone at Walden Pond to become deeply involved with a man who did.

This is the personal transaction that is at the heart of good nonfiction
80 writing. Out of it come two of the most important qualities that this book will go in search of: humanity and warmth. Good writing has an aliveness that keeps the reader reading from one paragraph to the next, and it's not a question of gimmicks to "personalize" the author. It's a question of using the English language in a way that will achieve the
85 greatest strength and the least clutter.

Can such principles be taught? Maybe not. But most of them can be learned.

Study Openers

1. This piece presents opposite styles of writing, the "Brock style" and the "Zinsser style." What are the key qualities of each? Which qualities do you share as a writer? Which qualities do you admire most or least? How do you think you might achieve the admirable ones and avoid the others?
2. What does Zinsser mean by "transaction"? What "transactions" have you already made—and how could you work them into writing something?
3. Comment on Zinsser's final comment that the principles of good writing cannot be taught, perhaps, but most of them can be learned. If you *can* learn without being taught, can you learn *better* that way?

Four Columns by Mike Royko

(One of the most inventive newspaper columnists in the U.S., Mike Royko published the following four pieces in the *Chicago Sun-Times,* all on the same subject, all within a matter of weeks. Read them to generalize about how he varied his attack, and how the same flexibility might help you to find several ways of developing one point.)

Pass Some More Ammunition:
Arsenals for All

(December 12, 1980)

The death of John Lennon is causing another national outcry for stronger gun controls. It happens every time a famous person is shot.

We're already seeing heated debates in the press and on TV between the anti-gun people and the forces of the National Rifle Association.

Naturally, being a good American and a macho guy, I am against gun   5
controls.

My position on this has been clear for many years, since I am the founder of the National Association for the Legalization of Machine-guns, Bazookas, Hand Grenades, Cannons, Land Mines and Anything Else That Goes Boom (NALMBHGCLMAETGB for short.)   10

I formed this organization because the present gun laws discriminate against those of us who are so weak-eyed or are such bad shots that we are useless with a pistol.

We need something that will really give us firepower, which is why we want to be able to walk into a store and buy choppers, bazookas,   15
grenades, etc., just as somebody like crazy Mark Chapman could go in and buy a .38-caliber pistol with which to kill Lennon.

You are probably asking why we want this kind of firepower. The answer is obvious: for the same reasons as those who like handguns.

Those who oppose strict controls of handguns say that it is their con-   20
stitutional right to bear arms. Actually it isn't. They always leave off the part that says the right to bear arms is so this country will have a strong "militia." That might have meant something in 1776, but not today.

But if somebody can claim it is his constitutional right to keep a .38 in his dresser drawer, I don't see why we can't buy machineguns.   25

After all, anything a .38-caliber pistol can do, a machinegun can do better.

For example, the gun lovers say that they need guns to defend them-selves from robbers, fiends and murderers who might come through their windows at night.   30

Unfortunately, for every robber, fiend or murderer who is shot dead by some citizen who snatches his pistol out of his dresser drawer, hun-dreds of innocent people are killed when their guns go off accidentally, or when they get drunk and have a domestic quarrel, or when some thief steals their gun and uses it to shoot someone else.   35

But that doesn't mean guns aren't effective. It probably means that most people don't move quickly enough, or aren't good enough handgun shots, to be effective against burglars and fiends.

Now, if it were possible for me to set up a machinegun on a tripod on my bed, I would be well prepared. Instead of having to look in a drawer for a pistol, I could simply sit up and begin spraying my bedroom windows with hundreds of rounds. Any criminal crawling through my window would be quickly dispatched, as would my next-door neighbors.

Or let us say that I hear someone rummaging about my basement. Sure, I could go down there with a pistol and confront him. But what if he also had a pistol? He might get off the first shot, and that would be the end of an honest citizen.

But if hand grenades were legal, I could just lob one or two down the basement stairs and the world would have one less criminal. My home repair bills would probably go up, but one has to pay the price for security.

Then there is the threat of foreign invaders. That is something frequently mentioned by the devoted gun lover. Many of them are concerned that the Russians or Chinese or somebody else might invade this country, and they want to be able to defend themselves. They want to be able to take a few of them russkies and gooks with them, as they go down in a blaze of glory.

Such patriotism is commendable. But the question is, how effective would handguns be if Russian tanks and troops made it as far as our city streets or country roads?

Ah, but cannons and bazookas would be something else. If I could set up a cannon on my lawn, I could keep the Russians off my street, by golly. Let them go to the next street, where some liberals live.

And the nice thing about a cannon is that it is difficult for a child to accidentally shoot himself or his sister while playing with it.

Many gun lovers also say that if people can't own guns, they are at the mercy of an oppressive government that might someday take over this country. Only the threat of being shot at by honest citizens keeps government from taking our liberties, they say.

Maybe. But once again, how effective is a handgun against the kind of weapons the government can muster—planes, tanks, etc.?

That's why my organization wants the heavy stuff legalized for home use. Land mines, for example. See how many government inspectors and other bureaucrats would come snooping around if they thought that they might step on a hidden mine as they cross your lawn.

And mines would also be effective against those rude people who let their dogs go on your grass.

So I would remind the anti-gun people of the favorite slogan of us gun
lovers: 80

"Guns don't kill; people kill."

Sure. Even if Mark Chapman hadn't been able to buy a handgun, he
could have then gotten himself a rifle or a baseball bat or a sword and
killed Lennon anyway. Of course, he might have had trouble walking
around unnoticed with a rifle or sword or baseball bat.   85

It's that wonderful slogan—"guns don't kill; people kill"—that has always made me wonder why certain poisons, such as arsenic, aren't sold
over the counter in drug stores.

After all, poisons don't kill; people kill, right?

And it's that spirit that makes me wonder why so many people are   90
concerned about the possible spread of nuclear weapons.

I don't see anything wrong with all kinds of little countries having
their own nuclear arsenals. Every country should have The Bomb.

After all, "nuclear bombs don't kill; people kill."

Come to think of it, why can't individual Americans have their own   95
little nuclear arsenals.

I'll have to bring that up at the next meeting.

Logic Shot Down: Letters, Calls, and Great Thoughts from Readers

(December 16, 1980)

RONALD HARRISON, Chicago: I own a handgun. I am also a member of the
National Rifle Association. You've probably heard this slogan: "Guns
don't kill; people do."

A gun is only a piece of metal, a tool, just as a knife or an ice pick or
an automobile is only a tool.   5

When that lady in Las Vegas ran down all those people with a car on
Thanksgiving Day, I didn't hear you bad-rap the car manufacturers. She
admitted she meant to do it, just as Lennon's slayer meant to kill him.

COMMENT: Yes, we all know that people can be killed with knives, ice
picks and cars. Or a fork, a corkscrew, or any blunt object, such as a   10
large crucifix. Or your thumb. But the purpose of these objects isn't to
kill. Only the handgun has as its sole purpose the shooting of human
beings. Or do you use it for stirring your coffee? The gun, I mean, not
your thumb.

ROBERT COVALL, Lombard: Ballistics has been my hobby for 21 years   15
and I have fired a lot of different guns. If you're going to print this stuff,

why don't you find out the facts? Do you know how many gun laws are on the books right now? They're not enforced by the judges, so why would any new law do any good?

20 The facts are these: The do-gooders believe if you take the guns away you're going to take away crime. This is a lot of bull. I can go into a hardware store and buy a piece of half-inch pipe; I could kill somebody with that.

Or you can roll up a Sun-Times. Lay it flat in front of you and roll it
25 up as tight as you can. Strike your desk with it. See? You have a minia-ture club. You hit someone in the adam's apple with it and you can kill them. Or if you put a piece of barbed wire between two clothespins, you can use it to strangle anybody.

Anybody with half a brain can make an instrument to commit violence
30 with. The guy that did in the Beatle, or the guy who shot Wallace, they were intent on committing murder.

I used to be a member of the NRA, and they always say, "Guns don't kill, people kill." I don't agree. Guns kill people when people use the guns to kill people. But a gun won't jump out of a case to shoot you
35 down. It takes a human being to pull the trigger. The 1968 gun laws never did any good, and the new ones won't either.

COMMENT: I agree that the present gun laws don't do much good. That's why I favor making the sale and possession of handguns illegal. I don't see why you should oppose that. After all, if a hunk of pipe, a
40 rolled-up newspaper or a piece of barbed wire are such fearsome weap-ons, you really don't need a handgun, do you? And I'll bet Yoko Ono, Mrs. Robert Kennedy and George Wallace would rather have taken their chances with an assassin armed with a rolled-up newspaper.

MICHAEL SMOLEK, Demotte, Ind.: What gripes me is that when some-
45 body well-known or famous gets killed with a gun, people try to con-demn gun manufacturers and the sale of guns.

Since John Lennon was killed, there have been several figures on TV, radio and newspapers on how many people have been killed with guns in the U.S.

50 Are these people trying to say that if the guns were not available that John Lennon would not be dead today? If Mark Chapman hadn't been allowed to buy a handgun, he would have been able to do the job he set out to do in one way or another.

COMMENT: Then why are the majority of murders committed with
55 handguns? Why aren't killers using more automobiles, ice picks, cork-screws and rolled-up newspapers? It must be that the gun nuts—besides being nutty—are also lazy. So if we get rid of handguns, at least we'll have assassins with initiative.

JACK WALLACE, Chicago: When you compare a handgun with a nuclear weapon, and say that every country should be allowed to have nuclear weapons because "nuclear bombs don't kill, people kill," you sound crazy.   60

You can't compare handguns with nuclear weapons. H-bombs can be used to wipe out great numbers of people.

COMMENT: What do you think all the thousands of victims of hand-   65
guns are—gnats?

An Unlicensed Drive: Ride on, Gun Lobby!

(December 17, 1980)

Of all the shrill arguments handgun lovers give when they scream against any kind of gun controls, my favorite goes this way:

"People are killed all the time by automobiles. But you don't say anything about doing away with cars."

It's my favorite because it shows how far the gun lovers have to reach   5
in trying to justify their ridiculous position that almost anybody in this country should be allowed to own a handgun.

I'm not talking about the obvious: That the purpose of a car is transportation, while the purpose of a handgun is shooting people. And that the purpose of almost any useful object, from a toothpick to an earth-   10
mover, can be perverted to make it a weapon; but that the only practical uses of a handgun are the killing or wounding of human beings.

No, what I'm talking about is the fact that there are thousands of times more governmental controls placed on automobiles and drivers and manufacturers than there are on guns and gun owners.   15

The gun lovers seem to forget that before you can legally get behind the wheel of a car, you have to take and pass a driver's test and be licensed by the state.

Passing the test can be difficult. That's why we have private driving schools and drivers' training offered in many public schools.   20

As soon as you get a license, a government file is opened on you. From then on, any serious violation of the driving laws becomes part of your record. If you commit some violations, you can lose your license for long periods of time.

The police expend far more manpower on cars and drivers than they   25
do on guns. It's the single biggest area of law enforcement—with everything from meter maids hanging tickets on windshields to radar units all

along the highway systems to elaborate computer systems that maintain
your driving record and violations.

30   If you own a car, the governmental controls increase. The car has to
be registered with the government. You cannot buy or sell a car without
the proper legal documents. Every year—or more often—you have to buy
a state license and, in most places, a city sticker in order to operate your
car. If you don't buy them, you can be arrested and taken to court.

35   There are financial liability laws that, if you have a serious accident,
can bring about the loss of your driving privileges.

The government constantly tells you how fast you can drive. It puts
up millions of traffic lights that tell you when you must stop and when
you can go. It puts up millions of signs that tell you where you can park
40   and where you can't. It puts up millions of parking meters and requires
you to pay a fee for parking on the streets. It paints millions of miles of
lines and requires that you stay on certain sides of them.

It has the right to seize your car, by towing, without notice or legal
proceedings or a warrant of any kind, if you leave it in the wrong place.
45   It can demand that you wear glasses while driving, that you scrape the
ice from your windows, that you have your lights on, that you use appropriate signals when making certain maneuvers.

And that's just a brief sketch of how the government regulates you, a
driver and car owner.

50   We could also talk about the mountain of government controls that
have been placed on the manufacturing and sale of automobiles.

These include the construction regulations, the pollution regulations,
the fuel consumption regulations. You have to have an engineer, a
lawyer, and a CPA at your side if you want to understand them.

55   If you tried to read all the state and federal and local laws applying
to cars and their drivers, it would take you until the next century. Then
you'd have to start catching up on the new ones.

These are laws controlling only one means of transporting people and
materials. And only an idiot would say we don't need most of them.

60   Yet, the laws controlling devices that have no other purpose than the
killing of people are only a tiny fraction of those having to do with
drivers and cars.

And the gun laws are so varied that they are virtually useless. You
have to be tested and licensed to drive a car. But in many parts of the
65   country, any maniac or criminal can buy a gun as easily as a loaf of
bread.

Cars, which are useful, have to be registered and licensed. But the
gun lovers scream about even the most modest forms of registration for
devices that are designed only to kill or wound.

The hard-core gun lobby and its supporters have consistently been against any kind of sale and ownership controls. If they had their way, guns and ammunition would be as available as cups and saucers.

But if you said their loose standards should apply to the driving and owning of automobiles, you would be considered a raving loony.

I just wish the gun people would stop tossing around their half-baked justifications for handgun ownership and would be truthful.

Go on, admit that you like the ways the gun feels in your hand, that it gives you a sense of power, that you have fantasies about blowing someone away. Be honest about how the long barrel of your pistol reminds you of your . . . well, you know.

We'll all understand. And if we don't, maybe a shrink would.

Top Gun Smells Smoke: The Snorting Life

(January 8, 1981)

I ran into my old friend George Loveguns the other day, and he was in a foul mood.

Loveguns is Top Pistol at his local National Rifle Association club, so I assumed he was upset by the recent outcry to ban all handguns.

But that wasn't the case.

"No, I'm not concerned about that," George said. "I know John Lennon's death was just another chance for you cowardly, commie, effeminate, naive, warped, sniveling un-American handgun-haters to blow off steam. Nothing will come of it because we keep Congress intimidated with our furious letter-writing barrage."

Then what's bothering you, old friend? Did you accidentally shoot a neighbor? Or worse, miss him?

"It has nothing to do with guns. It's my son, the college student."

You shot him?

"No, but I should. I came home tonight and went up to his room to ask him if he wanted to join me for a pleasant evening of cleaning my rifles. I found him staring at his toe, saying, 'Oh, wow, oh, wow!'"

That sounds like a normal college kid.

"You should have smelled his room. I spotted it right away. He was smoking dope! And I think he was taking pills. And he might have been snorting something, too."

That's no reason to get excited.

"No reason? I won't tolerate that stuff in my house. I hate it."

Why?

25   "Because it's dangerous. It can turn him into some kind of addict."

Nonsense. Dope doesn't addict—people addict.

"What?"

It's true. Here's an experiment: You take some dope and put it in a box and put it in your bedroom dresser drawer, which is where you keep
30   your .38.

"I keep a .45."

My apologies. Anyway, you put the dope there and just let it sit, or maybe you take it out and look at it once in awhile, and flick the dust off of it, or stroke it, or admire it, and what harm is it doing?
35   "Well, none, I guess."

That's right. When it is just sitting there, the dope isn't doing any harm. And it won't do any harm, either—not unless you smoke it or swallow it or snort it. Have you ever seen a dab or two of heroin? Perfectly harmless stuff. You could keep it around the house for years and not have
40   any problems—unless you stuck it in your arm. But would that be the heroin's fault? Of course not. Heroin can't think. It can't make decisions to be used or not to be used. It can't do anything by itself. It takes a person to do that.

"But that's the problem—my son might use it. Then he might do some-
45   thing crazy. Or turn into a lazy doper. Or become a thief to support his habit."

That's true. But think of all the people who use some kind of dope— marijuana or cocaine or others—and don't do anything crazy or become lazy dopers or become thieves. Should they be penalized because of
50   those irresponsible people who don't treat dope with proper respect? Of course not. The answer isn't to ban dope, but to punish those who misuse it.

"Yeah, but what if I had dope in my dresser drawer, and didn't use it, or used it in moderation, and somebody broke in and stole it and sold
55   it to children? That could happen."

True. But the answer is not to forbid you the right to have it. The answer is to punish the thief who stole it.

"I don't know. It seems to me that the only answer is to ban the stuff— to really crack down and make sure it isn't sold. I mean, what good
60   is it?"

Well, most dope has some medical use. Pain-killing, tranquilizing, things like that. Marijuana is now prescribed by some doctors.

"Then there should be stricter controls. You should only be able to get it when you can prove that you have a genuine need for it. But we can't
65   have anybody who wants it buying it the way it is now."

You mean you want the government stepping in and saying whether you can keep a few grams of some white powder in your dresser drawer? Or a few shreds of a weed? You want the government to decide what you can or cannot have in the privacy of your own home?

"You're damn right I do. That stuff can mess you up, it can addle your   70
brain, it can even kill."

Loveguns, I keep telling you: Dope doesn't mess up, dope doesn't addle brains, dope doesn't kill—people mess up, people addle brains, people kill. And besides, you don't need dope to get messed up. You can sniff glue. Should we ban all glue? Your kid could trip on a curb, hit   75
his head on the sidewalk and addle his brain. Should we ban all curbs? Your kid could inject kitchen cleanser into his vein and die. Should we ban kitchen cleanser?

"I don't care what you say. That stuff ruins lives. It has to be con-trolled."   80

Loveguns, I keep telling you: Dope doesn't ruin lives—people ruin lives.

"Enough! I can't talk to you anymore. You have no respect for human life. I'm going."

Where?   85
"Home. To clean my guns."

Study Openers

1. Note that these are *dramatic* arguments in that the different parties are presented as characters, some to be disapproved and some to be favored. How has Royko set up his characters (including himself as author) to be liked or disliked? To what extent do you think he has strengthened his argu-ment or weakened it by doing so? (Chapter 10 suggests further possibilities of dramatic argument; in particular, see "Special Applications to Persuasive Writing," page 108.)

2. How would you apply the technique of any one of Royko's pieces to one of the following?

       a. Drug control.
       b. Abortion.
       c. Prayer in public schools.

Add a few lines explaining Royko's technique and how you have tried to use it.

Oh, To Drive in England
by Barbara Hower

(two drafts of student paper, 1982)

1ST DRAFT

As an American tourist driving in England, I had the opportunity to observe some of the differences and similarities in automobile travel. To many, driving in England means driving on the "wrong" side of the road. This, however, represents only a small part of traveling in Great Britain.

To insure safety, driving laws are standardized in both countries. The English motorways are equivalent to our expressways, which are designed for high speed travel. While the speed limit in the United States is 55 miles per hour, the speed limit in England is 70 miles per hour. Expressway drivers, who have had cars race past them if they adhere to the 55 mile speed limit, should rest assured that they aren't alone; drivers on the English motorways, drive the same way. For those who want to pass another car, the English briefly flash their headlights to alert the other driver that they are being passed. In city driving, the motorist must be on the look out for pedestrians. Most of the major cities, like London, have few stop lights. The areas where pedestrians can cross safely are called Pelican, or Zebra crossings. These cross walks are marked with black-and-white stripes across the road, along with flashing amber lights. Once a pedestrian has stepped on to one of these crossings, they have the legal right-of-way. As in America, failure to concede the

REVISION

As an American tourist driving in England, I had the opportunity to observe some of the differences and similarities in automobile travel. To many, driving in England means driving on the "wrong" side of the road. However, after a first hand indoctrination in British driving, I found this to be only a small part of traveling in that country.

Driving laws are standardized in both countries in order to insure safety. The English motorways are equivalent to our expressways. These are multi-laned, divided roads which are designed for high speed travel. While the speed limit in the United States is 55 miles per hour, Britons are allowed to travel at 70 miles per hour. Americans who enjoy tacking a few extra miles on to the speedometer might look forward to driving at a legal 70 miles per hour. However, the motorist who adheres to the legal limit in England will find cars racing past him, just as in America. The shape of the road signs is standard to both countries. For example, all warning signs are triangular, and stop signs are the familiar octagonal shape. However, lane markings are quite different in each country.

Our roads have a solid yellow line which serves as the center marking, but the English have broken white lines instead. In city driving, a motorist must be on the lookout for pedestrians, as most of the major cities like London have few stop right of way to a pedestrian can result in heavy penalties.

45

50

One of the most obvious differences is in the overall construction and appearance of the roads. On the whole, the roads in England are maintained better than those in the United States. Even in remote, isolated areas, the pavement is free from pot holes. To the novice, British roads can seem rather intimidating. There are no shoulders along the side of the road; instead, there are hedgerows growing by the side of the road. In the northern areas, the hedgerows are replaced by stone "hedgerows." Another problem that most Americans don't have to contend with is coming upon a flock of sheep in the road. Suddenly coming upon a sheep standing in the road, with no place to go except into a hedgerow, resulted in a couple of close calls for me. On the motorways, instead of intersections or exit ramps, the English equivalent is the round about. It is essential that the driver know which road to take before entering into the round about. If not, you end up driving repeatedly in circles, becoming more bewildered by the minute. At least in the United States, if you're not sure which exit you need, you can always drive on to the next one. In England, you either make a rather hasty decision to choose a road, or circle for awhile.

55

60

65

70

75

80

85

90

lights. Instead, the areas where pedestrians can cross are called Pelican or Zebra crossings. These cross walks are marked with black-and-white stripes across the road, along with amber lights which flash when the pedestrian has the right of way. Once a pedestrian has stepped into one of these crossings, failure to yield can result in heavy penalties as well as an injured pedestrian.

One of the most obvious differences between driving in England and the United States is the overall construction and appearance of the roads. On the whole, the roads in England are better maintained than those in the United States. Even in remote, isolated areas, the pavement is free from potholes. In spite of this, British roads can seem rather intimidating to the novice. There are no shoulders along the side of the road; instead, there are hedgerows. In the northern regions, the hedgerows are replaced by stone walls. One other problem that few Americans have experienced is finding a flock of sheep in the road. Suddenly coming upon a sheep in the road, with no place to go except into a hedgerow, resulted in a couple of close calls for me. On the motorways, instead of intersections or exit ramps, the English equivalent is the roundabout. A roundabout resembles a wheel, with different roads radiating from a central circle. It is essential that the driver knows which road to take before entering the roundabout. If not, one ends up driving repeatedly in circles, becoming more bewildered by the minute. At least in the United States, if you're not sure which exit you need, you can always drive on to the next one. In England, one either makes a hasty choice of roads, or circles indefinitely.

Automobiles share a common resemblance, yet still maintain their own country's individuality. Compact cars are seen everywhere, both here and in England. The steady rise in gas prices have made the people of both countries favor the economy of small cars. Yet a driver in America is not likely to see an Austin Mini, Rover, or Vauxhall on the road. Both countries rely heavily on imported cars. However, many of the cars that England imports are American. The car I drove was a Ford Fiesta, typically American, except for the steering wheel on the right side. Even though the cars basically look the same, the terminology for their parts is different. In England, the hood is the bonnet, the trunk is the boot, the windscreen is the windshield, and instead of filling the car with gas, you fill up with petrol. Instead of our regular or lead-free gasoline, the English petrol is called two, three, or four star. The number of stars indicate the octane ratings, and, as in America, the higher octane gas costs more. For most people, these terms are easy enough to understand, and don't cause much confusion.

Despite the differences in some areas of driving, most tourists should find enough similarities to permit safe travel. Once the tourist adapts to some of the "typically English" rules of the road, driving becomes second nature to him. For the most part, common sense, along with some preliminary research on the topic, should allow most people to adapt with very little difficulty.

Automobiles share similar appearances, yet maintain their own country's individuality. Compact cars are popular both here and in England due to the steady rise in gas prices, which make the people of both countries favor the economy of small cars. Though popular in England, a driver is not likely to see an Austin Mini, Rover, or Vauxhall on American roads. While both countries rely heavily on imported cars, many of those that England imports are American. The car I drove was a Ford Fiesta, typically American, except for the steering wheel's placement on the right side. While the cars basically look the same, appearances can be deceiving, as the terminology for their parts is different. In English vernacular, the hood is the bonnet, the trunk is the boot and the windshield is the windscreen. Instead of filling the car with gas, one fills up with petrol. An American buys regular, super or lead-free gasoline, while an Englishman purchases petrol rated two, three, or four star. The number of stars indicates the octane ratings, and, as in America, the higher octane gas costs more. For most people, these terms are easy enough to understand, and don't cause much confusion.

Despite the differences in some aspects of driving, most American tourists find enough similarities to permit safe travel. Once the motorist adapts to some of the "typically English" rules of the road, driving becomes as natural as it is here. Common sense, along with some preliminary research on English driving conditions, should make for a safe and pleasant trip.

Study Openers

1. What kinds of change did Hower adopt in going to the second draft? Where do you find the greatest gains? Where might one expect more improvement in a further draft?
2. What do you conclude about what revision can do, and what seems to be the best way of going at it?

(Other elements)

3. The plan used for this paper illustrates *comparison* and *contrast*, patterns used in showing how A resembles and differs from B (as Chapter 7 will describe in more detail). What insights can a writer hope to get from this plan?
4. Notice that Hower discusses the driving conditions in the two countries by point matched to point (speed limits, road signs, etc.). As an alternative, one might first discuss one country thoroughly before taking up the second country. What could one gain or lose by this alternative?

The Use of Force
by William Carlos Williams

(from *Life Along the Passaic River*, 1938)

They were new patients to me, all I had was the name, Olson. Please come down as soon as you can, my daughter is very sick.

When I arrived I was met by the mother, a big startled looking woman, very clean and apologetic who merely said, Is this the doctor? and let me in. In the back, she added. You must excuse us, doctor, we have her in the kitchen where it is warm. It is very damp here sometimes.

The child was fully dressed and sitting on her father's lap near the kitchen table. He tried to get up, but I motioned for him not to bother, took off my overcoat and started to look things over. I could see that they were all very nervous, eyeing me up and down distrustfully. As often, in such cases, they weren't telling me more than they had to, it was up to me to tell them; that's why they were spending three dollars on me.

The child was fairly eating me up with her cold, steady eyes, and no expression to her face whatever. She did not move and seemed, inwardly, quiet; an unusually attractive little thing, and as strong as a heifer in appearance. But her face was flushed, she was breathing rapidly, and I real-

ized that she had a high fever. She had magnificent blonde hair, in profusion. One of those picture children often reproduced in advertising
20   leaflets and the photogravure sections of the Sunday papers.

She's had a fever for three days, began the father and we don't know
what it comes from. My wife has given her things, you know, like people
do, but it don't do no good. And there's been a lot of sickness around. So
we tho't you'd better look her over and tell us what is the matter.

25   As doctors often do I took a trial shot at it as a point of departure.
Had she had a sore throat?

Both parents answered me together, No . . . No, she says her throat
don't hurt her.

Does your throat hurt you? added the mother to the child. But the lit-
30   tle girl's expression didn't change nor did she move her eyes from my
face.

Have you looked?

I tried to, said the mother, but I couldn't see.

As it happens we had been having a number of cases of diphtheria in
35   the school to which this child went during that month and we were all,
quite apparently, thinking of that, though no one had as yet spoken of
the thing.

Well, I said, suppose we take a look at the throat first. I smiled in my
best professional manner and asking for the child's first name I said,
40   come on, Mathilda, open your mouth and let's take a look at your throat.

Nothing doing.

Aw, come on, I coaxed, just open your mouth wide and let me take a
look. Look, I said opening both hands wide, I haven't anything in my
hands. Just open up and let me see.

45   Such a nice man, put in the mother. Look how kind he is to you. Come
on, do what he tells you to. He won't hurt you.

At that I ground my teeth in disgust. If only they wouldn't use the
word "hurt" I might be able to get somewhere. But I did not allow myself to be hurried or disturbed but speaking quietly and slowly I ap-
50   proached the child again.

As I moved my chair a little nearer suddenly with one catlike movement both her hands clawed instinctively for my eyes and she almost
reached them too. In fact she knocked my glasses flying and they fell,
though unbroken, several feet away from me on the kitchen floor.

55   Both the mother and father almost turned themselves inside out in
embarrassment and apology. You bad girl, said the mother, taking her
and shaking her by one arm. Look what you've done. The nice man . . .

For heaven's sake, I broke in. Don't call me a nice man to her. I'm here
to look at her throat on the chance that she might have diphtheria and

possibly die of it. But that's nothing to her. Look here, I said to the child,   60
we're going to look at your throat. You're old enough to understand what
I'm saying. Will you open it now by yourself or shall we have to open it
for you?

VERSION A

Although she breathed more and
more rapidly, she made no move,
not even a change of expression.
Then the battle began—an absolute
necessity since I had to have a throat
culture for her own protection. First,
however, I explained the danger to
the parents and told them that if I
did not insist upon a throat culture
the responsibility would be entirely
theirs.

VERSION B

Not a move. Even her expression   65
hadn't changed. Her breaths however were coming faster and faster.
Then the battle began. I had to do
it. I had to have a throat culture for
her own protection. But first I told   70
the parents that it was entirely up to
them. I explained the danger but
said that I would not insist on a
throat examination so long as they
would take the responsibility.   75

If you don't do what the doctor says you'll have to go to the hospital,
the mother admonished her severely.

Oh yeah? I had to smile to myself. After all, I had already fallen in
love with the savage brat, the parents were contemptible to me. In the
ensuing struggle they grew more and more abject, crushed, exhausted   80
while she surely rose to magnificent heights of insane fury of effort bred
of her terror of me.

The father tried his best, and he was a big man but the fact that she
was his daughter, his shame at her behavior and his dread of hurting her
made him release her just at the critical moment several times when I   85
had almost achieved success, till I wanted to kill him. But his dread also
that she might have diphtheria made him tell me to go on, go on though
he himself was almost fainting, while the mother moved back and forth
behind us raising and lowering her hands in an agony of apprehension.

Put her in front of you on your lap, I ordered, and hold both her wrists.   90

But as soon as he did the child let out a scream. Don't, you're hurting
me. Let go of my hands. Let them go I tell you. Then she shrieked ter-
rifyingly, hysterically. Stop it! Stop it! You're killing me!

Do you think she can stand it, doctor! said the mother.

You get out, said the husband to his wife. Do you want her to die of   95
diphtheria?

Come on now, hold her, I said.

Then I grasped the child's head with my left hand and tried to get the
wooden tongue depressor between her teeth. She fought, with clenched
teeth, desperately! But now I also had grown furious—at a child. I tried   100
to hold myself down but I couldn't. I know how to expose a throat for in-

spection. And I did my best. When finally I got the wooden spatula behind the last teeth and just the point of it into the mouth cavity, she opened up for an instant but before I could see anything she came down again and gripping the wooden blade between her molars she reduced it to splinters before I could get it out again.

Aren't you ashamed, the mother yelled at her. Aren't you ashamed to act like that in front of the doctor?

Get me a smooth-handled spoon of some sort, I told the mother. We're going through with this. The child's mouth was already bleeding. Her tongue was cut and she was screaming in wild hysterical shrieks. Perhaps I should have desisted and come back in an hour or more. No doubt it would have been better. But I have seen at least two children lying dead in bed of neglect in such cases, and feeling that I must get a diagnosis now or never I went at it again. But the worst of it was that I too had got beyond reason. I could have torn the child apart in my own fury and enjoyed it. It was a pleasure to attack her. My face was burning with it.

The damned little brat must be protected against her own idiocy, one says to one's self at such times. Others must be protected against her. It is a social necessity. And all these things are true. But a blind fury, a feeling of adult shame, bred of a longing for muscular release are the operatives. One goes on to the end.

In a final unreasoning assault I overpowered the child's neck and jaws. I forced the heavy silver spoon back of her teeth and down her throat till she gagged. And there it was—both tonsils covered with membrane. She had fought valiantly to keep me from knowing her secret. She had been hiding that sore throat for three days at least and lying to her parents in order to escape just such an outcome as this.

Now truly she *was* furious. She had been on the defensive before but now she attacked. Tried to get off her father's lap and fly at me while tears of defeat blinded her eyes.

Study Openers

1. Stories usually represent a *time order* in which events are organized by clock or calendar order, as such events occur in external daily life. Stories also illustrate *parallel* development in that they often present an *analogy* to "real life" which conveys some meaning about real life.

   a. What does this story say about life—in particular "the use of force"?

   b. What do you see in the method of presentation which supports your inference? For example, what seems to be the point of the narrator's divided attitude toward the girl? (E.g., "damned little brat" versus "she rose to magnificent heights")

2. Try a brief first-person narrative for one of the following titles: "The Inferior Sex," "Winning Is the Only Thing," "Death Can Be Beautiful." The narrator can be any character you choose with whatever qualities you choose for making your point.
3. Take a recent non-fiction piece you have written, and write a story which brings out the same point. Submit both pieces.

(Other elements)

4. (Line 65) Which version, A or B, would you defend as better fitting the style of Williams' whole story?

Three Fables
by Augusto Monterroso

(from *The Blacksheep and Other Fables*, 1971)

Horse Imagining God

"In spite of what they say, the idea of Heaven inhabited by Horses and presided over by a God in equine form offends both good taste and elementary logic," the Horse explained recently.

"Everybody knows," his reasoning went, "that if Horses were capable of imagining God at all, they would think of him in the form of a rider."   5

Pygmalion

In ancient Greece there was a poet named Pygmalion who devoted himself to the sculpture of statues which were so perfect that they lacked   10
only the ability to talk.

When they were finished, he taught them many things he knew: literature in general, poetry in particular, a little politics, a bit of music and, finally, a smattering of witty sayings and small talk and something of the art of coming out ahead conversationally.   15

When the poet felt that they were finally ready, he contemplated them with satisfaction for a while, and then almost offhandedly, without conscious command, he made them speak.

Thenceforth, the statues took to dressing up and going out into the streets and whether in the streets or at home they talked ceaselessly,   20
about anything that entered their heads.

Pleased with his work, the poet let them carry on, and when visitors came he remained discreetly quiet (a relief for him actually) while his handiwork entertained the company with quite witty anecdotes—sometimes at the expense of the poet himself.

25   The best of it was that there came a time when the creations, as is wont to happen, considered themselves better than their creator, and they began to malign him.

Since they could speak, they argued, now the only thing lacking was to fly, and they began to try various kinds of wings, including some wax

30   ones, which shortly before had been completely discredited as the result of unfortunate adventure.

At times, red in the face with tremendous effort, they succeeded in rising two or three centimeters, a height which of course, since they weren't built for it, made them dizzy.

35   Some, remorsefully, gave it up and stuck to speaking and making others dizzy.

Others obstinately persisted in their design, and the Greeks passing by could only assume they were mad, seeing them continually making the little jumps that they considered flight.

40   Still others concluded that the poet was the cause of all their troubles, whether these were jumping or simply speaking, and tried to scratch his eyes out.

At times the poet got tired of the whole thing, gave them a kick in the tail, and they ended up in little chunks of marble.

45   The Origin of Old People

The other afternoon a child of five years was explaining to a four-year-old that many of them maintain the most rigorous sexual purity among themselves and hardly ever touch each other because they know—or at least they think—that if by chance they become careless and let them-

50   selves be carried away by the passion of the age and make love, the inevitable fruit of such unnatural union is unfailingly an old man or old woman; that they say that's how the old people we see in the streets and the parks were born and are born every day; and that maybe this belief was due to the fact that children never see their grandparents young and

55   nobody explains to them how these people came to be born or where they came from; but that actually that wasn't necessarily their origin at all.

Study Openers

1. Just as other fictions can often be taken as *parallels* or *analogies* of real life-patterns, the so-called *fable* analogizes such a pattern—but more

briefly, pointedly, and artificially than in longer stories which often seem real in themselves. Fables often use animals or legendary characters to give comic or satiric bite.

> a. What point about human nature is being made by each of Monterroso's fables?
> b. What is the effect of the fable framework in each case? For example, "Pygmalion" might have used God for its central character, or a teacher—but Monterroso chose instead the legendary sculptor Pygmalion whose statue came to life.

2. Think of about three observations you yourself could make about human weakness or foolishness—and write a fable for each.

The Roots of Serendipity
by James H. Austin

(*Saturday Review/World*, November 2, 1974)

What is life but a series of inspired follies? The difficulty is to find them to do. Never lose a chance: it doesn't come every day.
GEORGE BERNARD SHAW

It is never entirely in fashion to mention luck in the same breath as science. Science is considered a rational endeavor, and the investigator is supposed to make discoveries for logical reasons by virtue of his own intellectual hard work. As everyone no doubt knows, however, discoveries *do* come about through chance, but this fact becomes more impressive   5
only when it happens to you personally.

Take, for example, something that happened to me a few years ago. A physician-investigator, I was directing a laboratory team studying a rare form of hereditary epilepsy. The disorder is called Lafora's disease, after its discoverer, and in it the nerve cells contain distinctive round, red-   10
staining particles, called Lafora bodies. We knew if we could discover the chemical composition of these tiny spherules, it would help us eventually understand the metabolic cause of the disease. However, when we first analyzed the Lafora bodies isolated by my colleague, Dr. Yokoi, we drew a blank. We were up a blind alley, asking the wrong questions,   15
using the wrong analytical method.

At this point, my dog, Tom, led us to the answer—but only by a curious combination of circumstances. Tom was a high-spirited Brittany spaniel which frequently coursed far afield. One day we were out hunting— his hobby and mine—in thick cover, and to know where he was, I took   20
the precaution of tying a bell to the front of his collar. The bell is worth noting.

A few days later I noticed a rapidly growing mass on the front of

Tom's neck. The mass was hard enough to be a malignant growth, and
25 my surgical colleague, who was doing research on malignant tumors in
dogs, suggested that it be removed at once.

Tom turned only a few dog hairs during the operation and quickly returned to his usual frisky self. The mass, to everyone's surprise, was not
a malignant tumor after all. Instead, the microscopic slides showed a
30 subacute inflammatory response involving some lymph glands in Tom's
neck. We were baffled as to what might be the cause of this inflamma-
tion. Tuberculosis? Yeast? Fungi? Searching for these organisms, I asked
the technicians to treat further sections of the tissue with special staining
methods. These new sections showed an "unusual round fungus." Under
35 the microscope round structures were indeed there. Curiously, they lay
around the outside of the mass. None lay inside. No one had ever seen a
fungus quite like this before. Finally, someone on the surgical service
brightened with a happy thought. Perhaps these were not fungi but
round spherules of starch! Starch? Starch, we all now recalled, is used to
40 dust surgical gloves. Some of it could have remained on the gloves used
during Tom's operation and could have been transferred to the outside
of the mass when it was resected.

When I checked out this possibility and looked at starch dust under
the microscope, I finally realized that it is made up of round spherules.
45 Moreover, because starch is composed of many sugar molecules, the
starch in Tom's biopsy also turned red when stained with a special histo-
chemical stain for sugars. In fact, the starch spherules looked very much
like the human Lafora bodies we were trying to identify! When these
elementary facts entered my awareness, they completely transformed our
50 approach to Lafora's disease. Lafora bodies in humans not only looked
like starch but also could be a kind of starch! Starting afresh from this
new working hypothesis, we could next apply the appropriate chemical
test for sugar to the small amounts of Lafora bodies Dr. Yokoi had isolated. The tests permitted us to confirm our hypothesis. Some weeks later
55 we finally knew that Lafora bodies, like starch, were essentially made up
of many sugar units linked together in a long chain to form a polymer.

Now, nothing in this story is intended to convey the view that raising
dogs and running them afield is better than being hard working, persis-
tent, curious, imaginative, or enthusiastic. Nor would we downgrade the
60 sudden flash of insight that illuminates the scene or the whiff of intuition
that inclines us in the right—or wrong—direction.

But when this is said and done, much that is really novel in our creative efforts will still be decided at the pivotal moment when we confront chance. Like the lowly turtle, man, too, lurches forward only if he
65 first sticks his neck out and chances the consequences.

What is chance? Dictionaries define it as something fortuitous that happens unpredictably without discernible human intention. Chance is unintentional and capricious, but we needn't conclude that chance is immune from human intervention. Indeed, chance plays several distinct roles when humans react creatively with one another and with their environment.   70

We can readily distinguish four varieties of chance if we consider that they each involve a different kind of motor activity and a special kind of sensory receptivity. The varieties of chance also involve distinctive personality traits and differ in the way one particular individual influences 75 them.

Chance I is the pure blind luck that comes with no effort on our part. If, for example, you are sitting at a bridge table of four, it's "in the cards" for you to receive a hand of all 13 spades, but it will come up only once in every 6.3 trillion deals. You will ultimately draw this lucky hand—with 80 no intervention on your part—but it does involve a longer wait than most of us have time for.

Chance II evokes the kind of luck Charles Kettering had in mind when he said: "Keep on going and the chances are you will stumble on something, perhaps when you are least expecting it. I have never heard of 85 anyone stumbling on something sitting down."

In the sense referred to here, Chance II is not passive, but springs from an energetic, generalized motor activity. A certain basal level of action "stirs up the pot," brings in random ideas that will collide and stick together in fresh combinations, lets chance operate. When someone, *any-* 90 *one,* does swing into motion and keeps on going, he will increase the number of collisions between events. When a few events are linked together, they can then be exploited to have a fortuitous outcome, but many others, of course, cannot. Kettering was right. Press on. Something will turn up. We may term this the Kettering Principle.   95

In the two previous examples, a unique role of the individual person was either lacking or minimal. Accordingly, as we move on to Chance III, we see blind luck, but in camouflage. Chance presents the clue, the opportunity exists, but it would be missed except by that one person uniquely equipped to observe it, visualize it conceptually, and fully 100 grasp its significance. Chance III involves a special receptivity and discernment unique to the recipient. Louis Pasteur characterized it for all time when he said: "Chance favors only the prepared mind."

Pasteur himself had it in full measure. But the classic example of his principle occurred in 1928, when Alexander Fleming's mind instantly 105 fused at least five elements into a conceptually unified nexus. His mental sequences went something like this: (1) I see that a mold has fallen by accident into my culture dish; (2) the staphylococcal colonies residing

near it failed to grow; (3) the mold must have secreted something that
110   killed the bacteria; (4) I recall a similar experience once before; (5) if I
could separate this new "something" from the mold, it could be used to
kill staphylococci that cause human infections.

Actually, Fleming's mind was exceptionally well prepared for the penicillin mold. Six years earlier, while he was suffering from a cold, his own
115   nasal drippings had found their way onto a culture dish, for reasons not
made entirely clear. He noted that nearby bacteria were killed, and as-
tutely followed up the lead. His observations led him to discover a bac-
tericidal enzyme present in nasal mucus and tears, called lysozyme. Lysozyme proved too weak to be of medical use, but imagine how receptive
120   Fleming's mind was to the penicillin mold when it later happened on
the scene!

One word evokes the quality of the operations involved in the first three
kinds of chance. It is *serendipity.* The term describes the facility for encountering unexpected good luck, as the result of: accident (Chance I),
125   general exploratory behavior (Chance II), or sagacity (Chance III). The
word itself was coined by the Englishman-of-letters Horace Walpole, in
1754. He used it with reference to the legendary tales of the Three
Princes of Serendip (Ceylon), who quite unexpectedly encountered many
instances of good fortune on their travels. In today's parlance, we have
130   usually watered down *serendipity* to mean the good luck that comes
solely by accident. We think of it as a result, not an ability. We have
tended to lose sight of the element of sagacity, by which term Walpole
wished to emphasize that some distinctive personal receptivity is involved.

135   There remains a fourth element in good luck, an unintentional but
subtle personal prompting of it. The English Prime Minister Benjamin
Disraeli summed up the principle underlying Chance IV when he noted
that "we make our fortunes and we call them fate." Disraeli, a politician
of considerable practical experience, appreciated that we each shape
140   our own destiny, at least to some degree. One might restate the principle
as follows: *Chance favors the individualized action.*

In Chance IV the kind of luck is peculiar to one person, and like a personal hobby, it takes on a distinctive individual flavor. This form of
chance is one-man-made, and it is as personal as a signature. Indeed, it is
145   to motor behavior what Chance III is to sensory receptivity. But Chance
IV connotes no generalized activity, as bees might have in the anonymity
of a hive. Instead, it comprehends a discrete behavioral performance focused in a unique manner. Chance IV has an elusive, almost miragelike,
quality. Like a mirage, it is difficult to get a firm grip on, for it tends to
150   recede as we pursue it and advance as we step back. But we still accept

a mirage when we see it, because we vaguely understand the basis for the phenomenon. A strongly heated layer of air, less dense than usual, lies next to the earth, and it bends the light rays as they pass through. The resulting image may be magnified as if by a telescopic lens in the atmosphere, and real objects, ordinarily hidden far out of sight over the horizon, are brought forward and revealed to the eye. What happens in a mirage then, and in this form of chance, not only appears farfetched but indeed is farfetched. 155

About a century ago, a striking example of Chance IV took place in the Spanish cave of Altamira.* There, one day in 1879, Don Marcelino de Sautuola was engaged in his hobby of archaeology, searching Altamira for bones and stones. With him was his daughter, Maria, who had asked him if she could come along to the cave that day. The indulgent father had said she could. Naturally enough, he first looked where he had always found heavy objects before, on the *floor* of the cave. But Maria, unhampered by any such preconceptions, looked not only at the floor but also all around the cave with the open-eyed wonder of a child! She looked up, exclaimed, and then he looked up, to see incredible works of art on the cave ceiling! The magnificent colored bison and other animals they saw at Altamira, painted more than 15,000 years ago, might lead one to call it "the Sistine Chapel of Prehistory." Passionately pursuing his interest in archaeology, de Sautuola, to his surprise, discovered man's first paintings. In quest of Science, he happened upon Art. 160 165 170

Yes, a dog did "discover" the cave, and the initial receptivity was his daughter's, but the pivotal reason for the cave paintings' discovery hinged on a long sequence of prior events originating in de Sautuola himself. For when we dig into the background of this amateur excavator, we find he was an exceptional person. Few Spaniards were out probing into caves 100 years ago. The fact that he—not someone else—decided to dig that day in the cave of Altamira was the culmination of his passionate interest in his hobby. Here was a rare man whose avocation had been to educate himself from scratch, as it were, in the science of archaeology and cave exploration. This was no simple passive recognizer of blind luck when it came his way, but a man whose unique interests served as an active creative thrust—someone whose own actions and personality would focus the events that led circuitously but inexorably to the discovery of man's first paintings. 175 180 185

Then, too, there is a more subtle matter. How do you give full weight to the personal interests that imbue your child with your own curiosity,

* The cave had first been discovered some years before by an enterprising hunting dog in search of game. Curiously, in 1932 the French cave of Lascaux was discovered by still another dog.

190   that inspire her to ask to join you in your own musty hobby, and that then lead you to agree to her request at the critical moment? For many reasons, at Altamira, more than the special receptivity of Chance III was required—this was a different domain, that of the personality and its actions.

195   A century ago no one had the remotest idea our caveman ancestors were highly creative artists. Weren't their talents rather minor and limited to crude flint chippings? But the paintings at Altamira, like a mirage, would quickly magnify this diminutive view, bring up into full focus a distant, hidden era of man's prehistory, reveal sentient minds and well-

200   developed aesthetic sensibilities to which men of any age might aspire. And like a mirage, the events at Altamira grew out of de Sautuola's heated personal quest and out of the invisible forces of chance we know exist yet cannot touch. Accordingly, one may introduce the term *altamirage* to identify the quality underlying Chance IV. Let us define it as

205   the facility for encountering unexpected good luck as the result of highly individualized action. Altamirage goes well beyond the boundaries of serendipity in its emphasis on the role of personal action in chance.

   Chance IV is favored by distinctive, if not eccentric, hobbies, personal life-styles, and modes of behavior peculiar to one individual, usually in-

210   vested with some passion. The farther apart these personal activities are from the area under investigation, the more novel and unexpected will be the creative product of the encounter.

   For some classic examples of the four Chances in biology and medicine, let us again turn to Fleming.

215   Good examples of Chance I (pure blind luck) do not leap out from the medical literature, because researchers always feel a little guilty when they mention that luck has replaced more rational approaches. However, we can rely on Fleming for his candor as he described how it was to be visited by Chance I. He said: "There are thousands of differ-

220   ent molds, and there are thousands of different bacteria, and that chance put that mold in the right spot at the right time was like winning the Irish Sweepstakes."

   Many investigators are as energetic as bees, so their fast mental and physical pace stirs up a certain amount of Chance II for this reason

225   alone. Examples of Chance II are surely all around us, but it is difficult to prove with scientific certainty that they exist, because studies of twins would be required. No researcher seems to have a twin who is indolent, but equal in all other abilities, to serve as a basis for comparison.

   We have already considered Fleming under Chance III, and for an

230   example of the subtle workings of the personality in Chance IV, we can return to him. In Fleming's background was a boyhood shaped by the

frugal economy of a Scottish hill farm in Ayrshire. Later, we find that
much of his decision to train and work at old St. Mary's Hospital in London was not based on the excellence of its scientific facilities. Instead, his
decision hinged on the fact that he liked to play water polo and St.   235
Mary's had a good swimming pool. Without the hobby that drew him to
St. Mary's, Fleming would never have discovered penicillin! Still later,
when he is 47, let us observe this same thrifty Scot at his laboratory at
St. Mary's. His research facilities are primitive by today's standards. His
bench stands beneath a window, covered by a clutter of old culture   240
dishes, for Fleming is still reluctant to throw any dish out until he is certain that everything possible has been learned from it. He then picks up
one culture dish of staphylococci that, with ingrained thrift, he has
hoarded for many days. The delay has been crucial. Had he thrown the
dish out earlier, on schedule like the rest of us, the penicillin mold might   245
not have had the opportunity to grow. But there the mold is now, growing in the over-age culture dish, and he alone also has the prepared mind
to realize its implications.

We have now seen Sir Alexander Fleming's modest comment about his
Irish Sweepstakes luck under Chance I, and can infer that Chance II en-   250
tered his life from his many industrious years in the laboratory. We later
observed how receptive he was (Chance III) and finally how his hobby
and his thrifty habits coalesced in Chance IV. Fleming's discovery earned
him the Nobel Prize in Physiology and Medicine in 1945. (He shared it
with Florey and Chain, who achieved the large-scale production of peni-   255
cillin.) In Fleming's life, then, we see a fusion of all four forms of
chance, and from this there follows a simple conclusion: The most novel,
if not the greatest, discoveries occur when several varieties of chance coincide. Let us call this unifying observation the Fleming Effect. His life
exemplifies it, and it merits special emphasis.   260

Why do we still remember men like Fleming? We venerate them not
as scientists alone. As men, their total contribution transcends their scientific discoveries. In their lives we see demonstrated how malleable our
own futures are. In their work we perceive how many loopholes fate has
left us—how much of destiny is still in our hands. In them we find that   265
nothing is predetermined. Chance can be on our side, if we but stir it up
with our energies, stay receptive to its every random opportunity, and
continually provoke it by individuality in our hobbies and our approach
to life.

[For Study Openers, see p. 322.]

Hiram Walker and Sons, Inc.

(Advertisement, 1976)

The purpose of most bourbon ads is to get you to drink more bourbon.
The purpose of this one is to get you to drink <u>less</u>.

Maybe you drink bourbon when you relax. Perhaps it's true enjoyment.

That's fine. We're proud our Walker's De Luxe Bourbon can give you that pleasure.

But how much Walker's De Luxe should you drink? We say *less* than any other brand.

Of course, all liquor should be taken in moderation. But Walker's De Luxe is truly a bourbon to savor. It's meant to be sipped slowly—for a good reason.

Quality takes time.

We take eight long years to age Walker's De Luxe.

That aging gives our bourbon a smoothness and a well-rounded flavor that's hard to find.

A half hour for smoothness.

We feel you'll miss the flavor completely if you gulp it down without thinking.

In fact, we hope a responsible person will take at least one half hour to enjoy a De Luxe. That's the average time necessary to pour, sip, and enjoy.

In the end you'll drink less Walker's De Luxe Bourbon.

But you will get more drop for drop pleasure from our eight year old flavor when you do.

WALKER'S
DE LUXE BOURBON
AGED 8 YEARS

Study Openers

1. What patterns of development do you detect in this essay? (Chapter 7, page 62) Which seems to be the master pattern for the whole? How is that pattern appropriate?

(Other elements)

2. What reconciliation if any do you see between Austin's stress on *chance* and the determinism of thinkers like B. F. Skinner who maintain that nothing happens by chance?
3. Austin apparently offers little actual support in the way of footnotes, quotations, bibliography. What details justify your confidence (or lack of it) in Austin's credentials?
4. Present a plan for extending Austin's theory to increase the productivity of chance in a person's everyday life (your own in particular).

Study Openers

An effective advertisement uses many stylistic powers in concentration, and may therefore exhibit numerous principles. Notice what this Walker ad can show about coherence (Chapter 8, page 62).

1. Identify all the relationship signals which assist continuity of attention from one paragraph to the next.
2. Comment on the paragraphing. Only one paragraph contains more than two sentences. How might you consolidate these tiny paragraphs into two or three larger ones? What would be the effect?

(Other elements)

3. Are you favorably or unfavorably impressed by this presentation? Why?
4. Comment on the implied personality of the advertiser, as to competence and traits of character. How does it affect the impact of the ad? (Such matters are further explored in Chapter 10, page 101).
5. Construct a comparable advertisement urging the discriminating and moderate enjoyment of some product which many people believe to be harmful.

Inventing the Future
by James Burke

(from *Connections*, 1978)

Why should we look to the past in order to prepare for the future? Because there is nowhere else to look. The real question is whether the past contains clues to the future. Either history is a series of individual and unrepeated acts which bear no relation to anything other than their immediate and unique temporal environment, or it is a series of events triggered by recurring factors which manifest themselves as a product of human behavior at all times. If the latter is the case, it may be that the past illustrates a number of cause and effect sequences which may take place again, given similar circumstances. If it is not, then, as Henry Ford put it, "history is bunk," and there is no profit to be had from its study, or from anything not immediately and only concerned with the unchanging laws of nature.

Clearly, a preference for the cause and effect argument governs the approach to history expressed in this book. The process of innovation is shown to be influenced by several factors recurring at different times and places; although these may not be repeated exactly each time, the observer becomes aware that they may recur in his own future, and is therefore more able to recognize them should they do so. The structural device used here is to examine an event in the past which bears similarity to one in the present in order to see where such an event led. Thus we return from the modern ballistic missile to the development of cannonballs, from the telephone to medieval church postal services, from the atomic bomb to the stirrup, and so on. The purpose of this approach is to attempt to question the adequacy of the standard modern schoolbook treatment, in which history is represented in terms of heroes, themes or periods.

In the heroic treatment, historical change is shown to have been generated by the genius of individuals, conveniently labelled "inventors." In such a treatment, Edison invented the electric light, Bell the telephone, Gutenberg the printing press, Watt the steam engine, and so on. But no individual is responsible for producing an invention *ex nihilo*. The elevation of the single inventor to the position of sole creator at best exaggerates his influence over events, and at worst denies the involvement of those humbler members of society without whose work his task might have been impossible.

The thematic approach attempts to divide the past into subjects such

as Transport, Communications, Sail, Steam, Warfare, Metallurgy and
others, but this implies a degree of foreknowledge where none exists.
Thus Bouchon's use of perforated paper in 1725 to automate the Lyons
silk looms had nothing to do with the development of calculation or data   40
transmission, and yet it was an integral part of the development of the
computer. The Venturi principle, basic to the structure and operation of
the jet engine or the carburetor, was originally produced in an attempt
to measure the flow of water through pumps. Gutenberg's movable type-
face belonged as much to metallurgy or textiles as it did to the develop-   45
ment of literacy.

In the periodic treatment the past is seen as a series of sub-units
bounded by specific dates such as the beginning of a new royal dynasty,
the fall of an imperial capital city, the arrival of a new mode of transport, and these sub-units are conveniently labelled the Dark Ages, Mid-   50
dle Ages, Renaissance, Age of Enlightenment, and so forth. As this book
has shown, such a view of the past is over-simplified, for to give any period a specific label is to ignore the overlapping nature of the passage of
events. Elements of efficient Roman administration techniques continued
to operate throughout the so-called Dark Ages. The fall of Constantino-   55
ple meant little or nothing to the vast majority of the European population, if indeed they knew of it at all. There was no sudden and radical
alteration in English life when the Tudors gave way to the Stuarts.

These approaches to the study of history tend to leave the layman
with a linear view of the way change occurs, and this in turn affects the   60
way he sees the future. Most people, if asked how the telephone is likely
to develop during their lifetime, will consider merely the ways in which
the instrument itself may change. If such changes include a reduction in
size and cost and an increase in operating capability, it is easy to assume
that the user will be encouraged to communicate more frequently than   65
he does at present. But the major influence of the telephone on his life
might come from an interaction between communications technology
and other factors which have nothing to do with technology.

Consider, for instance, a point in the future at which depletion of energy resources makes Draconian governmental action necessary in order   70
to enforce severe energy rationing. In such a situation the government
might decide to tap telephones on a random national basis as part of a
campaign to discourage profiteering and, in a more subtle manner, dis-
sent. In these circumstances the telephone would become an instrument
which would act as a brake rather than a stimulus to communication.   75
This is typical of the way things happen. The triggering factor is more
often than not operating in an area entirely unconnected with the situation which is about to undergo change. A linear view of the past would,

for instance, place the arrival of the chimney in a sequence of developments relating to change in domestic living. Yet the alteration of life-
style brought about by the chimney included year-round administration
and increased intellectual activity, which in turn contributed to a general
increase in the economic welfare of the community to a point where the
increase in the construction of houses brought about a shortage of wood.
The consequent need for alternative sources of energy spurred the development of a furnace which would operate efficiently on coal, and this
led to the production of molten iron in large quantities, permitting the
casting of the cylinders which were used in the early steam engines.
Their use of air pressure led first to the investigation of gases and then
petroleum as a fuel for the modern automobile engine, without which, in
turn, powered flight would have been impossible.

Within this apparently haphazard structure of events we have seen
that there are certain recurring factors at work in the process of change.
The first is what one would expect: that an innovation occurs as the result of deliberate attempts to develop it. Napoleon presented the nation
with clearly defined goals when he established the Society for the Encouragement of National Industry. One of those goals was the development of a means of preserving food, and it was reached by Appert's bot-
tling process. When Edison began work on the development of the
incandescent light bulb, he did so in response to the inadequacy of the arc
light. All the means were available: a vacuum pump to evacuate the
bulb, electric current, the filament concept which the arc light itself
used, the use of carbon for the filament. The idea of serial motion in
Muybridge's early photographs of the trotting horse led, through Edison's friendship with Muybridge, to the deliberate development of the
kinetoscope as a money-making proposition. Von Linde perfected the domestic refrigeration system in answer to a specific request from the Mu-
nich beer brewers for a way of making and keeping beer in their cellars
all year round.

A second factor which recurs frequently is that the attempt to find one
thing leads to the discovery of another. William Perkin was in search of
an artificial form of quinine, using some of the molecular combinations
available in coal tar, when the black sludge with which one of his experiments ended turned out to be the first artificial aniline dye. Oersted's
attempt to illustrate that a compass needle was not affected by electric
current showed that in fact it was, and the electromagnet was the result
of that surprise discovery. Henri Moissan, attempting to make artificial
diamonds by subjecting common carbon to very high temperatures, failed
to do so, but trying his luck with other materials at hand he produced
calcium carbide, the basis for acetylene and fertilizer.

Another factor is one in which unrelated developments have a decisive
effect on the main event. The existence of a pegged cylinder as a control
mechanism for automated organs gave Bouchon the idea of using perforated paper for use in the silk loom. The medieval textile revolution,
which was based on the use of the spinning wheel in conjunction with   125
the horizontal loom, lowered the price of linen to the point where enough
of it became available in rag form to revolutionize the production of paper. C.T.R. Wilson's cloud chamber gave the physicists the tool they
needed to work on the splitting of the atom.

Motives such as war and religion may also act as major stimulants to   130
innovation. The use of the cannon in the fourteenth and fifteenth centuries led to defensive architectural developments which made use of as-
tronomical instruments that became the basic tools of map-making. The
introduction of the stirrup, and through it, the medieval armored shock-
troop, helped to change the social and economic structure of Europe.   135
The need to pray at predetermined times during the night and to know
when feast days would occur aroused interest in Arab knowledge of as-
tronomy. The water-powered alarm clock and the verge and foliot were
the direct result of this interest.

Accident and unforeseen circumstances play a leading role in innova-   140
tion. It was only when the bottom dropped out of the acetylene gas market that attempts were made to find a use for the vast amounts of calcium carbide in Europe and America: cheap fertilizer was the result.
When the Earl of Dundonald's coal distillation kiln exploded and the va-
pors ignited, investigation into the gases resulted in the production of   145
coal gas. The sudden arrival in Europe of the compass needle from
China led to work on the phenomenon of magnetic attraction, and this
in turn led to the discovery of electricity. A similarly unexpected Chinese
invention, gunpowder, stimulated mining for metals to make cannon,
and the money to pay for them. The flooding of these mines and the sub-   150
sequent failure of the pumps brought about the development of the
barometer.

Physical and climatic conditions play their part. As the European communities recovered after the withdrawal of the Roman legions and the
centuries of invasion and war that had followed, reclamation of the land   155
depended for its success on the development of a plow that would clear
the forests and till some of the toughest bottom land in the world. These
conditions helped to structure the moldboard and coulter, implements
that formed the basis for the radically new plow design that emerged in
Europe in the ninth century, and thus helped to move the center of eco-   160
nomic power north of the Alps. The change in the weather which struck
northern Europe like a sledgehammer in the twelfth and thirteenth cen-

turies provided urgent need for more efficient heating. The chimney answered that need, and in doing so had the most profound effect on the
165 economic and cultural life of the continent. In the early nineteenth century the prevalence of malaria in Florida, spread by the mosquitoes
breeding in the swamps surrounding the town of Apalachicola, spurred
John Gorrie to develop the ice-making machine and air-conditioning system in an attempt to cure his patients, in the mistaken belief that the dis-
170 ease was related directly to summer temperatures and miasma rising
from rotting vegetation.

Two points arise from this way of looking at the process of change
and innovation. One is that, as we have seen, no inventor works alone.
The myth of the lonely genius, filled with vision and driven to exhaustion
175 by his dream, may have been deliberately fostered by Edison, but even
he did not invent without help from his colleagues and predecessors. The
automobile, for example, as assembled from parts which included Volta's
electric pistol, using the electric spark to ignite gases. Its basic piston
and cylinder drive was Newcomen's. The carburetor owed its operation
180 to Venturi's jet principle and its scent spray derivative. Its gears were
descendants of the waterwheel. The elevation of the lonely inventor to a
position of ivory-tower isolation does more than deny such debts; it
makes more difficult the bridging of the gap between the technologist
and the man in the street.

185 The second point is that the ease with which information can be
spread is critical to the rate at which change occurs. The inventive out-
put of Western technology can be said to have occurred in three major
surges. The first—the Medieval Industrial Revolution—came after the establishment of safe lines of communication between the communities of
190 Europe as order was re-established in the wake of the invasions of the
tenth century. The second occurred in the seventeenth century when the
scientific community began to make use of printing to exchange ideas on
a major scale. The third followed the nineteenth-century development of
telecommunications.

195 It was with the second of these stages that the age of specialization
began, when scientists began to talk to each other in language that only
their fellows could understand. The more the knowledge in a certain
field increased, the more esoteric became the language. The reason for
this is simply that ordinary everyday language has proved incapable of
200 encompassing scientific subject matter. As the amount of knowledge in
each field increased, the percentage of language shared only by others
in the same field also grew. Today, the man in the street is often pre-
vented from sharing in scientific and technological discussions not by
mental inadequacy, but because he lacks certain key words and an un-

derstanding of their meaning. Has the rate of change become so high   205
that it is impossible for the layman to do more than keep up to date with
the *shape* of things around him? It has been said that if you understand
something today it must by definition be obsolete. And yet the rate at
which change now occurs is an integral part of the way our society
functions. The avalanche of ephemera that arrives in our homes every   210
day has to continue to flow if the economy is to operate to the general
advantage. Our industries are geared to high turnover, planned obsolescence, novelty. The basic components of the modern automobile have
not changed in a generation, but minor modifications such as fuel-
injection systems, suspension, lighting, seat cover material, body styling,   215
have done so. Without these modifications the consumer would have no
desire to change a machine which can operate efficiently, if well looked
after, for a decade or more. Thus change is good for the economy because it keeps the money going round and workers employed. The inter-
dependence of such a society, however, renders it vulnerable to compo-   220
nent failure. A small factory making one part of an automobile can bring
the entire industry to a halt if its workers go on strike. The New York
blackout of 1965 occurred because of the action of a single relay at Ni-
agara Falls.

The production-line style of manufacture has increasingly affected our   225
way of life, in some cases creating problems of alienation and dissatisfaction among wide sectors of the work force. But such difficulties go hand
in hand with a higher standard of living engendered by these very production processes. As the pace quickens, and the diffusion of innovative
ideas in the technological community is made easier by technological ad-   230
vance itself, the rate of change accelerates. At an obvious level this increases the avalanche of material goods and services provided, and makes
life more comfortable—if also more complicated. But the amount of innovation increases also at an "invisible" level—that at which a high degree of specialist knowledge is necessary to understand what is happening.   235
Unfortunately, it is at this level that many of the advances most critically
important to our future occur: developments in the field of genetic engineering, radioactive fuels, drugs, urban planning, and so on. It is in
these areas of innovation that the average citizen feels disfranchised. He
knows that they are happening, but does not know enough to be in-   240
volved in decisions relating to them. Indeed, in some cases, he is actively
discouraged from being so.

Thus the intelligent layman realizes that he is surrounded by man-
made objects—the products of innovation—that constantly serve as a
reminder of his ignorance. It may be this contradiction, coupled with   245
the possibility of resolving it provided by technology itself, which has

led to a growing desire in the community to assess the likely future effects of the present high rate of change.

250   Attitudes have tended to fall into four groups. The first maintains that we should give up the present system oriented toward high technology and return to an "intermediate" technology, making use of resources which cannot be depleted, such as wind, wave and solar power—in effect, that we should return to the land. The attraction of this idea is that it might
255   draw society closer together by reducing the present gulf between the technologist and the layman, thus encouraging participation on the part of the electorate in decision-making which would relate to simpler, more fundamental matters—a theory which has obvious appeal for the developing world, too. The question is whether such an alternative is possi-
260   ble for other than the simplest communities. Are we not in our advanced society already too dependent on technological life-support systems to make the switch?

The second attitude held is that we should assess scientific and technological research strictly according to its worth for society, and curtail all other forms of research. This presents more difficult problems. In
265   selecting which areas of research to encourage and which to curtail, to what extent are we depriving ourselves of the benefits of serendipity, which, as this book shows, is at the heart of the process of change? Without Apollo, would we have had minicomputers? Without Moissan's search for artificial diamonds, would cyanamide fertilizer have been
270   discovered? Without the atomic bomb, would fusion be feasible?

The third alternative is that we should allow technology to continue to solve the problems as it always has done. The result of this would be a continued rise in the standard of living, fuelled by cheaper consumer goods produced from cheaper power sources. Even if it worked, this
275   option would still leave the community with two major concerns. The first is the effect on the environment of the vast amounts of virtually free energy created by the fusion process. While undoubtedly attractive in its stimulating effect on manufacture, the use of energy on such a scale might create a major planet-wide problem of heat. The waste heat cre-
280   ated by the prolific use of this energy would have to go somewhere, and if it were not to have profound and long-term effects on the ecosphere, rationing measures might have to be taken. The next consideration is the inevitable frustration of the citizen should such rationing be enforced. This would surely increase, with potentially disruptive consequences.
285   The final alternative is that research and development should be directed toward producing more durable goods and less planned obsolescence. We should seek continued economic health in the markets as yet unsaturated by consumer products—in other words, "spread the wealth."

This offers a utopian concept of the future. Sharing the present level of advance on a world-wide scale would present the manufacturing indus- 290 tries with decades of opportunity. The gap between the haves and have-nots would narrow, eventually to disappear, and with it would go the divisions that endanger the survival of man on the planet. Scientific and technological talent would be diverted to serve the greater ends of education in bringing the community together on a more equal material and 295 intellectual footing. This vision is marred by the major dilemma it would present at its inception. How would it be possible to convince the haves that they had enough, and what would be the reaction of the have-nots if the richer communities would not accept a lower standard of living? The 1973 increase in oil prices demonstrated the power of countries 300 which are less well developed economically but rich in raw materials to cause universal recession in a matter of months.

Whichever of these alternatives is chosen, the key to success will be the use we make of what is undoubtedly the vital commodity of the future: information. It seems inevitable that, unless changes are made in 305 the way information is disseminated, we will soon become a society consisting of two classes: the informed elite, and the rest. The danger inherent in such a development is obvious.

In the meantime, we appear to be at another of the major crossroads in history. We are increasingly aware of the need to assess our use of 310 technology and its impact on us, and indeed it is technology which has given us the tools with which to make such an assessment. But the layman is aware too that he has not been adequately prepared to make that assessment. Now that computer systems are within the price range of most organizations, and indeed of many individuals, an avalanche of 315 data is about to be released on the man in the street. But what use are data if they cannot be understood?

In the last twenty years television has brought a wide spectrum of affairs into our living-rooms. Our emotional reaction to many of them—such as the problem of where to site atomic power stations, or the 320 dilemma of genetic enginering, or the question of abortion—reveals the paradoxical situation in which we find ourselves. The very tools which might be used to foster understanding and reason, as opposed to emotional reflex, are themselves forced to operate at a level which only enhances the paradox. The high rate of change to which we have become 325 accustomed affects the manner in which information is presented: when the viewer is deemed to be bored after only a few minutes of air time, or the reader after a few paragraphs, content is sacrificed for stimulus, and the problem is reinforced. The fundamental task of technology is to find a means to end this vicious circle, and to bring us all to a fuller com- 330 prehension of the technological system which governs and supports our lives. It is a difficult task, because it will involve surmounting barriers that have taken centuries to construct. During that time we have carried with us, and cherished, beliefs that are pre-technological in nature. These faiths place art and philosophy at the center of man's existence, and science and technology on the periphery. According to this view, the former lead and the latter follow.

Yet, as this book has shown, the reverse is true. Without instruments, how could the Copernican revolution have taken place? Why are we taught that we gain insight and the experience of beauty only through art, when this is but a limited and second-hand representation of the infinitely deeper experience to be gained by direct observation of the world around us? For such observation to become significant it must be made in the light of knowledge. The sense of wonder and excitement to be derived from watching the way an insect's wing functions, or an amoeba divides, or a fetus is formed comes in its greatest intensity only to those who have been given the opportunity to find out *how* these things happen.

Science and technology have immeasurably enriched our material lives. If we are to realize the immense potential of a society living in harmony with the systems and artifacts which it has created, we must learn —and learn soon—to use science and technology to enrich our intellectual lives.

Study Openers

Burke's essay introduces his book *Connections,* a history of science and technology on which his television series of that name was based. His essay shows the techniques of coherence working at their best—clearly and easily in holding together a long piece of writing. (See Chapter 8, page 77.)

1. Reading *only the first sentence of each paragraph,* see how far you can sketch in a topic outline of the whole essay. Be ready to point to the signals which show the relationship of each paragraph to the preceding one.
2. Looking now at the *interiors* of the paragraphs, identify some dozen relationship signals which help the reader to move from one sentence to the next.

(Other elements)

3. To what extent do Burke and Austin (page 314) agree on the way in which scientific breakthroughs occur? As a focusing question, take Burke's discussion of the development of the chimney and its consequences (lines 161–165): does it more closely illustrate Austin's Chance III or Chance IV?

The Case Against Man
by Isaac Asimov

(from *Science Past—Science Future*, 1975)

The first mistake is to think of mankind as a thing in itself. It isn't. It is part of an intricate web of life. And we can't think even of life as a thing in itself. It isn't. It is part of the intricate structure of a planet bathed by energy from the Sun.

The Earth, in the nearly 5 billion years since it assumed approximately its present form, has undergone a vast evolution. When it first came into being, it very likely lacked what we would today call an ocean and an atmosphere. These were formed by the gradual outward movement of material as the solid interior settled together.

Nor were ocean, atmosphere, and solid crust independent of each other after formation. There is interaction always: evaporation, condensation, solution, weathering. Far within the solid crust there are slow, continuing changes, too, of which hot springs, volcanoes, and earthquakes are the more noticeable manifestations here on the surface.

Between 2 billion and 3 billion years ago, portions of the surface water, bathed by the energetic radiation from the Sun, developed complicated compounds in organization sufficiently versatile to qualify as what we call "life." Life forms have become more complex and more various ever since.

But the life forms are as much part of the structure of the Earth as any inanimate portion is. It is all an inseparable part of a whole. If any animal is isolated totally from other forms of life, then death by starvation will surely follow. If isolated from water, death by dehydration will follow even faster. If isolated from air, whether free or dissolved in water, death by asphyxiation will follow still faster. If isolated from the Sun, animals will survive for a time, but plants would die, and if all plants died, all animals would starve.

It works in reverse, too, for the inanimate portion of Earth is shaped and molded by life. The nature of the atmosphere has been changed by plant activity (which adds to the air the free oxygen it could not otherwise retain). The soil is turned by earthworms, while enormous ocean reefs are formed by coral.

The entire planet, plus solar energy, is one enormous intricately interrelated system. The entire planet is a life form made up of nonliving portions and a large variety of living portions (as our own body is made up of nonliving crystals in bones and nonliving water in blood, as well as of a large variety of living portions).

In fact, we can pursue the analogy. A man is composed of 50 trillion cells of a variety of types, all interrelated and interdependent. Loss of some of those cells, such as those making up an entire leg, will seriously handicap all the rest of the organism: serious damage to a relatively few cells in an organ, such as the heart or kidneys, may end by killing all 50 trillion.

In the same way, on a planetary scale, the chopping down of an entire forest may not threaten Earth's life in general, but it will produce serious changes in the life forms of the region and even in the nature of the water runoff and, therefore, in the details of geological structure. A serious decline in the bee population will affect the numbers of those plants that depend on bees for fertilization, then the numbers of those animals that depend on those particular bee-fertilized plants, and so on.

Or consider cell growth. Cells in those organs that suffer constant wear and tear—as in the skin or in the intestinal lining—grow and multiply all life long. Other cells, not so exposed, as in nerve and muscle, do not multiply at all in the adult, under any circumstances. Still other organs, ordinarily quiescent, as liver and bone, stand ready to grow if that is necessary to replace damage. When the proper repairs are made, growth stops.

In a much looser and more flexible way, the same is true of the "planet organism" (which we study in the science called ecology). If cougars grow too numerous, the deer they live on are decimated, and some of the cougars die of starvation, so that their "proper number" is restored. If too many cougars die, then the deer multiply with particular rapidity, and cougars multiply quickly in turn, till the additional predators bring down the number of deer again. Barring interference from outside, the eaters and the eaten retain their proper numbers, and both are the better for it. (If the cougars are all killed off, deer would multiply to the point where they destroy the plants they live off, and more would then die of starvation than would have died of cougars.)

The neat economy of growth within an organism such as a human being is sometimes—for what reason, we know not—disrupted, and a group of cells begins growing without limit. This is the dread disease of cancer, and unless that growing group of cells is somehow stopped, the wild growth will throw all the body structure out of true and end by killing the organism itself.

In ecology, the same would happen if, for some reason, one particular type of organism began to multiply without limit, killing its competitors and increasing its own food supply at the expense of that of others. That, too, could end only in the destruction of the larger system—most or all of life and even of certain aspects of the inanimate environment.

And this is exactly what is happening at this moment. For thousands of years, the single species Homo sapiens, to which you and I have the dubious honor of belonging, has been increasing in numbers. In the past couple of centuries, the rate of increase has itself increased explosively.

At the time of Julius Caesar, when Earth's human population is estimated to have been 150 million, that population was increasing at a rate such that it would double in 1,000 years if that rate remained steady. Today, with Earth's population estimated at about 4,000 million (26 times what it was in Caesar's time), it is increasing at a rate which, if steady, will cause it to double in 35 years.

The present rate of increase of Earth's swarming human population qualifies Homo sapiens as an ecological cancer, which will destroy the ecology just as surely as any ordinary cancer would destroy an organism.

The cure? Just what it is for any cancer. The cancerous growth must somehow be stopped.

Of course, it will be. If we do nothing at all, the growth will stop, as a cancerous growth in a man will stop if nothing is done. The man dies and the cancer dies with him. And, analogously, the ecology will die and man will die with it.

How can the human population explosion be stopped? By raising the deathrate, or by lowering the birthrate. There are no other alternatives. The deathrate will rise spontaneously and finally catastrophically, if we do nothing—and that within a few decades. To make the birthrate fall, somehow (almost *any* how, in fact), is surely preferable, and that is therefore the first order of mankind's business today.

Failing this, mankind would stand at the bar of abstract justice (for there may be no posterity to judge) as the mass murderer of life generally, his own included, and mass disrupter of the intricate planetary development that made life in its present glory possible in the first place.

Am I too pessimistic? Can we allow the present rate of population increase to continue indefinitely, or at least for a good long time? Can we count on science to develop methods for cleaning up as we pollute, for replacing wasted resources with substitutes, for finding new food, new materials, more and better life for our waxing numbers?

Impossible! If the numbers continue to wax at the present rate.

Let us begin with a few estimates (admittedly not precise, but in the rough neighborhood of the truth).

The total mass of living objects on Earth is perhaps 20 trillion tons.

There is usually a balance between eaters and eaten that is about 1 to 10 in favor of the eaten. There would therefore be about 10 times as much plant life (the eaten) as animal life (the eaters) on Earth. There is, in other words, just a little under 2 trillion tons of animal life on Earth.

But this is all the animal life that can exist, given the present quantity of plant life. If more animal life is somehow produced, it will strip down the plant life, reduce the food supply, and then enough animals will starve to restore the balance. If one species of animal life increases in mass, it can only be because other species correspondingly decrease. For every additional pound of human flesh on Earth, a pound of some other form of flesh must disappear.

The total mass of humanity now on Earth may be estimated at about 200 million tons, or one ten-thousandth the mass of all animal life. If mankind increases in numbers ten thousandfold, then Homo sapiens will be, perforce, the *only* animal species alive on Earth. It will be a world without elephants or lions, without cats or dogs, without fish or lobsters, without worms or bugs. What's more, to support the mass of human life, all the plant world must be put to service. Only plants edible to man must remain, and only those plants most concentratedly edible and with minimum waste.

At the present moment, the average density of population of the Earth's land surface is about 73 people per square mile. Increase that ten thousandfold and the average density will become 730,000 people per square mile, or more than seven times the density of the workday population of Manhattan. Even if we assume that mankind will somehow spread itself into vast cities floating on the ocean surface (or resting on the ocean floor), the average density of human life at the time when the last nonhuman animal must be killed would be 310,000 people per square mile over all the world, land and sea alike, or a little better than three times the density of modern Manhattan at noon.

We have the vision, then, of high-rise apartments, higher and more thickly spaced than in Manhattan at present, spreading all over the world, across all the mountains, across the Sahara Desert, across Antarctica, across all the oceans; all with their load of humanity and with no other form of animal life beside. And on the roof of all those buildings are the algae farms, with little plant cells exposed to the Sun so that they might grow rapidly and, without waste, form protein for all the mighty population of 35 trillion human beings.

Is that tolerable? Even if science produced all the energy and materials mankind could want, kept them all fed with algae, all educated, all amused—is the planetary high-rise tolerable?

And if it were, can we double the population further in 35 more years?

And then double it again in another 35 years? Where will the food come from? What will persuade the algae to multiply faster than the light energy they absorb makes possible? What will speed up the Sun to add the energy to make it possible? And if vast supplies of fusion energy are added to supplement the Sun, how will we get rid of the equally vast supplies of heat that will be produced? And after the icecaps are melted and the oceans boiled into steam, what?

Can we bleed off the mass of humanity to other worlds? Right now, the number of human beings on Earth is increasing by 80 million per year, and each year that number goes up by 1 and a fraction percent. Can we really suppose that we can send 80 million people per year to the Moon, Mars, and elsewhere, and engineer those worlds to support those people? And even so, merely remain in the same place ourselves?

No! Not the most optimistic visionary in the world could honestly convince himself that space travel is the solution to our population problem, if the present rate of increase is sustained.

But when will this planetary high-rise culture come about? How long will it take to increase Earth's population to that impossible point at the present doubling rate of once every 35 years? If it will take 1 million years or even 100,000, then, for goodness sake, let's not worry just yet.

Well, we don't have that kind of time. We will reach that dead end in no more than 460 years.

At the rate we are going, without birth control, then even if science serves us in an absolutely ideal way, we will reach the planetary high-rise with no animals but man, with no plants but algae, with no room for even one more person, by A.D. 2430.

And if science serves us in less than an ideal way (as it certainly will), the end will come sooner, much sooner, and mankind will start fading long, long before he is forced to construct that building that will cover all the Earth's surface.

So if birth control *must* come by A.D. 2430 at the very latest, even in an ideal world of advancing science, let it come *now*, in heaven's name, while there are still oak trees in the world and daisies and tigers and butterflies, and while there is still open land and space, and before the cancer called man proves fatal to life and the planet.

Study Openers

1. Show several ways in which Asimov responds to a possible sensitivity in his audience over the issue of government control of population. (You might begin by sketching the "moral field" of this issue using the model provided on pages 91–92).

2. Show Asimov's use of *analogy* to make clear a scientific perspective for a lay audience.

(Other elements)

3. What moral and political demands do you think are made by population limitation on the scale urged by Asimov? Do you agree with him? How do you think it is possible for the world to respond?

On the Fear of Death
by Elisabeth Kübler-Ross

(from *On Death and Dying*, 1970)

Let me not pray to be sheltered from dangers but to be fearless
in facing them.
Let me not beg for the stilling of my pain but for the heart to
conquer it.
5   *Let me not look for allies in life's battlefield but to my own*
strength.
Let me not crave in anxious fear to be saved but hope for the
patience to win my freedom.
Grant me that I may not be a coward, feeling your mercy in my
10 *success alone; but let me find the grasp of your hand in my*
failure.

RABINDRANATH TAGORE, *Fruit-Gathering*

Epidemics have taken a great toll of lives in past generations. Death in infancy and early childhood was frequent and there were few families
15 who didn't lose a member of the family at an early age. Medicine has changed greatly in the last decades. Widespread vaccinations have practically eradicated many illnesses, at least in western Europe and the United States. The use of chemotherapy, especially the antibiotics, has contributed to an ever decreasing number of fatalities in infectious dis-
20 eases. Better child care and education has effected a low morbidity and mortality among children. The many diseases that have taken an impressive toll among the young and middle-aged have been conquered. The number of old people is on the rise, and with this fact come the number of people with malignancies and chronic diseases associated
25 more with old age.

Pediatricians have less work with acute and life-threatening situations as they have an ever increasing number of patients with psychosomatic disturbances and adjustment and behavior problems. Physicians have more people in their waiting rooms with emotional problems than they

have ever had before, but they also have more elderly patients who not 30
only try to live with their decreased physical abilities and limitations but
who also face loneliness and isolation with all its pains and anguish. The
majority of these people are not seen by a psychiatrist. Their needs have
to be elicited and gratified by other professional people, for instance,
chaplains and social workers. It is for them that I am trying to outline 35
the changes that have taken place in the last few decades, changes that
are ultimately responsible for the increased fear of death, the rising number of emotional problems, and the greater need for understanding of
and coping with the problems of death and dying.

When we look back in time and study old cultures and people, we are 40
impressed that death has always been distasteful to man and will probably always be. From a psychiatrist's point of view this is very under-
standable and can perhaps best be explained by our basic knowledge
that, in our unconscious, death is never possible in regard to ourselves. It
is inconceivable for our unconscious to imagine an actual ending of our 45
own life here on earth, and if this life of ours has to end, the ending is
always attributed to a malicious intervention from the outside by someone else. In simple terms, in our unconscious mind we can only be killed;
it is inconceivable to die of a natural cause or of old age. Therefore death
in itself is associated with a bad act, a frightening happening, something 50
that in itself calls for retribution and punishment.

One is wise to remember these fundamental facts as they are essential
in understanding some of the most important, otherwise unintelligible
communications of our patients.

The second fact that we have to comprehend is that in our uncon- 55
scious mind we cannot distinguish between a wish and a deed. We are
all aware of some of our illogical dreams in which two completely opposite statements can exist side by side—very acceptable in our dreams but
unthinkable and illogical in our wakening state. Just as our unconscious
mind cannot differentiate between the wish to kill somebody in anger 60
and the act of having done so, the young child is unable to make this
distinction. The child who angrily wishes his mother to drop dead for not
having gratified his needs will be traumatized greatly by the actual
death of his mother—even if this event is not linked closely in time with
his destructive wishes. He will always take part or the whole blame for 65
the loss of his mother. He will always say to himself—rarely to others—
"I did it, I am responsible, I was bad, therefore Mommy left me." It is
well to remember that the child will react in the same manner if he loses
a parent by divorce, separation, or desertion. Death is often seen by a
child as an impermanent thing and has therefore little distinction from a 70
divorce in which he may have an opportunity to see a parent again.

Many a parent will remember remarks of their children such as, "I will bury my doggy now and next spring when the flowers come up again, he will get up." Maybe it was the same wish that motivated the ancient
75 Egyptians to supply their dead with food and goods to keep them happy and the old American Indians to bury their relatives with their belongings.

When we grow older and begin to realize that our omnipotence is really not so omnipotent, that our strongest wishes are not powerful
80 enough to make the impossible possible, the fear that we have contributed to the death of a loved one diminishes—and with it the guilt. The fear remains diminished, however, only so long as it is not challenged too strongly. Its vestiges can be seen daily in hospital corridors and in people associated with the bereaved.

85 A husband and wife may have been fighting for years, but when the partner dies, the survivor will pull his hair, whine and cry louder and beat his chest in regret, fear and anguish, and will hence fear his own death more than before, still believing in the law of talion—an eye for an eye, a tooth for a tooth—"I am responsible for her death, I will have to
90 die a pitiful death in retribution."

Maybe this knowledge will help us understand many of the old customs and rituals which have lasted over the centuries and whose purpose is to diminish the anger of the gods or the people as the case may be, thus decreasing the anticipated punishment. I am thinking of the ashes,
95 the torn clothes, the veil, the *Klage Weiber* [hired female mourners] of the old days—they are all means to ask you to take pity on them, the mourners, and are expressions of sorrow, grief, and shame. If someone grieves, beats his chest, tears his hair, or refuses to eat, it is an attempt at self-punishment to avoid or reduce the anticipated punishment for the
100 blame that he takes on the death of a loved one.

This grief, shame, and guilt are not very far removed from feelings of anger and rage. The process of grief always includes some qualities of anger. Since none of us likes to admit anger at a deceased person, these emotions are often disguised or repressed and prolong the period of grief
105 or show up in other ways. It is well to remember that it is not up to us to judge such feelings as bad or shameful but to understand their true meaning and origin as something very human. In order to illustrate this I will again use the example of the child—and the child in us. The five-year-old who loses his mother is both blaming himself for her disappear-
110 ance and being angry at her for having deserted him and for no longer gratifying his needs. The dead person then turns into something the child loves and wants very much but also hates with equal intensity for this severe deprivation.

The ancient Hebrews regarded the body of a dead person as something unclean and not to be touched. The early American Indians talked about the evil spirits and shot arrows in the air to drive the spirits away. Many other cultures have rituals to take care of the "bad" dead person, and they all originate in this feeling of anger which still exists in all of us, though we dislike admitting it. The tradition of the tombstone may originate in this wish to keep the bad spirits deep down in the ground, and the pebbles that many mourners put on the grave are left-over symbols of the same wish. Though we call the firing of guns at military funerals a last salute, it is the same symbolic ritual as the Indian used when he shot his spears and arrows into the skies.

I give these examples to emphasize that man has not basically changed. Death is still a fearful, frightening happening, and the fear of death is a universal fear even if we think we have mastered it on many levels.

What has changed is our way of coping and dealing with death and dying and our dying patients.

Having been raised in a country in Europe where science is not so advanced, where modern techniques have just started to find their way into medicine, and where people still live as they did in this country half a century ago, I may have had an opportunity to study a part of the evolution of mankind in a shorter period.

I remember as a child the death of a farmer. He fell from a tree and was not expected to live. He asked simply to die at home, a wish that was granted without questioning. He called his daughters into the bedroom and spoke with each one of them alone for a few minutes. He arranged his affairs quietly, though he was in great pain, and distributed his belongings and his land, none of which was to be split until his wife should follow him in death. He also asked each of his children to share in the work, duties, and tasks that he had carried on until the time of the accident. He asked his friends to visit him once more, to bid good-bye to them. Although I was a small child at the time, he did not exclude me or my siblings. We were allowed to share in the preparations of the family just as we were permitted to grieve with them until he died. When he did die, he was left at home, in his own beloved home which he had built, and among his friends and neighbors who went to take a last look at him where he lay in the midst of flowers in the place he had lived in and loved so much. In that country today there is still no make-believe slumber room, no embalming, no false makeup to pretend sleep. Only the signs of very disfiguring illnesses are covered up with bandages and only infectious cases are removed from the home prior to the burial.

Why do I describe such "old-fashioned" customs? I think they are an indication of our acceptance of a fatal outcome, and they help the dying patient as well as his family to accept the loss of a loved one. If a patient is allowed to terminate his life in the familiar and beloved environment, it requires less adjustment for him. His own family knows him well enough to replace a sedative with a glass of his favorite wine; or the smell of a home-cooked soup may give him the appetite to sip a few spoons of fluid which, I think, is still more enjoyable than an infusion. I will not minimize the need for sedatives and infusions and realize full well from my own experience as a country doctor that they are sometimes life-saving and often unavoidable. But I also know that patience and familiar people and foods could replace many a bottle of intravenous fluids given for the simple reason that it fulfills the physiological need without involving too many people and/or individual nursing care.

The fact that children are allowed to stay at home where a fatality has stricken and are included in the talk, discussions, and fears gives them the feeling that they are not alone in the grief and gives them the comfort of shared responsibility and shared mourning. It prepares them gradually and helps them view death as part of life, an experience which may help them grow and mature.

This is in great contrast to a society in which death is viewed as taboo, discussion of it is regarded as morbid, and children are excluded with the presumption and pretext that it would be "too much" for them. They are then sent off to relatives, often accompanied with some unconvincing lies of "Mother has gone on a long trip" or other unbelievable stories. The child senses that something is wrong, and his distrust in adults will only multiply if other relatives add new variations of the story, avoid his questions or suspicions, shower him with gifts as a meager substitute for a loss he is not permitted to deal with. Sooner or later the child will become aware of the changed family situation and, depending on the age and personality of the child, will have an unresolved grief and regard this incident as a frightening, mysterious, in any case very traumatic experience with untrustworthy grownups, which he has no way to cope with.

It is equally unwise to tell a little child who lost her brother that God loved little boys so much that he took little Johnny to heaven. When this little girl grew up to be a woman she never solved her anger at God, which resulted in a psychotic depression when she lost her own little son three decades later.

We would think that our great emancipation, our knowledge of science and of man, has given us better ways and means to prepare ourselves and our families for this inevitable happening. Instead the days are gone when a man was allowed to die in peace and dignity in his own home.

The more we are making advancements in science, the more we seem to fear and deny the reality of death. How is this possible?

We use euphemisms, we make the dead look as if they were asleep, we

ship the children off to protect them from the anxiety and turmoil around   200
the house if the patient is fortunate enough to die at home, we don't allow children to visit their dying parents in the hospitals, we have long
and controversial discussions about whether patients should be told the
truth—a question that rarely arises when the dying person is tended by
the family physician who has known him from delivery to death and who   205
knows the weaknesses and strengths of each member of the family.

I think there are many reasons for this flight away from facing death
calmly. One of the most important facts is that dying nowadays is more
gruesome in many ways, namely, more lonely, mechanical, and dehu-   210
manized; at times it is even difficult to determine technically when the
time of death has occurred.

Dying becomes lonely and impersonal because the patient is often
taken out of his familiar environment and rushed to an emergency room.
Whoever has been very sick and has required rest and comfort especially   215
may recall his experience of being put on a stretcher and enduring the
noise of the ambulance siren and hectic rush until the hospital gates
open. Only those who have lived through this may appreciate the discomfort and cold necessity of such transportation which is only the beginning of a long ordeal—hard to endure when you are well, difficult to   220
express in words when noise, light, pumps, and voices are all too much
to put up with. It may well be that we might consider more the patient
under the sheets and blankets and perhaps stop our well-meant efficiency
and rush in order to hold the patient's hand, to smile, or to listen to a
question. I include the trip to the hospital as the first episode in dying,
as it is for many. I am putting it exaggeratedly in contrast to the sick man 225
who is left at home—not to say that lives should not be saved if they can
be saved by a hospitalization but to keep the focus on the patient's experience, his needs and his reactions.

When a patient is severely ill, he is often treated like a person with no
right to an opinion. It is often someone else who makes the decision if   230
and when and where a patient should be hospitalized. It would take so
little to remember that the sick person too has feelings, has wishes and
opinions, and has—most important of all—the right to be heard.

Well, our presumed patient has now reached the emergency room. He
will be surrounded by busy nurses, orderlies, interns, residents, a lab   235
technician perhaps who will take some blood, an electrocardiogram technician who takes the cardiogram. He may be moved to X-ray and he will
overhear opinions of his condition and discussions and questions to members of the family. He slowly but surely is beginning to be treated like a
thing. He is no longer a person. Decisions are made often without his   240

opinion. If he tries to rebel he will be sedated and after hours of waiting and wondering whether he has the strength, he will be wheeled into the operating room or intensive treatment unit and become an object of great concern and great financial investment.

245   He may cry.for rest, peace, and dignity, but he will get infusions, transfusions, a heart machine, or tracheotomy if necessary. He may want one single person to stop for one single minute so that he can ask one single question—but he will get a dozen people around the clock, all busily preoccupied with his heart rate, pulse, electrocardiogram or pul-

250 monary functions, his secretions or excretions but not with him as a human being. He may wish to fight it all but it is going to be a useless fight since all this is done in the fight for his life, and if they can save his life they can consider the person afterwards. Those who consider the person first may lose precious time to save his life! At least this seems to

255 be the rationale or justification behind all this—or is it? Is the reason for this increasingly mechanical, depersonalized approach our own defensiveness? Is this approach our own way to cope with and repress the anxieties that a terminally or critically ill patient evokes in us? Is our concentration on equipment, on blood pressure our desperate attempt to

260 deny the impending death which is so frightening and discomforting to us that we displace all our knowledge onto machines, since they are less close to us than the suffering face of another human being which would remind us once more of our lack of omnipotence, our own limits and failures, and last but not least perhaps our own mortality?

265   Maybe the question has to be raised: Are we becoming less human or more human? Though this book is in no way meant to be judgmental, it is clear that whatever the answer may be, the patient is suffering more— not physically, perhaps, but emotionally. And his needs have not changed over the centuries, only our ability to gratify them.

Study Openers

Kübler-Ross's writings and her work with dying patients have placed her at the center of the recent "death and dying" movement in medicine and psychology. This opening essay of *On Death and Dying* is presented here mainly for the ways in which the audience is made part of the discussion. (See Chapter 9, page 89).

1. Note where the essay refers to "I" or "me"; to "we" or "us"; or to "people," "one," and "they." Would Kübler-Ross have done better to use a single way of approaching her audience throughout? Can you distinguish the occasions on which she is likely to use each method of address?

2. How would you characterize the presumed audience of this piece as to age, education, probable virtues and vices, hopes and fears?

3. Without actually writing a new piece, discuss how you would put the same ideas before an audience of much different knowledge and disposition—for example, children, hospital patients, the very old.

(Other elements)

4. Several death scenes appear in this essay (e.g., lines 136, 188, 235). To what extent might they be considered undesirably sentimental?

5. What special features of sentence structure appear in the closing two paragraphs, and how are they appropriate to the writer's evident outlook? (Chapter 3, pages 25–28).

The Decline and Fall of Oratory
by Lance Morrow

(*Time*, August 18, 1980)

Tennessee's Governor Frank Clement, the most distinguished graduate of Mrs. Dockie Shipp Weems' School of Expression in Nashville, rose up before the 1956 Democratic Convention and demonstrated a dying art. His keynote address that night beside the Chicago stockyards was a symphony of rhetorical excess, a masterpiece of alliteration and allu- 5
sion, an epic of the smite-'em style of oratorical Americana.

"How long, O how long, America!" cried Clement, in a grandiloquent filch from Cicero's First Catiline Oration. "How long, O America, shall these things endure?" In Dwight Eisenhower's foreign policy, Clement declaimed, "Foster [Dulles] fiddles, frets, fritters and flits." Richard 10
Nixon was "the vice-hatchet man slinging slander and spreading half-truths while the top man peers down the green fairways of indifference." To farmers, the gusty Tennessean pleaded: "Come on home . . . Your lands are studded with the white skulls and crossbones of broken Republican promises." 15

The Republican Party in those days was not entirely speechless either. Connoisseurs of the genre remember the sublimely fogbound organ tones of Illinois' Everett McKinley Dirksen. In his early career, writes Biographer Neil MacNeil, Dirksen "bellowed his speeches in a mongrel mix of grand opera and hog calling." Over the years, he developed a style of 20
infinitely subtle fustian, whose effect can still be remotely approximated by sipping twelve-year-old bourbon, straight, while reading Dickens aloud, in a sort of sepulchral purr. Would he criticize an erring colleague? someone would ask. "I shall invoke upon him every condign im-

25   precation," Dirksen would intone, with a quiver of his basset's jowls and
     the gold-gray ringlets of his hair.
         Dirksen's oratory succeeded in part because it functioned simultane-
     ously as a satire upon oratory, in somewhat the way that Mae West has
     always been a walking satire upon sex. But all of Dirksen's splendor,
30   with his rapscallion rhapsodies and hints of the mountebank, could not
     conceal a small truth about what lay ahead for the ancient discipline of
     rhetoric: an art that wanes into self-mockery is dying.
         Today, oratory seems in serious, possibly terminal, decline. Americans
     rummaging in their memories for the last great speech they heard—great
35   in content and delivery—often find that they must fetch back at least to
     1963, to Martin Luther King Jr.'s soaring, preacherly performance during
     the March on Washington. Some think of John Kennedy's Inaugural
     Address; yet as the sixties wore on, the go-anywhere-pay-any-price rhet-
     oric of that bright January day on the New Frontier began to seem not
40   only suspect but even a symptom of the emptiness of eloquence and the
     woes that fancy talk can lead a country into. Some, with even longer
     memories, mention Churchill in Fulton, Mo., in 1946 ("An iron curtain
     has descended . . .") or F.D.R.'s first Inaugural ("The only thing we
     have to fear is fear itself").
45   Eloquence, of course, is a matter of political taste. Conservatives may
     rank Ronald Reagan's acceptance speech last month only a little short
     of Edmund Burke. Liberals might poignantly remember Edward Ken-
     nedy's speech to the 1972 Democratic Convention the night that George
     McGovern was nominated. Neoconservatives with a taste for the mysta-
50   gogic might wheel out Alexander Solzhenitsyn's "decline of the West"
     speech at Harvard two years ago. But of course that was delivered in
     Russian, and therefore flowed a little outside the American rhetorical
     mainstream.
         Heroic eloquence has made more difference in the world than West-
55   erners are now comfortable in admitting. That eloquence, like science,
     can do great evil is a truth this century acquired the hard way. Hitler's
     ranting persuasions worked enough disastrous black magic to send his
     audience pouring out of the stadium to conquer the world; Churchill's
     answering eloquence quite literally, physically, pushed back the Reich.
60   In each case, the spoken words alone, the voice, worked with an eerie,
     preternatural force. Perhaps in some instinctive recoil from its demon-
     strated, primitive powers, Westerners today have learned to treat elo-
     quence as either an amiable curio or a mild embarrassment. American
     TV audiences this summer see eloquence perfectly domesticated and
65   trivialized in an A.1 Steak Sauce commercial in which a bowler, feigning
     slightly lunatic oratorical inspiration, demands: "My friends, what *is*

hamburger?" In a culture that increasingly demands technical or bureau-
cratic solutions, passionate oratory seems a kind of gaudy irrelevance. It
also, rather curiously, makes people uncomfortable. Lord Shinwell, a
former British Labor Minister, remarks: "If Churchill came down to the   70
Commons today to call for blood, sweat and tears, many of his listeners
would probably titter or look plain embarrassed."

What has happened to eloquence, to the art of speechmaking? The greatest single factor in its decline has been television. The intrusion of TV   75
cameras into almost every significant public meeting in the U.S. has
vastly extended the range of speakers' voices, but also changed the nature of what they are doing. A play performed on the legitimate stage
but carried by TV somehow always seems dislocated and obscurely
fraudulent. The politician addressing a large rally in a speech that is   80
being televised has two audiences, the one in the hall and the one at
home. He works simultaneously in two media, an extraordinarily difficult
trick. TV has an intimate and pitiless eye that can make any exuberantly
talented stump speaker look a like a sweating and psychotic blowhard.
   Before his G.O.P. keynote speech in Detroit last month, Congressman   85
Guy Vander Jagt thought that the dual-medium problem was like "having one bullet and having to shoot north and south at the same time."
During his long campaign this year, Ted Kennedy often seemed on television to be bulging and strident, too angry, radiating heat; the same
performance in the hall usually seemed to come off rather well. Eventually, Kennedy began injecting into his thundering utterances a little of   90
the self-satirizing gaiety that Dirksen used.
   Ronald Reagan, of all the candidates this year, best understands TV's
intimate eye; he neither shouts nor gesticulates. Reagan owes his entire
career to his talent for persuasion; his long years on television gave him
just the right media reflexes for the age. Jimmy Carter also possesses a   95
shrewdly understated television style. A Carter speech that seems pale
and weak in person comes through coaxial cables giving off just the right
small personal glow.
   The procedures of television news reporting have very nearly disman-
tled what is left of oratorical integrity. TV news producers have in effect   100
become the editors of American speeches. The ancient disciplines of
rhetoric suffer disastrously as they are trimmed to the electronic purpose.
A politician's handlers try to schedule an event for some time around
2 or 3 P.M. to sluice neatly into Cronkite. Instead of constructing a
speech on the old Ciceronian blueprint (exordium, argument, refutation,   105
peroration and so on) or even on a less classical pattern (beginning,
middle and end would do) the politician contrives a speaking perfor-

mance that contains a few key and newsy sentences in oratorical neon to make the networks. As J.F.K. Aide William Haddad says, "A lot of writers figure out how they are going to get the part they want onto TV. They think of a news lead and write around it. And if the TV lights don't go on as the speaker is approaching that news lead, he skips a few paragraphs and waits until they are lit to read the key part. This does not make for a coherent, flowing speech." During the 1976 campaign, says Political Scientist James David Barber, Jimmy Carter made a useful discovery: "He put all his pauses in the middle of his sentences, and as he neared the period, he would speed up and pass it until the middle of the next sentence. He got more TV time because it was pretty hard for TV editors to chop him in midsentence."

Because of television's fragmenting procedures, it is hardly worth a politician's time to treat his speeches as works of art. Mark Twain said it took him three weeks to prepare a good impromptu speech, but few speakers rehearse their lines any more; Vander Jagt, who polished his keynote speech by orating at the squirrels and pine trees near his Luther, Mich., home, is an exception in his zeal.

Speeches simply no longer pulse as they once did at the center of political and cultural life. Once they were prized as entertainment. Today armies of business leaders, writers, politicians, actors and other celebrities are riding the lecture circuit, and yet they remain peripheral. Movies, then radio and television over the past several generations, have reduced oratory to the status almost of quaintness.

By beaming important speeches to the whole nation, TV has also ensured that most politicians and their committees of advisers will orchestrate all oratory to offend the least number of voters. William Jennings Bryan, whose 1896 "cross of gold" speech was one of the last to get Americans out of a chair and make them do something (they gave him the Democratic nomination on the spot), once described eloquence as "thought on fire." Today, in an age of single-issue politics, the ambitious are careful to see that they do not get burned. Says NBC-TV's Edwin Newman: "Advertising, public relations and polling techniques create attitudes that are designed to appeal to a large number of people. These attitudes tend to flatten out a speech." Political speeches may soon be written by computers: pretested paragraphs are tried out on people for reactions, then fed into a computer along with the speaker's philosophy, and out comes a speech. Audiences now wince wearily at the cute and canned self-deprecatory jokes that federal bureaucrats invariably tell when they go out of town to give a speech. Sample: "You know, the three lies most often told are 'I'll still love you in the morning,' 'The

check is in the mail,' and 'I'm from Washington and I'm here to help
you.'" Bureaucrats today invariably fall short of Gladstone, who once   150
kept the House of Commons enthralled for more than three hours with
a speech on the 1853 budget.

In America at least, a tradition of high rhetoric has always competed
with a sentimental worship of the inarticulate. In 1939's *Mr. Smith Goes
to Washington,* the sleekly senatorial Claude Rains attempts to conceal   155
his corruption behind an impressive tapestry of rhetoric. But Jimmy
Stewart, barely able to complete a sentence, engagingly stumbling over
his words, wins out because his sheer radiant American virtue shines
through the manipulative deceits inherent in language. It is possible that
Adlai Stevenson lost the presidency twice in part because he spoke a   160
little too well. This theme returned passionately in the counter-cultural
sixties, when inarticulate sincerity seemed the answer to the state's
mendacities. Some preached that imperialism, racism and sexism are
deeply embedded in the language—a fact that, if true, would tend to
discredit eloquence, to make it futile and wrong from the start.   165

Somehow, few speakers today make oratory seem the urgent and
necessary approach to the world that it once was. Eloquence implies
certitude. "Hear, O Israel," said Moses, his voice reverberating with
authority well beyond his own. It is not a posture much adopted now
when such previously safe topics as the family, progress and the future   170
become problematic. (Reagan's acceptance speech rejected doubts about
progress, the family and the future, which may explain why the speech
worked as oratory.) Eloquence implies premeditation in an age that has
made a virtue of spontaneity. It implies (at its historical best) a public
consciousness of serious issues in an age that in a profound way prefers   175
gossip. "The personality of the orator outweighs the issues," observes
John Leopold, professor of classical rhetoric at the University of California at Berkeley. A psychologically intimate age does not trust issues, but
rather impulses; a man would say anything, after all, to get elected, but
what is his mental weather? What makes the finger near the button   180
twitch?

Rhetoric—"Mere rhetoric"; "Oh, that's just rhetoric!"—is not taught
widely any more. In its Greco-Roman golden age, rhetoric was the key to
civilized persuasion, and therefore to society itself. The Greek apparatus
of rhetoric is a brilliantly elaborate armamentarium of speechmakers'   185
devices—synecdoche, syllepsis, symploce and so on. Almost from the beginning, the power of rhetoric troubled even those who were best at
wielding it. Wrote Cicero: "I have thought long and often over the problem of whether the power of speaking and the study of eloquence have
brought more good or harm to cities."   190

As Cicero knew, it depends. Rhetoric has started wars and stopped them. The eloquence of Bernard of Clairvaux dispatched tens of thousands on the catastrophic Second Crusade. Mindless oratory has also caused untold brain damage to audiences over the centuries. The out-
195 pouring of verbiage continues. As the political season ramshackles through the summer, the landscape is dense with BOMFOG (an acronym used by political reporters to designate one of the late Nelson Rockefeller's favorite oratorical clichés: Brotherhood of Man under the Fatherhood of God). Americans may sometimes wistfully miss a better
200 quality of oratory. They might grow even more wistful if they reflected on the Japanese, who regard eloquence as a potential threat to their stability-through-consensus. *Haragei*, their ultimate form of communication, can only be envied in the week of a convention. It consists of making oneself understood with silence.

Study Openers

Oratory lets us hear a specific human voice, often see a live speaker, feel ourselves present at a living event. Thus, above all, oratory is the art of dramatizing speaker, audience, and issues. If the art is dying, as Morrow claims, what happens to the notions about audience and writer which this textbook has proposed in Chapters 9 and 10?

1. Define "oratory" as Morrow uses the term.
2. Why, in his judgment, has it declined? To what extent does Morrow see this decline as healthy or unhealthy?
3. Americans seem to waver between an admiration of inarticulateness and a susceptibility to oratory. Can you give examples of speakers who belong at each end of the spectrum? Where do you belong? Have you stopped listening to certain speakers because their speeches seem to be "mere" oratory? Explain.
4. Write out two brief speeches taking a stand on some controversial issue. a) In the first speech play the part of a political leader *in office* near election time. b) In the second speech play the part of an *outside* candidate running hard to capture voters on the same stand.

(Other elements)

5. Morrow uses metaphors to clarify and sharpen his meanings. For each of the following, show how the italicized metaphor carries more or less force than its literal equivalent (in brackets):

   a. "His keynote address . . . was *a symphony* of rhetorical excess" [a harmonious blend] (line 5).
   b. "Connoisseurs . . . remember the sublimely *fogbound organ*

tones of Illinois' Everett McKinley Dirksen" [meaningless, sonorous speech] (line 18).

   c. "Attitudes that are designed to appeal to a large number of people . . . tend to *flatten out* a speech" [weaken the main positions of] (line 142).

   d. "Mindless oratory has . . . *caused untold brain damage to audiences*" [reduced the thoughtfulness of audiences] (line 193).

The Meaning of July Fourth for the Negro
by Frederick Douglass

(oration at Corinthian Hall, Rochester, N.Y., July 5, 1852)

Mr. President, Friends, and Fellow Citizens:

He who could address this audience without a quailing sensation, has
stronger nerves than I have. I do not remember ever to have appeared as
a speaker before any assembly more shrinkingly, nor with greater distrust of my ability, than I do this day. A feeling has crept over me quite   5
unfavorable to the exercise of my limited powers of speech. The task
before me is one which requires much previous thought and study for
its proper performance. I know that apologies of this sort are generally
considered flat and unmeaning. I trust, however, that mine will not be so
considered. Should I seem at ease, my appearance would much misrepre-   10
sent me. The little experience I have had in addressing public meetings,
in country school houses, avails me nothing on the present occasion.

The papers and placards say that I am to deliver a Fourth of July Oration. This certainly sounds large, and out of the common way, for me. It
is true that I have often had the privilege to speak in this beautiful Hall,   15
and to address many who now honor me with their presence. But neither
their familiar faces, nor the perfect gage I think I have of Corinthian
Hall seems to free me from embarrassment.

The fact is, ladies and gentlemen, the distance between this platform
and the slave plantation, from which I escaped, is considerable—and the   20
difficulties to be overcome in getting from the latter to the former are by
no means slight. That I am here to-day is, to me, a matter of astonishment as well as of gratitude. You will not, therefore, be surprised, if in
what I have to say I evince no elaborate preparation, nor grace my
speech with any high sounding exordium. With little experience and with   25
less learning, I have been able to throw my thoughts hastily and imperfectly together; and trusting to your patient and generous indulgence, I
will proceed to lay them before you.

This, for the purpose of this celebration, is the Fourth of July. It is the

30 birthday of your National Independence, and of your political freedom. This, to you, is what the Passover was to the emancipated people of God. It carries your minds back to the day, and to the act of your great deliverance; and to the signs, and to the wonders, associated with that act, and that day. This celebration also marks the beginning of another year

35 of your national life; and reminds you that the Republic of America is now 76 years old. I am glad, fellow-citizens, that your nation is so young. Seventy-six years, though a good old age for a man, is but a mere speck in the life of a nation. Three score years and ten is the allotted time for individual men; but nations number their years by thousands. According

40 to this fact, you are, even now, only in the beginning of your national career, still lingering in the period of childhood. I repeat, I am glad this is so. There is hope in the thought, and hope is much needed, under the dark clouds which lower above the horizon. The eye of the reformer is met with angry flashes, portending disastrous times; but his heart may

45 well beat lighter at the thought that America is young, and that she is still in the impressible stage of her existence. May he not hope that high lessons of wisdom, of justice and of truth, will yet give direction to her destiny? Were the nation older, the patriot's heart might be sadder, and the reformer's brow heavier. Its future might be shrouded in gloom, and

50 the hope of its prophets go out in sorrow. There is consolation in the thought that America is young.—Great streams are not easily turned from channels, worn deep in the course of ages. They may sometimes rise in quiet and stately majesty, and inundate the land, refreshing and fertilizing the earth with their mysterious properties. They may also rise in

55 wrath and fury, and bear away, on their angry waves, the accumulated wealth of years of toil and hardship. They, however, gradually flow back to the same old channel, and flow on as serenely as ever. But, while the river may not be turned aside, it may dry up, and leave nothing behind but the withered branch, and the unsightly rock, to howl in the abyss-

60 sweeping wind, the sad tale of departed glory. As with rivers so with nations. . . .

Fellow-citizens, pardon me, allow me to ask, why am I called upon to speak here to-day? What have I, or those I represent, to do with your national independence? Are the great principles of political freedom and

65 of natural justice, embodied in that Declaration of Independence, extended to us? and am I, therefore, called upon to bring our humble offering to the national altar, and to confess the benefits and express devout gratitude for the blessings resulting from your independence to us?

Would to God, both for your sakes and ours, that an affirmative an-

70 swer could be truthfully returned to these questions! Then would my task be light, and my burden easy and delightful. For *who is* there so cold,

that a nation's sympathy could not warm him? Who so obdurate and
dead to the claims of gratitude, that would not thankfully acknowledge
such priceless benefits? Who so stolid and selfish, that would not give
his voice to swell the hallelujahs of a nation's jubilee, when the chains   75
of servitude had been torn from his limbs? I am not that man. In a case
like that, the dumb might eloquently speak, and the "lame man leap as
an hart."

But such is not the state of the case. I say it with a sad sense of the
disparity between us. I am not included within the pale of this glorious   80
anniversary! Your high independence only reveals the immeasurable distance between us. The blessings in which you, this day, rejoice, are not
enjoyed in common.—The rich inheritance of justice, liberty, prosperity
and independence, bequeathed by your fathers, is shared by you, not by
me. The sunlight that brought light and healing to you, has brought   85
stripes and death to me. This Fourth of July is *yours*, not *mine*. *You* may
rejoice, *I* must mourn. To drag a man in fetters into the grand illuminated temple of liberty, and call upon him to join you in joyous anthems,
were inhuman mockery and sacrilegious irony. Do you mean, citizens, to
mock me, by asking to speak to-day? If so, there is a parallel to your   90
conduct. And let me warn you that it is dangerous to copy the example of
a nation whose crimes, towering up to heaven, were thrown down by the
breath of the Almighty, burying that nation in irrevocable ruin! I can
to-day take up the plaintive lament of a peeled and woe-smitten people!

"By the rivers of Babylon, there we sat down. Yea! we wept when we   95
remembered Zion. We hanged our harps upon the willows in the midst
thereof. For there, they that carried us away captive, required of us a
song; and they who wasted us required of us mirth, saying, Sing us one
of the songs of Zion. How can we sing the Lord's song in a strange land?
If I forget thee, O Jerusalem, let my right hand forget her cunning. If I   100
do not remember thee, let my tongue cleave to the roof of my mouth."

Fellow-citizens, above your national, tumultuous joy, I hear the mournful wail of millions! whose chains, heavy and grievous yesterday, are,
to-day, rendered more intolerable by the jubilee shouts that reach them.
If I do forget, if I do not faithfully remember those bleeding children of 105
sorrow this day, "may my right hand forget her cunning, and may my
tongue cleave to the roof of my mouth!" To forget them, to pass lightly
over their wrongs, and to chime in with the popular theme, would be
treason most scandalous and shocking, and would make me a reproach
before God and the world. My subject, then, fellow-citizens, is American   110
slavery. I shall see this day and its popular characteristics from the slave's
point of view. Standing there identified with the American bondman,
making his wrongs mine, I do not hesitate to declare, with all my soul,

that the character and conduct of this nation never looked blacker to me than on this 4th of July! Whether we turn to the declarations of the past, or to the professions of the present, the conduct of the nation seems equally hideous and revolting. America is false to the past, false to the present, and solemnly binds herself to be false to the future. Standing with God and the crushed and bleeding slave on this occasion, I will, in the name of humanity which is outraged, in the name of liberty which is fettered, in the name of the constitution and the Bible which are disregarded and trampled upon, dare to call in question and to denounce, with all the emphasis I can command, everything that serves to perpetuate slavery—the great sin and shame of America! "I will not equivocate; I will not excuse"; I will use the severest language I can command; and yet not one word shall escape me that any man, whose judgment is not blinded by prejudice, or who is not at heart a slaveholder, shall not confess to be right and just.

But I fancy I hear some one of my audience say, "It is just in this circumstance that you and your brother abolitionists fail to make a favorable impression on the public mind. Would you argue more, and denounce less; would you persuade more, and rebuke less; your cause would be much more likely to succeed." But, I submit, where all is plain there is nothing to be argued. What point in the anti-slavery creed would you have me argue? On what branch of the subject do the people of this country need light? Must I undertake to prove that the slave is a man? That point is conceded already. Nobody doubts it. The slaveholders themselves acknowledge it in the enactment of laws for their government. They acknowledge it when they punish disobedience on the part of the slave. There are seventy-two crimes in the State of Virginia which, if committed by a black man (no matter how ignorant he be), subject him to the punishment of death; while only two of the same crimes will subject a white man to the like punishment. What is this but the acknowledgment that the slave is a moral, intellectual, and responsible being? The manhood of the slave is conceded. It is admitted in the fact that Southern statute books are covered with enactments forbidding, under severe fines and penalties, the teaching of the slave to read or to write. When you can point to any such laws in reference to the beasts of the field, then I may consent to argue the manhood of the slave. When the dogs in your streets, when the fowls of the air, when the cattle on your hills, when the fish of the sea, and the reptiles that crawl, shall be unable to distinguish the slave from a brute, *then* will I argue with you that the slave is a man!

For the present, it is enough to affirm the equal manhood of the Negro race. Is it not astonishing that, while we are ploughing, planting, and reaping, using all kinds of mechanical tools, erecting houses, constructing

bridges, building ships, working in metals of brass, iron, copper, silver
and gold; that, while we are reading, writing and ciphering, acting as
clerks, merchants and secretaries, having among us lawyers, doctors,
ministers, poets, authors, editors, orators and teachers; that, while we are
engaged in all manner of enterprises common to other men, digging gold   160
in California, capturing the whale in the Pacific, feeding sheep and cattle
on the hill-side, living, moving, acting, thinking, planning, living in families as husbands, wives and children, and, above all, confessing and wor-
shipping the Christian's God, and looking hopefully for life and immor-
tality beyond the grave, we are called upon to prove that we are men!   165

Would you have me argue that man is entitled to liberty? that he is the
rightful owner of his own body? You have already declared it. Must I
argue the wrongfulness of slavery? Is that a question for Republicans? Is
it to be settled by the rules of logic and argumentation, as a matter beset
with great difficulty, involving a doubtful application of the principle of   170
justice, hard to be understood? How should I look to-day, in the presence
of Americans, dividing, and subdividing a discourse, to show that men
have a natural right to freedom? speaking of it relatively and positively,
negatively and affirmatively. To do so, would be to make myself ridiculous, and to offer an insult to your understanding.—There is not a man   175
beneath the canopy of heaven that does not know that slavery is wrong
for him.

What, am I to argue that it is wrong to make men brutes, to rob them
of their liberty, to work them without wages, to keep them ignorant of
their relations to their fellow men, to beat them with sticks, to flay their   180
flesh with the lash, to load their limbs with irons, to hunt them with dogs,
to sell them at auction, to sunder their families, to knock out their teeth,
to burn their flesh, to starve them into obedience and submission to their
masters? Must I argue that a system thus marked with blood, and stained
with pollution, is *wrong?* No! I will not. I have better employment for   185
my time and strength than such arguments would imply.

What, then, remains to be argued? Is it that slavery is not divine; that
God did not establish it; that our doctors of divinity are mistaken? There
is blasphemy in the thought. That which is inhuman, cannot be divine!
Who can reason on such a proposition? They that can, may; I cannot.   190
The time for such argument is passed.

At a time like this, scorching irony, not convincing argument, is needed.
O! had I the ability, and could reach the nation's ear, I would, to-day,
pour out a fiery stream of biting ridicule, blasting reproach, withering sarcasm, and stern rebuke. For it is not light that is needed, but fire; it is not   195
the gentle shower, but thunder. We need the storm, the whirlwind, and
the earthquake. The feeling of the nation must be quickened; the con-

science of the nation must be roused; the propriety of the nation must be startled; the hypocrisy of the nation must be exposed; and its crimes

200 against God and man must be proclaimed and denounced.

What, to the American slave, is your 4th of July? I answer: a day that reveals to him, more than all other days in the year, the gross injustice and cruelty to which he is the constant victim. To him, your celebration is a sham; your boasted liberty, an unholy license; your national great-

205 ness, swelling vanity; your sounds of rejoicing are empty and heartless; your denunciation of tyrants, brass fronted impudence; your shouts of liberty and equality, hollow mockery; your prayers and hymns, your sermons and thanksgivings, with all your religious parade and solemnity, are, to Him, mere bombast, fraud, deception, impiety, and hypocrisy—a

210 thin veil to cover up crimes which would disgrace a nation of savages. There is not a nation on the earth guilty of practices more shocking and bloody than are the people of the United States, at this very hour.

Go where you may, search where you will, roam through all the monarchies and despotisms of the Old World, travel through South America,

215 search out every abuse, and when you have found the last, lay your facts by the side of the everyday practices of this nation, and you will say with me, that, for revolting barbarity and shameless hypocrisy, America reigns without a rival. . . .

Annotation

This excerpt comes from the first half of an oration to a white audience, given by invitation of the Rochester Ladies' Anti-Slavery Society. Douglass went on to attack the domestic slave trade, the recent Fugitive Slave Act of 1850, the ineffectiveness of the American church on the slavery issue. He closed by arguing the unconstitutionality of slavery and by expressing his hopes for a new American dawn of freedom.

Study Openers

1. Explain Douglass' characterization of his audience and himself, his use of the immediate occasion (Chapters 9 and 10, pages 89, 101). Point out the psychological ordering by which he comes into his attack on slavery.

(Other elements)

2. How does this selection illustrate what Morrow calls "oratory" (page 344)? Would you admire this style or think it effective in a speaker of our own time? Why or why not?
3. In the paragraph beginning with line 153, note the climactic stress on the final word "men." How is this climax achieved, and what is its presumed effect?

Invisible Man
by Ralph Ellison

(from the Prologue, 1952)

I am an invisible man. No, I am not a spook like those who haunted Edgar Allan Poe; nor am I one of your Hollywood-movie ectoplasms. I am a man of substance, of flesh and bone, fiber and liquids—and I might even be said to possess a mind. I am invisible, understand, simply because people refuse to see me. Like the bodiless heads you see sometimes   5
in circus sideshows, it is as though I have been surrounded by mirrors of hard, distorting glass. When they approach me they see only my surroundings, themselves, or figments of their imagination—indeed, everything and anything except me.

Nor is my invisibility exactly a matter of a bio-chemical accident to my   10,
epidermis. That invisibility to which I refer occurs because of a peculiar disposition of the eyes of those with whom I come in contact. A matter of the construction of their *inner* eyes, those eyes with which they look through their physical eyes upon reality. I am not complaining, nor am I protesting either. It is sometimes advantageous to be unseen, although it   15
is most often rather wearing on the nerves. Then too, you're constantly being bumped against by those of poor vision. Or again, you often doubt if you really exist. You wonder whether you aren't simply a phantom in other people's minds. Say, a figure in a nightmare which the sleeper tries with all his strength to destroy. It's when you feel like this that, out of   20
resentment, you begin to bump people back. And, let me confess, you feel that way most of the time. You ache with the need to convince yourself that you do exist in the real world, that you're a part of all the sound and anguish, and you strike out with your fists, you curse and you swear to make them recognize you. And, alas, it's seldom successful.   25

One night I accidentally bumped into a man, and perhaps because of the near darkness he saw me and called me an insulting name. I sprang at him, seized his coat lapels and demanded that he apologize. He was a tall blond man, and as my face came close to his he looked insolently out of his blue eyes and cursed me, his breath hot in my face as he struggled.   30
I pulled his chin down sharp upon the crown of my head, butting him as I had seen the West Indians do, and I felt his flesh tear and the blood gush out, and I yelled, "Apologize! Apologize!" But he continued to curse and struggle, and I butted him again and again until he went down heavily, on his knees, profusely bleeding. I kicked him repeatedly, in a   35
frenzy because he still uttered insults though his lips were frothy with

blood. Oh yes, I kicked him! And in my outrage I got out my knife and
prepared to slit his throat, right there beneath the lamplight in the deserted street, holding him by the collar with one hand, and opening the
40   knife with my teeth—when it occurred to me that the man had not *seen*
me, actually; that he, as far as he knew, was in the midst of a walking
nightmare! And I stopped the blade, slicing the air as I pushed him away,
letting him fall back to the street. I stared at him hard as the lights of a
car stabbed through the darkness. He lay there, moaning on the asphalt;
45   a man almost killed by a phantom. It unnerved me. I was both disgusted
and ashamed. I was like a drunken man myself, wavering about on weakened legs. Then I was amused. Something in this man's thick head had
sprung out and beaten him within an inch of his life. I began to laugh at
this crazy discovery. Would he have awakened at the point of death?
50   Would Death himself have freed him for wakeful living? But I didn't
linger. I ran away into the dark, laughing so hard I feared I might rup-
ture myself. The next day I saw his picture in the *Daily News*, beneath a
caption stating that he had been "mugged." Poor fool, poor blind fool, I
thought with sincere compassion, mugged by an invisible man!
55   Most of the time (although I do not choose as I once did to deny the
violence of my days by ignoring it) I am not so overtly violent. I remember that I am invisible and walk softly so as not to awaken the sleeping
ones. Sometimes it is best not to awaken them; there are few things in
the world as dangerous as sleepwalkers. I learned in time though that it
60   is possible to carry on a fight against them without their realizing it. For
instance, I have been carrying on a fight with Monopolated Light &
Power for some time now. I use their service and pay them nothing at
all, and they don't know it. Oh, they suspect that power is being drained
off, but they don't know where. All they know is that according to the
65   master meter back there in their power station a hell of a lot of free current is disappearing somewhere into the jungle of Harlem. The joke, of
course, is that I don't live in Harlem but in a border area. Several years
ago (before I discovered the advantage of being invisible) I went through
the routine process of buying service and paying their outrageous rates.
70   But no more. I gave up all that, along with my apartment, and my old
way of life: That way based upon the fallacious assumption that I, like
other men, was visible. Now, aware of my invisibility, I live rent-free in
a building rented strictly to whites, in a section of the basement that was
shut off and forgotten during the nineteenth century. . . .
75   The point . . . is that I found a home—or a hole in the ground, as you
will. Now don't jump to the conclusion that because I call my home a
"hole" it is damp and cold like a grave; there are cold holes and warm
holes. Mine is a warm hole. And remember, a bear retires to his hole for

the winter and lives until spring; then he comes strolling out like the
Easter chick breaking from its shell. I say all this to assure you that it is   80
incorrect to assume that, because I'm invisible and live in a hole, I am
dead. I am neither dead nor in a state of suspended animation. Call me
Jack-the-Bear, for I am in a state of hibernation.

My hole is warm and full of light. Yes, *full* of light. I doubt if there is
a brighter spot in all New York than this hole of mine, and I do not ex-   85
clude Broadway. Or the Empire State Building on a photographer's
dream night. But that is taking advantage of you. Those two spots are
among the darkest of our whole civilization—pardon me, our whole *culture* (an important distinction, I've heard)—which might sound like a
hoax, or a contradiction, but that (by contradiction, I mean) is how the   90
world moves: Not like an arrow, but a boomerang. (Beware of those
who speak of the *spiral* of history; they are preparing a boomerang. Keep
a steel helmet handy.) I know; I have been boomeranged across my head
so much that I now can see the darkness of lightness. And I love light.
Perhaps you'll think it strange that an invisible man should need light,   95
desire light, love light. But maybe it is exactly because I *am* invisible.
Light confirms my reality, gives birth to my form. A beautiful girl once
told me of a recurring nightmare in which she lay in the center of a large
dark room and felt her face expand until it filled the whole room, becoming a formless mass while her eyes ran in bilious jelly up the chim-   100
ney. And so it is with me. Without light I am not only invisible, but
formless as well; and to be unaware of one's form is to live a death. I
myself, after existing some twenty years, did not become alive until I
discovered my invisibility.

That is why I fight my battle with Monopolated Light & Power. The   105
deeper reason, I mean: It allows me to feel my vital aliveness. I also fight
them for taking so much of my money before I learned to protect myself.
In my hole in the basement there are exactly 1,369 lights. I've wired the
entire ceiling, every inch of it. And not with fluorescent bulbs, but with
the older, more-expensive-to-operate kind, the filament type. An act of   110
sabotage, you know. I've already begun to wire the wall. A junk man I
know, a man of vision, has supplied me with wire and sockets. Nothing,
storm or flood, must get in the way of our need for light and ever more
and brighter light. The truth is the light and light is the truth. When I
finish all four walls, then I'll start on the floor. Just how that will go, I   115
don't know. Yet when you have lived invisible as long as I have you develop a certain ingenuity. I'll solve the problem. And maybe I'll invent a
gadget to place my coffeepot on the fire while I lie in bed, and even invent a gadget to warm my bed—like the fellow I saw in one of the picture magazines who made himself a gadget to warm his shoes! Though   120

invisible, I am in the great American tradition of tinkers. That makes me kin to Ford, Edison and Franklin. Call me, since I have a theory and a concept, a "thinker-tinker." Yes, I'll warm my shoes; they need it, they're usually full of holes. I'll do that and more.

125   Now I have one radio-phonograph; I plan to have five. There is a certain acoustical deadness in my hole, and when I have music I want to *feel* its vibration, not only with my ear but with my whole body. I'd like to hear five recordings of Louis Armstrong playing and singing "What Did I Do to Be so Black and Blue"—all at the same time. Sometimes now
130   I listen to Louis while I have my favorite dessert of vanilla ice cream and sloe gin. I pour the red liquid over the white mound, watching it glisten and the vapor rising as Louis bends that military instrument into a beam of lyrical sound. Perhaps I like Louis Armstrong because he's made poetry out of being invisible. I think it must be because he's unaware that
135   he *is* invisible. . . .
         Meanwhile I enjoy my life with the compliments of Monopolated Light & Power. Since you never recognize me even when in closest contact with me, and since, no doubt, you'll hardly believe that I exist, it won't matter if you know that I tapped a power line leading into the building
140   and ran it into my hole in the ground. Before that I lived in the darkness into which I was chased, but now I see. I've illuminated the blackness of my invisibility—and vice versa. And so I play the invisible music of my isolation. The last statement doesn't seem just right, does it? But it is; you hear this music simply because music is heard and seldom seen, ex-
145   cept by musicians. Could this compulsion to put invisibility down in black and white be thus an urge to make music of invisibility? But I am an orator, a rabble rouser—Am? I *was,* and perhaps shall be again. Who knows? All sickness is not unto death, neither is invisibility.
         I can hear you say, "What a horrible, irresponsible bastard!" And you're
150   right. I leap to agree with you. I am one of the most irresponsible beings that ever lived. Irresponsibility is part of my invisibility; any way you face it, it is a denial. But to whom can I be responsible, and why should I be, when you refuse to see me? And wait until I reveal how truly irresponsible I am. Responsibility rests upon recognition, and recognition is
155   a form of agreement. Take the man whom I almost killed: Who was responsible for that near murder—I? I don't think so, and I refuse it. I won't buy it. You can't give it to me. *He* bumped *me, he* insulted *me.* Shouldn't he, for his own personal safety, have recognized my hysteria, my "danger potential"? He, let us say, was lost in a dream world. But
160   didn't *he* control that dream world—which, alas, is only too real!—and didn't *he* rule me out of it? And if he had yelled for a policeman, wouldn't *I* have been taken for the offending one? Yes, yes, yes! Let me agree with

you, I was the irresponsible one; for I should have used my knife to protect the higher interests of society. Some day that kind of foolishness will cause us tragic trouble. All dreamers and sleepwalkers must pay the 165 price, and even the invisible victim is responsible for the fate of all. But I shirked that responsibility; I became too snarled in the incompatible notions that buzzed within my brain. I was a coward. . . .

Study Openers

1. Describe the apparent "character" of the writer, pointing to details which help to create your impression. (See Chapter 10, page 103.) How does the writer's character affect the point being made?
2. Write an account showing a white narrator becoming aware of Ellison's invisible man.

(Other elements)

3. What is the writer's definition of "invisibility"? What is the effect of defining it in this way rather than providing a formal definition?
4. Do you agree that this invisibility exists in U.S. society? Where is it likely to be found and why?
5. Both Ellison and Douglass (page 350) are black writers who address white readers, at least in part. How do they differ a) in their view of the race problem, and b) in their apparent stance toward it?

On Natural Death
by Lewis Thomas

(from *The Medusa and the Snail,* 1979)

There are so many new books about dying that there are now special shelves set aside for them in bookshops, along with the health-diet and home-repair paperbacks and the sex manuals. Some of them are so packed with detailed information and step-by-step instructions for performing the function that you'd think this was a new sort of skill which 5 all of us are now required to learn. The strongest impression the casual reader gets, leafing through, is that proper dying has become an extraordinary, even an exotic experience, something only the specially trained get to do.

Also, you could be led to believe that we are the only creatures capa- 10 ble of the awareness of death, that when all the rest of nature is being cycled through dying, one generation after another, it is a different kind of process, done automatically and trivially, more "natural," as we say.

An elm in our backyard caught the blight this summer and dropped
stone dead, leafless, almost overnight. One weekend it was a normal-
looking elm, maybe a little bare in spots but nothing alarming, and the
next weekend it was gone, passed over, departed, taken. Taken is right,
for the tree surgeon came by yesterday with his crew of young helpers
and their cherry picker, and took it down branch by branch and carted
it off in the back of a red truck, everyone singing.

The dying of a field mouse, at the jaws of an amiable household cat,
is a spectacle I have beheld many times. It used to make me wince. Early
in life I gave up throwing sticks at the cat to make him drop the mouse,
because the dropped mouse regularly went ahead and died anyway, but
I always shouted unaffections at the cat to let him know the sort of animal he had become. Nature, I thought, was an abomination.

Recently I've done some thinking about that mouse, and I wonder if
his dying is necessarily all that different from the passing of our elm. The
main difference, if there is one, would be in the matter of pain. I do not
believe that an elm tree has pain receptors, and even so, the blight seems
to me a relatively painless way to go even if there were nerve endings in
a tree, which there are not. But the mouse dangling tail-down from the
teeth of a gray cat is something else again, with pain beyond bearing,
you'd think, all over his small body.

There are now some plausible reasons for thinking it is not like that at
all, and you can make up an entirely different story about the mouse and
his dying if you like. At the instant of being trapped and penetrated by
teeth, peptide hormones are released by cells in the hypothalamus and
the pituitary gland; instantly these substances, called endorphins, are at-
tached to the surfaces of other cells responsible for pain perception; the
hormones have the pharmacologic properties of opium; there is no pain.
Thus it is that the mouse seems always to dangle so languidly from the
jaws, lies there so quietly when dropped, dies of his injuries without a
struggle. If a mouse could shrug, he'd shrug.

I do not know if this is true or not, nor do I know how to prove it if it
is true. Maybe if you could get in there quickly enough and administer
naloxone, a specific morphine antagonist, you could turn off the endorphins and observe the restoration of pain, but this is not something I
would care to do or see. I think I will leave it there, as a good guess
about the dying of a cat-chewed mouse, perhaps about dying in general.

Montaigne had a hunch about dying, based on his own close call in a
riding accident. He was so badly injured as to be believed dead by his
companions, and was carried home with lamentations, "all bloody, stained
all over with the blood I had thrown up." He remembers the entire episode, despite having been "dead, for two full hours," with wonderment:

It seemed to me that my life was hanging only by the tip of my lips. I closed my eyes in order, it seemed to me, to help push it out, and took pleasure in growing languid and letting myself go. It was an idea that was only floating on the surface of my soul, as delicate and feeble as all the rest, but in truth not only free from distress but mingled with that sweet feeling that people have who have let themselves slide into sleep. I believe that this is the same state in which people find themselves whom we see fainting in the agony of death, and I maintain that we pity them without cause. . . . In order to get used to the idea of death, I find there is nothing like coming close to it.

Later, in another essay, Montaigne returns to it:

If you know not how to die, never trouble yourself; Nature will in a moment fully and sufficiently instruct you; she will exactly do that business for you; take you no care for it.

The worst accident I've ever seen was on Okinawa, in the early days of the invasion, when a jeep ran into a troop carrier and was crushed nearly flat. Inside were two young MPs, trapped in bent steel, both mortally hurt, with only their heads and shoulders visible. We had a conversation while people with the right tools were prying them free. Sorry about the accident, they said. No, they said, they felt fine. Is everyone else okay, one of them said. Well, the other one said, no hurry now. And then they died.

Pain is useful for avoidance, for getting away when there's time to get away, but when it is end game, and no way back, pain is likely to be turned off, and the mechanisms for this are wonderfully precise and quick. If I had to design an ecosystem in which creatures had to live off each other and in which dying was an indispensable part of living, I could not think of a better way to manage.

Study Openers

Lewis Thomas has been a physician and professor, a medical scientist, a writer on biology for a serious general audience, and a medical administrator.

1. As a professional biologist, Thomas might well have chosen to characterize himself as a *scientist*—impersonal in manner, careful to cite scientific sources.

   a. How does the "character" of Thomas actually appear in this brief essay? Cover such points as his evident knowledge and his virtues, hopes, and fears. Also touch on his degree of directness of manner, his vantage-point with relation to the audience, and

his degree of formality. (See Chapter 10, page 106) How do all
these matters influence the impact of the essay on you?

b. Thomas considers four illustrations of death. What psychological effectiveness do you see in this order?

(Other elements)

2. This essay introduces several scientific terms not generally known. Show
how the following are defined by context, or, if they are not, whether a
fuller definition would be desirable.

> peptids (line 38)
> hypothalamus (line 38)
> endorphins (line 39)
> pharmacologic (line 41)
> naloxone (line 47)

3. How do Kübler-Ross (page 337) and Thomas differ: a) in what they say
about the nature of death; and b) in what they recommend as the attitude to take toward it?

American Cancer Society

(poster, 1976)

SMOKING IS VERY GLAMOROUS

AMERICAN CANCER SOCIETY

Study Openers

1. What is the real point of this poster?
2. Explain its ironic technique (Chapter 12). To what extent do you find it effective?
3. How would you put together a "straight" poster making the same point without irony? Why would it be more effective—or less?
4. Design an ironic poster using the tactics of this one to comment on the glamour of one of the following: alcohol, high-speed driving, cocaine. Use a photograph or, if you can, your own drawing.

(Other elements)

5. Although the picture of the woman smoking is visual and not verbal, it exhibits the force of well-chosen details. Which strike you as most telling?

Mum's the Word
by Russell Baker

(*New York Times Magazine*, August 29, 1982)

Biff is not his real name. Nor do the incidents related here have any con-nection with events in the life of the man whose real name is not Biff. I want this clearly understood on account of a recent court ruling that I can be sued to the eyeballs by the man whose real name is not Biff if
5 I publish a thinly disguised account of events in his life which rubs him the wrong way.

Let it be perfectly clear then: Hardly anything I shall now recount ac-tually happened. What did, in fact, happen to Biff was extraordinary, but, aware that lawyers are ready to seize my estate and, after extracting
10 a third for themselves, give the rest to the man whose real name is not Biff, I wouldn't print a word of that story though wild horses tried to drag it out of me.

This reminds me of another party—no relation to Biff—who keeps tele-phoning. He says he knows who is committing the baffling discothèque
15 murders and wants to tell me. "Why me?" I ask. "Why not tell the cops and put an end to these ghastly butcheries?"

Well, it seems if the killer finds out who squealed—"He has a very short temper," my caller says—he is likely to butcher the informer after the nuisance of his trial and a year or two in the jug are ended.

"But if I tell you," my caller says, "as a journalist you will be honor   20
bound to keep my name out of it."

"Don't you dare tell me the name of the discothèque butcher!" I yell at
him and hang up in terror. Every time he phones, I have a sleepless night
imagining what the courts would do to me if I printed the butcher's
name and refused to tell any lawyers who had slipped it to me.   25

For that kind of crime you can spend more time behind bars than the
discothèque butcher, who will probably be out on appeal while you're
celebrating your birthday next winter by watching the guards search the
cake for hacksaws.

Speaking of hacksaws, I'd love to tell you this hilarious story about a   30
man I know. You would absolutely die laughing. I guarantee it. I saw
the thing happen. Actually saw it happen. You wouldn't believe the absurdity that a man with three hacksaws can commit.

Nobody told me the story. I saw it. It's important that I make it clear
that nobody told me, because if anybody had told me, that person could   35
go to prison for a long, long time. The thing is, you see, that the fellow
in the hacksaw story works for the C.I.A., and Congress has just passed
a new law: Reveal the identity of somebody in the C.I.A., and off you go
to the Federal pen.

This is why I'm not going to tell you this riotous story, which you'd   40
love. In fact, I wish I'd never mentioned it. I probably wouldn't have if
it weren't so hard to find something you can print in a newspaper these
days without risking imprisonment or a multimillion-dollar lawsuit.

I did pick up a fantastic story the other day, but I've forgotten most
of the details. It was incredibly complicated and, of course, I didn't take   45
any notes, so it's all a muddle in my memory now.

"Shouldn't you be taking notes on a story as complicated as this?"
asked the man who was telling it to me, with the aid of diagrams.

Obviously, he was a man without the least grasp of a journalist's working problems these days. I explained that I'd quit taking notes a couple   50
of years back when the Supreme Court said it was perfectly fine for people to seize my notes.

I've been a happier man ever since. Now, when the doorbell interrupts dinner, I no longer quake in fear that it's Chief Justice Burger
come to seize my notes because I know I can get rid of him before the   55
hamburger chills by showing him an empty file cabinet.

This is probably why all the judges, lawyers and politicians who have
been designing ways to impoverish or imprison me keep saying their
schemes have no "chilling effect." Since I now do nothing that can possibly interest them or anybody else, they don't have to interrupt my life   60
long enough to let the hamburger chill.

I'm sure there are a lot of people, splendid people, in the hamburger industry ready to be outraged by the suggestion that hamburger, wonderful hamburger, splendid hamburger, could possibly become chilly
65 while a journalist is having his house searched or spending a few years in jail.

Before a jury awards them my car, shoes and house furnishings for slandering their superb product, let me make clear that I have not said that hamburger will chill spontaneously while sitting on the table. It is
70 the custom at our house, when it appears that a police search or a prison term impends, to put the warm hamburger into the refrigerator until normality resumes. I do not wish to be haled into court by the refrigerator industry to defend the libel that their marvelous products do not chill.

Nor would I be so arrogant as to publish the slightest intimation that
75 hamburger will ever let you down heatwise. In view of my eagerness to publish only what will not disturb a babe, I was distressed this week to receive a sneering letter stating that my work "illustrates how thoroughly the once fearless press has turned into a chicken press," and wish to assure the poultry industry here and now that I have never in my life
80 pressed a chicken.

Study Openers

1. How is irony involved in this piece? (Chapter 12, p. 124).
2. Teachers of composition are periodically plagued by the student who writes a whole paper about not being able to write. Does Baker get away with this old wheeze?

The Theory of Preemptive Revolution
by Aaron Wildavsky

(from *The Revolt Against the Masses,* 1971)

Criticizing American foreign policy has replaced baseball and Monopoly as the national pastime. And winning the game depends on making profound statements like: "The United States is always reacting to events instead of enacting them," or "America should be molding the New World,
5 instead of vainly trying to stem the forces of change," and "Born in revolution, the American government finds itself in the anomalous position of supporting conservative regimes." How much better it would be, the various critics seem to suggest, if the United States found itself part of the

revolutionary vanguard. Then, the American people would be loved abroad, instead of hated, and an American could raise his head in a foreign land with some small feeling of pride. It gives me great pride to announce that a new discovery in political science (or, rather, the adaptation of an old one) now permits the United States government to accomplish all of these goals—and many other desirable ends as well.

The new discovery is, of course, the *Theory of Preemptive Revolution.* As one would immediately suspect, this theory is merely a subtheory of Gresham's Law: "bad revolutions drive out good ones." In its opening phases, the Theory calls for the United States to single out the three most hopeless countries in Latin America, in Africa, and in Asia. These should be nations whose extraordinary dearth of natural resources is matched only by the virtually total incapacity of their populations. These countries must be such sinkholes that billions of dollars would disappear into their vast slums and vaster wastelands without producing a molecule of visible improvement. Unless, of course, it was to be found in the unremitting hostility of the populations of these countries to the nation that had supplied the funds.[1]

Once having chosen three unpromising countries in each area, the United States will immediately set about to cause Communist revolutions in them. If there is no nascent Communist movement, the United States will start one. Unlimited funds and weaponry will be supplied to all those who give promise of pulling off a Communist revolution at the earliest possible moment. No delays will be tolerated. All socialist, democratic, or conservative forces will be rigorously suppressed. The rallying cry will be: "All power to the Communist party—At Once."

Once the Communist revolutions have succeeded, the party leaders will be encouraged to ally themselves, as openly and loudly as possible, with the Soviet Union. Dedicated party members in each country, having introduced governments modeled on that of the Soviet Union, will make it unmistakably clear that their struggling but aspiring nations are truly and genuinely Communist, loyal parts of the socialist camp, and dedicated to following the Soviet lead—and to accepting Soviet aid—in all matters.

What alternatives will confront the Soviet Union? If she accepts these nine countries as part of her sphere of influence, she will be required to support them. At an enormously high expenditure. It is estimated that Cuba, one of the three wealthiest countries in Latin America before its revolution, currently costs the Soviet Union around a million dollars a day. How much more will these nine other countries cost? And for how

[1] Names of possible target countries have been omitted in order not to cause unnecessary offense at this stage and, also, not to alert our enemies to new policies.

long will they require support? Note that the Soviet Union will be supporting them, and the United States, once the revolution has succeeded,
will not be spending a penny. If the Soviet Union refuses to recognize
the claims of these countries to her protection and support, her hollow
pretensions to world leadership will be exposed. The Soviets will have to
choose between solvency and saving face. (Nor can the Chinese Communists take up the slack; they can afford it even less. At the moment, the
Chinese are specializing in places like Zanzibar, where much revolution
can be accomplished at minimal expenditure.) A third possibility for the
Soviet Union would be to attempt to stem the revolution in these Asian,
African, and Latin American countries. In this case, United States foreign
policy will have put the Soviet Union in the position of a status quo
power, which keeps insisting that various countries hurry, but very
slowly, along the road to Communism.

What about the so-called developing countries? The great problem at
the moment is that the United States keeps pursuing them, shouting at the
top of its lungs that they are in danger of being taken over by Communism. Naturally, these countries do not quite believe this, and wonder if
Uncle Sam does not have either some ulterior motive or paranoia. Their
best bet is to play both ends against the middle and to try to get the most
they can out of the Soviet Union and the United States. But, consider the
startling change that will overcome their policies the moment the United
States seriously undertakes to put into practice the Theory of Preemptive
Revolution. Instead of being able to take the status quo policies of the
United States for granted, the developing countries will suddenly find
themselves having to worry a great deal about the United States. If they
look too hopeless, they may find the United States not only leaving them
to the mercies of the local Communists, but perhaps even actively helping
the revolutionary process along. The developing countries will have to
demonstrate to the United States that they are worth saving from Communism. Countries who see their neighbors under Communist rule may
decide that the Communist menace is a possibility for them, too, and ask
for American assistance. The United States will then be in the much more
enviable position of being able to play hard to get. As a result, the Soviet
Union will end up supporting only the utterly hopeless countries—and
using the money it would have liked to spend on more prosperous countries to do so.

The image of the United States as a conservative status quo power will
be gone forever. No longer fear-ridden, no longer forever worrying about
which little piece of African, Asian, or Latin American real estate might
go Communist, it will be a proud and confident nation, which is continually in the enviable position of being asked to help others and must choose

carefully those lucky places to which it will lend its support. Instead of being a wall flower, or, what is worse, actively forcing partners to dance with it, the United States will be much sought after—and on its own terms. Its foreign policy will be both active and judicious. No longer will it be the passive reactor-to-events that it is now. On the contrary, it will always be actively contemplating the possibility of fomenting revolutions in the hopeless countries that need them most. The Communists will have little time, no incentive, and no funds to aid revolutions in countries that could really cause harm to American interests. Developing countries will have much greater incentive to defend themselves, and to call upon American assistance in doing so. By adopting the Theory of Preemptive Revolution, the United States will break out of the vicious cycle in which it now finds itself. . . .

Study Openers

1. Describe the apparent problem and solution which Wildavsky is presenting.
2. What signals lead you to suspect that he is being ironic? (Chapter 12)
3. What is Wildavsky really saying about U.S. foreign policy? How far do you agree?
4. Choose some alleged failing in federal, local, or institutional administration which is often criticized. (Examples: soaring costs, failure to take initiative, indifference to the individual.) Write an essay ironically recommending a plausible remedy. Your treatment should imply your real view of what needs to be done.

Security
by Germaine Greer

(*The Female Eunuch*, 1970)

There is no such thing as security. There never has been. And yet we speak of security as something which people are entitled to; we explain neurosis and psychosis as springing from the lack of it. Although security is not in the nature of things, we invent strategies for outwitting fortune, and call them after their guiding deity insurance, assurance, social security. We employ security services, pay security guards. And yet we know that the universe retains powers of unforeseen disaster that cannot be indemnified. We know that superannuation and pensions schemes are not proof against the fluctuations of modern currency. We know that money cannot repay a lost leg or a lifetime of headaches or scarred beauty, but we

arrange it just the same. In a dim way we realize that our vulnerability to fortune increases the more we rig up defenses against the unforeseeable. Money in the bank, our own home, investments, are extensions of the areas in which we can be damaged. The more superannuation one
15 amasses the more one can be threatened by the loss of it. The more the state undertakes to protect a man from illness and indigence, the more it has the right to sacrifice him to the common good, to demolish his house and kill his animals, to hospitalize his children or take them into approved homes; the more government forms upon which his name ap-
20 pears, the more numerous the opportunities for him to be calumniated in high places. John Greenaway fell for the mythology of the welfare state, and allowed the chimera to tantalize him before he was eighteen years old.

I don't feel very secure, and I'd like to marry one day. I sup-
25 pose it's for security.
You have to feel secure first and foremost. If you have no money in the bank to fall back on you can never be free from worry . . .
It's not that I have much insecurity at home, I have a good
30 home. I just can't feel secure because of the state of the world . . .
I daresay if I'm lucky enough to find a secure job bringing in really good money I'll get like the rest of them. It's amazing what a little money in the bank and a nice home will do for
35 you. You start thinking about running a car and keeping your garden tidy and life insurance, and two telly sets—and you don't have time to worry about the larger issues of how many people are starving in Africa.
Security can be a killer, and corrode your mind and soul. But
40 I wish I had it.[1]

Probably the only place where a man can feel really secure is in a maximum security prison, except for the imminent threat of release. The problem of recidivism ought to have shown young men like John Green-away just what sort of notion security is, but there is no indication that
45 he would understand it. Security is when everything is settled, when nothing can happen to you; security is the denial of life. Human beings are better equipped to cope with disaster and hardship than they are with unvarying security, but as long as security is the highest value in a community they can have little opportunity to decide this for themselves.
50 It is agreed that Englishmen coped magnificently with a war, and were more cheerful, enterprising and friendly under the daily threat of bom-

[1] Charles Hamblett and Jane Deverson, *Generation X* (London, 1964), pp. 41, 111.

bardment than they are now under benevolent peacetime, when we are
so far from worrying about how many people starve in Africa that we
can tolerate British policy in Nigeria. John Greenaway did not realize
that his bastions of security would provide new opportunities for threat.   55
The Elizabethans called the phenomenon *mutability*, and mourned the
passing of all that was fair and durable with a kind of melancholy ela-
tion, seeing in the Heraclitean dance of the elements a divine purpose
and a progress to a platonic immutability in an unearthly region of
ideas.[2] Greenaway cannot have access to this kind of philosophic detach-   60
ment; neither can he adopt the fatalism of the peasant who is always
mocked by the unreliability of the seasons. He believes that there is such
a thing as security: that an employer might pay him less but guarantee
him secure tenure, that he might be allowed to live and die in the same
house if he pays for it, that he can bind himself to a wife and family as   65
assurance against abandonment and loneliness.

The oddest thing about the twentieth-century chimera of security is
that it was forged in the age of greatest threat. No disaster so imminent
and so uncontrollable as total war was ever dreamt of before the atomic
age. It seems as if men have only to defuse one kind of threat before   70
another takes its place. Disease grows more complicated; the possibilities
of aggression and destruction exceed Pope Gregory's wildest dreams. An
international agreement proscribes the use of gas and so germ warfare
must be developed. And so forth. Insecurity in human life is a constant
factor, and I suppose efforts to eliminate it are just about as constant.   75

Greenaway mixes up security of life and possessions with emotional
security, and it is difficult to see how he could do otherwise. Part of the
mystery in our use of the idea is the suggestion of blame in the epithet
insecure when applied to a personality. Moreover, it is assumed that
women especially need to feel secure, reassured of love and buttressed   80
by the comforts of home. Women who refuse to marry are seen to be
daring insecurity, facing a desolate old age, courting poverty and degra-
dation. But husbands die, pensions are inadequate, children grow up and
go away and mothers become mothers-in-law. Women's work, married
or unmarried, is menial and low-paid. Women's right to possess property   85
is curtailed, more if they are married. How can marriage provide security? In any case a husband is a possession which can be lost or stolen
and the abandoned wife of thirty-odd with a couple of children is far
more desolate and insecure in her responsibility than an unmarried
woman with or without children ever could be. The laws which make   90

[2] E.g., Edmund Spenser, *Two Cantos of Mutabilitye*, published in 1609 "parcell of
some following Booke of the Faerie Queene" which was never completed.

divorce easier increase the insecurity of a wife. The gibe of emotional insecurity is a criticism of a woman's refusal to delude herself that she cannot be abandoned; it is hard indeed to rely upon an uncertain relationship which will become even more fragile if it is tested by demands
95 for reassurance. The marriage service promises security: for the religious it is a sacramental sign and the security is security in heaven where husband and wife can be one flesh; for women who understand it as a kind of life-long contract for personal management by one man it is a patently unsatisfactory document. The safeguards and indemnities ought to be
100 written into it at the outset as they are in management contracts and then it would have at least the value of a business document. A sacramental sign in an atheistic age has no value at all. It would be better for all concerned if its contractual nature were a little clearer.[3]

If marriage were a contract with safeguards and indemnities indicated
105 in it, it would still not provide emotional security. Its value would be in that it *did not appear to* provide it, so that women would not be encouraged to rely absolutely upon a situation which had no intrinsic permanence. The housewife is an unpaid worker in her husband's house in return for the security of being a permanent employee: hers is the *reduc-*
110 *tio ad absurdum* of the case of the employee who accepts a lower wage in return for permanence in his employment. But the lowest paid employees can be and are laid off, and so are wives. They have no savings, no skills which they can bargain with elsewhere, and they must bear the stigma of having been sacked. The only alternative for the worker and
115 the wife is to refuse to consider the bait of security and bargain openly. To do this a woman must have a different kind of security, the kind of personal security which enables her to consider insecurity as freedom.

Women are asked to exercise the virtue of personal security even if they do not have it, for they are supposed not to feel threatened within
120 their marriages and not to take measures to safeguard their interests, although they do do all these things. Self-reliance is theoretically necessary within marriage so logically there is no reason to accept a chimeric security which must not be relied upon if it is to eventuate. The search for security is undertaken by the weakest part of the personality, by fear,
125 inadequacy, fatigue and anxiety. Women are not gamblers even to the small extent that men are. Wives tend to limit their husbands' enterprise, especially if it involves risks, and consequently the opportunities for achievement, delight and surprise are limited.

[3] I suspect that a contract made by a man and a woman respecting the conditions of their cohabitation would be regarded by law as a contract for an immoral purpose, and hence not binding in law (!).

Marriage—having a home and a wife and children—has a very
important place in life. A man wouldn't be complete without   130
them—but I don't believe in tying yourself down until you've
done something on your own first.

Most people get the best job they can, work for promotion
and when they're earning enough money meet a girl and marry
her. Then you have to buy a house and a car, and there you   135
are—chained down for the rest of your life. When you get to
thirty-five you're frightened to try anything new in case you lose
your security. Then it means living with all the regrets about
things you wanted to do.[4]

This is how Mike Russell, the twenty-one-year-old reporter on the   140
Edinburgh Evening News saw marriage and security in 1964. What he
identified was the function of the wife in screwing her husband into his
place in the commercial machine. The welfare state justifies its existence
by the promise of security and forces the worker to insure against his
own restlessness and any accident that may befall him by taking con-   145
tributions for his old age and illness out of his wages, at the same time
as it uses some of his earnings to carry on developing the greatest threats
to his continuing existence in the name of defense. A wife is the ally in
such repression. The demands of home, mortgages, and hire-purchase
payments support the immobilizing tendencies of his employment, mili-   150
tating against his desires for job control and any interest in direct action.
If the correct level of remuneration is maintained, and the anomalies of
the situation are not too apparent, the married man is a docile and re-
liable worker. By playing upon insecurity fears about immigrants and
discontent with wage freezes and productivity deals, an adroit Tory can   155
convert the working class to the most arrant conservatism.

If women would reject their roles in this pattern, recognizing insecurity as freedom, they would not be perceptibly worse off for it. Cynics
notice that economically, unmarried couples are often better off on taxation deals and so forth than married ones. Spiritually a woman is better   160
off if she cannot be taken for granted. Obviously informal relationships
can be more binding than formal ones if patterns of mutual exploitation
develop, and they usually do, but if women were to keep spontaneous
association as an ideal, the stultifying effects of symbiosis could be les-
sened. The situation could remain open, capable of development into   165
richer fields. Adultery would hold no threat if women were sure that the
relationships they enjoyed were truly rewarding and not merely preserved by censorship of other possibilities. Loneliness is never more cruel
than when it is felt in close propinquity with someone who has ceased

---

[4] Hamblett and Deverson, *Generation X*, pp. 48–49.

170 to communicate. Many a housewife staring at the back of her husband's newspaper or listening to his breathing in bed is lonelier than any spinster in a rented room. Much of the loneliness of lonely people springs from distrust and egotism, not from their having failed to set themselves up in a conjugal arrangement. The marriage bargain offers what cannot

175 be delivered if it is thought to offer emotional security, for such security is the achievement of the individual. Possessive love, for all its seductiveness, breaks down that personal poise and leaves its victims newly vulnerable. Those miserable women who blame the men who *let them down* for their misery and isolation enact every day the initial mistake of sacri-

180 ficing their personal responsibility for themselves. They would not have been any happier if they had remained married. When a man woos a woman he strives to make himself as indispensable as any woman is to any man: he may even determine to impregnate her to break down her self-sufficiency. In the struggle to remain a complete person and to love

185 from her fullness instead of her inadequacy a woman may appear hard. She may feel her early conditioning tugging her in the direction of surrender, but she ought to remember that she was originally loved for herself; she ought to hang on to herself and not find herself nagging, helpless, irritable and trapped. Perhaps I am not old enough yet to promise

190 that the self-reliant woman is always loved, that she cannot be lonely as long as there are people in the world who need her joy and her strength, but certainly in my experience it has always been so. Lovers who are free to go when they are restless always come back; lovers who are free to change remain interesting. The bitter animosity and obscenity of

195 divorce is unknown where individuals have not become Siamese twins. A lover who comes to your bed of his own accord is more likely to sleep with his arms around you all night than a lover who has nowhere else to sleep.

Annotation

The Heraclitean dance of the elements: the ceaseless change of the universe, lacking permanent reality, according to the Greek philosopher Heraclitus.

Study Openers

1. How, in Greer's observation, do most people define "security"? Why is it nonexistent?
2. How does the myth of security relate to the institution of marriage, as Greer sees it? Do you agree? What changes would you recommend in our attitudes toward marriage?

(Other elements)

3. Is there, perhaps, a "security" which is real and desirable, and an "in-security" which is harmful? How might Greer resolve such a question?

Knowledge and Understanding
by Aldous Huxley

(from *Tomorrow and Tomorrow and Tomorrow*, 1956)

Knowledge is acquired when we succeed in fitting a new experience into the system of concepts based upon our old experiences. Understanding comes when we liberate ourselves from the old and so make possible a direct, unmediated contact with the new, the mystery, moment by moment, of our existence.   5

The new is the given on every level of experience—given perceptions, given emotions and thoughts, given states of unstructured awareness, given relationships with things and persons. The old is our home-made system of ideas and word patterns. It is the stock of finished articles fabricated out of the given mystery by memory and analytical reasoning,   10
by habit and the automatic associations of accepted notions. Knowledge is primarily a knowledge of these finished articles. Understanding is primarily direct awareness of the raw material.

Knowledge is always in terms of concepts and can be passed on by means of words or other symbols. Understanding is not conceptual, and   15
therefore cannot be passed on. It is an immediate experience, and immediate experience can only be talked about (very inadequately), never shared. Nobody can actually feel another's pain or grief, another's love or joy or hunger. And similarly nobody can experience another's understanding of a given event or situation. There can, of course, be knowl-   20
edge of such an understanding, and this knowledge may be passed on in speech or writing, or by means of other symbols. Such communicable knowledge is useful as a reminder that there have been specific understandings in the past, and that understanding is at all times possible. But we must always remember that knowledge of understanding is not   25
the same thing as the understanding, which is the raw material of that knowledge. It is as different from understanding as the doctor's prescription for penicillin is different from penicillin.

Understanding is not inherited, nor can it be laboriously acquired. It is something which, when circumstances are favorable, comes to us, so   30
to say, of its own accord. All of us are knowers, all the time; it is only occasionally and in spite of ourselves that we directly understand the

mystery of given reality. Consequently we are very seldom tempted to equate understanding with knowledge. Of the exceptional men and
35 women, who have understanding in every situation, most are intelligent enough to see that understanding is different from knowledge and that conceptual systems based upon past experience are as necessary to the conduct of life as are spontaneous insights into new experiences. For these reasons the mistake of identifying understanding with knowledge is
40 rarely perpetrated and therefore poses no serious problem.

How different is the case with the opposite mistake, the mistake of supposing that knowledge is the same as understanding and interchangeable with it! All adults possess vast stocks of knowledge. Some of it is correct knowledge, some of it is incorrect knowledge, and some of it only
45 looks like knowledge and is neither correct nor incorrect; it is merely meaningless. That which gives meaning to a proposition is not (to use the words of an eminent contemporary philosopher, Rudolf Carnap) "the attendant images or thoughts, but the possibility of deducing from it perceptive propositions, in other words the possibility of verification.
50 To give sense to a proposition, the presence of images is not sufficient, it is not even necessary. We have no image of the electro-magnetic field, nor even, I should say, of the gravitational field; nevertheless the propositions which physicists assert about these fields have a perfect sense, because perceptive propositions are deducible from them." Metaphysical
55 doctrines are propositions which cannot be operationally verified, at least on the level of ordinary experience. They may be expressive of a state of mind, in the way that lyrical poetry is expressive; but they have no assignable meaning. The information they convey is only pseudo-knowledge. But the formulators of metaphysical doctrines and the believers in
60 such doctrines have always mistaken this pseudo-knowledge for knowledge and have proceeded to modify their behavior accordingly. Meaningless pseudo-knowledge has at all times been one of the principal motivators of individual and collective action. And that is one of the reasons why the course of human history has been so tragic and at
65 the same time so strangely grotesque. Action based upon meaningless pseudo-knowledge is always inappropriate, always beside the point, and consequently always results in the kind of mess mankind has always lived in—the kind of mess that makes the angels weep and the satirists laugh aloud.

70 Correct or incorrect, relevant or meaningless, knowledge and pseudo-knowledge are as common as dirt and are therefore taken for granted. Understanding, on the contrary, is as rare, very nearly, as emeralds, and so is highly prized. The knowers would dearly love to be understanders; but either their stock of knowledge does not include the knowledge of

what to do in order to be understanders; or else they know theoretically   75
what they ought to do, but go on doing the opposite all the same. In
either case they cherish the comforting delusion that knowledge and,
above all, pseudo-knowledge *are* understanding. Along with the closely
related errors of over-abstraction, over-generalization and over-simplification, this is the commonest of all intellectual sins and the most dan-   80
gerous.

Of the vast sum of human misery about one third, I would guess, is
unavoidable misery. This is the price we must pay for being embodied,
and for inheriting genes which are subject to deleterious mutations. This
is the rent extorted by Nature for the privilege of living on the surface   85
of a planet, whose soil is mostly poor, whose climates are capricious and
inclement, and whose inhabitants include a countless number of micro-
organisms capable of causing in man himself, in his domestic animals
and cultivated plants, an immense variety of deadly or debilitating diseases. To these miseries of cosmic origin must be added the much larger   90
group of those avoidable disasters we bring upon ourselves. For at least
two-thirds of our miseries spring from human stupidity, human malice
and those great motivators and justifiers of malice and stupidity, idealism, dogmatism and proselytizing zeal on behalf of religious or political
idols. But zeal, dogmatism and idealism exist only because we are for-   95
ever committing intellectual sins. We sin by attributing concrete significance to meaningless pseudo-knowledge; we sin in being too lazy to
think in terms of multiple causation and indulging instead in over-
simplification, over-generalization and over-abstraction; and we sin by
cherishing the false but agreeable notion that conceptual knowledge and,   100
above all, conceptual pseudo-knowledge are the same as understanding.

Consider a few obvious examples. The atrocities of organized religion
(and organized religion, let us never forget, has done about as much
harm as it has done good) are all due, in the last analysis, to "mistaking
the pointing finger for the moon"—in other words to mistaking the ver-   105
balized notion for the given mystery to which it refers or, more often,
only seems to refer. This, as I have said, is one of the original sins of the
intellect, and it is a sin in which, with a rationalistic bumptiousness as
grotesque as it is distasteful, theologians have systematically wallowed.
From indulgence in this kind of delinquency there has arisen, in most   110
of the great religious traditions of the world, a fantastic over-valuation
of words. Over-valuation of words leads all too frequently to the fabrica-
tion and idolatrous worship of dogmas, to the insistence on uniformity of
belief, the demand for assent by all and sundry to a set of propositions
which, though meaningless, are to be regarded as sacred. Those who do   115
not consent to this idolatrous worship of words are to be "converted"

and, if that should prove impossible, either persecuted or, if the dog-
matizers lack political power, ostracized and denounced. Immediate experience of reality unites men. Conceptualized beliefs, including even
120   the belief in a God of love and righteousness, divide them and, as the
dismal record of religious history bears witness, set them for centuries on
end at each other's throats.

Over-simplification, over-generalization and over-abstraction are three
other sins closely related to the sin of imagining that knowledge and
125   pseudo-knowledge are the same as understanding. The over-generalizing
over-simplifier is the man who asserts, without producing evidence, that
"All X's are Y," or, "All A's have a single cause, which is B." The over-
abstractor is the one who cannot be bothered to deal with Jones and
Smith, with Jane and Mary, as individuals, but enjoys being eloquent on
130   the subject of Humanity, of Progress, of God and History and the Future.
This brand of intellectual delinquency is indulged in by every demagogue, every crusader. In the Middle Ages the favorite over-generalization was "All infidels are damned." (For the Moslems, "all infidels" meant
"all Christians"; for the Christians, "all Moslems.") Almost as popular
135   was the nonsensical proposition, "All heretics are inspired by the devil"
and "All eccentric old women are witches." In the sixteenth and seventeenth centuries the wars and persecutions were justified by the lumi-
nously clear and simple belief that "All Roman Catholics (or, if you
happened to be on the Pope's side, all Lutherans, Calvinists and Angli-
140   cans) are God's enemies." In our own day Hitler proclaimed that all the
ills of the world had one cause, namely Jews, and that all Jews were
sub-human enemies of mankind. For the Communists, all the ills of the
world have one cause, namely capitalists, and all capitalists and their
middle-class supporters are subhuman enemies of mankind. It is per-
145   fectly obvious, on the face of it, that none of these over-generalized statements can possibly be true. But the urge to intellectual sin is fearfully
strong. All are subject to temptation and few are able to resist.

•   •   •   •

Study Openers

Ordinary reading will rarely yield definitions at this high level of abstraction.
As such definitions succeed, they help one to address some of life's central
issues.

1. Explain and illustrate the distinction which Huxley draws between "knowledge" and "understanding."
2. Are you satisfied with the exactness of these definitions? Are there any addi-

tional challenges of the sort mentioned in Chapter 13 which you would like to see met?

3. Huxley argues that a confusion of knowledge with understanding has caused much human misery. How is this so?

4. Write on Huxley's distinction as you have experienced it in some occasion of your own life.

(Other elements)

5. Point to coherence devices used in this difficult essay and show how they help in the reading. (See Chapter 8, page 77)

The Principles of Newspeak
by George Orwell

(from *Nineteen Eighty-Four*, 1949)

[This appendix appeared in Orwell's nightmarish novel *Nineteen Eighty-Four*, which envisioned a future world dominated and brutalized by totalitarian socialism.]

Newspeak was the official language of Oceania and had been devised to meet the ideological needs of Ingsoc, or English Socialism. In the year 1984 there was not as yet anyone who used Newspeak as his sole means of communication, either in speech or writing. The leading articles in the *Times* were written in it, but this was a tour de force which could only   5
be carried out by a specialist. It was expected that Newspeak would have finally superseded Oldspeak (or Standard English, as we should call it) by about the year 2050. Meanwhile it gained ground steadily, all Party members tending to use Newspeak words and grammatical con-
structions more and more in their everyday speech. The version in use in   10
1984, and embodied in the Ninth and Tenth Editions of the Newspeak dictionary, was a provisional one, and contained many superfluous words and archaic formations which were due to be suppressed later. It is with the final, perfected version, as embodied in the Eleventh Edition of the dictionary, that we are concerned here.   15

   The purpose of Newspeak was not only to provide a medium of ex-
pression for the world-view and mental habits proper to the devotees of Ingsoc, but to make all other modes of thought impossible. It was intended that when Newspeak had been adopted once and for all and Oldspeak forgotten, a heretical thought—that is, a thought diverging   20
from the principles of Ingsoc—should be literally unthinkable, at least so far as thought is dependent on words. Its vocabulary was so constructed

as to give exact and often very subtle expression to every meaning that a
Party member could properly wish to express, while excluding all other
meanings and also the possibility of arriving at them by indirect methods. This was done partly by the invention of new words, but chiefly by
eliminating undesirable words and by stripping such words as remained
of unorthodox meanings, and so far as possible of all secondary meanings
whatever. To give a single example. The word *free* still existed in Newspeak, but it could only be used in such statements as "This dog is free
from lice" or "This field is free from weeds." It could not be used in its
old sense of "politically free" or "intellectually free," since political and
intellectual freedom no longer existed even as concepts, and were therefore of necessity nameless. Quite apart from the suppression of definitely
heretical words, reduction of vocabulary was regarded as an end in
itself, and no word that could be dispensed with was allowed to survive.
Newspeak was designed not to extend but to *diminish* the range of
thought, and this purpose was indirectly assisted by cutting the choice
of words down to a minimum.

Newspeak was founded on the English language as we now know it,
though many Newspeak sentences, even when not containing newly created words, would be barely intelligible to an English-speaker of our
own day. Newspeak words were divided into three distinct classes,
known as the A vocabulary, the B vocabulary (also called compound
words), and the C vocabulary. It will be simpler to discuss each class
separately, but the grammatical peculiarities of the language can be
dealt with in the section devoted to the A vocabulary, since the same
rules held good for all three categories.

The A vocabulary. The A vocabulary consisted of the words needed for
the business of everyday life—for such things as eating, drinking, working, putting on one's clothes, going up and down stairs, riding in vehicles,
gardening, cooking, and the like. It was composed almost entirely of
words that we already possess—words like *hit, run, dog, tree, sugar,
house, field*—but in comparison with the present-day English vocabulary,
their number was extremely small, while their meanings were far more
rigidly defined. All ambiguities and shades of meaning had been purged
out of them. So far as it could be achieved, a Newspeak word of this
class was simply a staccato sound expressing *one* clearly understood concept. It would have been quite impossible to use the A vocabulary for
literary purposes or for political or philosophical discussion. It was intended only to express simple, purposive thoughts, usually involving concrete objects or physical actions.

. . . . .

The B vocabulary. The B vocabulary consisted of words which had
been deliberately constructed for political purposes: words, that is to
say, which not only had in every case a political implication, but were   65
intended to impose a desirable mental attitude upon the person using
them. Without a full understanding of the principles of Ingsoc it was
difficult to use these words correctly. In some cases they could be translated into Oldspeak, or even into words taken from the A vocabulary,
but this usually demanded a long paraphrase and always involved the   70
loss of certain overtones. The B words were a sort of verbal shorthand,
often packing whole ranges of ideas into a few syllables, and at the same
time more accurate and forcible than ordinary language.

The B words were in all cases compound words. They consisted of
two or more words, or portions of words, welded together in an easily   75
pronounceable form. The resulting amalgam was always a noun-verb,
and inflected according to the ordinary rules. To take a single example:
the word *goodthink,* meaning, very roughly, "orthodoxy," or, if one chose
to regard it as a verb, "to think in an orthodox manner." This inflected
as follows: noun-verb, *goodthink;* past tense and past participle, *good-*   80
thinked; present participle, *goodthinking;* adjective, *goodthinkful;* ad-
verb, *goodthinkwise;* verbal noun, *goodthinker.*

·   ·   ·   ·

As we have already seen in the case of the word *free,* words which
had once borne a heretical meaning were sometimes retained for the
sake of convenience, but only with the undesirable meanings purged out   85
of them. Countless other words such as *honor, justice, morality, interna-*
tionalism, democracy, science, and *religion* had simply ceased to exist. A
few blanket words covered them, and, in covering them, abolished them.
All words grouping themselves round the concepts of liberty and equality, for instance, were contained in the single word *crimethink,* while all   90
words grouping themselves round the concepts of objectivity and ration-
alism were contained in the single word *oldthink.* Greater precision
would have been dangerous. What was required in a Party member was
an outlook similar to that of the ancient Hebrew who knew, without
knowing much else, that all nations other than his own worshiped "false   95
gods." He did not need to know that these gods were called Baal, Osiris,
Moloch, Ashtaroth, and the like; probably the less he knew about them
the better for his orthodoxy. He knew Jehovah and the commandments
of Jehovah; he knew, therefore, that all gods with other names or other
attributes were false gods. In somewhat the same way, the Party member   100
knew what constituted right conduct, and in exceedingly vague, generalized terms he knew what kinds of departure from it were possible. His

sexual life, for example, was entirely regulated by the two Newspeak words *sexcrime* (sexual immorality) and *goodsex* (chastity). *Sexcrime* covered all sexual misdeeds whatever. It covered fornication, adultery, homosexuality, and other perversions, and, in addition, normal intercourse practiced for its own sake. There was no need to enumerate them separately, since they were all equally culpable, and, in principle, all punishable by death. In the C vocabulary, which consisted of scientific and technical words, it might be necessary to give specialized names to certain sexual aberrations, but the ordinary citizen had no need of them. He knew what was meant by *goodsex*—that is to say, normal intercourse between man and wife, for the sole purpose of begetting children, and without physical pleasure on the part of the woman; all else was *sexcrime*. In Newspeak it was seldom possible to follow a heretical thought further than the perception that it *was* heretical; beyond that point the necessary words were nonexistent.

No word in the B vocabulary was ideologically neutral. A great many were euphemisms. Such words, for instance, as *joycamp* (forced-labor camp) or *Minipax* (Ministry of Peace, i.e., Ministry of War) meant almost the exact opposite of what they appeared to mean. Some words, on the other hand, displayed a frank and contemptuous understanding of the real nature of Oceanic society. An example was *prolefeed,* meaning the rubbishy entertainment and spurious news which the Party handed out to the masses. Other words, again, were ambivalent, having the connotation "good" when applied to the Party and "bad" when applied to its enemies. But in addition there were great numbers of words which at first sight appeared to be mere abbreviations and which derived their ideological color not from their meaning but from their structure.

· · · · ·

The C vocabulary. The C vocabulary was supplementary to the others and consisted entirely of scientific and technical terms. These resembled the scientific terms in use today, and were constructed from the same roots, but the usual care was taken to define them rigidly and strip them of undesirable meanings. They followed the same grammatical rules as the words in the other two vocabularies. Very few of the C words had any currency either in everyday speech or in political speech. Any scientific worker or technician could find all the words he needed in the list devoted to his own speciality, but he seldom had more than a smattering of the words occurring in the other lists. Only a very few words were common to all lists, and there was no vocabulary expressing the function of Science as a habit of mind, or a method of thought, irrespective of its particular branches. There was, indeed, no word for "Science," any

meaning that it could possibly bear being already sufficiently covered by
the word *Ingsoc*.

From the foregoing account it will be seen that in Newspeak the expres-   145
sion of unorthodox opinions, above a very low level, was well-nigh impossible. It was of course possible to utter heresies of a very crude kind,
a species of blasphemy. It would have been possible, for example, to say
Big Brother is ungood. But this statement, which to an orthodox ear
merely conveyed a self-evident absurdity, could not have been sustained   150
by reasoned argument, because the necessary words were not available.
Ideas inimical to Ingsoc could only be entertained in a vague wordless
form, and could only be named in very broad terms which lumped together and condemned whole groups of heresies without defining them
in doing so. One could, in fact, only use Newspeak for unorthodox pur-   155
poses by illegitimately translating some of the words back into Oldspeak.
For example, *All mans are equal* was a possible Newspeak sentence, but
only in the same sense in which *All men are redhaired* is a possible Oldspeak sentence. It did not contain a grammatical error, but it expressed
a palpable untruth, i.e., that all men are of equal size, weight, or   160
strength. The concept of political equality no longer existed, and this
secondary meaning had accordingly been purged out of the word *equal*.
In 1984, when Oldspeak was still the normal means of communication,
the danger theoretically existed that in using Newspeak words one might
remember their original meanings. In practice it was not difficult for any 165
person well grounded in *doublethink* to avoid doing this, but within a
couple of generations even the possibility of such a lapse would have
vanished. A person growing up with Newspeak as his sole language
would no more know that *equal* had once had the secondary meaning of
"politically equal," or that *free* had once meant "intellectually free,"   170
than, for instance, a person who had never heard of chess would be
aware of the secondary meanings attaching to *queen* and *rook*. There
would be many crimes and errors which it would be beyond his power to
commit, simply because they were nameless and therefore unimaginable.
And it was to be foreseen that with the passage of time the distinguish-   175
ing characteristics of Newspeak would become more and more pronounced—its words growing fewer and fewer, their meanings more and
more rigid, and the chance of putting them to improper uses always
diminishing.

When Oldspeak had been once and for all superseded, the last link   180
with the past would have been severed. History had already been rewritten, but fragments of the literature of the past survived here and

there, imperfectly censored, and so long as one retained one's knowledge of Oldspeak it was possible to read them. In the future such fragments,
185   even if they chanced to survive, would be unintelligible and untranslatable. It was impossible to translate any passage of Oldspeak into Newspeak unless it either referred to some technical process or some very simple everyday action, or was already orthodox (*goodthinkful* would be the Newspeak expression) in tendency. In practice this meant that no
190   book written before approximately 1960 could be translated as a whole. Prerevolutionary literature could only be subjected to ideological translation—that is, alteration in sense as well as language. Take for example the well-known passage from the Declaration of Independence:

195   *We hold these truths to be self-evident, that all men are created equal, that they are endowed by their Creator with certain inalienable rights, that among these are life, liberty and the pursuit of happiness. That to secure these rights, Governments are instituted among men, deriving their powers from the consent of the governed. That whenever any form of Government*
200   *becomes destructive of those ends, it is the right of the People to alter or abolish it, and to institute new Government . . .*

It would have been quite impossible to render this into Newspeak while keeping to the sense of the original. The nearest one could come to doing so would be to swallow the whole passage up in the single word
205   *crimethink*. A full translation could only be an ideological translation, whereby Jefferson's words would be changed into a panegyric on absolute government.

•   •   •   •

Study Openers

1. Distinguish the "A vocabulary," the "B vocabulary," and the "C vocabulary." Why is this distinction important? How does it relate to the functions of *definition* as discussed in Chapter 13 (page 141)?
2. Show how the language of Newspeak could be used as an instrument for achieving and maintaining cultural conformity.
3. Do you notice any parallel tendencies in the vocabularies used in our own culture, even though the tendencies may be unconscious? What strategy would you propose for intensifying or reducing such tendencies—and why?
4. Select a sample from any article or speech or news release which defends or attacks a public (or campus) policy. Rewrite it, using the principles of Newspeak. Submit it together with the original.

Our Own Baedeker
by John Updike

(*Assorted Prose*, 1965)

In Antarctica, everything turns left. Snow swirls to the left; seals, penguins, and skua gulls pivot to the left; the sun moves around the horizon
right to left; and lost men making a determined effort to bear right find
they have made a perfect left circle. Sunlight vibrating between white
snow and white clouds creates a white darkness, in which landmarks and   5
shadows disappear. A companion three feet away may vanish, and moments later rematerialize. On the other hand, whales and ships appear
inverted in the sky. The sun may appear to rise and set five times in a
day. Mountains actually over the horizon seem to loom close at hand.
Minor irregularities in the ice tower like steeples. All these illusions are   10
created by a combination of the oblique solar rays, the refraction and
reflection of light among strata of warm and cold air, and the appalling
lucidity of a dust-free, nearly vaporless atmosphere. In unclouded sunshine, the eye can follow an observation balloon for sixteen miles of its
ascent into an inky-purple sky. Sudden veils of intense blueness fall over   15
the world and in a few minutes are mysteriously lifted. When the sun is
low, the sky appears green. Men exhale, in their crystallized breath, iri-
descent rainbows. Weather rainbows are white. The wind-driven snow
charges men's noses and fingertips with static electricity, which is given
off as a phantom luminescence.   20
   For centuries, the continent itself was a phantom. From the time men
first recognized that the earth was spherical, a great land mass in the
south was imagined. In 1539, Emperor Charles V, of the Holy Roman
Empire, appointed Pedro Sancho de Hoz governor of an area shown on
maps of the period as stretching from the tip of South America across the   25
pole to China. European scholars equated southerliness with fecundating
warmth. Alexander Dalrymple, an eighteenth-century hydrographer for
England's East India Company, predicted that the human population of
the unknown continent would be found to exceed fifty million. In 1768,
Lieutenant James Cook was sent by the British on a secret mission to lo-   30
cate the southern land mass and "to observe the genius, temper, disposition, and number of the natives and endeavour by all proper means to
cultivate a friendship and alliance with them." Cook was unable to pene-
trate the ice pack, and concluded that if a continent lay beyond it, it
was uninhabitable and inhospitable. How true! Antarctica more nearly   35
resembles Mars than the earth we live on. It has no trees, no rivers, no

land animals except a few degenerate insects, no vegetation other than
some doughty moss and lichen, and no political or economic significance,
though it may have some any day now. Permanent bases are being es-
40   tablished by scientists of many of the nations involved in the antarctic
aspect of the International Geophysical Year 1957–58. Russia thus far
has not pressed the claims that the offshore explorations of Czar Alexander I's Admiral von Bellingshausen might justify. In 1948, though, the
Kremlin ominously resurrected and published his report. Hitler once
45   dropped thousands of swastika-stamped darts into a mammoth stretch of
ice, named it New Swabia, and left it at that. Britain, France, Norway,
Australia, New Zealand, Chile, and Argentina profess to own wedges of
the pie. The United States has recognized no claims. Our antarctic policy, reportedly due for an overhaul, was established by Secretary of State
50   Hughes in 1924, when he asserted that the *sine qua non* of territorial
rights is permanent settlement.*

Rain and disease are practically strangers to the antarctic. The air is
sterilized by ultraviolet rays, which are present in enormous quantities.
Penguins, tough birds in other ways, have no resistance to germs. Ex-
55   peditions never catch cold until they return to civilization. In a sense,
the continent lacks even time. In 1947, members of Byrd's expedition
visited the hut of the English explorer Scott. In thirty-five years, nothing
had changed. The London magazine on the table could have been
printed the day before. There was no rot in the timbers, no rust on
60   the nailheads, no soot on the windowsills. Outside, a sledge dog that had
frozen while standing up still stood there and looked alive. Explorers
have no qualms about eating food that was cached decades previously.
Admiral Byrd, the world's leading Antarcticophile, has suggested that
the land might be used as a refrigerator for the world's food surpluses.
65   Books could also be stored there, out of geopolitical harm's way and in
an air where even the tabloids would not yellow. Were it not for the

---

* This remains our policy. In 1959 the United States proposed a treaty, accepted by
twelve nations, which would preserve Antarctica as a territory of scientific research
free from national claims. Though several nations, including the United States and the
Soviet Union, have established year-round bases, Antarctica remains the most amicable
of continents. Russo-American amicability has a long history here: Captain Nathaniel
Palmer's claim to be its discoverer (In November, 1820, he sighted a strange coast-
line still named the Palmer Peninsula) was obligingly reinforced by von Bellingshausen, who habitually referred to the land mass as "Palmer's Land." Since 1956,
scientific exploration, besides collecting much meteorological data, has discovered several striking mountain ranges and unexpected warm patches. The thesis that the
continent is divided, beneath the bridging ice, by a strait between the Ross and
Weddell seas has been advanced and generally rejected. Admiral Richard Byrd, whose
lifelong devotion to the antarctic spanned the eras of individual heroism and of
massive mechanized assault, died in 1957.

lung-scorching effect of sub-zero temperatures, this highest and driest of
continents would make an excellent tuberculosis sanatorium. Antarctica
is a plateau. Its mean altitude is six thousand feet—twice that of Asia, its
tallest competitor. Its land area equals that of Australia and the United   70
States combined. The seas surrounding it are not only the roughest but
the richest in the world, with a greater weight of diatoms and plankton
than tropical waters have. The land probably contains all the baser metals. Its resources of coal are judged to be the largest in the world—a geological puzzle, since there is no reason to assume that the south-polar   75
region was ever warm enough for luxuriant vegetation. The most prominent thesis, supported by glacier scratches and the wide-ranging fossils
of the primitive fern Glossopteris, posits Gondwanaland—a vast continent in the southern hemisphere two hundred million years ago, when
the flat, swampy earth supported gigantic tree ferns, abundant mosses,   80
and the earliest vertebrates. According to the "continental drift" theory,
this mass of land shifted around a good bit, the surface of the earth being as loose as a puppy's skin, and eventually fragmented into the pieces
now called Africa, South America, Australia, New Zealand, and Antarctica—the last a once tropical realm brought to rest at the bottom of the   85
world and buried in ice.

   Ice—of two sorts, white (compressed snow) and blue-green (frozen
water)—is what Antarctica has lots of. Ten quadrillion tons, say, plus a
few billion created by the lack of centrifugal force near the poles. A man
weighs almost a pound more at the South Pole than he does at the equa-   90
tor. Glaciers, sliding on water melted by the pressure of their own
weight, flow away from the pole, squeeze through notches in the rim of
mountain ranges, and extend themselves over the sea in the form of ice
shelves. The largest shelf, the Ross, has the area of France. Chips as big
as Manhattan crack off the shelves. These icebergs are carved by wind   95
and waves into the shapes of palaces, cathedrals, pagodas, men, and angels before dissolving in temperate waters. In 1927, one was measured
and found to be a hundred miles square—the size of two Connecticuts.
The snow precipitation does not equal the ice lost in the form of bergs,
so a recession of the icecap is believed to be taking place. Were it to   100
melt completely, seeds held in suspension millions of years might germinate. Strange viruses and bacteria could be unleashed on the world. Now
York City would be under three hundred feet of water. This is not likely
to happen in our time.

Annotation
   Baedeker: a tourist's guidebook, after Karl Baedeker, publisher of a popular
series of such books.

Study Openers

This description of the strange and hostile continent of Antarctica is offered as an illustration of fine detail—highly specific and thoroughly cataloged.

1. "Our Own Baedeker" builds from a series of catalogs, each of which accumulates details to fill out a general topic (see Chapter 14, page 152). Thus the opening paragraph catalogs those details which bear upon the *visual qualities* of Antarctica. List the other catalogs which you can identify. Are they presented in any special order?
2. From what sources could such details be gathered? (Updike, though a well-known writer of fiction, has no reputation as a polar observer, nor does he cite personal experience for this piece.)
3. A reader's first reaction to this piece might be that Updike has thrown in everything but the kitchen sink—that he has packed in *too much* detail. What kind of material has he left out which he *might* have included—for example, a census of people now living on Antarctica? What is your final judgment about the quantity and range of Updike's detail?
4. Using a similar approach, find library and other materials to support a description of one of the following places: Sri Lanka, Afghanistan, Falkland Islands, Madagascar, Greenland. Write the description (at a suggested length of five pages) and add a list of your sources.

Ode to Thanksgiving
by Michael J. Arlen

(*The New Yorker*, November 27, 1978)

Here follows what is doubtless intended as a seasonal message from our Holiday Correspondent:

At last, it is time to speak the truth about Thanksgiving. The truth is this: it is not a really great holiday. Consider the imagery. Dried corn-
5   husks hanging on the door! Terrible wine! Cranberry jelly in little bowls of extremely doubtful provenance which everyone is required to handle with the greatest of care! Consider the participants, the merrymakers. Men and women (also children) who have survived passably well through the years, mainly as a result of living at considerable distances
10   from their dear parents and beloved siblings, who on this feast of feasts must apparently forgather (as if beckoned by an aberrant Fairy God-mother), usually by circuitous routes, through heavy traffic, at a common meeting place, where the very moods, distempers, and obtrusive personal habits that have kept them happily apart since adulthood are

then and there encouraged to slowly ferment beneath the cornhusks, and   15
gradually rise with the aid of the terrible wine, and finally burst forth
out of control under the stimulus of the cranberry jelly! No, it is a mockery of a holiday. For instance: *Thank you, O Lord, for what we are about
to receive.* This is surely not a gala concept. There are no presents, unless one counts Aunt Bertha's sweet rolls a present, which no one does.   20
There is precious little in the way of costumery: miniature plastic turkeys
and those witless Pilgrim hats. There is no sex. Indeed, Thanksgiving is
the one day of the year (a fact known to everybody) when all thoughts
of sex completely vanish, evaporating from apartments, houses, condo-
miniums, and mobile homes like steam from a bathroom mirror.   25

Consider also the nowhereness of the time of the year. The last week
or so in November. It is obviously not yet winter: winter, with its death-
dealing blizzards and its girls in tiny skirts pirouetting on the ice. On
the other hand, it is certainly not much use to anyone as fall: no golden
leaves or Oktoberfests, and so forth. Instead, it is a no man's land between 30
the seasons. In the cold and sobersides northern half of the country, it is
a vaguely unsettling interregnum of long, mournful walks beneath leafless trees: the long, mournful walks following the midday repast with the
dread inevitability of pie following turkey, and the leafless trees looming
or standing about like eyesores, and the ground either as hard as iron or   35
slightly mushy, and the light snow always beginning to fall when one is
halfway to the old green gate—flecks of cold, watery stuff plopping between neck and collar, for the reason that, it being not yet winter, one
has forgotten or not chosen to bring along a muffler. It is a corollary to
the long, mournful Thanksgiving walk that the absence of this muffler   40
is quickly noticed and that four weeks or so later, at Christmastime, instead of the Sony Betamax one had secretly hoped the children might
have chipped in together to purchase, one receives another muffler—by
then the thirty-third. Thirty-three mufflers! Some walk! Of course, things
are more fun in the warm and loony southern part of the country. No   45
snow there of any kind. No need of mufflers. Also, no long, mournful
walks, because in the warm and loony southern part of the country everybody drives. So everybody drives over to Uncle Jasper's house to watch
the Cougars play the Gators, a not entirely unimportant conflict, which
will determine whether the Gators get a bowl bid or must take another   50
post-season exhibition tour of North Korea. But no sooner do the Cougars
kick off (an astonishing end-over-end squiggly thing that floats lazily
above the arena before plummeting down toward K. C. McCoy and
catching him on the helmet) than Auntie Em starts hustling turkey. Soon
Cousin May is slamming around the bowls and platters, and Cousin   55
Bernice is oohing and ahing about "all the fixin's," and Uncle Bob is making low, insincere sounds of appreciation: "Yummy, yummy, Auntie Em,

I'll have me some more of these delicious yams!" Delicious yams? Uncle
Bob's eyes roll wildly in his head. Billy Joe Quaglino throws his long
60   bomb in the middle of Grandpa Morris saying grace, Grandpa Morris
speaking so low nobody can hear him—which is just as well, since he is
reciting what he can remember of his last union contract; and then, just
as J. B. (Speedy) Snood begins his ninety-two-yard punt return, Auntie
Em starts dealing second helpings of her famous stuffing to everyone, as
65   if she were pushing a controlled substance, which it well might be, since
there are no easily recognizable ingredients visible to the naked eye.

     Consider for a moment the Thanksgiving meal itself. It has become a
sort of refuge for endangered species of starch: sweet potatoes, cauliflower, pumpkin, mince (whatever "mince" is), those blessed yams.
70   Bowls of luridly colored yams, with no taste at all, lying torpid under a
lava flow of marshmallow! And then the sacred turkey. One might as
well try to construct a holiday repast around a fish—say, a nice piece of
boiled haddock. After all, turkey tastes very similar to haddock: same
consistency, same quite remarkable absence of flavor. But then, if the
75   Thanksgiving pièce de résistance were a nice piece of boiled haddock
instead of turkey, there wouldn't be all that fun for Dad when Mom
hands him the sterling-silver, bone-handled carving set (a wedding present from her parents and not sharpened since) and then everyone stands
around pretending not to watch while he saws and tears away at the
80   bird as if he were trying to burrow his way into or out of some grotesque,
fowl-like prison.

     What of the good side to Thanksgiving, you ask. There is always a
good side to everything. Not to Thanksgiving. There is only a bad side
and then a worse side. For instance, Grandmother's best linen tablecloth
85   is a bad side: the fact that it is produced each year, in the manner of a
red flag being produced before a bull, and then is always spilled upon by
whichever child is doing poorest at school that term and so is in need of
greatest reassurance. Thus: "Oh, my God, *Veronica,* you just spilled
grape juice [or "plum wine" or "tar"] on Grandmother's best linen table-
90   cloth!" But now comes worse. For at this point Cousin Bill, the one who
lost all Cousin Edwina's money on the car dealership three years ago and
has apparently been drinking steadily since Halloween, bizarrely chooses
to say, "Seems to me those old glasses are *always* falling over." To which
Auntie Meg is heard to add, "Somehow I don't remember *receivin'* any
95   of those old glasses." To which Uncle Fred replies, "That's because you
and George decided to go on vacation to *Hawaii* the summer Grandpa
Sam was dying." Now Grandmother is sobbing, though not so uncon-
trollably that she cannot refrain from murmuring, "I think that volcano
painting I threw away by mistake got sent me from Hawaii, heaven
100 knows why." But the gods are merciful, even the Pilgrim-hatted god of

cornhusks and soggy stuffing, and there is an end to everything, even to
Thanksgiving. Indeed, there is a grandeur to the feelings of finality and
doom which usually settle on a house after the Thanksgiving celebration
is over, for with the completion of Thanksgiving Day the year itself has
been properly terminated—shot through the cranium with a high-velocity   105
candied yam. At this calendrical nadir, all energy on the planet has gone,
all fun has fled, all the terrible wine has been drunk.

But then, overnight, life once again begins to stir, emerging, even by
the next morning, in the form of Japanese window displays and Taiwan-
ese Christmas lighting, from the primeval ooze of the nation's department 110
stores. Thus, a new year dawns, bringing with it immediate and cheering
possibilities of extended consumer debt, office-party flirtations, good—or,
at least, mediocre—wine, and visions of cheapskate excursion fares to
Montego Bay. It is worth noting, perhaps, that this true new year always
starts with the same mute, powerful mythic ceremony: the surreptitious   115
tossing out, in the early morning, of all those horrid aluminum-foil pack-
ages of yams and cauliflower and stuffing and red, gummy cranberry substance which have been squeezed into the refrigerator as if a reënact-
ment of the siege of Paris were expected. Soon afterward, the phoenix of
Christmas can be observed as it slowly rises, beating its drumsticks, once 120
again goggle-eyed with hope and unrealistic expectations.

Study Openers

1. Point to a dozen word-choices or so which most clearly convey the writer's
   feeling about Thanksgiving. (Chapter 15, page 159)
2. As an exercise in the use of connotative detail, write two comparable descriptions of Thanksgiving. Use the first to convey outright anger toward
   the values of Thanksgiving. Use the second to convey a sentimental nostal-
   gia for Thanksgiving.
3. Write a comparable description of either Christmas or New Year's Eve.

(Other elements)

4. Explain the effectiveness or ineffectiveness of such metaphoric language as
   the following:

   "as if beckoned by an aberrant Fairy Godmother" (line 11).
   "All thoughts of sex completely vanish . . . like steam from a
   bathroom mirror" (line 23).
   "The time of year . . . is a no man's land between the seasons"
   (line 30).
   "bowls of luridly colored yams . . . lying torpid under a lava
   flow of marshmallow" (line 70).

Marriage Is Better
by Suzanne Britt Jordan

(*Newsweek*, June 11, 1979)

My friends, after eighteen years of marriage, are getting a "civilized divorce." I object. I certainly do not assume that I know what demons lurk beneath the surface of an apparently happy marriage. I'm not even sure what a happy marriage is, having only my own to go by. The divorce's
5   being "civilized" bothers me even more than the divorce itself. It is rather like carefully controlled, mature adults spanking their children *after* they have cooled off. I think people should be upset about so serious a thing as divorce. There is a redeeming quality in the honest screech and howl that I miss in our psychoanalyzed "together" generation.
10   These friends are the last people, the very last, I would have expected to be having a lousy marriage. He is a kindly, chatty fellow, given to washing his car on Saturday morning and taking his dog for long walks. She is a neat, unassuming, mostly friendly woman who doesn't mind keeping an eye on our house when we go out of town.
15   You could set your clock by these people, so ordered and peaceful were their lives together. He always had his cocktail at five. Their pyracantha is sculptured to the garden wall, their grass is neatly edged, their ducks are in a row. But this quiet pair, without so much as a shout echoing through the neighborhood, is ready, as the husband put it, "to
20 hang it up after eighteen years." They made this momentous decision in the middle of a casual conversation. They had given the marriage everything they had, and *still* it wasn't exciting. She says they are more like friends, or brother and sister, than husband and wife. She says the marriage has no spark, no oomph. She is very much interested in the "spark"
25 business.
     Perhaps I was in the kitchen slinging hash when the decree went out that marriages in the twentieth century required pizzazz, romance, thrills. Perhaps I've got old-fashioned notions about this once venerable but now crumbling institution. But my insides tell me that what everybody else
30 is doing is not necessarily right. And what folks have dumped on marriage in the way of expectations, selfish interests and kinky kicks needs prompt removal before the marriage fortress is crushed by the barbarians.
     Marriage is nothing more nor less than a permanent promise between two consenting adults, and often, but not always, under God, to cling to
35 each other unto death. It sounds pretty grim, I know. But then we have a perfect model in our children and relatives for how marriage should be

viewed. I cannot, at any time, send my children back to some other
womb for a fresh start. I've got a few cousins, aunts, uncles, nieces and
nephews with whom I might like to deny kinship, but I can't, any more
than I can change the color of my eyes. My parents are my parents,   40
whether I speak to them or not. In the same way, the husband and wife
are one flesh, forever. If I divorce my husband, I am, in effect, cutting
off part of myself. I think we have forgotten the fundamental basis of
marriage, a notion that has nothing to do with moonlight and roses and
my own personal wishes.   45

Marriage is a partnership far more than a perpetual honeymoon. Anybody who stays married can tell you that. It may be made in heaven,
but it is lived on earth. And because earth is the way it is, marriage is
often irritating, hellatious, unsatisfying, boring and shaky. I myself, as a
human being, am not always such a prize. Some days I wouldn't have   50
me on a silver platter. But those seekers after the perfect marriage are
convinced that the spouse will display perfection. The perfect mate, despite what Cosmopolitan says, does not exist, no matter how many of
those tests you take.

We have all sorts of convenient excuses for not staying married these   55
days. In the old days, you are probably saying, people didn't live as long,
so a spouse could safely assume that his partner would kick the bucket
in five or ten years and the one still breathing could have another go at
it. Wrong. People are actually living only a few years longer than they
did in the last century if they survived the childhood diseases. The re- 60
ports of our increased longevity are greatly exaggerated.

We are also informed that marriage should be a place where we can
grow, find ourselves, be ourselves. Interestingly, we cannot be entirely
ourselves even with our best friends. Some decorum, some courtesy, some
selflessness are demanded. As for finding myself, I think I already know   65
where I am. I'm grown up; I have responsibilities; I am in the middle of
a lifelong marriage; I am hanging in there, sometimes enduring, sometimes enjoying. For some reason, we assume that people can't stay married for life, but we make no such assumption about staying on the same
job, keeping the same religion or voting the same ticket. "But marriage is   70
harder, more complex, more *intimate,*" you say. Well, yes, sort of. But the
difference is not as great as you think. I probably spend more waking
hours on my job with my colleagues than I do at home with my husband.
Intimate, yes. Prison, no.

It is true some people have marriages that defy hell itself in descrip-   75
tion. Spouses may be psychotic, alcoholic, sexually perverted or dangerous. Yet, we *do* promise to remain faithful in sickness and in health. And

certainly the above-mentioned abominations are evidences of deep mental and emotional sickness.

80   Conscientious adults should first ask themselves before they get a divorce whether their marriages are truly intolerable, cannot endure another instant, whether they risk life and limb by remaining. Most of the time, I submit, the answer will be no. People can get well, can change. Even if they don't, we would have to admit that we *chose* marriage, that

85   there is something of value even, or perhaps especially, in disinterested love, which goes on caring for the beloved long after whatever quality first attracted us to him has been lost. I am most emphatically *not* talking about martyrdom. I am talking about consciously striving to improve an intolerable situation by the cheerful performance of our marriage

90   duties.

My original objection was primarily to the flippancy with which we say goodbye to a mediocre or poor marriage. We are so selfish. We want our fun, and we want it *now*. We value pleasure above fidelity, loyalty, generosity and duty. My friends might have remained married if they

95   had stopped clutching greedily at pleasure. The "spark" might have returned if they had gently fanned the fire. And even if the spark never returned, they might nevertheless have lived lovingly and patiently and kindly together. There are worse fates—not the least of which is finding another, even less satisfactory, second mate.

Study Openers

1. Point to examples of the analogical language (i.e., metaphors or figures of speech) which Jordan uses. (Chapter 16, page 173) Which ones do you find rather commonplace—like "kick the bucket," line 57—and which seem more original? To what extent would you defend both categories in this essay?
2. Jordan uses analogical argument in lines 35–42 when she likens the permanence of marriage to the permanence of parenthood and other blood relationships. Do you find this argument effective?

(Other elements)

3. Show how this essay uses a contrast pattern of development. (Chapter 7, page 64)
4. Describe the characterization of the "writer" and how it affects the impact of this piece. (Chapter 10, page 101)
5. Write an imaginary dialog between Jordan and Germaine Greer (page 370) on the value of marriage.

United Technologies Corporation

(advertisement, 1981)

Aim So High You'll Never Be Bored

The
greatest waste
of our
natural resources
is the
number of
people
who never
achieve their
potential.
Get out
of that
slow lane.
Shift
into that
fast lane.
If you think
you can't,
you won't.
If you think
you can,
there's a
good chance
you will.
Even making
the effort
will make
you feel
like a new
person.
Reputations
are made
by searching
for things that
can't be done
and doing them.
Aim low:
boring.
Aim high:
soaring.

Study Openers

This ad illustrates some sophisticated possibilities in basic sentence building
(Chapter 17, page 184).

1. What do you make of its vertical format? What purposes might it serve?
2. Comment on the effectiveness of sentence variety in this ad.
3. Work out three alternate versions of this material as follows, and compare
   their presumed impact:

   a. The exact same text with traditional margins.
   b. The same passage reworked into only three sentences or less.
   c. The passage re-ordered.

(Other elements)

4. What do you observe about these additional features?

   a. Use of analogical language (metaphors or figures of speech,
      Chapter 16, page 173).
   b. Patterns in rhythm and sound. (Chapter 20 will cover this mat-
      ter in more detail.)

Maturity

(from Ann Landers' column of July 11, 1982)

DEAR ANN LANDERS: Over the past several years you have printed
many versions of your definition of maturity. My favorite is the one I
clipped when I was in high school. The date is blurred and I can't read
it, but I am sending it on in the hope that you will run it again. I want
5 to give it to my son, who is exactly the same age as I when I first read it.
Thanks a million for serving two generations.

                                          H. G., GROSSE POINT, MICH.

DEAR MICH.: Here it is—with pleasure.

10 Maturity is many things. First it is the ability to base a judgment on
the Big Picture—the Long Haul. It means being able to pass up the fun-
for-the-minute and select the course of action that will pay off later. One
of the characteristics of infancy is the I-want-it-NOW approach. Grownup
people are able to wait.

15 Maturity is the ability to stick with a project or a situation until it is
finished. The person who is constantly changing jobs, changing friends
and changing mates is immature. Everything seems to turn sour after
awhile.

Maturity is the ability to face unpleasantness, frustration, discomfort and defeat without complaint or collapse. The mature person knows he can't have everything his own way. Nobody wins 'em all. He is able to   20
defer to circumstances, to other people—and to time.

Maturity means doing what is expected of you, and this means being dependable. It means keeping your word. Bound in with dependability is personal integrity. Do you mean what you say—and say what you mean?

The world is filled with people who can't be counted on. They are   25
never around in a crisis. They break promises and substitute alibis for performance. They show up late—or not at all. They are confused and disorganized. Their lives are a maze of unfinished business. Such behavior suggests a lack of self-discipline—which is a large part of maturity.

Maturity is the ability to make a decision and stick with it, riding out   30
the storms that may follow. This requires clear thinking. And the courage to stand by your position once you've taken it.

Immature people spend a lifetime exploring possibilities and then doing nothing. Action requires courage. And courage means maturity.

Maturity is the ability to harness your abilities and your energies and   35
do more than is expected. The mature person refuses to settle for mediocrity. He would rather aim high and miss the mark than aim low—and make it.

Study Openers

1. This column exploits parallel sentence structure and climactic structure (Chapter 17, page 184). Evaluate the contribution of each.

(Other elements)

2. Defining a term by contrast with its opposite—here, maturity versus immaturity—is not usually put forward as an essential tactic in definition. (On definition, see Chapter 13, page 141.) Why not? To what extent does it succeed here?

On Being a Possibilist
by Max Lerner

(*Newsweek*, October 8, 1979)

In a time such as ours, when man acts like a wolf to man, it may seem more than a little absurd to question the prevailing gloom. Yet I want to break a lance in defense of the possible.

In my teaching, lecturing and column writing, I get a question thrust
at me constantly: "Are you an optimist or a pessimist?" At times I get
impatient. Do they think this is Wall Street, where you are bullish or
bearish about stocks you can't control? Our destiny as a people rests not
in our stars but in ourselves. I am neither optimist nor pessimist. I am a
possibilist.

To believe either that everything is bound to work out or that nothing
will ever work out is equally an exercise in mindlessness. There are no
blank-check guarantees that we will survive and prosper, and no inevitability that we won't. I believe in the possible. More options are
open for us than we dare admit. Everything depends on our collective
intelligence in making choices, and our will to carry them out.

The prevailing view is that all our options have narrowed. I don't believe it. There is a sense of being trapped—the feeling that nothing we
do makes much difference. Which leads to frantic group pressures and
single-issue politics, or to the cynical rejection of all forms of public life
and to a wallowing in our egos.

Let's face it. We used up our resources, polluted our environment and
laid staggering burdens on our government. Which means we must now
place limits on our desires, needs, greeds. The historians call it the Age
of Limits.

Civil-Rights Movement

But it is equally an Age of Breakthroughs which compensate for the narrowed options. It is hard to see this because the limits are concrete and
urgent while the breakthroughs are less visible.

But they are nonetheless real. I ask the black students in my seminars:
would you rather have come of age in the years before the civil-rights
movement—or now? I ask the women of every age: would you rather be
living in the days of male power and swagger, with slim options for jobs
and careers and meager life chances—or now?

I ask the professionals—the athletes, film and TV performers, photog-
raphers, playwrights, musicians, architects, writers, artists of every kind:
would you rather have plied your craft before the large audiences were
opened up to you—or now?

I ask the young scientists, the doctors and researchers, teachers, law
and medical students, staff workers, young business executives: would
you rather have lived and worked before the great breakthroughs of the
knowledge revolution—or now?

I ask the code breakers who deviate from the narrow social norms of
the past, and who have found new life-styles: would you rather have

lived before society accepted your life-ways, and before the breakthroughs that gave you a new identity—or now?   45

I say to the chronologically aging who still feel young in spirit: would
you rather have lived out your years at a time when elderly Americans
were shunted aside and were held to have lost their capacity to function
creatively—or now?

I hold with Freud that civilizations are caught between the twin gods,   50
Eros and Thanatos—love and death, the life-affirming and life-denying
principles. I find the conventional terms like "liberal" and "conservative"
less and less useful. What counts is whether we are on the side of life
affirmations or life denials. If I have to belong to a party, I am of the
party of Eros, not of Thanatos.   55

I am no believer in automatic progress. I have experienced too much
to wear blinders readily. But I can point to the real revolutions in process—in research, in access to life chances, in sexual attitudes, in awareness of the phases of the life cycle, in values and life-styles. The sixties
were the most revolutionary decade in American history. The revolutions   60
of the seventies—and those to come in the eighties—were and will be less
dramatic and visible but they may prove deeper.

An Age of Trade-offs

We have too long allowed ourselves to be blinkered by the naysayers of
our time. An Age of Limits can also be an Age of Trade-offs. As a possi-   65
bilist I believe there are practical ways to resolve conflicts by contriving
trade-offs in which you swap something marginal or formal to achieve
what neither camp can do without. We see it done every day in the Supreme Court decisions, which give trade-offs the authority of law. I have
to add, however, that you can't trade off the essential life principle for a   70
death principle.

I am aware of the uprootings and unravelings which threaten the cultural health of America. Every society has them, but ours seem to be
piling up—the fragmenting of life, the battering of the family, the erosion
of work, the breaking of connections, the intensity of pressure-group and   75
single-issue politics, the imperial ego, the conspiracy hunting, the cult of
the image, the moral relativism, the ethics of "anything goes," the refusal
to see anything in life as sacred.

Yet, to counter this, America for me, even today, is the world's most
revolutionary culture. It is in a phase of rapid change which belies the   80
familiar charge of decay. In every area of thought and action, those who
know most testify to the stunning, almost unimaginable transformations

they are witnessing in their fields. How then can the civilization as a whole be stagnant or dying?

85   Inner Changes

The great event of the twentieth century—greater than the Russian or Chinese revolutions—has been America's defining of itself as a complex civilization, growing and enduring amidst the wrack of change. People around the world recognize it. They want to come here—by boat, by
90   plane, by swimming, by cutting the barbed wire at the frontiers, by sneaking in. Their instinct is sounder than the self-hating doubts of some intellectuals.

The violences and excesses, the uprootings and unravelings of our culture are best seen as the agonizing inner changes of a social organism as
95   it moves toward a higher degree of complexity. They are evidences not of a senile but of a still-adolescent society, not of a dying civilization but of one that has not wholly found itself. If America dies, it will not be of a running down of energies but of an explosion of energies.

Call this the manifesto of a possibilist. When I am asked whether
100   America has come to the end of its tether, my answer is that of the lyric in "Porgy and Bess": "It ain't necessarily so." I believe, as yeasayers have insisted from Walt Whitman to Thomas Wolfe to our own day, that the true discovery of America still lies ahead.

Study Openers

1. Evaluate the following features of sentence structure in Lerner's essay. (See Chapters 17–19, pages 184–222).

      a. Sentence fragments.
      b. Sentence variety.
      c. Parallel structure.

(Other elements)

2. How does Lerner define "possibilism"? Has he sufficiently differentiated it from "optimism"? (See Chapter 13, page 141.) Do you share the convictions implicit in the term?
3. Note the heavy presence of the writer as "I." How do you think it reinforces or weakens the essay?

QUESTION

4

DO CIGARETTE COMPANIES WANT KIDS TO SMOKE?

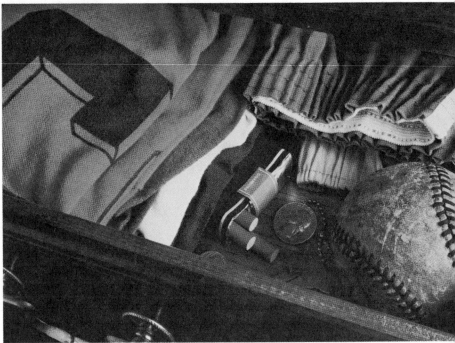

most asked questions about cigarettes.

No. As a matter of policy. No. As a matter of practice. No. As a matter of fact. No!

The unfortunate fact is that some kids do smoke. But, while cigarette sales continue to increase, fewer teenagers are smoking. For example, according to the American Cancer Society, smoking among young women has decreased 17 percent since 1974.

All of us need a time of "growing up" to develop the mature judgment to do so many things. Like driving. Voting. Raising a family. And knowing enough to make an informed decision about all sorts of adult activities.

In our view, smoking is an adult custom and the decision to smoke should be based on mature and informed individual freedom of choice.

For more information, write for our booklet, "Answers to the most asked questions about cigarettes." Address: The Tobacco Institute, Suite 841, 1875 Eye Street, Northwest, Washington, D.C. 20006. We offer it in the belief that full and free discussion of these important public issues is in the public interest.

Answers to the most asked questions about cigarettes.

WEIGH BOTH SIDES
BEFORE YOU TAKE SIDES.

Study Openers

1. Like many other effective ads, the Tobacco Institute message uses rhythm and sound. Show where these elements appear. Do you find them well used?

(Other elements)

2. Do you think that this message favors or disapproves of the use of cigarettes in general? Why do you think so?
3. How does the characterization of the "writer" (i.e., the Tobacco Institute) affect the impact of this message? (Chapter 10, page 101).
4. Devise a comparable public interest message which might be issued by a fictitious "handguns institute" or "alcohol institute" or "birth control institute." Either include a picture or indicate the possible contents of a supporting photo.

"Learning" to Give Up
by Albert Rosenfeld

(*Saturday Review*, September 3, 1977)

We all have an intuitive knowledge—supported by personal experience and common sense, reinforced by religious beliefs and folk wisdom—that our attitudes toward life are of critical importance to our enjoyment of it. Whether we overcome our problems or not (or in some crisis situations, whether we even survive or not) may depend on whether or not   5
we have hope, whether we give up or keep on trying.

Over the past few decades, biologists and psychologists have been carrying out some fascinating research that reconfirms how powerfully our mental outlook can affect the outcome of our life situations.

You can, for example, do a simple experiment (as Dr. Curt Richter of   10
Johns Hopkins has done repeatedly) with two rats: hold one rat in your hand firmly so that no matter how valiantly he struggles he cannot escape. He will finally give up. Now throw that quiescent rat into a tank of warm water. He will sink, not swim. He has "learned" that there is nothing he can do, that there is no point in struggling. Now throw an-   15
other rat into the water—one that doesn't "know" that his situation is hopeless and that he is therefore helpless. This rat will swim to safety.

Another experiment (done by Dr. Martin E. P. Seligman of the University of Pennsylvania), this time with dogs: suspend a dog in a hammock into which he fits so snugly that he cannot get loose. Give him   20

electric shocks. He will struggle for a while, then just lie there and submit. Later, take the same dog and put him down on one side of a grid that is only half electrified. Though he is perfectly free to get up and move to the unelectrified side, he will sit where he is, enduring the shock,
25 resigned to his fate. Put another dog down in the same spot—a dog that hasn't been taught to be helpless—and he'll move around until he finds an area that doesn't shock him.

Okay. Fine for rats and dogs. But what about people?

Seligman has been one of the pioneering investigators of the ways in
30 which people's perceptions of themselves as being helpless can in fact render them helpless. His seminal book, *Helplessness: On Depression, Development and Death,* has influenced many other psychologists to pursue this fruitful area of research. Here is a sample Seligman experiment:

35 Take two groups of college students and put them in rooms where they are blasted with noise turned up to almost intolerable levels. In one room there is a button that turns off the noise. The students quickly notice it, push it, and are rewarded with blissful silence. In the other room, however, there is no turn-off button. The students look for one, find
40 nothing, and finally give up. There is no way to escape the noise (except to leave the room before a previously agreed-upon time period has elapsed), so they simply endure.

Later, the same two groups are put in two other rooms. This time, *both* rooms contain a switch-off mechanism—though not a simple button this
45 time and not as easy to find. Nevertheless, the group that found the button the first time succeeds in finding the "off" switch the second time, too. But the second group, already schooled in the hopelessness of their circumstances, doesn't even search. Its members just sit it out again.

There is an obvious parallel here. In each of the three cases—rats, dogs,
50 and students—the situation had changed decisively, but because their efforts for alleviation didn't work in the first instance, the "helpless" subjects didn't even try the second time.

Yes, you may say, but the students knew that at a given point the experiment would be over and the noise would stop. Otherwise they would
55 have been more highly motivated to keep on looking. Besides, in the first instance, no matter how motivated they may have been, no matter how hard they may have tried, there simply *was* no way to turn off the noise. Their efforts would have been futile. Aren't many life situations like that—no matter how hard you try, you're doomed to lose?

60 True enough. In at least one of Richter's rat experiments, for example, he wanted to know how long a rat would keep swimming to try to save itself. The rat swam for 60 hours before it drowned. Were some other rat

intelligent and articulate, it might observe this and say: See, what was
the point? All that effort for nothing. Wasn't that a foolish rat, to try so
hard?   65

No one suggests there is a guarantee that you'll win if you try. But
most of the rats in these experiments did, after all, swim to safety. And
even in this one instance, the experimenter might have changed his mind
in the interim or been influenced by some outside event to stop the experiment. In most human life situations, the outcome is not rigidly pre-   70
ordained. Many studies in clinical medicine, psychology, and anthropol-
ogy indicate that seriously ill patients who have hope are more likely to
survive than those who don't, that those who are highly motivated tend
to last longer—and are happier in the knowledge that they are putting up
a fight.   75

Some population groups are more susceptible to feelings of helplessness than are others: the elderly, for instance; and, as one might suspect,
blacks; and women of any color.

In a series of classroom experiments, Dr. Carol Dweck of the University of Illinois found that when girls fail in school, they tend to blame   80
the failure on their inability to master the subject matter. But boys
ascribe failure to not trying hard enough. Because girls are considered to
be neater, better-behaved, and harder-working, teachers assume that
they are already doing the best they can. Because boys are considered
to be sloppier and less diligent by nature, teachers tend to tell them,   85
"You can do better. You're just not trying hard enough." The boys believe it. They do try harder, and do better. Thus, for paradoxical reasons,
girls are inadvertently programmed to feel more helpless about improving their situations.

Consider another series of classroom experiments being carried out by   90
Dr. Rita Smith, a former student of Seligman's who is now in the African
studies program at Temple University in Philadelphia. She has been comparing the helplessness quotients of black and white children. Though
the research is incomplete and the results not yet published, it is already
quite apparent to Smith that black children, especially those from poor   95
families, give up much more easily than do white children of similar
economic status. If you give the two groups a problem that has no solution (as in the case of Seligman's college students in the room with no
turn-off button), the black pupils not only quit trying sooner but when
given a solvable problem next, they are more likely to be convinced a   100
priori that it can't be done—at least not by them. The white kids tend to
stay with the problem longer, and they don't assume they can't solve one
problem because they failed to solve the other.

Smith attributes these results to the *experience* of black children in a

105 world that does not respond very reliably to their attempts to exercise more control over their lives. The giving-up attitude becomes even more pronounced in the tenth grade than it was in the second grade (the two age groups Smith has been working with). By then, the kids have had eight more years of experience to reconfirm the apparent uselessness of
110 trying.

Whether you look at rats, dogs, or people, it's now abundantly clear that those who try harder do better. Intelligent organisms, says Seligman, automatically know how to help themselves: they keep trying; they have hope. Nor does this healthy tendency have to be learned. In fact, it is so
115 built-in, says Seligman, that even special training doesn't enhance it. But *helplessness,* he is convinced, *must be taught.* Most of us, to one extent or another, are guilty of teaching others helplessness and of permitting ourselves to learn it.

Science has many uses. Experiments such as those described may not
120 provide us with any technological breakthroughs. They do not "conquer" any diseases. But they do give us scientific validation of, and therefore greater confidence in, the value of traditional virtues such as perseverance and hope—which, in these times, is no small service.

Thus through research are our homely truisms doubly confirmed: hope
125 is healthier than despair, perseverance is more sensible than giving up, and helplessness can be self-imposed and therefore self-defeating. The same can be true even in the affairs of nations. One wonders how guilty of defeatism we all, including our statesmen, may be, when we keep saying, There always have been wars, and there always will be wars;
130 people are no damned good, and you can't change human nature; and so on. Whatever the case in point, the fact that "it didn't work last time" has nothing to do with next time. Next time we may swim to safety. Next time we may find a spot on the grid that doesn't give us a shock. Next time the room may have a turn-off switch.

Study Openers

On a relatively brief scale, Rosenfeld's essay illustrates many qualities of the extended paper, and will bear explicit application of the concepts of Chapters 21–23.

1. Evaluate the kind of support on which Rosenfeld bases his discussion. Would the essay benefit by the addition of footnotes and bibliography?
2. What patterns of development are used?
3. What parts of the essay function as "reinforcement" (page 242) in meeting the reader's possible objections?

(Other elements)

4. Does Rosenberg take enough stock of the positive value of "giving up"—
the good sense in realizing that the game is over, that the time has come
to shift investments?

5. Write an extended documented essay on when to give up and when not to.

The Ethics of a Housewife
by Yvonne Streeter

﹒(two drafts of a student paper, 1980)

(Early draft)

I recently put my ego on the line and asked my husband what accomplishments of mine caused him to respect me. He didn't name my delicious apple torte, which is scrumptious and a hit each time I serve it. He also didn't mention my part in raising our two children, who at 11 & 14 seem to be turning out to be pretty nice people. What he mentioned   5
was my scholastic record here at NCC. And that points out one of the greatest ethical problems of my principal occupation: that of being a housewife.

This problem is largely one of a conflict of interest: one's personal goals: respect, perhaps, and a paycheck versus the interests of one's   10
family. Women can be crackerjack housekeepers and wonderful parents but still not receive too much respect from the "outside" world. This loss of respect causes them to feel as though they aren't really doing anything useful. T. Berry Brazelton, a Harvard pediatrician, author of seven books, and one of the country's recognized experts in child care, tells the   15
story of sitting with his wife when she was asked what she did. Her reply, "nothing." Brazelton was shocked: "There she was, raising four children, running a big house for me and mine, and really was the anchor for all of us—and she calls it nothing."[1]

Margaret Mead, known to us largely through her profession, addressed   20
this problem in 1963, in response to a report by the President's Commission on the Status of Women:

> . . . none of the specific recommendations of the report are directed to the emotional conflicts and problems created for a married woman and her family if the woman takes a job. Nothing   25
> ing is said about women who would rather center their lives in the home. There is no real discussion of the values involved in a

choice between working outside the home for money and inside
the home for love. There is no emphasis on the mother's role as
30   an educator of her children (except a lip-service speech about
passing on tradition), and the concept of a woman as a wife to
her husband is missing entirely from the report. In fact, the report assumes that once the children are grown, women can stay
away from home for months at a time, if a career should require
35   it, and no one will suffer. . . .

There is no real recognition of the principal historical difference between women's and men's roles—no recognition of the
fact that while men generally have devoted themselves to organizing and exploiting the outside world of nature and society,
40   women have devoted most of their time and attention to the
care and well-being of individuals, primarily to their families.[2]

In the cover story of a recent Money magazine, Jane Bryant Quinn
tells how she feels about this responsibility and the guilt involved in
being a working mother. Her job is undeniably an important one, par-
45   ticularly if money is used as a measurement. Though her husband is a
lawyer, she's the largest wage earner (1980 family income: $250,000).
When asked about the impact of her work on her children, she answers:

This gets down to the question of traditional roles. One never
considers the impact on the children of the man not being there.
50   One thinks only of what might result if the woman isn't there.
But sure, I had terrible attacks of working-mother guilt. I don't
know of any woman of my generation who has not.

But do you want to know a wonderful thing? You give the
best of your time that you possibly can to your children. When
55   you're not working, you're devoting the time to mommy duty.
The Little League games are at seven o'clock, so you get an
earlier commuter train and you attend the games. You muddle
through.

She indicates her guilt is a result of society's expectations. Later in the
60   article on Quinn, she tells of a friend who told her at her own dinner
table, "Women who go right back to work after their children are born
are a disgrace."[3]

This conflict is at the heart of the homemaker's ethical problems.
Dorothy Rodgers, wife of song-writer Richard Rodgers, who appears to
65   have great respect for herself and other homemakers, says this:

We believe that the greatest stabilizing influences in the world
stem from family and personal relationships, and that home is
where it all starts. Husbands, children, careers, and where and
how you live—each influences and is in turn influenced by the
70   others. They are the stuff a woman's life is made of.[4]

On the other hand, here is what a London feminist has to say in a chapter called, "Myths of Woman's Place: Motherhood":

> The myth of motherhood contains three popular assertions. The first is the most influential: that children need mothers, the second is the obverse of this: that mothers need their children. The third assertion is a generalization which holds that motherhood represents the greatest achievement of a woman's life: the sole true means of self-realization. Women, in other words, need to be mothers. "Need" here is always vaguely specified, but usually means damage to mental or emotional health following on the denial of mothers to children, children to mothers, or motherhood to women.[5]

Finally, from a Dr. De Hoyos, in a book described as "a rational approach to an emotional issue," has this to say,

> Some extreme Feminist groups feel that the family enslaves and exploits women and that, therefore, it must be done away with; less extreme groups challenge the traditional organization of the family unit and campaign for drastic changes in its division of labor; and almost half of the married women in the United States today, by choosing to work, are unconsciously bringing to pass crucial changes in attitudes, role expectations, and accommodations within the family unit. These attacks, challenges, and actual changes undermine the concept of the traditional family as an institution.
>
> We recognize and accept that these attacks and challenges against the family unit are real symptoms of discontent among women.
>
> However, we reject the notion that, because the family unit today, is not completely fulfilling, it must be done away with.[6]

The first problem in a discussion of the job of a housewife is a definition of the term; does it mean only those who have no outside paying job? I have defined it loosely here to include those women who may have outside jobs, but still consider their prime responsibility to be homemaking. In an informal survey I took, even the women who had full-time jobs did virtually 100% of the housework, grocery buying, etc. The one woman who said her husband did the majority of the cooking had no children. This introduces the other aspect of a wife's job: most of her job requirements are changed and redefined when she has children. This relates also to the fact that the job is virtually a woman's job, with at least one exception I'll talk about later.

One of the things that most contributes to discontent is the belief by many housekeepers that their job doesn't fulfill any of society's needs, as

Dr. Brazelton's wife mentioned earlier. One reason for this may be the
lack of a visible paycheck. Another is the fairly recent downgrading of
the job. Going back to Money magazine, here are two rather opposing
views of the dignity of running a home. The first, a 59-year old Nobel
prize winner (in medicine), says, "I'm from that older school that
teaches you that the wife takes complete charge of the household. That
same talent it takes to run a laboratory permits you to run a house very
efficiently."[7] Another 25-year old member of a two-income household
sees the job as a rather frivolous one: when asked about having children,
said, "But I'd continue working. I couldn't be content to redecorate my
living room every six months or attend gourmet cooking classes with the
ladies of the neighborhood."[8]

Many magazine articles and feminist writers imply that real enjoyment in life can be only found with outside jobs. The lead article in this
magazine states, "For wives, working can be a joy no matter how high
the dishes may pile up at home. Those on a career track find that a deep
sense of fulfillment usually accompanies a professional paycheck." It
goes on to quote a University of Michigan psychologist who says motherhood alone is unsatisfying as an occupation because it is so transitory.
"It's difficult to make it a career unless you keep having babies every 2½
years until menopause."[9]

One very interesting book on being a housewife was written by a
man. A journalist, Mike McGrady was raised with the standard role expectations, when he and his wife put into practice the old folk-tale "How
the Peasant Kept House,"[10] about a husband and wife who traded jobs.
McGrady was ready for a change; his wife wanted to run her own business. For one year he became the housewife; she became the breadwin-
ner. Some of his observations about the job: He couldn't keep the house
clean; he started feeling jealous of her contact with the outside world;
he discovered he was a very good cook (that was the creative aspect of
the job they both enjoyed); he couldn't think of anything to say in the
company of men at parties. At the same time, his wife began to feel the
stress of family financial responsibility. Two of the plusses in his unaccustomed role: much less stress and a closer relationship with his
children. One surprise: his recipe for mayonnaise was a smash hit with
the macho men at his favorite bar.[11] Here's what he had to say about the
cleaning of houses:

> I've since learned that cleaning a house is very much like iron-
> ing clothes—the first experience is dreadful and the second one,
> worse. These tasks require a numbness which, if one lacks at
> the outset, one soon tends to acquire . . . I've watched Corinne
> as she wades through a room, all motion and efficiency, and in

my attempts to imitate her, I come out as kind of a slow-motion   155
version, taking twice the time to accomplish half the work.[12]

Today, it seems that good housekeepers divide themselves neatly into
two groups: Those that get genuine pleasure out of the daily maintenance of the house, and those that develop efficient management techniques so they can get out of the house. Mrs. Rodgers takes the latter   160
view:

> Today the aim of a wife is the same as it has always been: to
> make things comfortable and pleasant for her family. Ideally
> she'd like to have everything beautiful and in perfect order,
> too . . . These days housekeeping is more and more like   165
> politics: the art of the possible. . . . I organize to have more
> time for baking bread or doing needlepoint or reading—or
> maybe taking a walk.[13]

Two home economists with doctoral degrees address the problem of the
mundaneness of housework while questioning a person's attitude toward   170
it. They talk of the conflict between the individual's conception of responsibilities of homemaker, wife, and mother and the desire for personal
fulfillment.

> When women say, "I'm *just* a housewife," we might wonder if
> they really do place a low value on their work and thus do little   175
> to enhance their satisfaction with it. It appears they do not rec-
> ognize the contribution they make to their husbands, children,
> and to society through the effective management of the home.[14]

It appears that one of the most fulfilling accomplishments of being a
housewife, while it causes women the most ethical problems, is that of   180
raising children. Margaret Mead, whom most of us see as being extraordinarily free for a woman of her generation, says in her autobiography
Blackberry Winter, that her future plans were changed dramatically
when she discovered she couldn't have the six children she'd always
planned on having.[15] That's when she went into professional partnership   185
with her second husband. Later, she talks about her hopes in having a
baby.

> I pointed out to Reo that one child would not interfere very
> much with our work. One child could always be put to bed in a
> bureau drawer. . . . Later, when Gregory and I were married   190
> and working in Bali, I continued to hope for a child, but once
> again I had several early miscarriages. . . . By the time we
> reached Chicago, on our way back to New York, I thought I was
> pregnant again . . . we went to a doctor, who said that I was

195   very pregnant or else I had a tumor and would have to be op-
       erated on immediately. . . . From the moment it was certain
       that I was pregnant, I took extreme precautions.[16]

After the baby was born, Dr. Mead relates, "Now there was Catherine,
a new person. We called her Cathy. She was fair-haired, her head was
200 unmarred by a hard birth or the use of instruments, and her expression
was already her own. I was completely happy."[17]

    Dr. Mead, of course, had very competent nurses to help in the day-to-
day care of her new baby, though she related how important her daughter was to both her and her husband. This importance is related by
205 another famous mother, Lillian M. Gilbreth, one of the parents in the
entertaining book *Cheaper by the Dozen*. She took over her husband's
responsibilities (he was one of the first experts in time management) at
his untimely death. She was the mother of 12 children and the co-author
of a book called *Management in the Home* where she talks about the
210 rewards of being a homemaker.

       It takes many different kinds of jobs to keep our world going,
       and homemaking is one of them. It's a good job and an im-
       portant job, and it ought to be an enjoyable one. They say it's
       love that makes the world go round. We willingly work for those
215   we love. If we can also love—or at least like—the work itself, the
       pleasure is doubles. The woman who likes her job of homemak-
       ing, who does it with skill and zest, whose home is well man-
       aged and whose family is contented, is a happy woman.
           We no longer say, "Woman's place is in the home," because
220   many women have their places outside the home. But the home
       belongs to the family, and it is still true that the family is wom-
       an's chief interest, it is even more a privilege and a trust, whether
       she has an outside job or not.[18]

    The conflicts between home and career has resulted in a new myth of
225 the perfect woman. The lead article in Money quotes Ellen Goodman,
a syndicated newspaper columnist, on the "perfect new Ms.":

       She wakes up in the morning brimming with energy. After feed-
       ing her husband and 2.3 children a grade A nutritional break-
       fast, the perfect Ms. sails off to her $40,000-a-year job. It is, of
230   course, creative and socially useful work. When she gets home,
       this paragon of a mother spends an hour with the kids; after all,
       it isn't the quantity of their time together but the quality that's
       important. Her husband's arrival is greeted with a perfect dry
       martini, followed by a gourmet dinner. Later, when the chil-
235   dren have been put to bed, husband and wife have time for a
       meaningful relationship. Then they go to bed themselves, where-
       upon the perfect Ms. is multi-orgasmic until midnight.[19]

Homemakers have a new image to live up to. There's no definitive answer to this ethical conflict for those who want to be both fulfilled and a responsible wife and parent. It comes down to what each of us considers important, and what our family expects of us (or what we've taught them to expect), and our own inclinations.   240

[Added note, handwritten] I have material, just ferreted out today, on pediatricians view of women working.
[Endnotes for the early draft are omitted here.]   245

(Final draft)

My mother once told me, "Even if he is wrong, you apologize if he doesn't" (knowing any argument takes two people). She was holding me responsible for the emotional health of my family. I accepted the responsibility. A few years later, my husband said, "You can work if you   250
don't neglect Alyson (our 10-month-old daughter) and the house." I accepted that responsibility also; I worked for only 3 months. I stayed at home till my younger child was in kindergarten. During that time my husband not only got a bachelor's degree, but for a while worked three part-time jobs to support us. As for me, I hated housework, and was an   255
incompetent housekeeper; floors were usually dusty, dishes stayed dirty through an entire day, and I was too undisciplined myself to teach my children regular habits of neatness. My job was that of a housewife, and I was terrible at my craft and chronically depressed.

Then I discovered feminism and realized that I was not alone in my   260
feeling; and furthermore, my very ill-suited qualifications for my job *must* mean my real vocation in the outside world! I read Gloria Steinem, Betty Friedan, and other feminist literature, at first appalled by their attitude, but more and more identifying myself with it.

This personal story isn't the beginning of a long and perhaps tiresome   265
tale of personal growth, but an introduction to what has been my own, and that of many women's biggest ethical problem: the tug-of-war between the needs of our families and our own personal needs.

The origin, I believe, of the ethical code for housewives is found in Proverbs 31, rather lengthy but important for listing all the expectations   270
still lingering in our society.

A good wife who can find? She is far more precious than jewels. The heart of her husband trusts in her, and he will have no lack of gain. She does him good, and not harm, all the days of her life. She seeks wool and flax, and works with willing hands.   275

. . . She rises while it is yet night and provides food for her
household and tasks for her maidens. She considers a field and
buys it; with the fruit of her hands she plants a vineyard. . . .
She perceives that her merchandise is profitable. Her lamp does
not go out at night. She puts her hands to the distaff, and her
hands hold the spindle. She opens her hand to the poor, and
reaches out her hands to the needy. She is not afraid of snow for
her household, for all her household are clothed in scarlet. She
makes herself coverings; her clothing is fine linen and pur-
ple. . . . She makes linen garments and sells them; she delivers
girdles to the merchant. Strength and dignity are her clothing
and she laughs at the time to come. She opens her mouth with
wisdom, and the teaching of kindness is on her tongue. She
looks well to the ways of her household, and does not eat the
bread of idleness. Her children rise up and call her blessed; her
husband also, and he praises her: "Many women have done excellently, but you surpass them all." (Revised Standard Version)

You will notice that this ideal woman is no mindless servant, but a
business-woman, an able administrator, and a person both dedicated to
and valued by her family. This older ethic is still reflected by women
such as Lillian Gilbreth and Dorothy Rodgers. Mrs. Rodgers has made a
priority of the creation of a haven in which her song-writer husband
Richard Rodgers can do his work, and she has this to say:

We believe that the greatest stabilizing influences in the world
stem from family and personal relationships, and that home is
where it all starts. Husbands, children, careers, and where and
how you live—each influences and is in turn influenced by the
others. They are the stuff a woman's life is made of.[1]

Lillian Gilbreth's husband, one of the first time-management experts,
involved his whole family in his experiments, discovering among other
things the fastest way to button your shirt, from top down, or bottom
up, and how to most efficiently do any domestic duty. At her husband's
untimely death, Mrs. Gilbreth took over his job and began lecturing and
visiting businesses to honor her husband's contracts, while still caring
for the remainder of her 12 children. While she recognized the possibility of women working, she still believed their main responsibility to, and
interest in, was their family. In a book on home management she co-
authored, she says this:

It takes many different kinds of jobs to keep our world going,
and homemaking is one of them. It's a good job and an important job, and it ought to be an enjoyable one. They say it's
love that makes the world go round. We willingly work for

those we love. If we can also love—or at least like—the work itself, the pleasure is doubled. The woman who likes her job of homemaking, who does it with skill and zest, whose home is well managed and whose family is contented, is a happy woman. 320

We no longer say, "Woman's place is in the home," because many women have their places outside the home. But the home belongs to the family, and it is still true that the family is woman's chief interest, it is even more a privilege and a trust, whether 325 she has an outside job or not.[2]

These two women have their feet firmly in the long-established standards of the past. Those standards still affect nearly all women. However, we're also being strongly influenced by the "new" woman, the one who disdains domestic responsibility, seeing it as a boring, non-fulfilling 330 job. One 25-year-old woman, after admitting she probably would eventually have children, said, "But I'd continue working. I couldn't be content to redecorate my living room every six months or attend gourmet cooking classes with the ladies of the neighborhood."[3]

Many magazine articles and feminist writers imply that real enjoy- 335 ment in life can only be found with outside jobs. The lead article of a recent magazine highlighting two-income families states, "For wives, working can be a joy no matter how high the dishes may pile up at home. Those on a career track find that a deep sense of fulfillment usually accompanies a professional paycheck." It goes on to quote a Univer- 340 sity of Michigan psychologist who says motherhood alone is unsatisfying as an occupation because it is so transitory. "It's difficult to make it a career unless you keep having babies every 2½ years until menopause."[4]

More and more women and men are questioning role expectations based on gender alone: cannot women be executives; are not some men 345 naturally nurturing people? There's literally tons of material available today on the subject. All this questioning performs a dual function: it causes people to re-examine their expectations of others, and it also gives us all, women *and* men, more freedom in what we choose to do.

The ethical considerations arise here in terms of responsibility to the 350 family unit. If both husband and wife have full-time jobs, who cares for the children? What happens to the family unit? Once again, reams of material have been written to offer solutions to this problem. Apparently, however, whatever the modern ideology and in whatever innovative ways some husbands and wives cope with this problem, in most homes 355 women (and their husbands) still feel it's *her* primary responsibility to care for both home and children. His job is the more important, and in situations where his wife earns more, he may feel threatened. One husband who doesn't is married to Jane Bryant Quinn, an advisor on money

360 management who writes a newspaper column and appears on television. Though her husband is an attorney, she will earn the greater amount of their $250,000 income this year. She answers a question on the impact of her work on their children:

365 > This gets down to the question of traditional roles. One never considers the impact on the children of the man not being there. One thinks only of what might result if the woman isn't there. But sure, I had terrible attacks of working-mother guilt. I don't know of any woman of my generation who has not.
370 > But do you want to know a wonderful thing? You give the best of your time that you possibly can to your children. When you're not working, you're devoting the time to mommy duty. The Little League games are at seven o'clock, so you get an earlier commuter train and you attend the games. You muddle through.[5]

375 By any standards a busy person, Quinn still sees herself as responsible for "mommy duty." Whether or not this feeling of responsibility is thrust upon women or willingly shouldered has not been answered, and probably depends on the person, but the long-held tradition of the importance of motherhood is being challenged by radical feminists who see mother-
380 hood as a neat trap. In a chapter entitled "Myths of Woman's Place: Motherhood," a London feminist has this to say:

> The myth of motherhood contains three popular assertions. The first is the most influential: that children need mothers, the second is the obverse of this: that mothers need their children. The
385 > third assertion is a generalization which holds that motherhood represents the greatest achievement of a woman's life: the sole true means of self-realization. Women, in other words, need to be mothers. "Need" here is always vaguely specified, but usually means damage to mental or emotional health following on the
390 > denial of mothers to children, children to mothers, or motherhood to women.[6]

Those of us who have two or three children under six read that and say to ourselves, "Yeah, why should I spend so much of my time on my children? I'm not neurotic; I don't *need* my children in some kind of sick
395 way!" Independence is very tempting on the days the two-year-old has just spilled ink on the rug and the five-year-old, who has had a bad day, is spoiling for a fight. That's when you wonder if motherhood is worth all the effort, especially if your education prepared you to be the next Madame Curie. Running a home, particularly one with children in it,
400 is not easy for anyone, and it's very tempting sometimes to consider just walking out.

These pressures on housewives and mothers haven't always existed to the extent they do today. There are several conditions in America that make today's families different than those of 30 or 40 years ago, one of which is the practical necessity of two incomes to cope with modern   405
economic needs. Also, the respect for the job of homemaking has diminished. When it became obvious women could handle jobs in business, medicine, and law, the role of housewife seemed less and less meaningful and rewarding, because it dealt with so many daily boring tasks, supposedly easily handled by any simpleton. Mike McGrady became a   410
housewife for a year while his wife ran her own business, and talks about his realization of the mundane quality of the tasks involved, giving his wife recognition for abilities previously unnoticed:

> I've since learned that cleaning a house is very much like iron-
> ing clothes—the first experience is dreadful and the second one,   415
> worse. These tasks require a numbness which, if one lacks at
> the outset, one soon tends to acquire. . . . I've watched Corinne
> as she wades through a room, all motion and efficiency, but in
> my attempts to imitate her, I come out as kind of a slow-motion
> version, taking twice the time to accomplish half the work.[7]   420

The truth is, the same skills that run an efficient business will manage an efficient home, but though we teach men and women accounting and business management, we do not train anyone how to manage a house. That occupation is virtually always learned on-the-job. Our grandmothers proudly kept clean houses, but also helped run the farm in rural   425
communities, or in the city devoted many afternoons to charity work and other activities, having gotten housework out of the way easily that morning. When we started educating our daughters, we stopped expecting them to learn household skills; many of them come ill-prepared to handle the job efficiently.   430
Another situation that has changed in this country is the isolation of many of today's women. Americans have moved from the farm to the city, and families are more dependent than ever on an outside income, since we no longer grow any of our own produce. Because of that dependence, employers gain more control over their employees; men be-   435
come more and more mobile, and women lose stable contact with the "outside" world at the same time their husbands invest greater emotional energy in their jobs. Women are increasingly dependent on their husbands' ability to be a source of companionship while their husbands' employers are placing less value on family responsibilities (though there   440
are signs this trend is beginning to reverse).
Dr. Genevieve De Hoyos, a sociologist in Utah and advocate of family

life, acknowledges women's discontent and examines the changes in the
traditional family division of labor; she says a marriage originally con-
445   sisted of two partnerships:

> 1. The *providing partnership* to which the wife has tradi-
> tionally contributed fully, but headed by the husband who is
> ultimately responsible for it;
> 2. The *socializing partnership* within which the husband en-
450 > forces basic patterns of conduct but which is the traditional
> domain of the wife.[8]

Industrialization had the effect of modifying this division of labor, so
that father became the provider and disciplinarian and mother became
homemaker and nurturer. The next change resulted from the father's
455   often long hours away from home and his gradual shift in emphasis of
goals directed toward his job instead of his home, which now became his
refuge after a hard day's work. Gradually, says Dr. De Hoyos, a man
came to see the family unit as primarily expressive (satisfying emotional
needs) when he had previously been the instrumental (goal-oriented)
460   leader in the family. Because the only source of income now came from
the husband's job (husband and wife are no longer co-providers), wives
began protecting their husbands from daily decision-making and dis-
ciplining of children. Thus the wife, who still saw the family as an
instrumental unit, took over the role of disciplinarian, in charge of all
465   day-to-day functions of the home. On the other hand, father and children
were perceiving the family as an answer to their emotional needs. Dr. De
Hoyos relates why the position of apparent power which modern wives
have is instead a cause of frustration.

> So, many of the responsibilities of the home are being shoved
470 > onto the wife. Unfortunately at this time of our industrial de-
> velopment, most of what she does is typically regarded as not
> particularly important. Children, for whom she is particularly
> responsible, are not really wanted by society, her efforts to
> maintain her home as well as her ability to fulfill her husband's
475 > emotional needs are too private to be consistently and accu-
> rately evaluated by those around. Moreover, she is seldom in-
> volved in her husband's work. Therefore, she cannot expect any
> stable recognition from society at large.[9]

As more and more women respond to this lack of recognition by going
480   to work, it seems that this solution instead just adds to their responsibilities. Besides discovering that fact in much of the reading I've done, I
surveyed women with whom I daily associate, and found concordance.
One woman in the survey is a CPA, teaches accounting, works with her

husband in an accounting firm they recently purchased, and is the
mother of two pre-school boys. She said she is also responsible for 100%   485
of the maintenance, cleaning, cooking, shopping, etc. Another woman,
though childless, listed as her main activities: full-time accountant 50%,
part-time student 50%, full-time wife 50%, and concluded, "In other words,
I'm doing more than is physically possible, with each area equally important."   490

What is happening, then, is not really emancipation for women as
much as it is simply more work, or work left undone. My own experience
with a part-time job (20 hrs. a week) coincided with a period of time
in which we had all-day Sunday dinner guests about twice a month. Because my husband helped me with household cleaning on the weekends,   495
the traditional "men's" jobs of house maintenance, car repairs, etc., simply didn't get done.

One of the biggest problems in my own and other families is the willingness on both my part and my husband's, to see all home-related jobs,
including child care, as only my responsibility, though as a full-time   500
student, I ostensibly spend 45 hours a week on school responsibilities.
Any work he or my children do is "helping out Mom," not "taking care
of the chores."

In a study of women physicians, it was found that most of them state
that their husbands helped them, but their help was in the negative   505
sense—they just expected less of their wives, without actually sharing the
responsibilities. Women physicians see themselves as strong and capable,
and also feel guilty about the requirements of their jobs; consequently,
they feel they should be able to handle everything. Here one woman
talks about the ways in which her husband helps: 510

> He does a lot. I don't ask him to clean up the living room or to
> wash the diapers—I have a maid to clean. It's the little things
> that are most important. If I am tired, he will take the baby.
> . . . And he is not at all demanding. If I am busy, he doesn't
> mind having a TV dinner for supper.[10]   515

Referring to Proverbs, it is obvious that the "ideal" woman could
conduct business activities and care for her family too, but that her
family was her *primary responsibility*. How could this woman appear so
contented and secure, though, when today's woman feels overworked or
dissatisfied? I think there are several reasons. One is the obvious—the   520
woman in Proverbs had servants. Modern equivalents would be child
care, a housekeeper, and modern appliances, aids that are sometimes
limited by economics, availability, or the quality of what's available. I've
come to believe the main reason she was contented (remember we're

525 dealing with an ideal), is that her husband and the community *also* had as their prime concern the family. Not only in Proverbs, but in other parts of the Bible, it's obvious that the role of the father was vitally important to the family, and not only through his economic contribution. (Whether or not a person believes the Bible isn't important here—what

530 we can assume is that it has had an enormous influence on American values.)

The ethical problem discussed here is an important one to me, as I will soon become, at the age of 37, the mother of my third child, an event that totally changes my plan to return to the labor force (no pun in-

535 tended) after graduation. With much thought and assessment of priorities, I've opted to put the needs of my new baby ahead of my own. The decision was not made easily, though I will enjoy much of the caring for a baby again. In addition I have concluded that the ethical considerations aren't mine alone. What I've discovered in the reading I have done is

540 that the ethics involved here does not concern only housewives, but their husbands, and to a more diffused extent, the whole community.

Social changes have been largely responsible for the changes in attitude toward family responsibilities, and the role each member of the family shares. If we choose to think the family is important (and I do)

545 then we have the responsibility to individually act on that importance. We must decide that all persons involved in family life are responsible for its health. If I as a mother willingly make the decision to stay home and care for children, I should be able to expect the same willingness on the part of my husband and community to recognize my worth (since

550 they expect that from me), and give me any kind of assistance necessary. How to get others to share this recognition? I was amused just this week to read in another book an acknowledgment of that problem, talking about the importance of husbands helping their wives with small children:

555   Husbands who recognize this fact can help their wives feel understood, loved and supported in the vital jobs they are doing. (Don't ask me, please, how to convince husbands to accept that responsibility. I'm like the mouse who recommended that a bell be put around the neck of the cat, but had no idea how to

560   get it there!)[11]

There is a way, of course—effective communication to not only husbands, but to others, at any opportunity—supporting the value of family life, and a positive outlook on our own self-worth will help all of us mothers at home to change not only our own attitudes, but the attitudes

565 of our family and community.

NOTES

[1] Dorothy Rodgers and Mary Rodgers, *A Word to the Wives* (New York: Alfred A. Knopf, 1970), p. xii.

[2] Lillian M. Gilbreth, Orpha Mae Thomas, and Eleanor Clymer, *Management in the Home: Happier Living through Saving Time and Energy* (New York: Dodd, Mead & Company, 1955), p. 1.

[3] Robert Runde, "Now, the Us Generation," *Money*, 9 (November 1980), 63.

[4] Robert Runde, "How to Make the Most of Two Incomes," *Money*, 9 (November 1980), 54.

[5] "A Professional Adviser's Personal Advice," *Money*, 9 (November 1980), 58.

[6] Ann Oakley, *Woman's Work: The Housewife, Past and Present* (New York: Pantheon Books, 1974), p. 186.

[7] Mike McGrady, *The Kitchen Sink Papers: My Life as a Househusband* (New York: Doubleday & Co., Inc., 1975), p. 46.

[8] Genevieve De Hoyos, *Feminism or Familism* (Provo, Utah: Northbridge Publishing Company, 1978), p. 72.

[9] De Hoyos, p. 83.

[10] Margaret M. Poloma and T. Neal Garland, "The Myth of the Egalitarian Family: Familian Roles and the Professionally Employed Wife," *The Professional Woman*, edited by Athena Theodore (Cambridge: Schenkman Publishing Co., Inc., 1971), p. 750, cited in *Feminism or Familism*, p. 113.

[11] James Dobson, *The Strong-Willed Child: Birth through Adolescence* (Wheaton, Illinois: Tyndale House Pub., Inc., 1978), p. 45.

BIBLIOGRAPHY

De Hoyos, Genevieve. *Feminism or Familism*. Provo, Utah: Northbridge Publishing Company, 1978.

> *Authoritativeness:* High; the author is a sociologist and obviously researched her subject carefully.
>
> *Currency:* High; the book was published just two years ago.
>
> *Soundness:* Reasonably high: The author approached the subject with a bias in favor of family unity. There's a lot of evidence she's of the Mormon religion, which is spending a lot of effort now in the interests of family preservation. However, her arguments are so soundly presented in the book, she strongly affected my paper, and I am purchasing the book.

Dobson, James. *The Strong-Willed Child: Birth through Adolescence*. Wheaton, Illinois: Tyndale House Publ., Inc., 1978).

> Evaluation not really applicable; did not use for any material; was just happening to read it during preparation of the paper. Dr. Dobson is a psychologist who has worked with many teen-aged children and is a source of much good advice on raising children.

Gilbreth, Lillian M., Orpha Mae Thomas, and Eleanor Clymer. *Management in the Home: Happier Living through Saving Time and Energy*. New York: Dodd, Mead & Company, 1955.

> *Authoritativeness:* Adequate for purposes of this paper, since I was looking for attitudes rather than practical advice.
>
> *Currency:* Once again, adequate for my purposes. Since I wanted an example of past attitudes, 1955 was a good year.
>
> *Soundness:* Adequate.

McGrady, Mike. *The Kitchen Sink Papers: My Life as a Househusband*. New York: Doubleday & Co., Inc., 1975.

> *Authoritativeness:* Excellent: Obviously raised with all the biases of a man, his views on housework are seen through the eyes of someone new to it all.
>
> *Currency:* Good.
>
> *Soundness:* The only flaw I could find was that his reactions could have been influenced by recent literature. Many of his reactions seemed to be what he might have *expected* to feel— all the complaints of women were in there.

Money articles—

> *Authoritativeness:* Adequate—once again, I was looking for attitudes; the biases would have been mine, therefore. *Money* is published by Time, Inc., and would reflect their research methods & attitudes.
>
> *Currency:* Obviously excellent.
>
> *Soundness:* Excellent: I was looking for attitudes of modern women; obviously an article on two-income families would be an excellent source.

Oakley, Ann. *Woman's Work: The Housewife, Past and Present*. New York: Pantheon Books, 1974.

> *Authoritativeness:* Adequate—she is not a parent, and as a feminist, would be biased on the subject of the expectations on women. I tried to get Betty Friedan, but couldn't get the book.
>
> *Currency:* High.
>
> *Soundness:* Not too good, though she is a sound representative of other feminist literature I've read.

Annotation

This paper formed the major project of a course in professional ethics. It illustrates the growth, organization, and documentation of an excellent longer paper at the undergraduate level.

Study Openers

1. Make informal notes of the apparent organization or sequence of topics for each draft.

    a. What change in purpose and main idea can you detect between the two drafts?
    b. Admitting that the first draft seems to ramble, what plan of development was worked out for the final draft?

2. Streeter shifted her use of sources in several ways. What do you find significant in the following?

    a. The dropping of Margaret Mead.
    b. The adding of Streeter's own testimony in several places.
    c. The relative treatments of De Hoyos (lines 83 and 442), of Rodgers (lines 64 and 160; 299), and of Gilbreth (lines 205 and 307).

3. Compare the openings and endings of the two drafts. What changes do you see and how are they important?

4. How useful a contribution do you think is made by the annotation of the bibliography at the end? (For annotated bibliography see Chapter 23, page 278.)

The Reading Machine
by Morris Bishop

(*The New Yorker,* 1947)

"I have invented a reading machine," said Professor Entwhistle, a strident energumen whose violent enthusiasms are apt to infect his colleagues with nausea or hot flashes before the eyes.

Every head in the smoking room of the Faculty Club bowed over a magazine, in an attitude of prayer. The prayer was unanswered, as usual.   5

"It is obvious," said Professor Entwhistle, "that the greatest waste of our civilization is the time spent in reading. We have been able to speed up practically everything to fit the modern tempo—communication, transportation, calculation. But today a man takes just as long to read a book as Dante did, or—"   10

"Great Caesar!" said the Professor of Amphibology, shutting his magazine with a spank.

"Or great Caesar," continued Professor Entwhistle. "So I have invented a machine. It operates by a simple arrangement of photoelectric cells,
15 which scan a line of type at lightning speed. The operation of the photoelectric cells is synchronized with a mechanical device for turning the pages—rather ingenious. I figure that my machine can read a book of three hundred pages in ten minutes."

"Can it read French?" said the Professor of Bio-Economics, without
20 looking up.

"It can read any language that is printed in Roman type. And by an alteration of the master pattern on which the photoelectric cells operate, it can be fitted to read Russian, or Bulgarian, or any language printed in the Cyrillic alphabet. In fact, it will do more. By simply throwing a
25 switch, you can adapt it to read Hebrew, or Arabic, or any language that is written from right to left instead of from left to right."

"Chinese?" said the Professor of Amphibology, throwing himself into the arena. The others still studied their magazines.

"Not Chinese, as yet," said Professor Entwhistle. "Though by inserting
30 the pages sidewise . . . Yes, I think it could be done."

"Yes, but when you say this contrivance reads, exactly what do you mean? It seems to me—"

"The light waves registered by the photoelectric cells are first converted into sound waves."
35 "So you can listen in to the reading of the text?"

"Not at all. The sound waves alter so fast that you hear nothing but a continuous hum. If you hear them at all. You can't, in fact, because they are on a wave length inaudible to the human ear."

"Well, it seems to me—"
40 "Think of the efficiency of the thing!" Professor Entwhistle was really warming up. "Think of the time saved! You assign a student a bibliography of fifty books. He runs them through the machine comfortably in a weekend. And on Monday morning he turns in a certificate from the machine. Everything has been conscientiously read!"
45 "Yes, but the student won't remember what he has read!"

"He doesn't remember what he reads now."

"Well, you have me there," said the Professor of Amphibology. "I confess you have me there. But it seems to me we would have to pass the machine and fail the student."
50 "Not at all," said Professor Entwhistle. "An accountant today does not think of doing his work by multiplication and division. Often he is unable to multiply and divide. He confides his problem to a business ma-

chine and the machine does his work for him. All the accountant has to know is how to run the machine. That is efficiency."

"Still, it seems to me that what we want to do is to transfer the con-   55
tents of the book to the student's mind."

"In the mechanized age? My dear fellow! What we want is to train the student to run machines. An airplane pilot doesn't need to know the history of aerodynamics. He needs to know how to run his machine. A lawyer doesn't want to know the development of theories of Roman law.   60
He wants to win cases, if possible by getting the right answers to logical problems. That is largely a mechanical process. It might well be possible to construct a machine. It could begin by solving simple syllogisms, you know—drawing a conclusion from a major premise and a minor premise—"

"Here, let's not get distracted. This reading machine of yours, it must   65
do something, it must make some kind of record. What happens after you get the sound waves?"

"That's the beauty of it," said Professor Entwhistle. "The sound waves are converted into light waves, of a different character from the original light waves, and these are communicated to an automatic typewriter,   70
working at inconceivable speed. This transforms the light impulses into legible typescript, in folders of a hundred pages each. It tosses them out the way a combine tosses out sacked wheat. Thus, everything the machine reads is preserved entire, in durable form. The only thing that remains is to file it somewhere, and for this you would need only the   75
services of a capable filing clerk."

"Or you could read it?" persisted the Professor of Amphibology.

"Why, yes, if you wanted to, you could read it," said Professor Entwhistle.

An indigestible silence hung over the Faculty Club.   80

"I see where the Athletic Association has bought a pitching machine," said the Assistant Professor of Business Psychology (Retail). "Damn thing throws any curve desired, with a maximum margin of error of three centimetres over the plate. What'll they be thinking of next?"

"A batting machine, obviously," said Professor Entwhistle.   85

Annotation
Energumen: one possessed by an evil spirit; an enthusiast.
Amphibology: double meanings.

["Study Openers" are here left to the reader, in light of Chapter 24, page 283.]

Zen and the Art of Motorcycle Maintenance
by Robert M. Pirsig

(from Chapter 1, 1974)

I can see by my watch, without taking my hand from the left grip of the cycle, that it is eight-thirty in the morning. The wind, even at sixty miles a hour, is warm and humid. When it's this hot and muggy at eight-thirty, I'm wondering what it's going to be like in the afternoon.

5   In the wind are pungent odors from the marshes by the road. We are in an area of the Central Plains filled with thousands of duck hunting sloughs, heading northwest from Minneapolis toward the Dakotas. This highway is an old concrete two-laner that hasn't had much traffic since a four-laner went in parallel to it several years ago. When we pass a marsh

10   the air suddenly becomes cooler. Then, when we are past, it suddenly warms up again.

    I'm happy to be riding back into this country. It is a kind of nowhere, famous for nothing at all and has an appeal because of just that. Tensions disappear along old roads like this. We bump along the beat-up

15   concrete between the cattails and stretches of meadow and then more cattails and marsh grass. Here and there is a stretch of open water and if you look closely you can see wild ducks at the edge of the cattails. And turtles. . . . There's a red-winged blackbird.

    I whack Chris's knee and point to it.

20   "What!" he hollers.

    "Blackbird!"

    He says something I don't hear. "What?" I holler back.

    He grabs the back of my helmet and hollers up, "I've seen *lots* of those, Dad!"

25   "Oh!" I holler back. Then I nod. At age eleven you don't get very impressed with red-winged blackbirds.

    You have to get older for that. For me this is all mixed with memories that he doesn't have. Cold mornings long ago when the marsh grass had turned brown and cattails were waving in the northwest wind. The pun-

30   gent smell then was from muck stirred up by hip boots while we were getting in position for the sun to come up and the duck season to open. Or winters when the sloughs were frozen over and dead and I could walk across the ice and snow between the dead cattails and see nothing but grey skies and dead things and cold. The blackbirds were gone then. But

35   now in July they're back and everything is at its alivest and every foot of these sloughs is humming and cricking and buzzing and chirping, a

whole community of millions of living things living out their lives in a kind of benign continuum.

You see things vacationing on a motorcycle in a way that is completely different from any other. In a car you're always in a compartment, and because you're used to it you don't realize that through that car window everything you see is just more TV. You're a passive observer and it is all moving by you boringly in a frame.

On a cycle the frame is gone. You're completely in contact with it all. You're *in* the scene, not just watching it anymore, and the sense of presence is overwhelming. That concrete whizzing by five inches below your foot is the real thing, the same stuff you walk on, it's right there, so blurred you can't focus on it, yet you can put your foot down and touch it anytime, and the whole thing, the whole experience, is never removed from immediate consciousness.

Chris and I are traveling to Montana with some friends riding up ahead, and maybe headed farther than that. Plans are deliberately indefinite, more to travel than to arrive anywhere. We are just vacationing. Secondary roads are preferred. Paved county roads are the best, state highways are next. Freeways are the worst. We want to make good time, but for us now this is measured with emphasis on "good" rather than "time" and when you make that shift in emphasis the whole approach changes. . . .

Unless you're fond of hollering you don't make great conversations on a running cycle. Instead you spend your time being aware of things, and meditating on them. On sights and sounds, on the mood of the weather and things remembered, on the machine and the countryside you're in, thinking about things at great leisure and length without being hurried and without feeling you're losing time.

What I would like to do is use the time that is coming now to talk about some things that have come to mind. We're in such a hurry most of the time we never get much chance to talk. The result is a kind of endless day-to-day shallowness, a monotony that leaves a person wondering years later where all the time went and sorry that it's all gone. Now that we do have some time, and know it, I would like to use the time to talk in some depth about things that seem important.

What is in mind is a sort of Chautauqua—that's the only name I can think of for it—like the traveling tent-show Chautauquas that used to move across America, *this* America, the one that we are now in, an old-time series of popular talks intended to edify and entertain, improve the mind and bring culture and enlightenment to the ears and thoughts of the hearer. The Chautauquas were pushed aside by faster-paced radio,

movies and TV, and it seems to me the change was not entirely an improvement. Perhaps because of these changes the stream of national consciousness moves faster now, and is broader, but it seems to run less deep.
The old channels cannot contain it and in its search for new ones there
seems to be growing havoc and destruction along its banks. In this Chautauqua I would like not to cut any new channels of consciousness but
simply dig deeper into old ones that have become silted in with the
debris of thoughts grown stale and platitudes too often repeated. "What's
new?" is an interesting and broadening eternal question, but one which,
if pursued exclusively, results only in an endless parade of trivia and
fashion, the silt of tomorrow. I would like, instead, to be concerned with
the question "What is best?," a question which cuts deeply rather than
broadly, a question whose answers tend to move the silt downstream.
There are eras of human history in which the channels of thought have
been too deeply cut and no change was possible, and nothing new ever
happened, and "best" was a matter of dogma, but that is not the situation now. Now the stream of our common consciousness seems to be
obliterating its own banks, losing its central direction and purpose, flooding the lowlands, disconnecting and isolating the highlands and to no
particular purpose other than the wasteful fulfillment of its own internal
momentum. Some channel deepening seems called for.

Up ahead the other riders, John Sutherland and his wife, Sylvia, have
pulled into a roadside picnic area. It's time to stretch. As I pull my machine beside them Sylvia is taking her helmet off and shaking her hair
loose, while John puts his BMW up on the stand. Nothing is said. We
have been on so many trips together we know from a glance how one another feels. Right now we are just quiet and looking around.

The picnic benches are abandoned at this hour of the morning. We
have the whole place to ourselves. John goes across the grass to a cast-
iron pump and starts pumping water to drink. Chris wanders down
through some trees beyond a grassy knoll to a small stream. I am just
staring around.

After a while Sylvia sits down on the wooden picnic bench and
straightens out her legs, lifting one at a time slowly without looking up.
Long silences mean gloom for her, and I comment on it. She looks up
and then looks down again.

"It was all those people in the cars coming the other way," she says.
"The first one looked so sad. And then the next one looked exactly the
same way, and then the next one and the next one, they were all the
same."

"They were just commuting to work."

She perceives well but there was nothing unnatural about it. "Well,
you know, *work*," I repeat. "Monday morning. Half asleep. Who goes to   120
work Monday morning with a grin?"

"It's just that they looked so *lost*," she says. "Like they were all dead.
Like a funeral procession." Then she puts both feet down and leaves
them there.

I see what she is saying, but logically it doesn't go anywhere. You   125
work to live and that's what they are doing. "I was watching swamps,"
I say.

After a while she looks up and says, "What did you see?"

"There was a whole flock of red-winged blackbirds. They rose up sud-
denly when we went by."   130

"Oh."

"I was happy to see them again. They tie things together, thoughts and
such. You know?"

She thinks for a while and then, with the trees behind her a deep green,
she smiles. She understands a peculiar language which has nothing to do   135
with what you are saying. A daughter.

"Yes," she says. "They're beautiful."

"Watch for them," I say.

"All right."

John appears and checks the gear on the cycle. He adjusts some of the   140
ropes and then opens the saddlebag and starts rummaging through. He
sets some things on the ground. "If you ever need any rope, don't hesitate," he says. "God, I think I've got about *five* times what I need here."

"Not yet," I answer.

"Matches?" he says, still rummaging. "Sunburn lotion, combs, shoe-   145
laces . . . *shoelaces?* What do we need shoelaces for?"

"Let's not start *that*," Sylvia says. They look at each other deadpan and
then both look over at me.

"Shoelaces can break anytime," I say solemnly. They smile, but not at
each other.   150

Chris soon appears and it is time to go. While he gets ready and climbs
on, they pull out and Sylvia waves. We are on the highway again, and I
watch them gain distance up ahead.

The Chautauqua that is in mind for this trip was inspired by these two
many months ago and perhaps, although I don't know, is related to a   155
certain undercurrent of disharmony between them.

Disharmony I suppose is common enough in any marriage, but in their
case it seems more tragic. To me, anyway.

It's not a personality clash between them; it's something else, for which

160 neither is to blame, but for which neither has any solution, and for which I'm not sure I have any solution either, just ideas.

The ideas began with what seemed to be a minor difference of opinion between John and me on a matter of small importance: how much one should maintain one's own motorcycle. It seems natural and normal to
165 me to make use of the small tool kits and instruction booklets supplied with each machine, and keep it tuned and adjusted myself. John demurs. He prefers to let a competent mechanic take care of these things so that they are done right. Neither viewpoint is unusual, and this minor difference would never have become magnified if we didn't spend so much
170 time riding together and sitting in country roadhouses drinking beer and talking about whatever comes to mind. What comes to mind, usually, is whatever we've been thinking about in the half hour or forty-five minutes since we last talked to each other. When it's roads or weather or people or old memories or what's in the newspapers, the conversation just natu-
175 rally builds pleasantly. But whenever the performance of the machine has been on my mind and gets into the conversation, the building stops. The conversation no longer moves forward. There is a silence and a break in the continuity. It is as though two old friends, a Catholic and Protestant, were sitting drinking beer, enjoying life, and the subject of birth control
180 somehow came up. Big freeze-out.

And, of course, when you discover something like that it's like discovering a tooth with a missing filling. You can never leave it alone. You have to probe it, work around it, push on it, think about it, not because it's enjoyable but because it's on your mind and it won't get off your mind.
185 And the more I probe and push on this subject of cycle maintenance the more irritated he gets, and of course that makes me want to probe and push all the more. Not deliberately to irritate him but because the irritation seems symptomatic of something deeper, something under the surface that isn't immediately apparent.

190 When you're talking birth control, what blocks it and freezes it out is that it's not a matter of more or fewer babies being argued. That's just on the surface. What's underneath is a conflict of faith, of faith in empirical social planning versus faith in the authority of God as revealed by the teachings of the Catholic Church. You can prove the practicality of
195 planned parenthood till you get tired of listening to yourself and it's going to go nowhere because your antagonist isn't buying the assumption that anything socially practical is good per se. Goodness for him has other sources which he values as much as or more than social practicality.

So it is with John. I could preach the practical value and worth of mo-
200 torcycle maintenance till I'm hoarse and it would make not a dent in him. After two sentences on the subject his eyes go completely glassy and he

changes the conversation or just looks away. He doesn't want to hear about it.

Sylvia is completely with him on this one. In fact she is even more emphatic. "It's just a whole other thing," she says, when in a thoughtful   205
mood. "Like garbage," she says, when not. They want *not* to understand it. Not to *hear* about it. And the more I try to fathom what makes me enjoy mechanical work and them hate it so, the more elusive it becomes. The ultimate cause of this originally minor difference of opinion appears to run way, way deep.   210

Inability on their part is ruled out immediately. They are both plenty bright enough. Either one of them could learn to tune a motorcycle in an hour and a half if they put their minds and energy to it, and the saving in money and worry and delay would repay them over and over again for their effort. And they *know* that. Or maybe they don't. I don't know.   215
I never confront them with the question. It's better to just get along.

But I remember once, outside a bar in Savage, Minnesota, on a really scorching day when I just about let loose. We'd been in the bar for about an hour and we came out and the machines were so hot you could hardly get on them. I'm started and ready to go and there's John pumping away   220
on the kick starter. I smell gas like we're next to a refinery and tell him so, thinking this is enough to let him know his engine's flooded.

"Yeah, I smell it too," he says and keeps on pumping. And he pumps and pumps and jumps and pumps and *I* don't know what more to say. Finally, he's really winded and sweat's running down all over his face   225
and he can't pump anymore, and so I suggest taking out the plugs to dry them off and air out the cylinders while we go back for another beer.

Oh my God no! He doesn't want to get into all that stuff.

"All what stuff?"

"Oh, getting out the tools and all that stuff. There's no reason why it   230
shouldn't start. It's a brand-new machine and I'm following the instructions perfectly. See, it's right on full choke like they say."

"Full *choke!*"

"That's what the instructions say."

"That's for when it's *cold!*"   235

"Well, we've been in there for a half an hour at least," he says.

It kind of shakes me up. "This is a hot day, John," I say. "And they take longer than that to cool off even on a freezing day."

He scratches his head. "Well, why don't they tell you that in the instructions?" He opens the choke and on the second kick it starts. "I guess   240
that was it," he says cheerfully. . . .

I might have thought this was just a peculiar attitude of theirs about

motorcycles but discovered later that it extended to other things. . . .
Waiting for them to get going one morning in their kitchen I noticed the
245 sink faucet was dripping and remembered that it was dripping the last
time I was there before and that in fact it had been dripping as long as I
could remember. I commented on it and John said he had tried to fix it
with a new faucet washer but it hadn't worked. That was all he said. The
presumption left was that that was the end of the matter. If you try to fix
250 a faucet and your fixing doesn't work then it's just your lot to live with a
dripping faucet.

This made me wonder to myself if it got on their nerves, this drip-drip-
drip, week in, week out, year in, year out, but I could not notice any irritation or concern about it on their part, and so concluded they just aren't
255 bothered by things like dripping faucets. Some people aren't.

What it was that changed this conclusion, I don't remember . . . some
intuition, some insight one day, perhaps it was a subtle change in Sylvia's
mood whenever the dripping was particularly loud and she was trying to
talk. She has a very soft voice. And one day when she was trying to talk
260 above the dripping and the kids came in and interrupted her she lost her
temper at them. It seemed that her anger at the kids would not have been
nearly as great if the faucet hadn't also been dripping when she was trying to talk. It was the combined dripping and loud kids that blew her
up. What struck me hard then was that she was *not* blaming the faucet,
265 and that she was *deliberately* not blaming the faucet. She wasn't ignoring
that faucet at all! She was *suppressing* anger at that faucet and that god-
damned dripping faucet was just about *killing* her! But she could not admit the importance of this for some reason.

Why suppress anger at a dripping faucet? I wondered.
270 Then that patched in with the motorcycle maintenance and one of
those light bulbs went on over my head and I thought, Ahhhhhhhh!

It's not the motorcycle maintenance, not the faucet. It's all of technology they can't take. And then all sorts of things started tumbling into
place and I knew that was it. Sylvia's irritation at a friend who thought
275 computer programming was "creative." All their drawings and paintings
and photographs without a technological thing in them. Of course she's
not going to get mad at that faucet, I thought. You always suppress mo-
mentary anger at something you deeply and permanently hate. Of course
John signs off every time the subject of cycle repair comes up, even when
280 it is obvious he is suffering for it. That's technology. And sure, of course,
obviously. It's so simple when you see it. To get away from technology
out into the country in the fresh air and sunshine is why they are on the
motorcycle in the first place. For me to bring it back to them just at the

point and place where they think they have finally escaped it just frosts both of them, tremendously. That's why the conversation always breaks and freezes when the subject comes up.   285

I disagree with them about cycle maintenance, but not because I am out of sympathy with their feelings about technology. I just think that their flight from and hatred of technology is self-defeating. The Buddha, the Godhead, resides quite as comfortably in the circuits of a digital com-   290 puter or the gears of a cycle transmission as he does at the top of a mountain or in the petals of a flower. To think otherwise is to demean the Buddha—which is to demean oneself. That is what I want to talk about in this Chautauqua.

We're out of the marshes now, but the air is still so humid you can look   295 straight up directly at the yellow circle of the sun as if there were smoke or smog in the sky. But we're in the green countryside now. The farmhouses are clean and white and fresh. And there's no smoke or smog.

["Study Openers" are here left to the reader, in light of Chapter 24, page 283.]

Usage Reminders: An Appendix

This appendix describes the most common trouble spots in writing. Its recommendations are compatible with the Ebbitts' *Index to English*, 6th edition, one of the rare guides to document itself point by point from the view of linguistic scholarship. But no brief appendix can substitute for the *Index* itself or any other grammar handbook. If you have frequent difficulty, consult an English teacher or a librarian for the title of a good handbook to meet your needs. You can also consult the table of contents of your desk dictionary, which may include a "style manual" or articles on punctuation and grammar.

The Conservatism of Serious Written English

Your serious written work, except for literary creation, will usually follow the conventions of general English toward the formal end of its range (see pp. 106–107). When you have a choice between a usage established among educated people for serious writing and another usage which is not, you would prefer the established usage. Thus:

Usage still debated for formal usage (though practiced informally):
> The experiment worked *like* he hoped.

Usage established:
> The experiment worked *as* he hoped.

A good college desk dictionary will often explain the level of usage for words under question.

435

P   *Punctuation*

P1 *Sentence division.* The most important single use of punctuation is to divide one sentence from another. The following failures to use conventional divisional signals can seriously damage the reader's attention.

a *The "sentence fragment."*

> I mean to study hard this term. Especially in chemistry.

The first period mistakenly implies that the sentence is ended; the remaining fragment is presented as if it were a complete second sentence. Solution: substitute a comma after "term." Some fragments do justify themselves through providing vigorous but unambiguous stress (see page 193).

b *The "fused sentence."*

> So the war came to an end the enemy could no longer effectively resist.

Here two sentences are rammed together as if they were one. Solution: insert a period or semicolon after "end."

c *The "comma fault" or "comma splice."*

> Huxley went to bed, the next day he started the job all over again.

The comma in serious prose is usually too weak a mark to separate complete sentences. Solution: substitute a period or semicolon after "bed." Comma splices do appear without confusion where the continuity is self-evident:

> The crew had had enough, they were fed up, they saw no hope except through mutiny.

P2   *Period* .

Called in British the "full stop." ("There is not much to be said about the period except that most writers don't reach it soon enough"—William Zinsser.) Besides signaling the end of a sentence, the period is used:

a *To set aside a topic heading, number, or letter.*

> I. How the West was won.

b *To signal an ellipsis or omission* in the quotation of a source, by use of three spaced periods.

ORIGINAL The King had just learned from Halvek, his chancellor, that the
rebellion had begun.

AS QUOTED "The King had just learned . . . that the rebellion had begun."

If the ellipsis occurs at the end of a sentence, the terminal punctuation
is added (usually a fourth period).

c *To designate an abbreviation.*

> Dec.
> no.
> Mr. and Mrs. (but in British: Mr and Mrs)

P3 *Comma* ,

The many common uses of this most versatile of all punctuation marks
can be reduced to seven.

a *To separate clauses.* The comma usually appears before coordinate
clauses—those introduced by *and, but, for, or, nor, so,* and *yet*—except
where very brief clauses are involved.

> We have planned long and hard for this opportunity, *and* now
> we intend to take it.
>
> We have planned for this and we are ready for it. (Brief clauses;
> no comma.)

Similarly, the comma sets off many types of subordinate clause as they
precede or follow the main clause. Most common are those subordinate
clauses opening with *although, as, as if, because, since, unless.* Again,
the comma is often omitted where clauses are brief.

> The Company has decided that it must close down operations
> this month, *although* the government had specifically asked for
> a delay.
>
> I had a great time although we didn't plan it. (Brief clauses; no
> comma.)

Commas do *not* set off subordinate clauses which are used as complements and thus fit directly into the main sentence structure. Such clauses
often open with *what, why, how, that.*

> The Company has decided *that it must close down.*
>
> I don't care *what the whole town says.*

See next item for subordinate clauses which help to define nouns—especially clauses opening with *who* or *which.*

b *To set off "nonrestrictive" modifiers.* A "restrictive" modifier is one absolutely needed to identify, define, restrict the meaning of the word it modifies. Because of the close relationship, no comma is used.

> The lathe operator *who had served longest* was promoted. (The *who*-clause is needed to pick out the promotee from among the other lathe operators.)

But if only *one* lathe operator worked in the shop, the *who*-clause is *not* essential for identification. It merely provides additional information. Being less indispensable to the main assertion, it *is* set off by commas.

> The lathe operator, who had served longer than the other workers, was promoted.

This same distinction between restrictive (or defining) modifiers and nonrestrictive (or nondefining modifiers) applies not only to clauses but to phrases as well.

> The hay, *mowed yesterday,* was raked and stacked.
>
> The hay *in the nearest field* was the first to be raked and stacked. (The first example implies, by use of commas, that *all* the hay is being processed. The second example identifies which of several fields of hay is being processed first.)
>
> Fred Korbas, *newly elected as councilor,* has offered a new transit plan. (Since Korbas is already identified, the modifier is punctuated as "nondefining.")
>
> The councilor *from the fifth district* has offered a new transit plan. (The modifier is needed to show which councilor is meant; hence it is not separated by commas.)

c *To set off interrupters.* Commas are used to set off a word or group of words which markedly delays or interrupts the normal sentence order (subject-verb-complement).

> OPENING *Still,* we can hardly blame taxes alone.
> INTERRUP-   s   v   c
> TION *When Dad returned,* Mother had the car packed.
>   s   v   c
> (Very short opening clauses or phrases may sometimes not carry a comma.)
>
> INSERTED I believe, *however,* that we must do better.
> INTERRUP- s   v   c
> TION The highest achievement, *in my opinion,* requires at least a touch
>   s   v   c
> of luck.

d *To separate the elements of a series.*

> I have held jobs as *secretary, public relations officer, and assistant to the president.* (Practice varies on whether to include the final comma in a series when "and" introduces the final item. Many writers favor the comma, since it will sometimes prevent misreading as in the next example.)

> Jones has served as foreman, assistant to the superintendent and president. (A final comma before "and" would prevent a reading of the sentence to imply that Jones has been assistant to *both* the superintendent and the president.)

e *To set off the compound elements of a date or address.*

> May 20, 1916
> 119 Ellsworth St., Clindale, Virginia 22029
> (No comma before ZIP code.)

Occasional usage without commas: 29 May 1916. May 1916.

f *To introduce dialog or quotation.*

> On reading the message, the President turned to his aide and said, "Good news from the Middle East!"

Commas are sometimes omitted where the continuity is tight:

> He had not learned that "conscience makes cowards of us all."

A colon may be preferred in formal contexts:

> The central logic of the Declaration appears in the following passage: [quotation].

g *To prevent run-on readings* which would confuse reader.

> I will oppose Gloria's plan to cut the budget and explain why. (Who is to "explain why"—the speaker or Gloria? A comma before "and" would clearly designate the speaker.)

P4 *Semicolon* ⟨ ; ⟩

a This mark is used mainly: *as a weak period* or as a "semiperiod" where the writer wants an interruption weaker than a period but stronger than a comma in separating independent clauses.

> My mother went to Harvard; my father attended Parsons College.

Thus the semicolon both separates the clauses and holds together closely related ideas. Two or more clauses can be linked in this way.

b *To separate series elements which contain internal commas.*

> I should like to order these titles: John Holliwell, *Wheel of Fire;*
> Henry Sok, *The Flaming Wind,* just published; and Elisabeth
> Baugh, *The Hot Road.*

P5 *Colon* **:**

The colon is used mainly to signal that what follows is an amplification,
particularization, or explanation of what has preceded. It most commonly
announces a series or list, as in the example just above.

P6 *Quotation marks* **" "**

a Or in British usage, inverted commas (' '). These marks set off dialog,
words referred to as words, short quotations (for longer quotations see **Q2,**
page 274), and references to titles of short literary and artistic works
(for longer works see **P11** below). They are *not* used for titles which head
articles, essays, or themes unless the title itself is a quotation. The writer's
main problem is how to place " " in relation to other punctuation marks.

b *When sentence closes with quoted matter:* The terminal period comes inside the quotation marks in the United States—not logically but in practice. If the terminal mark is ? or !, it appears inside or outside the quotation marks depending on whether the quoted matter includes it. (British
usage often follows the same principle for the terminal period.)

> Have you read "The Purloined Letter"?
>
> The boss shouted, "Don't come back without real proof!"
>
> POSSIBLE Have you read "Is It Too Late?"?

c *When the quoted matter is interrupted by the text:* The interrupter is set
off by commas if the quoted sentence is not yet completed. If the quotation is to resume with a new sentence, a period replaces the second
comma.

> "We cannot have civilization," someone has observed, "unless
> we have taxes."
>
> "Now we do have taxes," was the retort. "See what they've done
> to civilization!"

Notice that the first comma falls *within* the quotation marks, whereas the
second does not. In British usage the first comma may come *after* the
quotation marks if it is not part of the quoted matter.

d *When quotes include quotes.* Use single quotation marks (' ') within any quotation enclosed in double quotation marks (" "). The British practice is the reverse. The principle is to alternate these marks for each further level of quotation. Thus:

> "Mr. Farquhar did not say that he had been 'misinformed,'" said the manager. "His exact words were, 'I have been told an outright lie.'"

P7 *Apostrophe*

a This troublesome mark has actually only three main uses: a) *To form possessive case:* add *'s* to any noun unless it ends with an *s*. If it ends with an *s*, add the *'* alone. Thus:

> John's car. Thomas' car (but in British usage, Thomas's car).
>
> The horse's mouth. The horses' mouths.

Pronouns, however, have their own possessive forms and therefore do *not* take the apostrophe:

> Your car. Its engine (*not* it's engine). Is this ticket yours or hers or theirs?

b *To show omission of a letter or letters.*

> It's [it is] time to go. He'd [he would] like to join us. There's [there is] a party tonight.

c *To form certain plurals.* The apostrophe is used to form the plural of letters and may be used to form the plural of figures. It is *not* used to form other plurals.

> In the early 1980's (or 1980s), he earned three A's. We invited the Johnsons (*not* Johnson's).

P8 *Parentheses* ( )

Parentheses appear most often in formal writing and suggest a decided setting-off of the interrupting material. In fact, the parenthetic matter need not be grammatically related to the main sentence, as illustrated by the first example below.

> The rising automobile fatality rate (127 deaths were reported last weekend for this state alone) requires a total review of all preventive measures.
>
> After Ezra finished his chores (feeding, milking, manure spreading), he still had enough energy for night school.

Note that the closing parenthesis is placed *before* any punctuation required by the main sentence.

P9   *Dash*

Dashes can be used as dramatic parentheses giving special stress to the interruption; and the *single* dash can set up a remarkable fact or comment to follow. Extensive use of the dash is regarded by many as an affectation.

> I ordered the diet lunch—as penance, of course—and my usual double malt.

> I've had no time to examine Doreen's report—the trustees are here.

> Dr. Terapin believes that surgery is close to the ultimate transplant—that of the human brain.

To type a dash, use two hyphens together without spacing before or after.

P10   *Brackets* [ ]

Brackets enclose explanatory information being added to a quoted passage by someone other than the author quoted.

> "In 1969 a woman [in the United States] made only 60 cents for every dollar made by a man."

Brackets rarely appear outside of documented writing such as term papers, theses, and reports. Parentheses are *not* a substitute for brackets; if brackets do not appear on your keyboard, they should be inked in.

P11   *Italics*

Italics are print which slants to the right as in the heading to this section, or typewriting and handwriting which is underlined. Italics are used:

a *To emphasize a word or passage.*

> Taking a tennis lesson is not the same as *playing.*

> If you believe in a free nation, *be worthy of a free nation.*

b *To refer to words as words.* (The same function can be served by quotation marks.)

Inoperative statement is a fancy way of labeling a lie.

c *To designate foreign words; names of books, pamphlets, magazines, newspapers, ships; titles of plays, films, longer literary and artistic works when separately published.* (Quotation marks are used for shorter works such as stories, poems of less than book length, book chapters, articles, and essays.)

> I read in *The Atlantic City Bugle* that Horatio Dixby, the *enfant terrible* who had given the world that grotesque novel, *The Piebald Pheasant,* had arrived on the *S. S. Orestes.*

P12   *Hyphen* [-]

a ("If you take the hyphen seriously, you will surely go mad"—John Benbow.) This mark is used: *at the end of a line* to show that the final word is being continued on the next line because of lack of space.

> From all medical signs, the President was mending at a phenomenal rate.

Words are not divided except between syllables and never so as to leave only a single letter on one line. The syllabication of a word can be found in the dictionary and is shown by dots in the listing of that word: "phe·nom·e·nal."

b *In the customary spelling of two or more words used as one, or of a word containing a prefix otherwise easily misread.* The dictionary usually shows such hyphenations.

freeze-dry   re-create
heart-stricken   co-opt
safe-deposit   de-escalate

When such hyphenated words are commonly used, the hyphen tends to disappear after a time of divided usage.

c *To join two or more words used as a single modifier.*

> A dozen *high-school* seniors dropped out of the club.
>
> The party was a *never-to-be-forgotten* fiasco.
>
> I am fond of *light-brown* sweaters.

In general the joining of words by hyphens is a conservative practice, most important when ambiguity might otherwise result (as in "light-brown sweaters" which might otherwise be read as "light, brown sweaters").

S   *Sentence Structure*

S1 *Exact coordination and subordination.* Although "and" and "so" constantly appear in everyday speech as all-purpose connectors, formal usage aims at a tighter joining of ideas.

> LOOSE   We were in a frantic hurry to head west, *so* we didn't read the road signs, *and* we found ourselves dashing east along the expressway, *and* we couldn't get off for the next twenty miles.

> TIGHTER   In a frantic hurry to head west, we failed to read the road signs, thus finding ourselves on the expressway dashing east without an exit for the next twenty miles.

Also see "The Flexibility of Sentence Management," pages 215–217.

S2 *Placement of modifiers.* Since a modifier tends to make connection with the nearest possible headword, a careless placement can produce an undesirable ambiguity:

> PUZZLING   To become really proficient, the piano should be practiced daily. (Which is to be proficient, the piano or the player?)

> CLEAR   To become really proficient, a player should practice the piano daily.

> PUZZLING   Cecil was strolling down the boulevard to impress the old ladies, with freshly waxed whiskers.

> CLEAR   Cecil, with freshly waxed whiskers, was strolling down the boulevard to impress the old ladies.

S3 *Parallel structure.* You can obtain both smoothness and force by using similar structures for similar ideas (see pp. 210–214).

> AWKWARD   He failed to come to class and in doing his work.

> REVISED   He failed to come to class and to do his work.

On the other hand, avoid forcing parallel structure upon nonparallel ideas:

> ILLOGICAL   Henry's performance fell short of Philip.

> REVISED   Henry's performance fell short of Philip's.

S4 *Pronoun reference.* In formal writing a pronoun refers to a specific noun. A pronoun which refers loosely to a whole clause or sentence can result in vague or ambiguous expression.

> AMBIGUOUS   The newspaper favored reform, but the people neglected to vote. *This* meant that the machine gots its own candidates elected without trouble. (What does "this" refer to—the newspaper campaign or the people's negligence?)

CLEAR . . . *This public indifference* meant that the machine got its own candidates elected without trouble.

S5 *Use of impersonal pronouns.* "You" in the general sense of "the reader" is appropriate in instructional writing (as in this book) and in deliberately making the reader visible as a participant (see page 104). "You" and "they" in the sense of "anybody" are inadvisable in formal writing: the reader may take "you" in the personal sense or may wonder what people are meant by "they." Although "one" is the traditional impersonal pronoun, it seems stilted to many; and because in longer passages it takes the pronoun "he," it may seem sexist to others. The whole problem can be solved with some ingenuity by substituting specific nouns or alternate sentence structure.

CONFUSING When *one* visits Paris, *they* should see the Eiffel Tower. *They* take *you* to the top in an elevator.

POSSIBLY
SEXIST When *one* visits Paris, *he* should see the Eiffel Tower. . . .

LABORED When *one* visits Paris, *he or she* should see the Eiffel Tower. *He or she* is taken to the top in an elevator.

SAMPLE Any visit to Paris should include the Eiffel Tower and the eleva-
SOLUTIONS tor ride to its top.

A tourist visiting Paris should see the Eiffel Tower and take the elevator to its top.

S6 *Verb agreement.*

Agreement with subject. Obviously the subject and verb should agree in number, but sometimes an intervening noun can distract the writer into making the wrong choice. Example: "An *analysis* of recent market statistics *show* a decided increase in prices." (Standard: "analysis *shows.*" The noun "statistics" does not govern the verb.)

Agreement in tenses. Avoid shifting between past and present tenses unless your material requires a shift in time orientation. Random shifts of tense are especially likely to occur in discussions of an author's work. Thus:

Philip, the chief character, did not want supper, but he has no choice. As the meal wears on, he felt sick to his stomach.

Either past tense or present tense, used consistently, would serve. However, since a written work is thought of as existing *now*, the present (and present perfect) tenses are commonly used in discussing it. Thus:

Philip, the chief character, has not wanted supper, but he has no choice. As the meal wears on, he feels sick to his stomach.

Sx   *Sexist Language*

We live in a male-centered culture, and our language reflects this orientation both directly and subtly. Although this fact may not disturb you, many of your readers may take offence at male-biased language, all the more if used unknowingly. Hence you might consider avoiding the following:

Sx1   *Occupational labels implying the gender of the worker,* as wrongly suggesting that the sex difference is essential. Examples: usher*ette* (for usher), *lady* doctor, poet*ess,* news*boy* (for news carrier), working*man,* police*man* (for police officer), mail*man* (for mail carrier).

Certain terms like "chairman" and "spokesman" have become so ingrained that many people flinch at their neutralized equivalents: "chairperson," "chair," "spokesperson." It is tempting to satirize this allergy to masculine terms by inventing such atrocities as "personhole cover," "mispersonagement," "sportspersonship," "fisherperson." On the other hand, the ear quickly adapts to new language, and the history of vocabulary abounds in "atrocities" once despised but long since quietly naturalized.

Sx2   *Casual references to the sexual attributes of women* when irrelevant to context. Examples: busty, curvaceous, well-stacked, leggy, the Mayor's blonde wife.

Sx3   *Diminutive references to women,* as in "girl" for "secretary," "the little woman" for "wife," "the weaker sex" for "women," "chick," "broad," "doll," "babe," "dame."

Sx4   *Impersonal references to humans as "men,"* as implying that males are the norm while females are a variant form. Try "humanity" for "mankind," "people and their careers" instead of "man and *his* career." Pronouns with antecedents in the singular offer spiny problems for any writer sensitive to sexism, as in "the writer and *his* reader." Certain solutions seem grotesque (he/she, s/he, wo/man) or unwieldy (his or her). Judicious use of plurals will resolve most difficulties of this sort: "writers and *their* readers." Or the antecedent can simply be dropped: "the writer and *the* reader."

You may argue, as many humane writers have done, that general references to people as "he" or "man" have really lost any sexist tinge and should be accepted as a neutral convention, the simplest available in English. But why risk the possible resistance of your reader, when both of you have better fish to fry?

Bibliography

Allen, Walter, ed. *Writers on Writing*. Boston: The Writer, Inc., 1948.

Altick, Richard D. *Preface to Critical Reading*. 4th edition. New York: Holt, Rinehart, and Winston, 1960.

Aristotle. *Rhetoric*.

Auerbach, Erich. *Mimesis: The Representation of Reality in Western Literature*. Trans. Willard R. Trask. Princeton: Princeton Univ. Press, 1953.

Bazerman, Charles. "A Relationship Between Reading and Writing: The Conversational Model." *College English,* 41 (February 1980), 656–661.

Christensen, Francis, and Bonnijean Christensen. *Notes Toward a New Rhetoric*. 2nd edition. New York: Harper and Row, 1978.

Comprone, Joseph. "Kenneth Burke and the Teaching of Writing." *College Composition and Communication,* 29 (December 1978), 336–340.

Cooper, Charles R., and Lee Odell. *Research on Composing: Points of Departure*. Urbana: National Council of Teachers of English, 1978.

Corbett, Edward P. J. *Classical Rhetoric for the Modern Student*. 2nd edition. New York: Oxford Univ. Press, 1971.

———. *The Little Rhetoric*. New York: Wiley, 1977.

Ebbitt, Wilma R., and David R. Ebbitt. *Writer's Guide and Index to English*. 6th edition. Glenview, Illinois: Scott, Foresman, 1978.

———. 7th edition. 1982.

Elbow, Peter. *Writing Without Teachers*. New York: Oxford Univ. Press, 1973.

Flower, Linda S. and John R. Hayes. "Problem-Solving Strategies and the Writing Process." *College English,* 39 (December 1977), 449–461.

Ford, James E., and Dennis R. Perry. "Research Paper Instruction in the Undergraduate Writing Program." *College English*, 44 (December 1982), 825–831.

Fulkerson, Richard. "Four Philosophies of Composition." *College English*, 30 (December 1979), 343–348.

Gage, John T. "Philosophies of Style and Their Implications for Composition." *College English*, 41 (February 1980), 615–622.

Gordon, Ian. *The Movement of English Prose*. Bloomington: Indiana Univ. Press, 1966.

Green, Lawrence D. "Enthymemic Invention and Structural Prediction." *College English*, 41 (February 1980), 623–634.

Harrington, David V. "Teaching Students the Art of Discovery." *College Composition and Communication*, 19 (February 1968), 7–14.

Hartwell, Patrick, with Robert H. Bentley. *Open to Language: A New College Rhetoric*. New York: Oxford Univ. Press, 1982.

Hayakawa, S. I. *Language in Thought and Action*. 2nd edition. New York: Harcourt, Brace, and World, 1964.

Hirsch, E. D., Jr. *The Philosophy of Composition*. Chicago: Univ. of Chicago Press, 1977.

Irmscher, William. *Teaching Expository Writing*. Holt, Rinehart and Winston, 1979.

Knaus, William J. *Do It Now: How to Stop Procrastinating*. Englewood Cliffs, N.J.: Prentice Hall, 1979.

Knuepper, Charles W. "Revising the Tagmemic Heuristic: Theoretical and Practical Considerations." *College Composition and Communication*, 31 (May 1980), 160–168.

Koch, Carol, and James M. Brazil. *Strategies for Teaching the Composition Process*. Urbana: National Council of Teachers of English, 1978.

Kolb, Harold H., Jr. *A Writer's Guide: The Essential Points*. New York: Harcourt Brace Jovanovich, 1980.

Macrorie, Ken. *Telling Writing*. 3rd edition. Rochelle Park, N.Y.: Hayden, 1980.

Martin, Harold C., and Richard M. Ohmann. *The Logic and Rhetoric of Exposition*. Revised edition. New York: Holt, Rinehart and Winston, 1963.

Milic, Louis T. "Theories of Style and Their Implications for the Teaching of Composition." *College Composition and Communication*, 16 (May 1965), 66–69, 126.

MLA Handbook: for Writers of Research Papers, Theses, and Dissertations. New York: Modern Language Association, 1977.

O'Hare, Frank. *Sentence Combining: Improving Student Writing without Formal Grammar Instruction*. Urbana: National Council of Teachers of English, 1973.

Ohmann, Richard M. "Prolegomena to the Analysis of Prose Style." In *Style in Prose Fiction*. Ed. H. C. Martin. New York: Columbia Univ. Press, 1959.

Plato. *Phaedrus*.

Plimpton, George. *Writers at Work: The PARIS REVIEW Interviews*. Second series. New York: Viking Press, 1963.

Roberts, Paul. *Understanding English*. New York: Harper and Row, 1958.

Schwegler, Robert A., and Linda K. Shamoon. "The Aims and Process of the Research Paper." *College English*, 44 (December 1982), 817–824.

Stewart, Donald C. "Composition Textbooks and the Assault on Tradition." *College Composition and Communication*, 29 (May 1978), 171–176.

Tate, Gary, ed. *Teaching Composition: 10 Bibliographical Essays*. Fort Worth: Texas Christian Univ. Press, 1976.

————, and Edward P. J. Corbett, eds. *The Writing Teacher's Sourcebook*. New York: Oxford Univ. Press, 1981.

Thale, Jerome. "Style and Anti-Style: History and Anti-History." *College English*, 29 (January 1968), 286–302.

Turabian, Kate L. *Student's Guide for Writing College Papers*. 3rd edition. Chicago: Univ. of Chicago Press, 1976.

Wiener, Harvey S. *The Writing Room: A Resource Book for Teachers of English*. New York: Oxford Univ. Press, 1981.

Wilkie, Brian. "What Is Sentimentality?" *College English*, 28 (May 1967), 564–575.

Williams, Joseph. *Style: Ten Lessons in Clarity and Grace*. Glenview, Ill.: Scott, Foresman, 1981.

Young, Richard E., Alton L. Becker, and Kenneth L. Pike. *Rhetoric: Discovery and Change*. New York: Harcourt, Brace and World, 1970.

Zinsser, William. *On Writing Well: An Informal Guide to Writing Nonfiction*. 2nd edition. New York: Harper and Row, 1980.

Index

451

QUICK REFERENCE CHART
USAGE, DOCUMENTATION, COMMON
DIFFICULTIES IN STYLE

Usage

Common Difficulties in Style

(Here are symbols and page references for those more conspicuous stylistic difficulties to which instructors most commonly refer individual students. Such quick reference is *not* offered for subtle or sensitive matters (like audience, writer's image, sentimentality) which usually require extended comment. Complete locator service is, of course, furnished by the Contents and the Index.)